Casenote® Legal Briefs

COMMERCIAL LAW

Keyed to Courses Using

Whaley and McJohn's
Problems and Materials on Commercial Law

Tenth Edition

Wolters Kluwer
Law & Business

Published by Wolters Kluwer Law & Business in New York.

Wolters Kluwer Law & Business serves customers worldwide with CCH, Aspen Publishers, and Kluwer Law International products. (www.wolterskluwerlb.com)

To contact Customer Service, e-mail customer.service@wolterskluwer.com, call 1-800-234-1660, fax 1-800-901-9075, or mail correspondence to:

Wolters Kluwer Law & Business
Attn: Order Department
P.O. Box 990
Frederick, MD 21705

Printed in the United States of America.

1 2 3 4 5 6 7 8 9 0

ISBN 978-1-4548-0800-8

SFI Certified Chain of Custody
Product Line Contains At Least 20% Certified Forest Content
www.sfiprogram.org
SFI-00756

About Wolters Kluwer Law & Business

Wolters Kluwer Law & Business is a leading global provider of intelligent information and digital solutions for legal and business professionals in key specialty areas, and respected educational resources for professors and law students. Wolters Kluwer Law & Business connects legal and business professionals as well as those in the education market with timely, specialized authoritative content and information-enabled solutions to support success through productivity, accuracy and mobility.

Serving customers worldwide, Wolters Kluwer Law & Business products include those under the Aspen Publishers, CCH, Kluwer Law International, Loislaw, Best Case, ftwilliam.com and MediRegs family of products.

CCH products have been a trusted resource since 1913, and are highly regarded resources for legal, securities, antitrust and trade regulation, government contracting, banking, pension, payroll, employment and labor, and healthcare reimbursement and compliance professionals.

Aspen Publishers products provide essential information to attorneys, business professionals and law students. Written by preeminent authorities, the product line offers analytical and practical information in a range of specialty practice areas from securities law and intellectual property to mergers and acquisitions and pension/benefits. Aspen's trusted legal education resources provide professors and students with high-quality, up-to-date and effective resources for successful instruction and study in all areas of the law.

Kluwer Law International products provide the global business community with reliable international legal information in English. Legal practitioners, corporate counsel and business executives around the world rely on Kluwer Law journals, looseleafs, books, and electronic products for comprehensive information in many areas of international legal practice.

Loislaw is a comprehensive online legal research product providing legal content to law firm practitioners of various specializations. Loislaw provides attorneys with the ability to quickly and efficiently find the necessary legal information they need, when and where they need it, by facilitating access to primary law as well as state-specific law, records, forms and treatises.

Best Case Solutions is the leading bankruptcy software product to the bankruptcy industry. It provides software and workflow tools to flawlessly streamline petition preparation and the electronic filing process, while timely incorporating ever-changing court requirements.

ftwilliam.com offers employee benefits professionals the highest quality plan documents (retirement, welfare and non-qualified) and government forms (5500/PBGC, 1099 and IRS) software at highly competitive prices.

MediRegs products provide integrated health care compliance content and software solutions for professionals in healthcare, higher education and life sciences, including professionals in accounting, law and consulting.

Wolters Kluwer Law & Business, a division of Wolters Kluwer, is headquartered in New York. Wolters Kluwer is a market-leading global information services company focused on professionals.

Format for the Casenote® Legal Brief

Nature of Case: This section identifies the form of action (e.g., breach of contract, negligence, battery), the type of proceeding (e.g., demurrer, appeal from trial court's jury instructions), or the relief sought (e.g., damages, injunction, criminal sanctions).

Party ID: Quick identification of the relationship between the parties.

Fact Summary: This is included to refresh your memory and can be used as a quick reminder of the facts.

Rule of Law: Summarizes the general principle of law that the case illustrates. It may be used for instant recall of the court's holding and for classroom discussion or home review.

Facts: This section contains all relevant facts of the case, including the contentions of the parties and the lower court holdings. It is written in a logical order to give the student a clear understanding of the case. The plaintiff and defendant are identified by their proper names throughout and are always labeled with a (P) or (D).

Concurrence/Dissent: All concurrences and dissents are briefed whenever they are included by the casebook editor.

Analysis: This last paragraph gives you a broad understanding of where the case "fits in" with other cases in the section of the book and with the entire course. It is a hornbook-style discussion indicating whether the case is a majority or minority opinion and comparing the principal case with other cases in the casebook. It may also provide analysis from restatements, uniform codes, and law review articles. The analysis will prove to be invaluable to classroom discussion.

Palsgraf v. Long Island R.R. Co.

Injured bystander (P) v. Railroad company (D)

N.Y. Ct. App., 248 N.Y. 339, 162 N.E. 99 (1928).

NATURE OF CASE: Appeal from judgment affirming verdict for plaintiff seeking damages for personal injury.

FACT SUMMARY: Helen Palsgraf (P) was injured on R.R.'s (D) train platform when R.R.'s (D) guard helped a passenger aboard a moving train, causing his package to fall on the tracks. The package contained fireworks which exploded, creating a shock that tipped a scale onto Palsgraf (P).

RULE OF LAW

The risk reasonably to be perceived defines the duty to be obeyed.

FACTS: Helen Palsgraf (P) purchased a ticket to Rockaway Beach from R.R. (D) and was waiting on the train platform. As she waited, two men ran to catch a train that was pulling out from the platform. The first man jumped aboard, but the second man, who appeared as if he might fall, was helped aboard by the guard on the train who had kept the door open so they could jump aboard. A guard on the platform also helped by pushing him onto the train. The man was carrying a package wrapped in newspaper. In the process, the man dropped his package, which fell on the tracks. The package contained fireworks and exploded. The shock of the explosion was apparently of great enough strength to tip over some scales at the other end of the platform, which fell on Palsgraf (P) and injured her. A jury awarded her damages, and R.R. (D) appealed.

ISSUE: Does the risk reasonably to be perceived define the duty to be obeyed?

HOLDING AND DECISION: (Cardozo, C.J.) Yes. The risk reasonably to be perceived defines the duty to be obeyed. If there is no foreseeable hazard to the injured party as the result of a seemingly innocent act, the act does not become a tort because it happened to be a wrong as to another. If the wrong was not willful, the plaintiff must show that the act as to her had such great and apparent possibilities of danger as to entitle her to protection. Negligence in the abstract is not enough upon which to base liability. Negligence is a relative concept, evolving out of the common law doctrine of trespass on the case. To establish liability, the defendant must owe a legal duty of reasonable care to the injured party. A cause of action in tort will lie where harm, though unintended, could have been averted or avoided by observance of such a duty. The scope of the duty is limited by the range of danger that a reasonable person could foresee. In this case, there was nothing to suggest from the appearance of the parcel or otherwise that the parcel contained fireworks. The guard could not reasonably have had any warning of a threat to Palsgraf (P), and R.R. (D) therefore cannot be held liable. Judgment is reversed in favor of R.R. (D).

DISSENT: (Andrews, J.) The concept that there is no negligence unless R.R. (D) owes a legal duty to take care as to Palsgraf (P) herself is too narrow. Everyone owes to the world at large the duty of refraining from those acts that may unreasonably threaten the safety of others. If the guard's action was negligent as to those nearby, it was also negligent as to those outside what might be termed the "danger zone." For Palsgraf (P) to recover, R.R.'s (D) negligence must have been the proximate cause of her injury, a question of fact for the jury.

ANALYSIS

The majority defined the limit of the defendant's liability in terms of the danger that a reasonable person in defendant's situation would have perceived. The dissent argued that the limitation should not be placed on liability, but rather on damages. Judge Andrews suggested that only injuries that would not have happened but for R.R.'s (D) negligence should be compensable. Both the majority and dissent recognized the policy-driven need to limit liability for negligent acts, seeking, in the words of Judge Andrews, to define a framework "that will be practical and in keeping with the general understanding of mankind." The Restatement (Second) of Torts has accepted Judge Cardozo's view.

Quicknotes

FORESEEABILITY A reasonable expectation that change is the probable result of certain acts or omissions.

NEGLIGENCE Conduct falling below the standard of care that a reasonable person would demonstrate under similar conditions.

PROXIMATE CAUSE The natural sequence of events without which an injury would not have been sustained.

Issue: The issue is a concise question that brings out the essence of the opinion as it relates to the section of the casebook in which the case appears. Both substantive and procedural issues are included if relevant to the decision.

Holding and Decision: This section offers a clear and in-depth discussion of the rule of the case and the court's rationale. It is written in easy-to-understand language and answers the issue presented by applying the law to the facts of the case. When relevant, it includes a thorough discussion of the exceptions to the case as listed by the court, any major cites to the other cases on point, and the names of the judges who wrote the decisions.

Quicknotes: Conveniently defines legal terms found in the case and summarizes the nature of any statutes, codes, or rules referred to in the text.

Note to Students

Wolters Kluwer Law & Business is proud to offer *Casenote® Legal Briefs*—continuing thirty years of publishing America's best-selling legal briefs.

Casenote® Legal Briefs are designed to help you save time when briefing assigned cases. Organized under convenient headings, they show you how to abstract the basic facts and holdings from the text of the actual opinions handed down by the courts. Used as part of a rigorous study regimen, they can help you spend more time analyzing and critiquing points of law than on copying bits and pieces of judicial opinions into your notebook or outline.

Casenote® Legal Briefs should never be used as a substitute for assigned casebook readings. They work best when read as a follow-up to reviewing the underlying opinions themselves. Students who try to avoid reading and digesting the judicial opinions in their casebooks or online sources will end up shortchanging themselves in the long run. The ability to absorb, critique, and restate the dynamic and complex elements of case law decisions is crucial to your success in law school and beyond. It cannot be developed vicariously.

Casenote® Legal Briefs represents but one of the many offerings in Legal Education's Study Aid Timeline, which includes:

- *Casenote® Legal Briefs*
- *Emanuel® Law Outlines*
- Emanuel® *Law in a Flash* Flash Cards
- Emanuel® *CrunchTime®* Series
- *Siegel's Essay and Multiple-Choice Questions and Answers Series*

Each of these series is designed to provide you with easy-to-understand explanations of complex points of law. Each volume offers guidance on the principles of legal analysis and, consulted regularly, will hone your ability to spot relevant issues. We have titles that will help you prepare for class, prepare for your exams, and enhance your general comprehension of the law along the way.

To find out more about Wolters Kluwer Law & Business' study aid publications, visit us online at *www.wolterskluwerlb.com* or email us at *legaledu@wolterskluwer.com*. We'll be happy to assist you.

How to Brief a Case

A. Decide on a Format and Stick to It

Structure is essential to a good brief. It enables you to arrange systematically the related parts that are scattered throughout most cases, thus making manageable and understandable what might otherwise seem to be an endless and unfathomable sea of information. There are, of course, an unlimited number of formats that can be utilized. However, it is best to find one that suits your needs and stick to it. Consistency breeds both efficiency and the security that when called upon you will know where to look in your brief for the information you are asked to give.

Any format, as long as it presents the essential elements of a case in an organized fashion, can be used. Experience, however, has led *Casenote® Legal Briefs* to develop and utilize the following format because of its logical flow and universal applicability.

NATURE OF CASE: This is a brief statement of the legal character and procedural status of the case (e.g., "Appeal of a burglary conviction").

There are many different alternatives open to a litigant dissatisfied with a court ruling. The key to determining which one has been used is to discover *who is asking this court for what.*

This first entry in the brief should be kept as *short as possible.* Use the court's terminology if you understand it. But since jurisdictions vary as to the titles of pleadings, the best entry is the one that addresses who wants what in this proceeding, not the one that sounds most like the court's language.

RULE OF LAW: A statement of the general principle of law that the case illustrates (e.g., "An acceptance that varies any term of the offer is considered a rejection and counteroffer").

Determining the rule of law of a case is a procedure similar to determining the issue of the case. Avoid being fooled by red herrings; there may be a few rules of law mentioned in the case excerpt, but usually only one is *the* rule with which the casebook editor is concerned. The techniques used to locate the issue, described below, may also be utilized to find the rule of law. Generally, your best guide is simply the chapter heading. It is a clue to the point the casebook editor seeks to make and should be kept in mind when reading every case in the respective section.

FACTS: A synopsis of only the essential facts of the case, i.e., those bearing upon or leading up to the issue.

The facts entry should be a short statement of the events and transactions that led one party to initiate legal proceedings against another in the first place. While some cases conveniently state the salient facts at the beginning of the decision, in other instances they will have to be culled from hiding places throughout the text, even from concurring and dissenting opinions. Some of the "facts" will often be in dispute and should be so noted. Conflicting evidence may be briefly pointed up. "Hard" facts must be included. Both must be *relevant* in order to be listed in the facts entry. It is impossible to tell what is relevant until the entire case is read, as the ultimate determination of the rights and liabilities of the parties may turn on something buried deep in the opinion.

Generally, the facts entry should not be longer than three to five *short* sentences.

It is often helpful to identify the role played by a party in a given context. For example, in a construction contract case the identification of a party as the "contractor" or "builder" alleviates the need to tell that that party was the one who was supposed to have built the house.

It is always helpful, and a good general practice, to identify the "plaintiff" and the "defendant." This may seem elementary and uncomplicated, but, especially in view of the creative editing practiced by some casebook editors, it is sometimes a difficult or even impossible task. Bear in mind that the *party presently* seeking something from this court may not be the plaintiff, and that sometimes only the cross-claim of a defendant is treated in the excerpt. Confusing or misaligning the parties can ruin your analysis and understanding of the case.

ISSUE: A statement of the general legal question answered by or illustrated in the case. For clarity, the issue is best put in the form of a question capable of a "yes" or "no" answer. In reality, the issue is simply the Rule of Law put in the form of a question (e.g., "May an offer be accepted by performance?").

The major problem presented in discerning what is *the* issue in the case is that an opinion usually purports to raise and answer several questions. However, except for rare cases, only one such question is really the issue in the case. Collateral issues not necessary to the resolution of the matter in controversy are handled by the court by language known as "*obiter dictum*" or merely "*dictum.*" While dicta may be included later in the brief, they have no place under the issue heading.

To find the issue, ask *who wants what* and then go on to ask *why did that party succeed or fail in getting it.* Once this is determined, the "why" should be turned into a question.

The complexity of the issues in the cases will vary, but in all cases a single-sentence question should sum up the issue. *In a few cases,* there will be two, or even more rarely, three issues of equal importance to the resolution of the case. Each should be expressed in a single-sentence question.

Since many issues are resolved by a court in coming to a final disposition of a case, the casebook editor will reproduce the portion of the opinion containing the issue or issues most relevant to the area of law under scrutiny. A noted law professor gave this advice: "Close the book; look at the title on the cover." Chances are, if it is Property, you need not concern yourself with whether, for example, the federal government's treatment of the plaintiff's land really raises a federal question sufficient to support jurisdiction on this ground in federal court.

The same rule applies to chapter headings designating sub-areas within the subjects. They tip you off as to what the text is designed to teach. The cases are arranged in a casebook to show a progression or development of the law, so that the preceding cases may also help.

It is also most important to remember to *read the notes and questions* at the end of a case to determine what the editors wanted you to have gleaned from it.

HOLDING AND DECISION: This section should succinctly explain the rationale of the court in arriving at its decision. In capsulizing the "reasoning" of the court, it should always include an application of the general rule or rules of law to the specific facts of the case. Hidden justifications come to light in this entry: the reasons for the state of the law, the public policies, the biases and prejudices, those considerations that influence the justices' thinking and, ultimately, the outcome of the case. At the end, there should be a short indication of the disposition or procedural resolution of the case (e.g., "Decision of the trial court for Mr. Smith (P) reversed").

The foregoing format is designed to help you "digest" the reams of case material with which you will be faced in your law school career. Once mastered by practice, it will place at your fingertips the information the authors of your casebooks have sought to impart to you in case-by-case illustration and analysis.

B. Be as Economical as Possible in Briefing Cases

Once armed with a format that encourages succinctness, it is as important to be economical with regard to the time spent on the actual reading of the case as it is to be economical in the writing of the brief itself. This does not mean "skimming" a case. Rather, it means reading the case with an "eye" trained to recognize into which "section" of your brief a particular passage or line fits and having a system for quickly and precisely marking the case so that the passages fitting any one particular part of the brief can be easily identified and brought together in a concise and accurate manner when the brief is actually written.

It is of no use to simply repeat everything in the opinion of the court; record only enough information to trigger your recollection of what the court said. Nevertheless, an accurate statement of the "law of the case," i.e., the legal principle applied to the facts, is absolutely essential to class preparation and to learning the law under the case method.

To that end, it is important to develop a "shorthand" that you can use to make marginal notations. These notations will tell you at a glance in which section of the brief you will be placing that particular passage or portion of the opinion.

Some students prefer to underline all the salient portions of the opinion (with a pencil or colored underliner marker), making marginal notations as they go along. Others prefer the color-coded method of underlining, utilizing different colors of markers to underline the salient portions of the case, each separate color being used to represent a different section of the brief. For example, blue underlining could be used for passages relating to the rule of law, yellow for those relating to the issue, and green for those relating to the holding and decision, etc. While it has its advocates, the color-coded method can be confusing and time-consuming (all that time spent on changing colored markers). Furthermore, it can interfere with the continuity and concentration many students deem essential to the reading of a case for maximum comprehension. In the end, however, it is a matter of personal preference and style. Just remember, whatever method you use, underlining must be used sparingly or its value is lost.

If you take the marginal notation route, an efficient and easy method is to go along underlining the key portions of the case and placing in the margin alongside them the following "markers" to indicate where a particular passage or line "belongs" in the brief you will write:

N (NATURE OF CASE)
RL (RULE OF LAW)
I (ISSUE)
HL (HOLDING AND DECISION, relates to the RULE OF LAW behind the decision)
HR (HOLDING AND DECISION, gives the RATIONALE or reasoning behind the decision)
HA (HOLDING AND DECISION, APPLIES the general principle(s) of law to the facts of the case to arrive at the decision)

Remember that a particular passage may well contain information necessary to more than one part of your brief, in which case you simply note that in the margin. If you are using the color-coded underlining method instead of marginal notation, simply make asterisks or checks in the margin next to the passage in question in the colors that indicate the additional sections of the brief where it might be utilized.

The economy of utilizing "shorthand" in marking cases for briefing can be maintained in the actual brief writing process itself by utilizing "law student shorthand" within the brief. There are many commonly used words and phrases for which abbreviations can be substituted in your briefs (and in your class notes also). You can develop abbreviations that are personal to you and which will save you a lot of time. A reference list of briefing abbreviations can be found on page xii of this book.

C. Use Both the Briefing Process and the Brief as a Learning Tool

Now that you have a format and the tools for briefing cases efficiently, the most important thing is to make the time spent in briefing profitable to you and to make the most advantageous use of the briefs you create. Of course, the briefs are invaluable for classroom reference when you are called upon to explain or analyze a particular case. However, they are also useful in reviewing for exams. A quick glance at the fact summary should bring the case to mind, and a rereading of the rule of law should enable you to go over the underlying legal concept in your mind, how it was applied in that particular case, and how it might apply in other factual settings.

As to the value to be derived from engaging in the briefing process itself, there is an immediate benefit that arises from being forced to sift through the essential facts and reasoning from the court's opinion and to succinctly express them in your own words in your brief. The process ensures that you understand the case and the point that it illustrates, and that means you will be ready to absorb further analysis and information brought forth in class. It also ensures you will have something to say when called upon in class. The briefing process helps develop a mental agility for getting to the *gist* of a case and for identifying, expounding on, and applying the legal concepts and issues found there. The briefing process is the mental process on which you must rely in taking law school examinations; it is also the mental process upon which a lawyer relies in serving his clients and in making his living.

Abbreviations for Briefs

acceptance	acp
affirmed	aff
answer	ans
assumption of risk	a/r
attorney	atty
beyond a reasonable doubt	b/r/d
bona fide purchaser	BFP
breach of contract	br/k
cause of action	c/a
common law	c/l
Constitution	Con
constitutional	con
contract	K
contributory negligence	c/n
cross	x
cross-complaint	x/c
cross-examination	x/ex
cruel and unusual punishment	c/u/p
defendant	D
dismissed	dis
double jeopardy	d/j
due process	d/p
equal protection	e/p
equity	eq
evidence	ev
exclude	exc
exclusionary rule	exc/r
felony	f/n
freedom of speech	f/s
good faith	g/f
habeas corpus	h/c
hearsay	hr
husband	H
injunction	inj
in loco parentis	ILP
inter vivos	I/v
joint tenancy	j/t
judgment	judgt
jurisdiction	jur
last clear chance	LCC
long-arm statute	LAS
majority view	maj
meeting of minds	MOM
minority view	min
Miranda rule	Mir/r
Miranda warnings	Mir/w
negligence	neg
notice	ntc
nuisance	nus
obligation	ob
obscene	obs
offer	O
offeree	OE
offeror	OR
ordinance	ord
pain and suffering	p/s
parol evidence	p/e
plaintiff	P
prima facie	p/f
probable cause	p/c
proximate cause	px/c
real property	r/p
reasonable doubt	r/d
reasonable man	r/m
rebuttable presumption	rb/p
remanded	rem
res ipsa loquitur	RIL
respondeat superior	r/s
Restatement	RS
reversed	rev
Rule Against Perpetuities	RAP
search and seizure	s/s
search warrant	s/w
self-defense	s/d
specific performance	s/p
statute	S
statute of frauds	S/F
statute of limitations	S/L
summary judgment	s/j
tenancy at will	t/w
tenancy in common	t/c
tenant	t
third party	TP
third party beneficiary	TPB
transferred intent	TI
unconscionable	uncon
unconstitutional	unconst
undue influence	u/e
Uniform Commercial Code	UCC
unilateral	uni
vendee	VE
vendor	VR
versus	v
void for vagueness	VFV
weight of authority	w/a
weight of the evidence	w/e
wife	W
with	w/
within	w/i
without	w/o
without prejudice	w/o/p
wrongful death	wr/d

Table of Cases

CHAPTER 1

Basic Concepts

Quick Reference Rules of Law

Milau Associates, Inc. v. North Avenue Development Corp.

Contractors (D) v. Plaintiff (P)

N.Y. Ct. App., 42 N.Y.2d 482, 368 N.E.2d 1247, 398 N.Y.S.2d 882 (1977).

NATURE OF CASE: Appeal from denial of damages for breach of implied warranty.

FACT SUMMARY: After an underground section of pipe connecting a sprinkler system to the city's water line burst, causing substantial damage to textiles stored in a warehouse, the textile companies whose bolts of textiles were damaged filed suit against Milau Associates, Inc. (D), the general contractor which built the warehouse, and Higgins Fire Protection Inc. (D), the subcontractor which designed and installed the sprinkler system.

RULE OF LAW

The reasonable care and competence owed generally by practitioners in a particular trade or profession defines the limits of an injured party's justifiable demands.

FACTS: When an underground section of pipe, connecting a sprinkler system to the city water line, burst, it caused substantial water damage to bolts of textiles stored in a warehouse. The commercial tenants of the building sought recovery against both Milau Associates, Inc. (Milau) (D), the general contractor which built the warehouse, and Higgins Fire Protection Inc. (Higgins) (D), the subcontractor which designed and installed the sprinkler system. The suit was brought on the alternative theories of negligence and breach of implied warranty of fitness for a particular purpose. Expert testimony suggested that a pressure phenomenon known as a "water hammer" caused a crack to develop at the root of a V-shaped notch discovered toward the end of the conduit. The "stress-raising" notch was alleged to have been produced by a dull tooth on the hydraulic squeeze cutter used by Higgins (D) to cut sections of the commercially marketed pipe furnished by the subcontractor. The textile companies alleged that only a few months of use had caused enough rusting at the base of the notch to affect the integrity of the entire system. Milau (D) and Higgins (D) produced offsetting expert opinion that the pipe itself was neither defective as manufactured nor improperly installed. The case was submitted to the jury on the sole question of negligent installation, and the jury returned a verdict in favor of Milau (D) and Higgins (D). The appellate division found no evidence that the pipe installed by Higgins (D) was unfit for its intended purpose and concluded that neither the Uniform Commercial Code (U.C.C.) nor the case law could be invoked to grant the extension of warranty protection sought by the textile companies. This appeal followed. [North Avenue Development Corp. is not identified in the casebook excerpt.]

ISSUE: Does the reasonable care and competence owed generally by practitioners in a particular trade or profession define the limits of an injured party's justifiable demands?

HOLDING AND DECISION: (Wachtler, J.) Yes. The reasonable care and competence owed generally by practitioners in a particular trade or profession defines the limits of an injured party's justifiable demands. Reasonable expectations, not perfect results in the face of any and all contingencies, will be ensured under a traditional negligence standard of conduct. U.C.C. § 2-313 requires that a seller's affirmation of fact to a buyer be made as part of the basis of the bargain, that is, the contract for the sale of goods. The express warranty section would therefore be no more applicable to a service contract than the U.C.C.'s implied warranty provisions. Of course, where the party rendering services can be shown to have expressly bound itself to the accomplishment of a particular result, the courts will enforce that promise. Both the subcontract and the agreement between Milau (D) and the owner were no more than a series of performance undertakings, plans, schedules, and specifications for the incorporation of the specialized system during the erection of a building—a predominantly labor-intensive endeavor. Thus, neither the U.C.C. nor New York common law can be read to imply an undertaking to guard against economic loss stemming from nonnegligent performance by a construction firm which has not contractually bound itself to provide perfect results. Affirmed.

ANALYSIS

The court noted that where courts in other jurisdictions have purported to apply an implied warranty of fitness to transactions which in essence contemplated the rendition of services, what was actually imposed was no more than a "warranty that the performer would not act negligently," or a "warranty of workmanlike performance" imposing only the degree of care and skill that a reasonably prudent, skilled, and qualified person would have exercised under the circumstances, or an "implied warranty of competence and ability ordinarily possessed by those in the profession." The court found that the performance of Higgins (D) and Milau (D) had been tested under precisely this standard and was free from any actionable departure. In the words of the court, those who hire experts for the predominant

Continued on next page.

purpose of rendering services, relying on their special skills, cannot expect infallibility.

Quicknotes

REASONABLE CARE The degree of care observed by a reasonably prudent person under similar circumstances; synonymous with due care or ordinary care.

Analysts Intern. Corp. v. Recycled Paper Products, Inc.

Corporation (P) v. Corporation (D)

1987 WL 12917, 45 U.C.C. Rep. Serv. 746 (N.D. Ill. 1987).

NATURE OF CASE: Motion for summary judgment on a counterclaim of breach of contract and warranty.

FACT SUMMARY: Recycled Paper Products, Inc. (RPP) (D) contracted with Analysts International Corporation (AIC) (P) for a computerized reordering system known as a computer-assisted merchandising program (CAMP). After CAMP was implemented, it failed to perform and, instead, disrupted RPP's (D) business. AIC (P) attempted to fix the program, but eventually RPP (D) refused to pay and AIC (P) sued under breach of contract to recover the unpaid balance. RPP (D) countersued for breach of contract and warranty.

RULE OF LAW

A contract for a computerized reordering system is a transaction in goods subject to the Uniform Commercial Code (U.C.C.).

FACTS: Recycled Paper Products, Inc. (RPP) (D) entered into a contract with Analysts International Corporation (AIC) (P) whereby AIC (P) would create a custom-made computerized reordering system known as a computer-assisted merchandising program (CAMP). The parties disagreed about the material terms of their agreement. RPP (D) claimed that AIC (P) agreed to provide the system within 36 months, by October 1984, and for a set price. AIC (P) claimed that the price was only a rough estimate and that RPP (D) had agreed to pay on an hourly basis. In October 1984, AIC (P) announced CAMP would not be completed on time, and when CAMP was implemented in December, it did not perform any of its intended functions. Instead, RPP's (D) business was severely disrupted from January to June 1985. Throughout this period, AIC (P) tried to fix the program, and RPP (D) continued to pay AIC's (P) invoices. Outside auditors concluded that the system would have to be replaced, and in October 1985, despite AIC's (P) claim that the system was substantially operational, RPP (D) refused to pay an outstanding bill of $330,386. AIC (P) sued in federal district court for breach of contract and fraud. RPP (D) countersued for, among other things, breach of contract and breach of an express warranty, implied warranty of merchantability, and warranty of fitness for a particular purpose. AIC (P) moved for summary judgment on these counterclaims.

ISSUE: Is a contract for a computerized reordering system a transaction in goods subject to the U.C.C.?

HOLDING AND DECISION: (Grady, C.J.) Yes. A contract for a computerized reordering system is a transaction in goods subject to the U.C.C. The claims for breach of implied warranty, brought under §§ 2-314 and 2-315 of the U.C.C., apply only to sales of goods. AIC (P) argues that the contract called for performance of services, not the sale of goods. Although RPP (D) concedes that the contract called for substantial design and programming services to be rendered by AIC (P), this alone does not entitle AIC (P) to judgment as a matter of law. The legal issue is whether the U.C.C. applies to CAMP, and that, in turn, depends on whether the agreement is for a "transaction in goods." The reasoning in cases holding that the subject of computer program contracts is the skill of programmers is unpersuasive. Software has both tangible and intangible elements; focusing on the intangible elements (as those cases do) to the exclusion of the tangible aspects loses sight of the whole of the contract. The knowledge of the programmer is important, but only to the extent that it enables production of the contracted-for software. Here, the contract, which was not altogether explicit on this point, called for "system delivery." Where an agreement involves both goods and services, state law requires use of the "dominant purpose" test to determine whether the agreement is one for goods. Here, under this test, the dominant factor of the contract was the provision of a good—a computerized recording system. But for this end product, the contract would have had no purpose. Accordingly, RPP's (D) agreement with AIC (P) was a transaction in goods and is therefore within the U.C.C.'s purview. Summary judgment is denied.

ANALYSIS

The issue of whether transactions involving the creation and sale of software are transactions in goods has been a vexing one for the courts, and has produced all sorts of stands as to the applicability of U.C.C. Article 2. The majority of courts, like the majority in this case, have found that Article 2 is applicable.

Quicknotes

BREACH OF CONTRACT Unlawful failure by a party to perform its obligations pursuant to contract.

BREACH OF WARRANTY The breach of a promise made by one party to a contract on which the other party may rely, relieving that party from the obligation of determining whether the fact is true and indemnifying the other party from liability if that fact is shown to be false.

Anthony Pools v. Sheehan

Contractor (D) v. Diver (P)

Md. Ct App., 295 Md. 285, 455 A.2d 434 (1983).

NATURE OF CASE: Appeal from remand for a new trial, reversing a denial of damages for breach of implied warranty and for strict liability in tort.

FACT SUMMARY: After he injured himself when he slipped on the diving board installed by Anthony Pools (D), a company that builds swimming pools, Sheehan (P) filed suit based on the theories of implied warranty of merchantability and strict liability in tort.

RULE OF LAW

Where one sells consumer goods which retain their character as consumer goods after completion of performance, the provisions of the Uniform Commercial Code (U.C.C.) dealing with implied warranties apply, even if the transaction is predominantly one for the rendering of consumer services.

FACTS: After Anthony Pools (D) installed a swimming pool and diving board for the Sheehans (P), Sheehan (P) sustained bodily injuries when, walking toward the pool end of the diving board, he slipped and fell from the right side of the board and struck the coping of the pool. Sheehan (P) filed two causes of action for damages: (1) breach of an implied warranty of merchantability because the skid-resistant material built into the surface of the top of the diving board did not extend to the very edge on each side and (2) strict liability in tort because use of the "defective" diving board, particularly as positioned in the alcove of the pool, was unreasonably dangerous. The trial court directed a verdict for Anthony Pools (D) as to liability founded on warranty because the contract between the parties contained express warranties which superseded any other warranties, express or implied. The jury verdict on the strict liability issue was also in favor of Anthony Pools (D). The court of special appeals reversed and remanded for a new trial on the grounds that the swimming pool package constituted consumer goods, rendering ineffective an attempt by Anthony Pools (D) to limit the implied warranty of merchantability. Anthony Pools (D) petitioned the Maryland Supreme Court for certiorari.

ISSUE: Where one sells consumer goods which retain their character as consumer goods after completion of the promised performance, do the provisions of the U.C.C. dealing with implied warranties apply, even if the transaction is predominantly one for the rendering of consumer services?

HOLDING AND DECISION: (Rodowsky, J.) Yes. Where one sells consumer goods which retain their character as consumer goods after completion of the promised performance, the provisions of the U.C.C. dealing with implied warranties apply, even if the transaction is predominantly one for the rendering of consumer services. The subject contract presents a mixed or hybrid transaction. It is in part a contract for the rendering of services and in part a contract for the sale of goods. To determine the applicability of the U.C.C. in such a contract, the predominant purpose test has generally been applied. Were that test to be mechanically applied to the facts of this case, there would be no quality warranty implied as to the diving board. However, the diving board itself is not structurally integrated into the swimming pool. Anthony Pools (D) offered the board as an optional accessory. Thus, the diving board, considered alone, is goods. Had it been purchased by the Sheehans (P) in a transaction distinct from the pool construction agreement with Anthony (D), there would have been an implied warranty of merchantability. In addition, C.L. § 2-316.1 declares that a seller of consumer services may not contractually disclaim implied warranties. An all-or-nothing classification of the instant transaction under the predominant purpose test would be contrary to the legislative policy implicit in § 2-316.1. Therefore, the better test to apply is the gravamen test, focusing on whether the gravamen of the action involves goods or services. Using that test, the diving board carried an implied warranty of merchantability. Anthony Pools' (D) contractual disclaimer of that warranty was ineffective under C.L. § 2-316.1. As a result, the trial court erred in relying on the disclaimer as a basis for directing a verdict in favor of Anthony Pools (D) on the warranty count. Affirmed.

ANALYSIS

The court observed that a number of commentators advocated a more policy-oriented approach to determining whether warranties of quality and fitness were implied with respect to goods sold as part of a hybrid transaction in which service predominated. The gravamen test enunciated by the court was formulated by W. Hawkland in "Uniform Commercial Code Series (1982)," § 2-102:04, at Art. 2, p. 12. Another commentator, R. Anderson, had previously noted that: "It is probable that a goods-service transaction will come to be subjected to Article 2 of the Code insofar as the contractor's obligations with respect to the goods themselves are involved."

Continued on next page.

Quicknotes

IMPLIED WARRANTY OF MERCHANTABILITY An implied promise made by a merchant in a contract for the sale of goods that such goods are suitable for the purpose for which they are purchased.

STRICT LIABILITY Liability for all injuries proximately caused by a party's conducting of certain inherently dangerous activities without regard to negligence or fault.

Siemen v. Alden

Operator of sawmill (P) v. Manufacturer of saws (D)

Ill. App. Ct., 34 Il. App. 3d 961, 341 N.E.2d 713 (1975).

NATURE OF CASE: Appeal from summary judgment denying damages for strict liability and breach of warranty.

FACT SUMMARY: After he was injured while using an automated multirip saw manufactured by Alden (D) and purchased from Korleski (D), Siemen (P) sought damages based on theories of strict tort liability for sale of a defective product, breach of warranties, and negligence.

RULE OF LAW

A person making an isolated sale of goods is not a merchant within the scope of Article 2 of the Uniform Commercial Code (U.C.C.).

FACTS: When Siemen (P), owner and operator of a sawmill, tried to purchase a multirip saw from Alden (D), manufacturer of the saws, he was told that a new saw could not be delivered in less than six months. However, Alden (D) suggested that Siemen (P) contact Korleski (D), who owned two of the Alden (D) saws. Korleski (D) used one of the saws, while the other older saw sat partially dismantled and covered with boards and sawdust. After Korleski (D) informed Siemen (P) that he would have to supply and install various parts in order to use the saw, the parties agreed on a purchase price. Siemen (P) was later injured while operating the saw. He sought damages against both Alden (D) and Korleski (D) in strict tort liability for sale of a defective product, breach of warranties, and negligence. Alden (D) argued that it was not a merchant under the U.C.C. The trial court granted Alden's (D) motion for summary judgment on counts one and two. Siemen (P) filed this appeal against Korleski (D) only, contending that summary judgment in Korleski's (D) favor should be reversed because Korleski (D) had sufficient relationship to the saw to subject Korleski (D) to strict liability for sale of the defective product and, under the U.C.C., for breach of implied warranties.

ISSUE: Is a person making an isolated sale of goods a merchant within the scope of Article 2 of the U.C.C.?

HOLDING AND DECISION: (Moran, J.) No. A person making an isolated sale of goods is not a merchant within the scope of Article 2 of the U.C.C. U.C.C. § 2-314 states in pertinent part, "Unless excluded or modified . . . a warranty that the goods shall be merchantable is implied in a contract for their sale if the seller is a merchant with respect to goods of that kind." Korleski (D) was engaged in the sawmill business. The sale in the instant case was an isolated transaction and therefore did not come within the terms of § 2-314. In addition, U.C.C. § 2-315 provides that, where the seller has reason to know any particular purpose for which the goods are required and that the buyer is relying on the seller's skill or judgment to select or furnish suitable goods, there is an implied warranty that the goods shall be fit for such purpose. Here, the first requirement was met in that it was undisputed that Korleski (D) knew Siemen's (P) purpose for buying the saw. As to the second requirement, Siemen (P) failed to show sufficiently that he relied on Korleski's (D) skill and expertise in making the decision to purchase the saw. Rather, the uncontroverted facts established that Siemen (P) had decided to purchase an Alden (D) saw prior to his initial contact with Korleski (D). Therefore, the trial court properly granted Korleski's (D) motion for summary judgment. Affirmed.

ANALYSIS

U.C.C. § 2-104 defines a merchant as: "A person who deals in goods of the kind or otherwise by his occupation holds himself out as having knowledge or skill peculiar to the practices or goods involved in the transaction or to whom such knowledge or skill may be attributed by his employment of an agent or broker or other intermediary who by his occupation holds himself out as having such knowledge or skill." However, the court noted that the comments to § 2-314 make clear that the definition of a merchant within that section is a narrow one and that the warranty of merchantability is applicable only to a person who, in a professional status, sells the particular kind of goods giving rise to the warranty. Clearly, this narrow interpretation of the definition of a merchant does not apply to sawmill owner Korleski (D).

Quicknotes

NEGLIGENCE Conduct falling below the standard of care that a reasonable person would demonstrate under similar conditions.

STRICT LIABILITY Liability for all injuries proximately caused by a party's conducting of certain inherently dangerous activities without regard to negligence or fault.

SUMMARY JUDGMENT Judgment rendered by a court in response to a motion by one of the parties, claiming that the lack of a question of material fact in respect to an issue warrants disposition of the issue without consideration by the jury.

CHAPTER 2

Contract Formation

Quick Reference Rules of Law

St. Ansgar Mills, Inc. v. Streit

Grain dealer (P) v. Livestock farmer (D)

Iowa Sup. Ct., 613 N.W.2d 289, 42 U.C.C. Rep. Serv. 2d 58 (2000).

NATURE OF CASE: Appeal from an order of summary judgment in action to enforce an oral contract.

FACT SUMMARY: Duane Streit (Duane) (D) entered into an oral contract with St. Ansgar Mills, Inc. (St. Ansgar Mills) (P), a grain dealer, for 60,000 bushels of corn. Despite Duane's (D) long-standing custom of accepting delivery of grain from St. Ansgar Mills (P), notwithstanding the absence of, or long delay in obtaining, written confirmation of the parties' oral contracts, Duane (D) refused delivery in this instance because the market price of corn had plummeted between the time he placed his order and the delivery date. St. Ansgar Mills (P) sued for contract damages, and Duane (D) moved for summary judgment under the statute of frauds.

RULE OF LAW

For purposes of an exception to the statute of frauds, a delay in the delivery of a written confirmation of an oral contract of over a month is not unreasonable as a matter of law where the sale price is large and the market is volatile but where the parties have developed a custom and practice of delaying written confirmation.

FACTS: Duane Streit (Duane) (D), a livestock farmer, and his father, John, who helped with the farming operations, called St. Ansgar Mills, Inc. (St. Ansgar Mills) (P), a grain dealer, via telephone on July 1, 1996, to place two orders for 60,000 bushels of corn to be delivered in December 1996 and May 1997. Duane (D) later refused delivery of the corn that had been orally purchased. The custom between the parties for many years had been that Duane (D) would enter into an oral contract with St. Ansgar Mills (P). St. Ansgar Mills (P) would prepare a written confirmation of the sale and then would either mail it to Duane (D) to sign and return or wait for Duane (D) or John to sign the confirmation when they would stop into the business, which they regularly did on a monthly basis. Sometimes the confirmation would not be signed for a very long time, or it would never be returned, but in any event, Duane (D) had never before refused delivery. Departing from their monthly routine, the Streits did not come to the business in July and did not receive the written confirmation until John stopped by on August 10, 1996. St. Ansgar Mills (P) did not have an explanation for why it did not send the confirmation to Duane (D) immediately after John failed to make his July stop at the business. Between July and December, the market price of corn plummeted. St. Ansgar Mills (P) brought an action for contract damages of $152,100 (the difference between the contract price and the market price at the time of delivery refusal), and Duane (D) moved for summary judgment, claiming the oral contract was unenforceable as a matter of law under the Universal Commercial Code's (U.C.C.'s) statute of frauds. The trial court granted the motion on the ground that St. Ansgar Mills's (P) delay of getting written confirmation to Duane (D) until August 10 was, as a matter of law, unreasonable.

ISSUE: For purposes of an exception to the statute of frauds, is a delay in the delivery of a written confirmation of an oral contract of over a month unreasonable as a matter of law where the sale price is large and the market is volatile but where the parties have developed a custom and practice of delaying written confirmation?

HOLDING AND DECISION: (Cady, J.) No. For purposes of an exception to the statute of frauds, a delay in the delivery of a written confirmation of an oral contract of over a month is not unreasonable as a matter of law where the sale price is large and the market is volatile but where the parties have developed a custom and practice of delaying written confirmation. The statute of frauds, which is codified in the U.C.C. (Iowa Code § 554.2201), requires certain types of contracts for the sale of goods for $500 or more to be in writing. One statutory exception to the writing requirement applies to merchants where written confirmation of an oral contract is received within a reasonable time. The standard of reasonableness to establish the time in which the confirmation must be received is a flexible one and is defined in relationship to the "nature, purpose and circumstances" of the action. The "circumstances" include the custom and practice—course of dealings—of the parties and must be considered in determining what constitutes a reasonable time. Generally, the question of reasonableness of conduct is a jury question, and usually the question of what constitutes a reasonable time under the written confirmation exception of the U.C.C. is a jury question unless the evidence is so one-sided that one party should prevail as a matter of law. As demonstrated by a host of cases, the resolution of each case depends on the particular facts and circumstances. Here, the trial court relied on the large amount of the sale, volatile market conditions, and lack of an explanation by St. Ansgar Mills (P) for failing to send the written confirmation to Duane (D) to determine that St. Ansgar Mills (P) acted unreasonably as a matter of law. However, other relevant factors that must be considered are the custom and

Continued on next page.

practice of the parties to delay delivery of the confirmation and that the parties had engaged in many other similar transactions without incident. The evidence also supports an inference that St. Ansgar Mills (P) did not suspect John's failure to follow his customary practice in July of stopping by the business was a concern at the time. Accordingly, there is a genuine dispute over the reasonableness of the delay in delivering the written confirmation, and the resolution of this issue is appropriate for a jury. Reversed and remanded.

ANALYSIS

Merchant confirmation letters are one of four of the exceptions to the written contract requirement under the statute of frauds, along with special manufacture, part performance, and admission in legal proceedings. As this case demonstrates, many issues can arise with regard to each exception. For example, in this case, in addition to the issue on appeal, an issue that had come before the trial court was whether Duane (D) was a merchant. Unlike its decision with regard to written confirmation, the trial court's decision on the "merchant" issue was that a jury question was presented.

Quicknotes

STATUTE OF FRAUDS A statute that requires specified types of contracts to be in writing in order to be binding.

Columbia Nitrogen Corp. v. Royster Co.

Purchaser (D) v. Manufacturer (P)

451 F.2d 3 (4th Cir. 1971).

NATURE OF CASE: Appeal in breach of contract action for exclusion of evidence.

FACT SUMMARY: Following a drastic drop in the price of phosphate, Columbia Nitrogen Corp. (Columbia) (D) insisted that evidence of the course of dealing and trade usage should be admitted into evidence to show that Columbia (D) was not obliged to purchase a yearly minimum quantity of phosphate from Royster Co. (P) at the original contract price.

RULE OF LAW

Even if a court finds a sales contract to be intended by the parties as a complete and exclusive statement of the terms of the agreement, those terms may still be explained or interpreted by parol evidence as to the course of dealing, usage of the trade, or course of performance.

FACTS: Royster Co. (P), a manufacturer and seller of mixed fertilizers, had for many years been a major purchaser of nitrogen from Columbia Nitrogen Corp. (Columbia) (D), although, previous to the contract in question, Columbia (D) had never been a significant customer of Royster (P). However, in 1966 both companies contracted for Royster (P) to sell a minimum of 31,000 tons of phosphate yearly to Columbia (D) at a stated price. Soon thereafter, phosphate prices dropped so steeply that Columbia (D) was unable to resell the phosphate at a competitive price. Although Royster (P) made some concessions, it came to the point where Columbia (D) finally refused to accept delivery. Royster (P), therefore, sold the unaccepted phosphate for Columbia's (D) account at a price substantially below the contract price and brought this suit for the balance. During the trial, Columbia (D) had offered evidence: (1) that due to numerous factors (weather, farming practices, etc.), it was the practice of the trade to regard express price and quantity terms of this type of contract to be a mere projection subject to adjustment according to market forces; (2) that during the six years' course of dealing in which Columbia (D) had sold to Royster (P), there had been a pattern of repeated and substantial deviation from the contract price, and there were four instances in which Royster (P) had taken none of the goods for which it had contracted. However, the district court excluded this evidence on the grounds that "custom and usage or course of dealing are not admissible to contradict the express, plain, and unambiguous language of a valid written contract which, by virtue of its detail, negates the proposition that the contract is open to variances in its terms." Columbia (D) cited this as error and appealed the judgment in the amount of $75,000 for Royster (P).

ISSUE: Even if a court finds a sales contract to be intended by the parties as a complete and exclusive statement of the terms of the agreement, may those terms still be explained or interpreted by parol evidence as to the course of dealing, usage of the trade, or course of performance?

HOLDING AND DECISION: (Butzner, J.) Yes. Even if a court finds a sales contract to be intended by the parties as a complete and exclusive statement of the terms of the agreement, those terms may still be explained or interpreted by parol evidence as to the course of dealing, usage of the trade, or course of performance. This is in accord with Universal Commercial Code (U.C.C.) § 1-102, which speaks of expanding "commercial practices through custom, usage, and agreement of the parties." Also, U.C.C. § 2-202 explicitly authorizes evidence of the usage of the trade and course of dealing between the parties to explain or supplement a contract. The official comment states that the latter section rejects the old rule that such evidence may be introduced only when the contract is ambiguous. A finding of ambiguity is not necessary for the admission of such evidence. Royster's (P) next argument was based on the premise that the evidence should be excluded because this contract was complete on its face. However, reading U.C.C. § 2-202 in the light of U.C.C. § 1-205(4), the test of admissibility is not whether the contract appears on its face to be complete in every detail but whether the proffered evidence of the course of dealing and usage of the trade can reasonably be construed as consistent with the express terms of the contract. But the evidence offered here—indicating that dealers usually adjust prices due to various factors—is consistent with the terms of this contract since (1) the contract does not exclude the use of such evidence; (2) the contract is silent or neutral about adjusting prices and quantities to reflect a declining market; (3) the contract's description for minimum tonnages and additional quantities is consistent with what the proffered testimony purports to show; and (4) the default clause in the contract refers only to the buyer's failure to pay, whereas this default is based on Columbia's (D) failure to take delivery. Further, the problem cannot be solved by applying general contract law, as Royster (P) insisted. Before a court can reach the point of allowing damages under contract law, it must determine if there has been a default. This requires interpreting the agreement by such evidence as is here offered.

Continued on next page.

Finally, Royster (P) argued that the contract excludes "verbal misunderstandings." However, according to U.C.C. § 2-202, the course of dealing and usage of the trade are not synonymous with verbal misunderstandings and can be used to modify a complete statement unless carefully negated. Therefore, Columbia's (D) evidence about the course of dealing and usage of the trade should have been admitted. Reversed and remanded for new trial.

ANALYSIS

In non-U.C.C. transactions, the parol evidence rule generally operates both as a rule of evidence and of substantive law, excluding evidence of verbal representations or understandings which would alter or vary the terms of the written document. The basic assumption is that if the parties have executed a written statement, they intended it to be a complete and final statement of the agreed-upon terms. However, as to sales contracts, the Code rejects the assumption that because a writing has been worked out which is final on some matters, it is to be taken as including all matters agreed upon. Instead, before the writing can operate to exclude parol evidence, the court must find that the parties intended the writing to be the complete and exclusive statement of the terms of the agreement. As indicated above, even those terms may be explained or interpreted by parol evidence as to course of dealing, usage of trade, or course of performance.

Quicknotes

COURSE OF DEALING Previous conduct between two parties to a contact which may be relied upon to interpret their actions.

COURSE OF PERFORMANCE Previous conduct between two parties to a contact which may be relied upon to interpret their actions.

USAGE OF TRADE A course of dealing or practice commonly used in a particular trade.

Diamond Fruit Growers, Inc. v. Krack Corp.

Buyer (P) v. Manufacturer (D)

794 F.2d 1440 (9th Cir. 1986).

NATURE OF CASE: Appeal from award of consequential damages for breach of warranty.

FACT SUMMARY: Krack Corp. (D) and Metal Matic (D) disputed the effectiveness of a disclaimer of consequential damages that Metal Matic (D) included on order acknowledgment forms.

RULE OF LAW

Under Universal Commercial Code (U.C.C.) § 2-207, when an offeree conditions its acceptance on assent to additional terms and the parties have proceeded as if there is a contract, if the offeror does not give specific unequivocal assent, the provisions of § 2-207(3) will supply the terms of the contract.

FACTS: Metal Matic (D) sold tubing to Krack Corp. (Krack) (D) for use in the cooling systems that Krack (D) manufactured. Krack (D) sent a blanket purchase order to Metal Matic (D) at the beginning of the year for its tubing requirements for that year. As the tubing was needed, Krack (D) sent release purchase orders requesting that the tubing be delivered. Metal Matic (D) returned an acknowledgment form and shipped the tubing. Metal Matic's (D) acknowledgment made its acceptance conditional on the purchaser's assent to the terms of the acknowledgment. It also contained a provision that disclaimed all liability for consequential damages. Krack's (D) purchase orders did not contain this provision. In previous dealings, Krack (D) had attempted to have the disclaimer eliminated but Metal Matic (D) refused. Diamond Fruit Growers, Inc. (Diamond) (P) purchased a cooling system from Krack (D) which failed due to defective tubing. Diamond (P) filed suit against Krack (D), which in turn filed a third-party complaint against Metal Matic (D), seeking contribution. At trial, the jury ruled for Diamond (P) and that Krack (D) was entitled to contribution from Metal Matic (D). Metal Matic (D) appealed, contending that the disclaimer of consequential damages prevented contribution liability.

ISSUE: Under U.C.C. § 2-207, when an offeree conditions its acceptance on assent to additional terms and the parties have proceeded as if there is a contract, if the offeror does not give specific unequivocal assent, will the provisions of § 2-207(3) supply the terms of the contract?

HOLDING AND DECISION: (Wiggins, J.) Yes. Under U.C.C. § 2-207, when an offeree conditions its acceptance on assent to additional terms and the parties have proceeded as if there is a contract, if the offeror does not give specific unequivocal assent, the provisions of § 2-207(3) will supply the terms of the contract. U.C.C. § 2-207 replaces the last shot doctrine of common law. Under the last shot rule, the terms contained in the last form to which no objection is made control the contract. Under § 2-207, the terms on which the parties disagree drop out, and the U.C.C. supplies the missing terms. If the offeror fails to give specific assent to a different term in the offeree's form, that term is eliminated. Metal Matic's (D) acknowledgment form contained a consequential damages disclaimer not contained on Krack's (D) purchase order. Although Krack (D) accepted delivery of the tubing, this was not sufficient to show that Krack (D) assented to the different term. Therefore, the disclaimer was ineffective, and the U.C.C. supplies the contract's warranty terms. The U.C.C. allows for consequential damages unless disclaimed, so Krack (D) is entitled to those damages since the disclaimer was ineffective. Here, the verdict was supported by the evidence and was consistent with the U.C.C., so that denial of motion for a judgment n.o.v. was not erroneous. Affirmed.

ANALYSIS

The decision is in accord with the White and Summer viewpoint. They acknowledge that when § 2-207(3) supplies the contract's terms, it often works to the disadvantage of the seller. This is due to the fact that sellers typically desire to limit their liability when the U.C.C. seeks to hold them liable.

Quicknotes

CONSEQUENTIAL DAMAGES Monetary compensation that may be recovered in order to compensate for injuries or losses sustained as a result of damages that are not the direct or foreseeable result of the act of a party, but that nevertheless are the consequence of such act and which must be specifically pled and demonstrated.

CONTRIBUTION The right of a person or party who has compensated a victim for his injury to seek reimbursement from others who are equally responsible for the injury in proportional amounts.

Bayway Refining Co. v. Oxygenated Marketing and Trading A.G.

Seller (P) v. Buyer (D)

215 F.3d 219 (2d Cir. 2000).

NATURE OF CASE: Appeal from summary judgment order finding that, as a matter of law, an additional term to a contract did not materially alter the contract.

FACT SUMMARY: Bayway Refining Co. (Bayway) (P) sold to Oxygenated Marketing and Trading A.G. (OMT) (D) a petroleum product, and, as required by federal law, paid an excise tax on the transaction. Bayway's (P) acceptance confirmation incorporated by reference the company's general terms and conditions, which included a provision that shifted responsibility of any excise taxes in a transaction to the buyer. OMT (D) did not object to the acceptance and accepted delivery. Bayway (P) demanded payment of the excise tax in addition to the purchase price. OMT (D) argued it had not agreed to make the tax payment and refused to pay it. Bayway (P) sued for breach of contract.

RULE OF LAW

In a "battle of the forms" case, the party opposing the inclusion of an additional term bears the burden of proving that the term works a material alteration of the contract.

FACTS: Bayway Refining Co. (Bayway) (P) sold to Oxygenated Marketing and Trading A.G. (OMT) (D) 60,000 barrels of a gasoline blendstock known as MTBE. In response to OMT's (D) written confirmation, which served as an offer, Bayway (P) faxed its confirmation, which served as the acceptance, the next day. That acceptance incorporated by reference Bayway's (P) "General Terms and Conditions," which had not been transmitted with the confirming fax. Those terms and conditions contained a clause (the Tax Clause) that shifted to the buyer the responsibility of paying any non-income taxes related to a certain transaction. Federal law imposes an excise tax, payable by the seller, on the sale of gasoline blendstocks to any buyer who is not registered under federal law for a tax exemption. After delivery, Bayway (P) learned that OMT (D) was not registered for the exemption and that, therefore, the transaction created a tax liability of $464,035.12, which Bayway (P) paid. Invoking the Tax Clause, Bayway (P) demanded payment by OMT (D) of the tax. OMT (D) denied it had agreed to pay the tax and refused to pay it. Bayway (P) filed suit in federal district court for breach of contract. The district court held that the Tax Clause had been properly incorporated into the contract, and granted summary judgment in favor of Bayway (P), concluding that OMT (D) had failed to carry its burden of proving that the Tax Clause materially altered the contract.

ISSUE: In a "battle of the forms" case, does the party opposing the inclusion of an additional term bear the burden of proving that the term works a material alteration of the contract?

HOLDING AND DECISION: (Jacobs, J.) Yes. In a "battle of the forms" case, the party opposing the inclusion of an additional term bears the burden of proving that the term works a material alteration of the contract. Bayway's (P) confirming fax was effective to form a contract even though it referenced additional terms, such as the Tax Clause. Therefore, under the Universal Commercial Code (U.C.C.), the Tax Clause is a proposal for an addition to the contract, and (as between two merchants, as here) is presumed to become part of the contract unless one of three exceptions applies. Here, OMT (D) invokes the "material alteration" exception. Because the general provision provides that the additional term becomes part of the contract, it is a presumption of the intent of the contracting parties. To implement that presumption, the burden of proving the materiality of the alteration must fall on the party that opposes inclusion. Here, OMT (D) has failed to carry that burden. A material alteration is one that would "result in surprise or hardship if incorporated without express awareness by the other party." Certain terms are deemed material per se. Here, the Tax Clause is not per se material because it does not provide for open-ended tax liability, but merely allocates responsibility for a tax payable on one specific transaction; it is limited, discrete, and the subject of no special protection. Therefore, OMT (D) must prove that the Tax Clause resulted in surprise or hardship. With regard to surprise, OMT (D) must show not only that it was subjectively surprised, but also that it was objectively surprised, i.e., what it should have known. OMT (D) established that it was subjectively surprised—the company truly felt ambushed—but it failed to show that a reasonable petroleum merchant would have been surprised by the Tax Clause. Moreover, Bayway (P) introduced evidence that the Tax Clause reflected custom and practice in the petroleum industry. OMT (D) challenged this evidence as raising a genuine issue of fact. A review of the evidence shows that shifting tax liability to a buyer is the custom and practice in the petroleum industry. Expert opinions and other contracts from the industry support that conclusion, as does common sense, because it is the buyer who controls whether any tax liability will be incurred in a transaction, since it is within the buyer's control as to whether it will be registered for a tax exemption. Because allocating tax

Continued on next page.

liability to the buyer is the custom and practice in the petroleum industry, OMT (D) could not objectively be surprised by the incorporation of the Tax Clause, which merely reflected that practice. As to hardship, OMT (D) failed to raise a genuine issue of material fact. Its only evidence on this issue was that it is a small business that would suffer a loss it cannot afford by having to shoulder the tax liability. This does not amount to hardship. Typically, hardship comes about from an additional contract term that creates open-ended or prolonged liability. Here, any loss that the Tax Clause imposed on OMT (D) would be limited, routine, and self-inflicted [because OMT (D) could have avoided the liability by registering for the exemption]. Affirmed.

ANALYSIS

The result of this case, like the result of many "battle of the forms" cases under U.C.C. § 2-207, should serve as a warning to merchants to carefully read the boilerplate on standard preprinted purchase order and acknowledgment forms that they receive. Had OMT (D) read Bayway's (P) acceptance fax, it could at the very least have requested and reviewed Bayway's (P) General Terms and Conditions and could have objected to Bayway's (P) acceptance or the incorporation of the Terms and Conditions if it so chose.

Quicknotes

BATTLE OF THE FORMS Refers to the exchange of forms, pursuant to a contract for the sale of goods, between a buyer and seller.

MATERIAL TERMS OF CONTRACT A fact without the existence of which a contract would not have been entered.

U.C.C. § 2-207 Provides that a definite expression of acceptance sent within a reasonable time operates as an acceptance even though it states terms additional to or different from those offered, unless acceptance is expressly made conditional on assent to the additional terms.

Northrop Corp. v. Litronic Industries

Purchasing merchant/defense contractor (P) v. Selling merchant/manufacturer (D)

29 F.3d 1173 (7th Cir. 1994).

NATURE OF CASE: Appeal from judgment for plaintiff in action for breach of warranty.

FACT SUMMARY: Litronic Industries (Litronic) (D) contended that under Uniform Commercial Code (U.C.C.) § 2-207, a 90-day warranty contained in its offer for the sale of printed wire boards to Northrop Corp. (P) became part of the contract between the parties notwithstanding that Northrop's (P) purchase order, which was part of Northrop's (P) acceptance, contained an unlimited warranty.

RULE OF LAW

Under U.C.C. § 2-207, where an offer and acceptance contain different terms, the discrepant terms fall out and are replaced by a suitable U.C.C. gap-filler.

FACTS: Northrop Corp. (P) solicited offers for the sale of printed wire boards. Northrop's (P) request stated that any purchase would be made by means of a purchase order that would set forth terms and conditions that would override any inconsistent terms in the offer. In response, Litronic Industries (Litronic) (D) mailed an offer to sell Northrop (P) four boards. The offer contained a 90-day warranty stated to be in lieu of any other warranties, and provided that the terms of the offer would take precedence over any terms proposed by the buyer. Lynch, Northrop's (P) purchasing agent, accepted the offer, indicating to Lair, a Litronic's (D) employee, a formal purchase order would follow. Northrop's (P) purchase order form provided for a warranty that contained no time limit. Litronic (D) had done business with Northrop (P) before, and was familiar with its purchase order terms. The purchase order was sent after Litronic (D) began manufacturing several boards. Thereafter, Litronic (D) delivered several boards. Northrup (P) took between five and six months to inspect the boards, which Northrup (P) found to be defective and returned. Litronic (D) refused to accept the return of the boards, on the ground that its 90-day warranty had lapsed. Northrop's (P) position was that it had an unlimited warranty, as stated in the purchase order. Northrup (P) brought suit for breach of warranty, and sought a refund of the monies it had paid to Litronic (D) for the boards. The district court, finding that under U.C.C. § 2-207 the discrepant warranty terms of the offer and acceptance fell out and were replaced by a suitable U.C.C. gap-filler provision, determined that under U.C.C. § 2-309, which provides that nonconforming goods may be rejected within a "reasonable" time, held that the six months that Northrop (P) took to reject Litronic's (D) boards was a reasonable time because of the complexity of the required testing. The court of appeals granted review.

ISSUE: Under U.C.C. § 2-207, where an offer and acceptance contain different terms, do the discrepant terms fall out and are they replaced by a suitable U.C.C. gap-filler?

HOLDING AND DECISION: (Posner, C.J.) Yes. Under U.C.C. § 2-207, where an offer and acceptance contain different terms, the discrepant terms fall out and are replaced by a suitable U.C.C. gap-filler. Section 2-207(1) provides that "a definite and seasonable expression of acceptance or a written confirmation which is sent within a reasonable time operates as an acceptance even though it states terms additional to or different from those offered or agreed upon, unless acceptance is made conditional on assent to the additional or different terms." Section 2-207(2) provides that if additional terms in the acceptance are not materially different from those in the offer, then, subject to certain other qualifications, they become part of the contract, while if the additional terms are materially different they operate as proposals and so have no effect unless the offeror agrees to them. Thus, if the offeror does not agree to them, the terms of the contract are those in the offer. The U.C.C. does not explain, however, what happens if the offeree's response contains different terms (rather than additional ones). The majority view is that the discrepant terms in both the nonidentical offer and the acceptance drop out, and default terms found elsewhere in the U.C.C. fill the resulting gap. This approach was the one taken by the district court. The minority view is that the offeree's discrepant terms drop out and the offeror's become part of the contract. A third view, adopted by only one state's courts (those of California), equates "different" with "additional" and makes the outcome turn on whether the new terms in the acceptance are materially different from the terms in the offer—in which event they operate as proposals, so that the offeror's terms prevail unless he agrees to the variant terms in the acceptance—or not materially different from the terms in the offer, in which event they become part of the contract. The state courts, the case law of which must be followed in this case, have not had occasion to choose among these approaches to the issue. Given, however, that this state's courts tend to adopt the majority position and because the interest in the uniform nationwide application of the U.C.C. argues for moving majority views toward unanimity, the majority view will be adopted unless there is good reason not to—

Continued on next page.

which there is not. Accordingly, that approach will be applied here. Under that approach, Litronic's (D) 90-day warranty was part of the offer. Lynch's acceptance was sufficiently definite to satisfy the requirement of definiteness in § 2-207(1), since it impelled Litronic (D) to begin production immediately, and there is no suggestion that it acted precipitately in doing so. Northrop's (P) acceptance was not expressly conditioned on Litronic's (D) yielding to Northrop's (P) demand for an open-ended warranty. Although Lynch's reference to the purchase order might have alerted Litronic (D) to Northrop's (P) desire for a warranty not limited to 90 days, Lynch did not purport to make the more extensive warranty a condition of acceptance. Therefore, there was a contract, and the issue becomes on what terms, and, more specifically, what the terms of the warranty were. Lynch did not accept Litronic's (D) offer and leave it at that. He said that he would issue a Northrop (P) purchase order, and both he and Lair knew (or at least should have known) that the purchase order form contained a different warranty from Litronic's (D) sale order form. In other words, Lynch said enough to make clear to Lair that the acceptance contained different terms from the offer. Therefore, the discrepant terms fall out, and the U.C.C. gap-filler provision (U.C.C. § 2-309) is applied. That provision applies a reasonable (rather than unlimited) warranty period. Here, it seems that given the complexity of the boards at issue, it was not unreasonable for Northrop (P) to take six months to inspect the boards. Accordingly, the district court's application of this provision was not erroneous. Furthermore, Northrop's (P) argument that the 90-day warranty period was unconscionable is rejected; the defense of unconscionability was not invented to protect multi-billion dollar corporations (like Northrop (P)) against mistakes committed by their employees. Affirmed.

ANALYSIS

The idea behind the majority view adopted by the court in this case is that the presence of different terms in the acceptance suggests that the offeree didn't really accede to the offeror's terms, yet both parties wanted to contract, so why not find a neutral term to govern the dispute that has arisen between them? Of course the offeree may not have had any serious objection to the terms in the offer at the time of contracting; he may have mailed a boilerplated form without giving any thought to its contents or to its suitability for the particular contract in question. But it is just as likely that the discrepant terms in the offer itself were the product of a thoughtless use of a boilerplate form rather than a considered condition of contracting. And if the offeror doesn't want to do business other than on the terms in the offer, he can protect himself by specifying that the offeree must accept all those terms for the parties to have a contract. The offeror goes first and therefore has a little more time for careful specification of the terms on which he is willing to make a contract. Under the leading minority view, the offeror may be tempted to spring a surprise on the offeree, hoping the latter won't read the fine print. Under the majority view, if the offeree tries to spring a surprise (the offeror can't, since his terms won't prevail if the acceptance contains different terms), the parties move to neutral ground. According to Judge Posner, the California approach is the best one because it "dissolves all these problems."

Quicknotes

ACCEPTANCE Assent to the specified terms of an offer resulting in the formation of a binding agreement.

BREACH OF WARRANTY The breach of a promise made by one party to a contract on which the other party may rely, relieving that party from the obligation of determining whether the fact is true and indemnifying the other party from liability if that fact is shown to be false.

OFFER A proposed promise to undertake performance of an action, or to refrain from acting, that is to become binding upon acceptance by the offeree.

U.C.C. § 2-207 Provides that a definite expression of acceptance sent within a reasonable time operates as an acceptance even though it states terms additional to or different from those offered, unless acceptance is expressly made conditional on assent to the additional terms.

U.C.C. § 2-207 (1) Provides that a valid contract may exist where the acceptance contains additional terms not present in the offer, unless the offer specifically limits acceptance from including additional terms.

U.C.C. § 2-309 Provides that reasonable notification of termination be given if successive performance has come to be expected over an indefinite time period.

Klocek v. Gateway, Inc.

Consumer (P) v. Computer vendor (D)

104 F. Supp. 2d 1332 (D. Kan. 2000).

NATURE OF CASE: Motion to dismiss on the ground that claims brought by the purchaser of a computer must be arbitrated pursuant to the vendor's standard agreement included with the computer.

FACT SUMMARY: William Klocek (P) purchased a computer from Gateway, Inc. (D), which included a copy of its Standard Terms and Conditions Agreement (Standard Terms) with the computer. The Standard Terms provided that they would be accepted by the purchaser if the computer was kept beyond five days and also provided for arbitration of any claims arising from the agreement. Klocek (P) sued Gateway (D) for breach of contract and of warranty. Gateway (D) moved to dismiss, asserting that the claims had to be arbitrated under the Standard Terms agreement.

RULE OF LAW

Terms shipped with a computer do not become part of the sales contract where the vendor does not expressly make its acceptance conditional on the buyer's assent to the additional, shipped terms and where the buyer does not expressly agree to the terms.

FACTS: William Klocek (P) purchased a computer from Gateway, Inc. (D), which included a copy of its Standard Terms and Conditions Agreement (Standard Terms) in the box that contained the computer battery power cables and instruction manuals. The Standard Terms provided in bold type that they would be accepted by the purchaser if the computer was kept beyond five days. Paragraph 10 of the Standard Terms provided for arbitration of any claims arising from the agreement. Klocek (P) sued Gateway (D) for breach of contract and of warranty, and Gateway (D) moved to dismiss, asserting that the claims had to be arbitrated under the Standard Terms agreement.

ISSUE: Do terms shipped with a computer become part of the sales contract where the vendor does not expressly make its acceptance conditional on the buyer's assent to the additional, shipped terms, and where the buyer does not expressly agree to the terms?

HOLDING AND DECISION: (Vratil, J.) No. Terms shipped with a computer do not become part of the sales contract where the vendor does not expressly make its acceptance conditional on the buyer's assent to the additional, shipped terms and where the buyer does not expressly agree to the terms. Gateway (D) bears an initial burden of showing that it is entitled to arbitration. To do so, it must demonstrate that an enforceable agreement to arbitrate exists. When deciding if such an agreement exists, the court applies state law contract formation principles. Here, the Universal Commercial Code (U.C.C.) governs the parties' transaction under both Kansas and Missouri law. The fact that Klocek (P) paid for and received a computer is evidence of a contract for the sale of a computer. Here, the issue is whether terms received with a product become part of the parties' agreement—an issue not decided by either Kansas or Missouri state courts. Authority from other courts is split, and seems to depend on whether the court finds that the parties formed their contract before or after the vendor communicated its terms to the purchaser. Gateway (D) urges following the approach taken by the Seventh Circuit, which enforced an arbitration clause in a situation similar to the one in this case. The Seventh Circuit reasoned that by including the license with the software, the vendor proposed a contract that the buyer could accept by using the software after having an opportunity to read the license. The Seventh Circuit, however, concluded, without support, that U.C.C. § 2-207 was irrelevant because the case involved only one written form, and that the vendor was the master of the offer. The Missouri or Kansas courts would not follow this reasoning because nothing in the language of § 2-207 precludes its application in a case that involves only one form. By its terms, § 2-207 applies to an acceptance or written confirmation. Therefore, the state courts would apply § 2-207 to the facts of this case. In addition, in typical consumer transactions, it is the purchaser who is the offeror, and the vendor is the offeree. Here, Gateway (D) has provided no evidence that would support a finding that it was the offeror—and therefore could propose limitations on the kind of conduct that constituted acceptance. Instead, the court assumes that plaintiff offered to purchase the computer and that Gateway (D) accepted plaintiff's offer. Under § 2-207, the Standard Terms are either an expression of acceptance or written confirmation. As an expression of acceptance, they would constitute a counteroffer only if Gateway (D) expressly made its acceptance conditional on Klocek's (P) assent to the additional or different terms, but, here, Gateway (D) has not shown that its mere shipment of the Standard Terms with the computer communicated to the plaintiff that the sale was conditioned on his acceptance of the Standard Terms. Because Klocek (P) was not a merchant, any additional or different terms contained in the Standard Terms did not become part of the parties' agreement unless Klocek (P) expressly agreed to them. Gateway (D) has not shown that

Continued on next page.

Klocek (P) expressly agreed to the Standard Terms. It provided no evidence that it informed Klocek (P) of the five-day review-and-return period as a condition of the sales transaction, or that the parties contemplated additional terms to the agreement. The fact that Klocek (P) kept the computer past five days was insufficient to demonstrate that he expressly agreed to the Standard Terms. Therefore, Gateway (D) has not shown that Klocek (P) agreed to the arbitration provision, and its motion to dismiss is overruled.

ANALYSIS

The decision in this case would find support from legal commentators who have found that software shrinkwrap agreements are a form of adhesion contracts and who have criticized the line of cases that support such agreements, such as those in the Seventh Circuit, on the grounds that they ignore the issue of informed consumer consent. Nonetheless, several courts have followed the Seventh Circuit line of cases.

Quicknotes

ADHESION CONTRACT A contract that is not negotiated and is usually prepared by the dominant party on a "take it or leave it" basis.

SHRINKWRAP LICENSE Terms of restriction packaged inside a product.

U.C.C. § 2-207 Provides that a definite expression of acceptance sent within a reasonable time operates as an acceptance even though it states terms additional to or different from those offered, unless acceptance is expressly made conditional on assent to the additional terms.

CHAPTER 3

Warranties

Quick Reference Rules of Law

CHAPTER 3

Moore v. Pro Team Corvette Sales, Inc.

Buyer (P) v. Seller (D)

Ohio Ct. App., 152 Ohio App. 3d 71, 786 N.E.2d 903 (2002).

NATURE OF CASE: Appeal from the County Common Pleas Court's dismissal of a breach of warranty suit.

FACT SUMMARY: Bryon Moore (P) brought a breach of warranty action against Pro Team Corvette Sales, Inc. (Pro Team) (D), for having sold him a stolen vehicle.

RULE OF LAW

A sales contract must contain precise and unambiguous language in order to disclaim the implied warranty of good title, codified in Uniform Commercial Code (U.C.C.) § 2-312.

FACTS: Bryon Moore (P), a Michigan resident, purchased a 1974 Corvette from Pro Team Corvette Sales, Inc. (Pro Team) (D), an Ohio corporation. When he attempted to register it he discovered that it had been stolen in Texas. Consequently, the Michigan State Police, where Moore (P) lived, confiscated the vehicle and returned it to the Texas authorities. Moore (P) brought suit against Pro Team (D) under multiple theories, but ultimately dismissed all allegations except a breach of statutory warranty claim. The County Common Pleas Court dismissed the suit, finding that Pro Team (D) had disclaimed the statutory warranty by stating in the sales contract that the car was being sold "as is" and that all warranties were excluded from the agreement. Moore (P) appealed.

ISSUE: Must a sales contract contain precise and unambiguous language in order to disclaim the implied warranty of good title, codified in U.C.C. § 2-312?

HOLDING AND DECISION: (Walters, J.) Yes. A sales contract must contain precise and unambiguous language in order to disclaim the implied warranty of good title, codified in U.C.C. § 2-312. Section 2-312 of the U.C.C., as adopted by Ohio, adds to any sales contract, absent an express exclusion or modification, a warranty by the seller that the title conveyed "shall be good and its transfer rightful." This statutory warranty requires the seller to convey a good title, free from any security interest, lien, or encumbrance of which the buyer is not aware at the time of contracting. The contractual language required to disclaim this statutory warranty of good title must clearly convey to the buyer that the disclaimer applies to the title. The disclaimer must be so precise and unambiguous as to eliminate any idea in the buyer's mind that it only applies to the quality of the item being sold. Pro Team's (D) sales contract with Moore (P) stated, "All Warranties pursuant to U.C.C. § 2-312 are hereby excluded from this transaction." This language appears to limit the seller's liability and does not specifically and clearly inform the buyer that the disclaimer applies to the title. The court found the disclaimer to be ineffective in relieving Pro Team (D) from its statutory warranty. Dismissal was inappropriate under these circumstances. Reversed and remanded.

ANALYSIS

The U.C.C. specifically divides warranties into the two basic categories of title and quality. These supplemental contractual terms are designed to add substance to a seller's oral or written representations about a product to prevent deceptive sales practices. In order for a seller to disclaim one of these warranties, they must do so with clear, express language in the contract so a buyer is fully aware of what he or she is purchasing and what he or she is not purchasing. The courts will, in most cases, construe any ambiguity against the seller.

Quicknotes

IMPLIED WARRANTY An implied promise made by one party to a contract that the other party may rely on a fact, relieving that party from the obligation of determining whether the fact is true and indemnifying the other party from liability if that fact is shown to be false.

Lindholm v. Brant

Painting's owner (P) v. Purchaser of painting from dealer unauthorized to sell (D)

Conn. Sup. Ct., 283 Conn. 65, 925 A.2d 1048 (2007).

NATURE OF CASE: Appeal from judgment holding that a purchaser was a buyer in the ordinary course of business and therefore not liable in an action for conversion.

FACT SUMMARY: Lindholm (P), who had entrusted her painting to Malmberg, an art dealer, but who had not authorized him to sell the painting, contended that Brant (D), who purchased the painting from Malmberg, was not a buyer in the ordinary course of business, and, therefore, could be held liable to her for conversion of the painting.

RULE OF LAW

A merchant buyer of goods who follows the usual or customary practices of, and observes reasonable commercial standards of fair dealing in, a certain industry is a buyer in the ordinary course of business for purposes of purchasing the rights of an entruster who has entrusted the goods to a dealer who deals in goods of that kind.

FACTS: Lindholm (P) owned the painting by Andy Warhol known as *Red Elvis.* She entrusted the painting to Malmberg, a respected art dealer known for his honesty and integrity, for the sole purpose of having the painting exhibited in museums around the world. She did not authorize Malmberg to sell the painting. Nonetheless, Malmberg (contrary to his otherwise solid reputation) sold the painting to Brant (D), an art merchant, for $2.9 million. Before purchasing the painting, Brant (D) took the extraordinary step of hiring counsel to conduct an investigation and to negotiate a formal contract of sale on his behalf. He also insisted on and obtained a formal contract containing representations and warranties that Malmberg had title to the painting. Counsel conducted a lien search and an Art Loss Register search relating to *Red Elvis.* Neither search revealed a claim or lien by Lindholm (P) or any other individual. Brant's (D) counsel cautioned, however, that these searches only provided "minimal assurances" that Malmberg had good title to the painting. Another dealer, Holm, who informed Brant (D) that Malmberg was offering the painting for sale, also assured Brant (D) that Malmberg had title to the painting and had bought it from Lindholm (P), who needed the money due to her divorce. Holm, like Malmberg, had a reputation for being honest, trustworthy and reliable. In the art world, it is customary for buyers to rely on the assurances of respected art dealers. Moreover, Brant (D) was further assured that Malmberg owned the painting because it was delivered by a respected museum to a bonded warehouse and released to Malmberg. Brant (D) knew that it was the museum's policy to release artwork only to its true owner or authorized representatives. Brant (D), however, had not been informed that Lindholm (P) had authorized release to Malmberg for the sole purpose of lending the painting to a different museum. Further, it is the custom in the art world to not require a merchant buyer to obtain documentary proof that the seller owns the work of art even if there are reasonable doubts or questions regarding the seller's authority to sell. It is also the custom for buyers to deal exclusively with a dealer, rather than the principal, where it is known that the principal works exclusively with that dealer. Accordingly, following this custom, Brant (D) did not contact Lindholm (P) directly. The reason that documentary proof of ownership customarily is not required is to protect the confidentiality of the owner and the buyer. Requiring a merchant buyer to obtain an invoice or other supporting documentation proving the seller's ownership would in every transaction destroy the privacy and confidentiality that buyers and sellers of art have come to desire and expect. Brant (D) did, however, obtain proof that Lindholm (P) had title to the painting. Lindholm (P) brought suit for conversion. Brant (D) defended by arguing that under the state's version of Uniform Commercial Code (U.C.C.) §§ 1-201(9) and 2-403, he was a buyer in the ordinary course of business, and, therefore, could not be held liable to her for conversion of the painting, as he took all her rights to *Red Elvis.* The trial court agreed with Brant (D) and granted judgment for him. The state's highest court granted review.

ISSUE: Is a merchant buyer of goods who follows the usual or customary practices of, and observes reasonable commercial standards of fair dealing in, a certain industry a buyer in the ordinary course of business for purposes of purchasing the rights of an entruster who has entrusted the goods to a dealer who deals in goods of that kind?

HOLDING AND DECISION: (Sullivan, J.) Yes. A merchant buyer of goods who follows the usual or customary practices of, and observes reasonable commercial standards of fair dealing in, a certain industry is a buyer in the ordinary course of business for purposes of purchasing the rights of an entruster who has entrusted the goods to a dealer who deals in goods of that kind. The state's version of U.C.C. § 2-403(2) provides that "[a]ny entrusting of possession of goods to a merchant who deals in goods of that kind gives him power to transfer all rights of the entruster to a buyer in ordinary course of business."

Continued on next page.

"Entrusting" is defined in § 2-403(3) as "any delivery and any acquiescence in retention of possession regardless of any condition expressed between the parties to the delivery or acquiescence and regardless of whether the procurement of the entrusting or the possessor's disposition of the goods have been such as to be larcenous under the criminal law." There is no dispute here that the Lindholm's (P) letter authorizing the museum to release *Red Elvis* to Malmberg constituted an entrustment, or that Malmberg, an art dealer, is a merchant dealing in "goods of that kind." Under the plain language of § 2-403 (2) and (3), therefore, Malmberg, as a merchant dealing in art entrusted with the painting, had the power to transfer all the rights of the entruster to a buyer in the ordinary course of business. Therefore, the key issue is whether Brant (D) was such a buyer Under § 1-201(9), a "[b]uyer in [the] ordinary course of business" is defined as "a person that buys goods in good faith, without knowledge that the sale violates the rights of another person in the goods, and in the ordinary course from a person . . . in the business of selling goods of that kind. A person buys goods in the ordinary course if the sale to the person comports with the usual or customary practices in the kind of business in which the seller is engaged or with the seller's own usual or customary practices. . . ." Under § 1-201(20), a person buys goods in good faith if there is "honesty in fact and the observance of reasonable commercial standards of fair dealing" in the conduct or transaction concerned. Therefore, it must be determined whether Brant (D) followed the usual or customary practices and observed reasonable commercial standards of fair dealing in the art industry in his dealings with Malmberg. The evidence shows that he did, given the nature of the art industry. In that industry, the vast majority of transactions are completed on a handshake and an exchange of an invoice. Here, however, Brant (D) had had good reason to be concerned that Lindholm (P) might have claims to the painting. Several courts have held that, under such circumstances, a handshake and an exchange of invoice is not sufficient to confer status as a buyer in the ordinary course. Thus, Brant (D) had a heightened duty of inquiry. The steps he took fulfilled this duty. He reasonably relied on Holms and Malmberg, who had impeccable reputations; he hired counsel who investigated whether there were liens or other claims to the painting; he reasonably believed—and had no reason to doubt—that Malmberg had title to the painting based on the museum's release of the painting to Malmberg; and he also insisted on and obtained a formal contract containing representations and warranties that Malmberg had title to the painting. These steps were sufficient to conform to reasonable commercial standards for the sale of artwork under the circumstances and, therefore, that Brant (D) had status as a buyer in the ordinary course of business. Based on all the circumstances surrounding the sale, and the art world's unwillingness to destroy, through greater documentation, the privacy and confidentiality that buyers and sellers have come to desire and expect, Brant's (D) failure to obtain an invoice from the Lindholm (P) to Malmberg or a signed copy of the letter showing Lindholm's (P) title does not strip him of his status as a buyer in the ordinary course of business, and, for the same reasons, he was not required to contact directly Lindholm (P) or other parties who might have had knowledge concerning *Red Elvis*' title. Affirmed.

ANALYSIS

This case pointedly illustrates how the customary practice in the art industry of not requiring a merchant buyer to obtain documentary proof that the seller owns the work of art whenever there are reasonable doubts or questions regarding the seller's authority to sell imposes risks on persons who entrust art to an art dealer. It also illustrates how courts adhering to the legislative mandate of U.C.C. § 1-201(9) are not at liberty to impose the type of business practices that they might prefer; they must take an industry as it is, with its customs, no matter how risky those customs might be.

Quicknotes

BUYER IN THE ORDINARY COURSE OF BUSINESS (BOCB) A person who purchases merchandise from another in the ordinary course of the seller's business in good faith, and without knowledge of another party's interest in the goods.

CONVERSION The act of depriving an owner of his property without permission or justification.

FAIR DEALING An implied warranty that the parties will deal honestly in the satisfaction of their obligations and without an intent to defraud.

U.C.C. § 2-201 Statute of Frauds; a statute that requires specified types of contracts to be in writing in order to be binding.

In re Toshiba America HD DVD Marketing and Sales Practices Litigation

[Parties not identified.]

69 U.C.C. Rep. Serv. 2d 1085 (D.N.J. 2009).

NATURE OF CASE: Action for breach of an express warranty.

FACT SUMMARY: Consumers (P) who bought a Toshiba (D) HD DVD player contended that Toshiba (D) breached an express warranty by advertising the player as "For Today, Tomorrow and Beyond" even though at the time the consumers (P) purchased the player, Toshiba (D) had already decided to discontinue future production of the player.

RULE OF LAW

A seller's statement does not create an express warranty of a product's future performance where the statement is mere puffery, general in its terms, and cannot reasonably be understood as containing an affirmation or representation that the product possesses a certain quality or capacity relating to future performance.

FACTS: Toshiba (D) produced an HD DVD player that competed with the Blu-ray Disc format for playing high definition DVDs. The competition between Blu-ray and HD DVD was well reported in the media. Eventually, the major movie studios decided to support the Blu-ray format, and it became clear that Toshiba's HD DVD format lost the battle for technological supremacy. Notwithstanding the obvious lack of market support for its format, Toshiba (D) continued to aggressively market its player for a couple of months with the slogan "For Today, Tomorrow and Beyond." Then, Toshiba (D) abruptly announced that it was exiting the HD DVD market. Consumers (P) who bought the HD DVD player brought suit in federal district court for, inter alia, breach of express warranty. The consumers (P) claimed that Toshiba (D) was aware of market trends and knew, despite its misleading marketing campaign, that it was only a matter of time before the company withdrew from the marketplace abandoning its customer base. They also claimed that, as a direct result of Toshiba's (D) abrupt exit from the HD DVD market, their investments in the HD DVD players lost significant value. The consumers (P) alleged that Toshiba's (D) affirmations of fact and/or promises relating to the HD DVD players created express warranties that Toshiba (D) would continue to support the HD DVD format and continue to manufacture such players.

ISSUE: Does a seller's statement create an express warranty of a product's future performance where the statement is mere puffery, general in its terms, and cannot reasonably be understood as containing an affirmation or representation that the product possesses a certain quality or capacity relating to future performance?

HOLDING AND DECISION: (Debevoise, J.) No. A seller's statement does not create an express warranty of a product's future performance where the statement is mere puffery, general in its terms, and cannot reasonably be understood as containing an affirmation or representation that the product possesses a certain quality or capacity relating to future performance. Here, the consumers (P) do not allege that the HD DVD Players cannot still play HD DVDs. The real problem is that the availability of new HD DVDs has severely decreased. They argue that Toshiba's (D) tag line that its HD DVD Players were for "Today, Tomorrow, and Beyond" created an express warranty that, essentially, Toshiba (D) would remain in the HD DVD market forever. However, this tag line was puffery and not specific enough to create an express warranty. Although a statement relating to future performance may create an express warranty, even if not intended by the seller, Toshiba's (D) statement regarding its HD DVD players did not rise to that level. It was not specific enough to create an affirmation about the HD DVD's future performance. In addition, even if Toshiba (D) created an express warranty of future performance, there was no allegation that the HD DVD players did not perform as intended—i.e., to play HD DVDs. Therefore, the claim must be dismissed.

ANALYSIS

In addition to needing to be sufficiently specifically related to the goods at issue, and not mere "puffing," as demonstrated by this case, an express warranty must also form the "basis of the bargain." This means that the natural tendency of the statement is to induce a buyer to purchase. Here, the consumers (P) asserted that the long-term viability of the HD DVD market was a large part of the basis of the bargain between Toshiba (D) and the consumers (P), who were concerned with choosing a high definition DVD player that would have long-term viability. According to the consumers (P), Toshiba's (D) exit from the HD DVD market substantially limited that viability. The court did not address the consumers' (P) "basis of the bargain" argument, presumably because it determined that Toshiba's (D) statement was puffery and not specific enough to create an express warranty, so that

Continued on next page.

it did not need to reach the basis of the bargain requirement.

Quicknotes

EXPRESS WARRANTY A promise made by one party to a contract that the other party may rely on a fact, relieving that party from the obligation of determining whether the fact is true and indemnifying the other party from liability if that fact is shown to be false.

PUFFING The communication of an opinion not intended as a representation of fact and upon which an action for fraud or misrepresentation cannot be based.

Shaffer v. Victoria Station, Inc.

Wine drinker (P) v. Restaurant (D)

Wash. Sup. Ct., 91 Wash. 2d 295, 588 P.2d 233 (1978).

NATURE OF CASE: Appeal from dismissal of action for damages for negligence, breach of implied warranty, and strict liability.

FACT SUMMARY: After Shaffer's (P) hand was permanently injured when the glass containing wine he had ordered in Victoria Station, Inc.'s (D) restaurant broke, Shaffer (P) sought damages for negligence, breach of implied warranty, and strict liability.

RULE OF LAW

The serving for value of food or drink to be consumed either on the premises or elsewhere is a sale, and such food and drink must be adequately contained, packaged, and labeled as the agreement may require.

FACTS: Shaffer (P) ordered a glass of wine at the "Victoria Station" restaurant operated by Victoria Station, Inc. (D). While drinking the wine, the wine glass broke in Shaffer's (P) hand, resulting in permanent injury. Shaffer (P) sued Victoria Station (D), seeking damages for negligence, breach of implied warranty under the Uniform Commercial Code (U.C.C.), and strict liability under the Restatement (Second) of Torts § 402A. [Prior to trial, Shaffer's (P) attorney, indicating he could not prove negligence, took a voluntary nonsuit on the negligence issue.] Victoria Station (D) argued that the U.C.C. did not apply since it was not a merchant with respect to wine glasses. Shaffer (P), however, argued that U.C.C. § 2-314 was controlling. The trial court, ruling that the case sounded in negligence alone, granted Victoria Station's (D) motion for dismissal. The court of appeals affirmed, and Shaffer (P) appealed.

ISSUE: Is the serving for value of food or drink to be consumed either on the premises or elsewhere a sale such that the food and drink must be adequately contained, packaged, and labeled as the agreement may require?

HOLDING AND DECISION: (Dolliver, J.) Yes. The serving for value of food or drink to be consumed either on the premises or elsewhere is a sale, and such food and drink must be adequately contained, packaged, and labeled as the agreement may require. Section 2-314 embodies the rule stated above. The wine could not be served as a drink or consumed without an adequate container. The drink sold thus includes the wine and the container, both of which must be fit for the ordinary purpose for which used. Shaffer (P) has a cause of action both on the face of the statute and under the principles of prior case law. An action also lies under the strict liability theory of Restatement (Second) of Torts § 402A. Confirmation of the applicability of § 402A to this case is given in comment h, which says in pertinent part: "No reason is apparent for distinguishing between the product itself and the container in which it is supplied, and the two are purchased by the user or consumer as an integrated whole. Where the container is itself dangerous, the product is sold in a defective condition. The container cannot logically be separated from the contents when the two are sold as a unit." Shaffer (P) has thus also stated a cause of action under the theories of implied warranty of fitness and strict liability. Reversed.

ANALYSIS

Victoria Station (D) contended that the restaurant was not a merchant with respect to wine glasses as defined in § 2-104, and, since the glass itself was not sold, there was no passing of title as required under § 2-106. The court of appeals expressed concern over an uncontrollable broadening of the doctrine of strict liability, stating that the argument could be made that numerous aspects of a restaurant's operation were integral to each sale. Thus, to ignore the fact that this allegedly defective glass was never sold would create great uncertainty as to the limits of strict liability. However, in finding that U.C.C. § 2-314 controlled here, the Washington Supreme Court declared that if the court of appeals's predictions as to future lawsuits came to pass, it would deal with the situation at that time.

Quicknotes

BREACH OF CONTRACT Unlawful failure by a party to perform its obligations pursuant to contract.

NEGLIGENCE Conduct falling below the standard of care that a reasonable person would demonstrate under similar conditions.

STRICT LIABILITY Liability for all injuries proximately caused by a party's conducting of certain inherently dangerous activities without regard to negligence or fault.

Webster v. Blue Ship Tea Room, Inc.

Customer (P) v. Restaurant (D)

Mass. Sup. Jud. Ct., 347 Mass. 421, 198 N.E.2d 309 (1964).

NATURE OF CASE: Appeal of award of damages for breach of an implied warranty.

FACT SUMMARY: After a fish bone became lodged in Webster's (P) esophagus while she was eating a bowl of fish chowder at the Blue Ship Tea Room (D), she sought damages for breach of an implied warranty of food served in the restaurant.

RULE OF LAW

The possible presence of fish bones in fish chowder is so well known that it can be reasonably anticipated and guarded against by anyone eating such fish chowder, thus precluding a breach of implied warranty under the Uniform Commercial Code (U.C.C.).

FACTS: While eating a bowl of New England fish chowder in the Blue Ship Tea Room (Blue Ship) (D), Webster (P), a native New Englander, felt something lodge in her throat preventing her from swallowing and/or clearing her throat by gulping. During the second of two esophagoscopies at Massachusetts General Hospital, a fish bone was found and removed. As a result of her injuries, Webster (P) sought damages, under applicable provisions of the U.C.C., for breach of implied contract, of food served by the Blue Ship Tea Room (D). An auditor, whose findings of fact were not final, found for Webster (P). On a retrial in the superior court, the jury returned a verdict for Webster (P). Blue Ship (D) appealed on exceptions to the judge's refusal to strike certain portions of the auditor's report, to direct a verdict for Blue Ship (D), and to allow Blue Ship's (D) motion for the entry of a verdict in its favor under leave reserved.

ISSUE: Is the possible presence of fish bones in fish chowder so well known that it can be reasonably anticipated and guarded against by anyone eating such fish chowder, thus precluding a breach of implied warranty under the U.C.C.?

HOLDING AND DECISION: (Reardon, J.) Yes. The possible presence of fish bones in fish chowder is so well known that it can be reasonably anticipated and guarded against by anyone eating such fish chowder, thus precluding a breach of implied warranty under the Uniform Commercial Code. According to the cookbooks consulted, fish chowder has for many years been made with fish that have not been filleted. The recipes indicate that, in the preparation of chowders in New England over the years, worries about fish bones played no part whatsoever. This broad outlook on chowders persists in more modern cookbooks, and this court is not inclined to tamper with age-old recipes by any amendment reflecting Webster's (P) view of the effect of the U.C.C. upon them. The joys of life in New England include the ready availability of fresh fish chowder. Diners should be prepared to cope with the hazards of fish bones, the occasional presence of which in chowder is to be anticipated and does not impair fitness or merchantability. Thus, while this court sympathizes with Webster (P), who has suffered a peculiarly New England injury, Blue Ship's (D) exceptions must be sustained. Judgment for the defendant.

ANALYSIS

In reaching its decision, the court cited cookbooks, a New England dictionary, and Nathaniel Hawthorne's *The House of the Seven Gables*, with publication dates ranging from 1883 to 1957. The court observed that while there is a heavy body of case law involving foreign substances in food, there is a strong distinction between those cases and a fish bone in fish chowder. Some jurisdictions make a distinction between natural and foreign objects found in food, with some denying liability for natural substances and others allowing recovery if the consumer had a "reasonable expectation" that the substance in question would have been removed.

Quicknotes

FORESEEABILITY A reasonable expectation that an act or omission would result in injury.

IMPLIED WARRANTY An implied promise made by one party to a contract that the other party may rely on a fact, relieving that party from the obligation of determining whether the fact is true and indemnifying the other party from liability if that fact is shown to be false.

Bell Sports, Inc. v. Yarusso

Manufacturer (D) v. Helmet wearer (P)

Del. Sup. Ct., 759 A.2d 582, 42 U.C.C. Rep. Serv. 2d 714 (2000).

NATURE OF CASE: Appeal from denial of judgment as a matter of law on breach of warranty claims.

FACT SUMMARY: Although he was wearing a helmet made by Bell Sports, Inc. (D), Yarusso (P) became a quadriplegic after he landed on his head when his off-road motorcycle hit a bump and catapulted him. Yarusso (P) claimed that the helmet's design was defective and alleged negligence, breach of express warranties, and breach of an implied warranty of merchantability.

RULE OF LAW

(1) An express warranty that arises from textual representations that are not labeled as such may not be disclaimed under Universal Commercial Code (U.C.C.) § 2-313.

(2) A finding of breach of express warranty is not inconsistent with a finding of no negligence.

FACTS: Yarusso (P) was riding his off-road motorcycle when he hit a mogul and was catapulted off the vehicle and onto his head. He sustained a burst fracture of the C5 vertebral body, rendering him a quadriplegic. At the time, he was wearing Bell Sports, Inc.'s (Bell) (D) Bell Moto-5, a full-face motocross helmet designed for off-road use. Yarusso (P) filed suit, alleging negligence in the design and construction of the helmet, breach of express warranties, and breach of an implied warranty of merchantability. His express warranty claim arose from textual representations in the helmet's owner's manual, which included the statement: "the primary function of a helmet is to reduce the harmful effects of a blow to the head" and which described how the helmet would work on impact. The express warranty also attempted to limit itself to five years and warned in bold, capital letters that "no helmet can protect the wearer against all foreseeable impacts." Experts for both parties disagreed as to whether the helmet had functioned properly at the time of impact. At the close of the evidence, Bell (D) moved for judgment as a matter of law as to liability, but the court sent the claims to the jury, which ultimately found that Bell (D) had not been negligent but had breached an express or implied warranty that proximately caused Yarusso's (P) injuries (the jury was permitted to find liability under alternative theories of breach of warranty, express or implied, without differentiating between the two). Bell (D) appealed, claiming that Yarusso (P) failed as a matter of law to establish an evidentiary basis for recovery under express or implied warranty.

ISSUE:

(1) May an express warranty that arises from textual representations that are not labeled as such be disclaimed under U.C.C. § 2-313?

(2) Is a finding of breach of express warranty inconsistent with a finding of no negligence?

HOLDING AND DECISION: (Walsh, J.)

(1) No. An express warranty that arises from textual representations that are not labeled as such may not be disclaimed under U.C.C. § 2-313. According to the U.C.C.'s official commentary, the U.C.C.'s warranty provisions are intended to be liberally construed and applied in favor of a buyer of goods. Formal wording is not necessary to create a warranty, and a seller does not have to express any specific intention to create one. Here, the helmet's owner's manual contained textual representations of fact on which a buyer was entitled to rely, even though they were not expressly labeled as warranties. Because the U.C.C. and its state counterparts are restrictive, any effort to disclaim these express warranties is ineffective. Even though the manual contained disclaimers warning that use of the helmet could not prevent all injuries, such disclaimers are ineffective to disclaim the express warranties. Because the evidence presented to the jury by both parties was inconclusive, the jury could come to a logical conclusion that express warranties were made and that they were breached. Therefore, the trial court did not err in submitting this issue to the jury. Evidence that the helmet could have been designed to reduce certain neck injuries also provided a sufficient factual predicate for submitting the implied warranty claim to the jury.

(2) No. A finding of breach of express warranty is not inconsistent with a finding of no negligence. Bell (D) argues that the jury's finding that it was not negligent is inconsistent with its finding of a breach of an express or implied warranty because, it argues, the jury found no product defect that could support negligence and, therefore, could not properly find a defect that would support a warranty claim. However, a claim for breach of warranty is conceptually distinct from a negligence claim because the latter focuses on the manufacturer's conduct, whereas a warranty claim focuses on the product itself. Therefore, there is no inconsistency between

Continued on next page.

the jury's verdict negating negligence but finding a breach of warranty. Affirmed.

ANALYSIS

The instant case demonstrates the difficulty of disclaiming any express warranties, even when they are mere statements of fact that serve to create buyer expectations or interest. Accordingly, a seller must carefully weigh the benefits of such statements (e.g., in advertising) against the potential exposure to liability they can entail.

Quicknotes

BREACH OF EXPRESS WARRANTY The breach of an express promise made by one party to a contract on which the other party may rely, relieving that party from the obligation of determining whether the fact is true and indemnifying the other party from liability if that fact is shown to be false.

Cate v. Dover Corp.

Customer (P) v. Manufacturer (D)

Texas Sup. Ct., 790 S.W.2d 559, 12 U.C.C. Rep Serv. 2d 47 (1990).

NATURE OF CASE: Appeal of summary judgment denying damages for breach of warranty.

FACT SUMMARY: Cate (P) purchased lifts manufactured by Dover Corp. (D), which came with a warranty which disclaimed the implied warranty of merchantability.

RULE OF LAW

A disclaimer of the implied warranty of merchantability is ineffective unless it is conspicuous or the party has actual knowledge of the disclaimer.

FACTS: Cate (P) purchased three lifts from Beech Tire Mart. The lifts were manufactured and designed by Dover Corp. (D). Dover's (D) warranty for the lifts contained a disclaimer of the implied warranty of merchantability. The text of the warranty appeared in regular size print. The disclaimer appeared in a separate paragraph, but in the same typeface, size, and color as the remainder of the text. Cate (P) was aware of the warranty and read it. The lifts never functioned properly and Cate (P) filed suit against Dover (D) for breach of the implied warranty of merchantability. Dover (D) contended that the claim was barred by the disclaimer in the written warranty. The trial court upheld the disclaimer and granted summary judgment to Dover (D), and Cate (P) appealed.

ISSUE: Does a disclaimer of the implied warranty of merchantability have to be conspicuous in order to be effective?

HOLDING AND DECISION: (Doggett, J.) Yes. Disclaimers of the implied warranty of merchantability must be conspicuous, or the party must have actual knowledge of it, in order to be effective. A clause is conspicuous when it is written so that a reasonable person against whom it will operate should have noticed it. Contrasting typefaces or colors are evidence that a clause is conspicuous. Although a disclaimer is not conspicuous, it will be effective if the party has actual knowledge of it at the time of purchase. Dover's (D) disclaimer clause was contained within a section outlining the terms of the warranty and was not in different typeface or color. Therefore, it failed to alert a reasonable person that an exclusion was intended. Although Cate (P) admitted to reading the warranty, the evidence did not establish that he understood the limitation which would constitute actual knowledge of the disclaimer. Thus, Dover's (D) disclaimer was ineffective. Reversed and remanded.

CONCURRENCE: (Spears, J.) The implied warranty of merchantability is designed to protect consumers who don't read limitations or understand the effect of disclaimers. Therefore, disclaimers should be prohibited by the state legislature.

CONCURRENCE AND DISSENT: (Ray, J.) The statute allowing disclaimers requires conspicuousness and does not provide for an actual knowledge exception, which should be irrelevant to the determination.

ANALYSIS

Some commentators support the position of the dissent that actual knowledge of the buyer should not play a role in determining the validity of a disclaimer. They claim that a rule requiring conspicuousness reduces the need for courts to make difficult evaluations of actual awareness. See W. Powers, *Texas Products Liability Law* § 2.0723 (1989).

Quicknotes

IMPLIED WARRANTY OF MERCHANTABILITY An implied promise made by a merchant in a contract for the sale of goods that such goods are suitable for the purpose for which they are purchased.

Bowdoin v. Showell Growers, Inc.

Chicken growers (P) v. Chicken buyers (D)

817 F.2d 1543 (11th Cir. 1987).

NATURE OF CASE: Appeal from summary judgment denying damages for breach of implied warranties of fitness and merchantability.

FACT SUMMARY: While cleaning out their chicken house and chicken coop pallets with a spray rig lent to them by Showell Growers, Inc. (D), with whom the Bowdoins (P) contracted as chicken raisers, Mrs. Bowdoin (P) suffered severe injuries when the spray rig malfunctioned.

RULE OF LAW

A manufacturer may disclaim the implied warranties of merchantability and fitness provided that the disclaimer is in writing, is conspicuous, and is part of the parties' bargain.

FACTS: The Bowdoins (P), under their contract to raise chickens for Showell Growers, Inc. (Showell) (D), were required to thoroughly clean their chicken house and chicken coop pallets once a year. To accomplish this task, Showell (D) lent the Bowdoins (P) a high-pressure spray rig Showell (D) had purchased from the manufacturers. Two weeks after Showell (D) purchased the spray rig it was delivered with an instruction manual which included a purported warranty disclaimer on the last page. Usually, the manufacturer required its dealer and the purchaser to complete an "agriculture delivery report," containing a disclaimer of the implied warranties of fitness and merchantability, before a sale. However, the record showed that no agriculture delivery report was completed in connection with the purchase of the spray rig by Showell (D). Mrs. Bowdoin (P) was using the spray rig to clean the pallets when an article of her clothing caught in the safety shield covering the spray rig's power takeoff shaft, pulling her into the shaft and causing her to suffer severe injuries. The Bowdoins (P) filed a diversity action in federal court against Showell (D) and the manufacturers, seeking to recover on a number of counts, including one alleging breach of the implied warranties of fitness and merchantability. The manufacturers moved for summary judgment, which the district court granted, concluding that, under Alabama law, the manufacturers had effectively disclaimed the implied warranties in the instruction manual. The Bowdoins (P) appealed.

ISSUE: May a manufacturer disclaim the implied warranties of merchantability and fitness provided that the disclaimer is in writing, is conspicuous, and is part of the parties' bargain?

HOLDING AND DECISION: (Wisdom, J.) Yes. A manufacturer may disclaim the implied warranties of merchantability and fitness provided that the disclaimer is in writing, is conspicuous, and is part of the parties' bargain. This "basis of the bargain" rule protects purchasers from unexpected and coercive disclaimers. However, Showell (D) purchased the spray rig at least two weeks before it was delivered, and the instruction manual delivered with the spray rig was never brought to Showell's (D) attention. Such a post-sale disclaimer is ineffective. By definition, a disclaimer that appears for the first time after the sale in a manual supplied by the seller is not a part of the basis of the bargain and therefore is not binding on the buyer. Decisions of other courts construing Universal Commercial Code (U.C.C.) § 2-316 have also concluded that a post-sale disclaimer is not effective. Reversed [with instructions to reinstate the Bowdoins' (P) breach of implied warranties of fitness and merchantability claims against the manufacturers].

ANALYSIS

The court noted that to be effective, a disclaimer must be conspicuous before the sale, for only then will the law presume that the disclaimer was part of the bargain. However, whether or not a post-sale disclaimer was conspicuous was immaterial. As the court observed, by definition, a post-sale disclaimer is not conspicuous in the full sense of that term because the reasonable person against whom it is intended to operate could not have noticed it before the consummation of the transaction. A post-sale disclaimer is therefore not effective merely because it was otherwise conspicuous.

Quicknotes

IMPLIED WARRANTY OF MERCHANTABILITY An implied promise made by a merchant in a contract for the sale of goods that such goods are suitable for the purpose for which they are purchased.

Rinaldi v. Iomega Corp.

Consumer (P) v. Manufacturer (D)

Del. Super. Ct., 41 U.C.C. Rep. Serv. 2d 1143 (1999).

NATURE OF CASE: Motion to dismiss class action for breach of implied warranty of merchantability.

FACT SUMMARY: Plaintiffs (P), as a class, purchased "Zip drives" from Iomega Corp. (D) that were allegedly defective and caused irreparable damage to computer data. They brought suit for breach of warranty of merchantability, negligence, fraud, and negligent failure to warn. Iomega (D) moved to dismiss the breach of warranty claim because its disclaimer, shipped with the drive, disclaimed all liability.

RULE OF LAW

A disclaimer of the warranty of merchantability that is otherwise conspicuous and that is contained inside the packaging of a product is sufficiently conspicuous to be effective.

FACTS: Iomega Corp. (D) manufactured the Zip drive, a large capacity computer data storage drive. A class action on behalf of all persons who purchased purportedly defective Zip drives was brought against Iomega (D). The plaintiffs (P) alleged, inter alia, that a defect in the drive caused the "Click of Death," which caused irreparable damage to computer data, and could be transferred to other drives. Plaintiffs (P) brought suit for breach of warranty of merchantability, negligence, fraud, and negligent failure to warn. The breach of warranty count of the complaint asserted that Iomega (D) manufactured a product that was not fit for the ordinary purpose for which such products are used and that Iomega's (D) disclaimer of this implied warranty that was contained in the packaging of the drive was ineffective because it was not sufficiently "conspicuous" as required by the state counterpart to the Uniform Commercial Code (U.C.C.). Iomega (D) moved to dismiss this count of the complaint on the ground that it failed to state a claim because the disclaimer in the drive packaging was sufficiently conspicuous and effectively disclaimed all liability.

ISSUE: Is a disclaimer of the warranty of merchantability that is otherwise conspicuous and that is contained inside the packaging of a product sufficiently conspicuous to be effective?

HOLDING AND DECISION: (Cooch, J.) Yes. A disclaimer of the warranty of merchantability that is otherwise conspicuous and that is contained inside the packaging of a product is sufficiently conspicuous to be effective. The state's counterpart to the U.C.C. (6 Del. C. § 2-316(2)) requires that to disclaim the warranty of merchantability, the language in a writing must mention merchantability and must be conspicuous. Various aspects of "conspicuousness" are not at issue here, e.g., type size, wording, readability, location of the disclaimer in the warranty itself, etc. Instead, the only issue is whether by being located in the packaging of the product, the disclaimer could not realistically be called to the attention of the consumer until after the sale had been consummated and, therefore, was not "conspicuous" as a matter of law. To determine this issue, the purpose of the U.C.C. must be looked to. That purpose is to protect a buyer from unexpected and unbargained-for language of disclaimer. An analogous case, relating to software shrinkwrap license agreements, is the Seventh Circuit's *ProCD, Inc. v. Zeidenberg*, 86 F.3d 1447 (1996), which reasoned that it would be impractical to print additional terms of the sales contract on the outside of the box in microscopic print. That case also reasoned that the consumer had the ability to reject the goods if it found the additional terms unacceptable. Other courts have also held that various contract terms, like arbitration clauses, are effective even though located inside the packaging of a product. Still, other courts have held that a disclaimer of the warranty of merchantability is conspicuous so long as it can be noticed and understood. Here, the sales of the Zip drives were not consummated until after each plaintiff (P) had a chance to inspect and then to reject or accept the drive with the additional terms that were enclosed along with it. The commercial practicalities of modern retail purchasing make it "eminently reasonable" for sellers to place disclaimers inside their products' packaging, and for buyers to reject the contract terms if they so choose. Therefore, the disclaimer physically placed inside the Zip drive packing was conspicuous, and Iomega's (D) motion to dismiss is granted.

ANALYSIS

Other courts have held that to be effective, a disclaimer such as the one in the instant case must be conspicuous before the sale. Those courts would hold that by definition a postsale disclaimer could not be conspicuous because the buyer could not have noticed it before consummation of the transaction. It seems the court here is implying that the sale transaction is not complete until the buyer has had a chance to review the additional terms that are inside the packaging and has either rejected or accepted them by either using the product or returning it.

Continued on next page.

Quicknotes

FRAUD A false representation of facts with the intent that another will rely on the misrepresentation to his detriment.

IMPLIED WARRANTY OF MERCHANTABILITY An implied promise made by a merchant in a contract for the sale of goods that such goods are suitable for the purpose for which they are purchased.

NEGLIGENCE Conduct falling below the standard of care that a reasonable person would demonstrate under similar conditions.

Wilson Trading Corp. v. David Ferguson, Ltd.

Yarn seller (P) v. Yarn buyer (D)

N.Y. Ct. App., 23 N.Y.2d 398, 244 N.E.2d 685 (1968).

NATURE OF CASE: Appeal from affirmance of summary judgment awarding damages for breach of contract.

FACT SUMMARY: When David Ferguson, Ltd. (Ferguson) (D) discovered a defect in the yarn it had purchased from Wilson Trading Corp. (Wilson) (P), Ferguson (D) refused to pay for the goods, despite the fact that its notice to Wilson (P) of the defect was made after the 10-day limitation period stipulated in the contract of sale.

RULE OF LAW

A buyer who accepts goods has a reasonable time after he discovers or should have discovered a breach to notify the seller of such breach.

FACTS: After Wilson Trading Corp. (Wilson) (P) sold a specified quantity of yarn to David Ferguson, Ltd. (Ferguson) (D), the yarn was cut and knitted into sweaters, which were then washed. It was during this washing that Ferguson (D) discovered that the color of the yarn varied from piece to piece and within the pieces. Ferguson (D) claimed the defect rendered the sweaters unmarketable. The contract for sale of the yarn foreclosed claims made after weaving, knitting, or processing, or made more than 10 days after receipt of shipment. Wilson (P) sought to recover the contract price of the yarn after Ferguson (D) refused to pay for the yarn purchased. As a defense and as a counterclaim for damages, Ferguson (D) alleged that Wilson (P) delivered defective and unworkmanlike goods. Special terms granted Wilson's (P) motion for summary judgment for the contract price of the yarn on the grounds that notice of an alleged breach of warranty for defect in shading was not given within the time expressly limited by the contract and was not now available by way of defense or counterclaim. The appellate division affirmed, and this appeal followed.

ISSUE: Does a buyer who accepts goods have a reasonable time after he discovers or should have discovered a breach to notify the seller of such breach?

HOLDING AND DECISION: (Jasen, J.) Yes. A buyer who accepts goods has a reasonable time after he discovers or should have discovered a breach to notify the seller of such breach. However, the Universal Commercial Code (U.C.C.) allows the parties, within limits established by it, to modify or exclude warranties and to limit remedies for breach of warranty. Under the U.C.C., parties are given broad latitude within which to fashion their own remedies for breach of contract. Nevertheless, it is clear from the official comment to § 2-719 that it is the very essence of a sale contract that at least minimum adequate remedies be available for its breach. Official comment to § 2-719 explains that "where an apparently fair and reasonable clause because of circumstances fails in its purpose or operates to deprive either party of the substantial value of the bargain, it must give way to the general remedy provisions of this Article." Here, the time provision of the contract eliminated all remedies for defects not discoverable before knitting and processing; thus, § 2-719 applies. Ferguson's (D) affidavits alleged that sweaters manufactured from the yarn were rendered unmarketable because of latent shading defects not reasonably discoverable before knitting and processing. If these factual allegations are established at trial, the limited remedy established by the contract has failed its "essential purpose," and the buyer is, in effect, without remedy. The time limitation clause of the contract must then give way to the general code rule stated above. Ferguson's (D) affidavits are thus sufficient to create a question of fact concerning whether notice was given within a reasonable time after the shading defect should have been discovered. The order of the appellate division should be reversed, and Wilson's (P) motion for summary judgment should be denied.

CONCURRENCE: (Fuld, C.J.) There should be a reversal—but on the sole ground that a substantial question of fact has been raised as to whether the clause limiting the time in which to make a claim is "manifestly unreasonable" as applied to the type of defect of which Ferguson (D) complained, without discussing unconscionability.

ANALYSIS

As noted by the concurrence, the majority also discussed unconscionability, before stating that it did not need to decide that specific issue here. In its analysis, the court noted that the contract between the parties not only limited remedies for its breach but also purported to modify the warranty of merchantability. The court declared that an attempt to both warrant and refuse to warrant goods creates an ambiguity which can only be resolved by making one term yield to the other. U.C.C. § 2-316 provides that warranty language prevails over the disclaimer if the two cannot be reasonably reconciled. Under these circumstances, the contract language creating the unlimited express warranty must prevail over the time limitation insofar as the latter modifies the warranty.

Continued on next page.

Quicknotes

BREACH OF CONTRACT Unlawful failure by a party to perform its obligations pursuant to contract.

UNCONSCIONABILITY Rule of law whereby a court may excuse performance of a contract, or of a particular contract term, if it determines that such term(s) are unduly oppressive or unfair to one party to the contract.

Pierce v. Catalina Yachts, Inc.

Boat purchaser (P) v. Boat manufacturer (D)

Alaska Sup. Ct., 2 P.3d 618, 41 U.C.C. Rep. Serv. 2d 737 (1999).

NATURE OF CASE: Appeal from denial of consequential damages in action for tort and contract damages.

FACT SUMMARY: The Pierces (P) purchased a new sailboat from Catalina Yachts, Inc. (Catalina) (D), which gave them a limited warranty for the repair of any below waterline blisters appearing in the boat's gel coat. The warranty expressly disclaimed Catalina's (D) responsibility for consequential damages. The Pierces (P) discovered blistering on the hull and promptly notified Catalina (D) with an estimate, which Catalina (D) refused to accept. The Pierces (P) sued, and a jury awarded them monetary damages for repair, as well as finding that Catalina (D) had acted in bad faith. However, before trial, the trial court had ruled that their claim for consequential damages was barred by the warranty disclaimer.

RULE OF LAW

Where a limited warranty is breached in bad faith, consequential damages are available despite an express disclaimer in the warranty that excludes such damages.

FACTS: In 1992, the Pierces (P) purchased a new sailboat from Catalina Yachts, Inc. (Catalina) (D), which gave them a limited warranty promising to repair or pay for the repair of any below waterline blisters appearing in the boat's gel coat—an outer layer of resin on the boat's hull. The warranty expressly disclaimed Catalina's (D) responsibility for consequential damages. In 1994, the Pierces (P) discovered blistering on the hull and promptly notified Catalina (D) with a repair estimate of $10,645, which Catalina (D) refused to accept. Catalina (D) insisted that the hull only needed minor patching. Six months later, the Pierces (P) sued, claiming tort and contract damages. Before trial, the trial court ruled that their claim for consequential damages was barred by the warranty disclaimer. The jury awarded them monetary damages for repair, as well as finding that Catalina (D) had acted in bad faith. The Pierces (P) appealed, claiming that the trial court had erred in striking their consequential damages claim.

ISSUE: Where a limited warranty is breached in bad faith, are consequential damages available despite an express disclaimer in the warranty that excludes such damages?

HOLDING AND DECISION: (Bryner, J.) Yes. Where a limited warranty is breached in bad faith, consequential damages are available despite an express disclaimer in the warranty that excludes such damages. The issue is whether the failure of a warranty provision that creates a limited remedy requires failure of another provision that excludes consequential damages. Under the state's Universal Commercial Code counterpart (AS 45.02.719(b)), a limited remedy is the exclusive remedy. When that limited remedy fails, the warranty's limitations are nullified and the remedy available is the remedy provided by the code. Thus, it would seem that here the gel-coat warranty failed its essential purpose and that the Pierces (P) can pursue any remedy available under the code, including consequential damages. However, another code provision (.719(c)) separately provides that consequential damages may be limited or excluded unless the limitation or exclusion is unconscionable. Thus, there is tension between these two subsections because .719(c) casts doubt on .719(b)'s implication that when a limited remedy fails, consequential damages may be available. The code itself does not resolve this tension. The majority of courts find that the two subsections are independent, ruling that when a warranty fails, the provision barring consequential damages survives unless it is unconscionable. Because this approach serves the purpose of the code and allows parties flexibility to contract around consequential damages, the court adopts the independent approach. However, courts applying this approach examine the totality of the circumstances surrounding the limited remedy's failure to see if there is anything unconscionable about enforcing the parties' allocation of risk. One consideration is whether the seller acted unreasonably or in bad faith. Here, Catalina's (D) actions weigh heavily against enforcing the consequential damages exclusion, and the finding by the jury that Catalina (D) acted in bad faith establishes a "circumstance resulting in failure of performance that makes it unconscionable to enforce the parties' allocation of risk." Because Catalina (D) consciously deprived the Pierces (P) of their rights, Catalina (D) cannot conscionably demand to enforce its own warranty rights. Therefore, the trial court erred in ruling that it would be conscionable to enforce the consequential damages exclusion. Vacated and remanded.

ANALYSIS

In the instant case, the court found it significant that the Pierces (P) were consumers, rather than merchants, who were not sophisticated business people and who were not bargaining on equal footing with Catalina (D). In a commercial setting, where the buyer is not a consumer,

Continued on next page.

the courts are more likely to uphold the consequential damages exclusion, even where the limited remedy portion of the warranty has failed.

Quicknotes

BREACH OF CONTRACT Unlawful failure by a party to perform its obligations pursuant to contract.

CONSEQUENTIAL DAMAGES Monetary compensation that may be recovered in order to compensate for injuries or losses sustained as a result of damages that are not the direct or foreseeable result of the act of a party, but that nevertheless are the consequence of such act and which must be specifically pled and demonstrated.

Fitl v. Strek

Sports card purchaser (P) v. Sports card dealer (D)

Neb. Sup. Ct., 269 Neb. 51, 690 N.W.2d 605 (2005).

NATURE OF CASE: Appeal from award of damages to plaintiff in warranty action brought under the Universal Commercial Code (U.C.C.)

FACT SUMMARY: Strek (D) contended that Fitl's (P) notice, two years after purchase of a rare sports card, that the card was worthless, was unreasonable under U.C.C. § 2-607(3)(a).

RULE OF LAW

It is reasonable under U.C.C. § 2-607(3)(a) for a purchaser of an item from a dealer in items of that kind to give notice immediately after investigation reveals that the item is defective, even if that notice is two years after the date of purchase.

FACTS: Based on representations by Strek (D), a sports card dealer, that a rare baseball card was in near mint condition, Fitl (P) purchased it for $17,750. He immediately placed it in a safe-deposit box. Two years later, Fitl (P) sent the card for authentication, and discovered that the card had been doctored and was worthless. Fitl (P) gave Strek (D) notice that he intended to sue, and Strek (D) responded that Fitl (P) should have returned the card within a typical grace period of a month. Fitl (P) sued Strek (D), asserting that Strek (D) knew of the alterations and that Fitl (P) had relied on his representations. Evidence was presented that typically there is a lifetime guarantee of sports memorabilia. The trial court awarded Fitl (P) the purchase price. Strek (D) appealed, claiming that Fitl's (P) notice to him had been untimely under U.C.C. § 2-607(3)(a). The state's highest court granted review.

ISSUE: Is it reasonable under U.C.C. § 2-607(3)(a) for a purchaser of an item from a dealer in items of that kind to give notice immediately after investigation reveals that the item is defective, even if that notice is two years after the date of purchase?

HOLDING AND DECISION: (Wright, J.) Yes. It is reasonable under U.C.C. § 2-607(3)(a) for a purchaser of an item from a dealer in items of that kind to give notice immediately after investigation reveals that the item is defective, even if that notice is two years after the date of purchase. The issue is whether the trial court's determination that notice after discovery but two years after purchase was reasonable under U.C.C. § 2-607(3)(a) was clearly erroneous. That section requires notification within a reasonable time from discovery or from when discovery should have been made. The issue, therefore, becomes what is reasonable under the statute, which is a question of fact. The three purposes of the section are to provide the seller with an opportunity to correct any defect, to prepare for negotiation and litigation, and to protect itself against stale claims asserted after it is too late for the seller to investigate them. The most important of these is the first—to give the seller an opportunity to cure the breach. Here, Fitl (P) could rely on Strek's (D) representations as to authenticity, so immediate investigation was not required, and Fitl (P) gave notice right after investigation was made. Regardless of what point in time Fitl (P) had given notice, there was nothing Strek (D) could have done to cure the breach, since the card was worthless. Also, earlier notification would not have helped Strek (D) prepare for litigation or negotiation. Even if, as Strek (D) asserts, he could have had recourse against the source from which he obtained the card, that would have been immaterial to Fitl's (P) claim and would not have altered his damages. Accordingly, the trial court's determination was supported by the evidence and was not clearly erroneous. Affirmed.

ANALYSIS

If it is determined that the purchaser's notice has not been reasonable under U.C.C. § 2-607(3)(a), the purchaser loses all U.C.C. rights. Thus, it is incumbent upon purchasers to give notice immediately after they discover (or should have discovered) a nonconforming defect and they may not sleep on their rights or else they will lose them.

Quicknotes

CURE In a commercial transaction, the seller has a right to correct a delivery of defective goods within the time originally provided for performance as specified in the contract.

Flippo v. Mode O'Day Frock Shops of Hollywood

Pants purchaser (P) v. Apparel store (D)

Ark. Sup. Ct., 48 Ark. 1, 449 S.W.2d 692 (1970).

NATURE OF CASE: Appeal from judgment for defendants in action for breach of the implied warranty of merchantability, strict tort liability, and negligence, on the grounds that the trial court's refusal to submit the case upon implied warranty and strict tort liability theories was erroneous.

FACT SUMMARY: Flippo (P), who was bitten by a spider when she tried on pants being sold by a woman's clothing store named Mode O'Day Frock Shops of Hollywood (D), contended that the store had breached the implied warranty of merchantability, and was liable under a theory of strict tort liability, because the pants were not fit for the purpose for which they were purchased, given that a spider had been in the pants and had bitten Flippo (P).

RULE OF LAW

Manufactured goods are not unfit for their intended use, and therefore do not breach the implied warranty of merchantability, where an insect or animal attaches itself to the goods and happens to bite a purchaser of the goods.

FACTS: Flippo (P) was trying on slacks at a woman's clothing store named Mode O'Day Frock Shops of Hollywood (Mode O'Day Frock Shops) (D), which was owned by Goforth (D). As she put on a pair of slacks, Flippo (P) suddenly felt a burning sensation on her thigh; she immediately removed the pants, shook them, and a spider fell to the floor. An examination of her thigh revealed a reddened area, which progressively grew worse. Flippo (P) was subsequently hospitalized for approximately 30 days, and, according to her physician, the injury was caused by the bite of a brown recluse spider. Despite the bite, Flippo (P) bought the pants, wore them, and laundered them several times after purchase. Flippo (P) brought suit against Mode O'Day Frock Shops (D) and Goforth (D) on grounds of negligence, strict tort liability, and breach of the implied warranty of merchantability. Flippo (P) contended, inter alia, that the slacks were unreasonably dangerous and that there was an implied warranty that the slacks were fit for the purpose for which they were purchased, though actually not fit, because of the poisonous spider concealed therein. The trial court refused requested instructions offered by Flippo (P) on theories of implied warranty, and strict tort liability, and instructed the jury only on the issue of negligence as the proximate cause of the injury. The jury returned a verdict for Mode O'Day Frock Shops (D) and Goforth (D), finding no negligence on their part. Flippo (P) appealed the trial court's refusal to submit the implied warranty and strict tort liability claims to the jury. The state's highest court granted review.

ISSUE: Are manufactured goods unfit for their intended use, and therefore breach the implied warranty of merchantability, where an insect or animal attaches itself to the goods and happens to bite a purchaser of the goods?

HOLDING AND DECISION: (Harris, C.J.) No. Manufactured goods are not unfit for their intended use, and therefore do not breach the implied warranty of merchantability, where an insect or animal attaches itself to the goods and happens to bite a purchaser of the goods. The state's version of Uniform Commercial Code (U.C.C.) § 2-314 provides that in order to be merchantable, goods must, inter alia, be fit for the ordinary purposes for which such goods are used. That provision is inapplicable here because the pants themselves were fit for their intended purpose; there was nothing wrong from a manufacturing standpoint. There was absolutely no evidence that the goods were defective in any manner. The spider was not a part of the product, and there was no evidence that either the manufacturer or retailer had any control of the spider, or caused it to be in the pants. Regardless of where the spider attached itself to the pants—whether at the manufacturer's factory or during shipping or at the store—the fact remains that the spider was not part of the pants, and it was the spider, not the pants, that injured Flippo (P). Affirmed as to this issue.

ANALYSIS

The court also affirmed as to the theory of strict tort liability, finding that the slacks sold were neither defective nor unreasonably dangerous, and that it was not the pants that injured Flippo (P), since the spider was not part of the pants. Thus, the case illustrates the principle that for a purchaser to prevail on a claim of breach of the implied warranty of merchantability, the purchaser must show, inter alia, that the goods themselves proximately caused the purchaser's harm.

Quicknotes

IMPLIED WARRANTY OF MERCHANTABILITY An implied promise made by a merchant in a contract for the sale of goods that such goods are suitable for the purpose for which they are purchased.

Reed v. City of Chicago

Estate administrator/Non-purchaser (P) v. Buyer and manufacturer (D)

263 F. Supp. 2d 1123 (N.D. Ill. 2003).

NATURE OF CASE: Defendant's motion to dismiss for failure to state a claim.

FACT SUMMARY: Acting as the Administrator of her son's estate, Ruby Reed (P) brought a breach of warranty action against the City of Chicago (D) and the manufacturers of a jail cell gown for the death of her son.

RULE OF LAW

A plaintiff does not, in all cases, have to establish privity to bring a breach of warranty claim against a manufacturer of a good.

FACTS: Ruby Reed (P) sued the City of Chicago (City) (D), four Chicago police officers (Officers) (D), Edwards Medical Supply, Inc. (Edwards) (D), Cypress Medical Products, Ltd. and Cypress Medical Products, Inc. (together, Cypress) (D), and Medline Industries (Medline) (D) for the death of her son, J.C., which occurred in a Chicago jail cell. J.C. had been arrested and placed in a detention cell and had been provided with a paper gown because the Officers (D) were allegedly aware that J.C. was mentally unstable. J.C. used the paper gown to hang himself. The gown, which was used for the safety of inmates who might hurt themselves or others, failed to tear away as it was designed and marketed to do to prevent it from being used in such a fashion. Cypress (D) filed a motion pursuant to Rule 12(B)(6) of the Federal Rules of Civil Procedure seeking to have the suit dismissed for failure to state a claim upon which relief could be granted.

ISSUE: Must a plaintiff, in all cases, establish privity to bring a breach of warranty claim against a manufacturer of a good?

HOLDING AND DECISION: (Moran, J.) No. A plaintiff does not, in all cases, have to establish privity to bring a breach of warranty claim against a manufacturer of a good. Privity is no longer an absolute requirement for breach of warranty actions. Section 2-318 of the Universal Commercial Code (U.C.C.) lists specific exceptions to the privity requirement, and comment 3 of this section states that it "is not intended to enlarge or restrict the developing case law on whether a seller's warranties, given to his buyer who resells, extend to other persons in the distributive chain." While, historically, the Illinois courts have required both horizontal and vertical privity in breach of warranty actions, the plaintiff class may need to be expanded to provide the necessary protection to the ultimate user of the good(s) in question. Such was the situation in the instant case, where if protection were not extended to J.C., then any warranty as to the safety of the paper isolation gown would be meaningless. The motion to dismiss was denied.

ANALYSIS

Breach of warranty actions are based in contract and the legal connection between the parties of a contract is called privity. Vertical privity refers to the chain of distribution and lack of vertical privity occurs when the consumer of a good is too remote from a member of the distribution chain to allege they were involved in the sale to the consumer. Horizontal privity is the connection between the retailer and the ultimate user of the product, and lack of horizontal privity occurs when the product injures a user who is too far removed from the purchaser. Traditionally, manufacturers of goods could offer a defense if both forms of privity were not satisfied; however, as the case law and the U.C.C. evolved, a need was recognized to protect certain users of goods who were not in the immediate chain of buyers or distributors. Attorneys should look to their own jurisdictions to determine which comments to § 2-318 of the U.C.C. have been adopted. Some jurisdictions apply a foreseeable personal injury test and some allow for property damages as well as for personal injury. It should be noted that, to survive a motion to dismiss based upon an affirmative defense of lack of privity, as Reed (P) did in the instant case, does not guarantee success on the merits of this or any other breach of warranty action.

Quicknotes

PRIVITY Commonality of rights or interests between parties.

Lincoln General Insurance Co. v. Detroit Diesel Corp.

Insurer (P) v. Engine producer (D)

Tenn. Sup. Ct., 293 S.W.3d 487 (2009).

NATURE OF CASE: Question certified from federal district court to state's highest court in action for breach of express and implied warranties, negligence, and strict products liability.

FACT SUMMARY: After Lincoln General Insurance Company (Lincoln General) (P) paid its insured for damage to the insured's bus, which caught fire due to an alleged engine defect, Lincoln General (P) brought suit for breach of express and implied warranties, negligence, and strict products liability against the bus manufacturer, Prevost Car (US) Inc. (Prevost) (D), and the engine producer, Detroit Diesel Corporation (Detroit Diesel) (D). Prevost (D) moved to dismiss, contending that Lincoln General's (P) tort claims were barred by the economic loss doctrine.

RULE OF LAW

Tennessee law does not recognize an exception to the economic loss doctrine under which recovery in tort is possible for damage to the defective product itself when the defect renders the product unreasonably dangerous and causes the damage by means of a sudden, calamitous event.

FACTS: Senators Rental, Inc. (Senators Rental), an insured of Lincoln General Insurance Company (Lincoln General) (P), purchased a bus manufactured by Prevost Car (US) Inc. (Prevost). The engine in the bus was produced by Detroit Diesel Corporation (Detroit Diesel) (D). As it was travelling in Tennessee, the bus caught fire due to an alleged engine defect. The fire did not cause personal injury or damage to any property other than the bus itself. Lincoln General (P) paid Senators Rental $405,250 for the fire damage pursuant to its insurance policy. Lincoln General (P) then sued Prevost (D) and Detroit Diesel (D) for breach of express and implied warranties, negligence, and strict products liability. Prevost (D) and Detroit Diesel removed the case to federal district court, where Prevost (D) moved to dismiss for failure to state a claim, arguing that Lincoln General's (P) tort claims were barred by the economic loss doctrine, a judicially created principle that reflects an attempt to maintain separation between contract law and tort law by barring recovery in tort for purely economic loss. The doctrine is implicated in products liability cases when a defective product damages itself without causing personal injury or damage to other property. In this context, "economic loss" is defined generally as "the diminution in the value of the product because it is inferior in quality and does not work for the general purposes for which it was manufactured and sold." The district court certified a question to the Tennessee Supreme Court as to whether Tennessee law recognizes an exception to the economic loss doctrine under which recovery in tort is possible for damage to the defective product itself when the defect renders the product unreasonably dangerous and causes the damage by means of a sudden, calamitous event. The Tennessee Supreme Court answered the certified question.

ISSUE: Does Tennessee law recognize an exception to the economic loss doctrine under which recovery in tort is possible for damage to the defective product itself when the defect renders the product unreasonably dangerous and causes the damage by means of a sudden, calamitous event?

HOLDING AND DECISION: (Holder, C.J.) No. Tennessee law does not recognize an exception to the economic loss doctrine under which recovery in tort is possible for damage to the defective product itself when the defect renders the product unreasonably dangerous and causes the damage by means of a sudden, calamitous event. First, the certified question presupposes that the state recognizes the economic loss doctrine. Although the doctrine has never been expressly adopted, this court has expressed agreement with the policies underlying the doctrine, i.e., that product liability claims resulting in pure economic loss can be better resolved on theories other than negligence. Similarly, the United States Supreme Court has also adopted the doctrine, and has set forth the bright-line rule that precludes recovery in tort when a product damages itself without causing personal injury or damage to other property. In such instances, damage to a defective product is merely a failure of the product to meet the purchaser's expectations, a risk that the parties had the opportunity to allocate by negotiating contract terms and acquiring insurance. Therefore, the purchaser's remedies must be limited to contractual remedies. Moreover, permitting recovery in tort for purely economic loss could subject a manufacturer to an indefinite amount of damages, whereas a warranty action has built-in limitations on liability. A minority of jurisdictions do not distinguish at all between economic loss and personal injury or property damage because, in either circumstance, the damage was caused by the defendant's conduct. An intermediate approach permits tort recovery for damage to the defective product alone under limited exceptions that "turn on the nature of the defect, the type of risk, and the manner in which the injury arose." Here, Lincoln General (P) urges that the court adopt this intermediate approach, which would permit recovery for unreasonably dangerous

Continued on next page.

products that cause damage to themselves during sudden, calamitous events. This exception would require courts to distinguish between those products that expose a product owner to an unreasonable risk of injury during an abrupt and disastrous occurrence and those products that merely disappoint a product owner's expectations. However, the dichotomy between disappointed and endangered product owners is too indeterminate to enable manufacturers easily to structure their business behavior. Regardless of this dichotomy, the owners of damaged products, whether merely "disappointed" or "endangered," end up in the same position, and the only injury experienced is purely economic. It follows that the remedies available to these similarly situated product owners should derive from the parties' agreements, not from the law of torts, lest the courts disrupt the parties' allocation of risk. To hold otherwise would make it more difficult for parties to predict the consequences of their business transactions, the cost of which ultimately falls on consumers in the form of increased prices. Additionally, it is difficult for parties and courts to apply a rule that focuses on the degree of risk and the manner in which the product was damaged as opposed to a rule that hinges on harm the plaintiff actually sustains. Rejected, too, is Lincoln General's (P) argument that failing to adopt its approach will lead to decreased safety; there is sufficient deterrence of defective products in tort law that permits recovery for personal injury and damage to property other than the product itself. Finally, adopting the economic loss doctrine with no exception is not inconsistent with the state's product liability act, since that act does not apply to purely economic losses. The certified question is answered in the negative.

ANALYSIS

In this opinion, the Tennessee Supreme Court joined the majority of state appellate courts that had considered—and rejected—the adoption of an exception to the economic loss doctrine based on unreasonably dangerous products; sudden, calamitous events; or both. Those courts have concluded that the remedies provided under the Uniform Commercial Code—repair and replacement costs and, in appropriate circumstances, consequential economic loss—are sufficient. This holding is also consistent with Section 21 of the Restatement (Third) of Torts: Products Liability (1998), which specifically excludes harm to "the defective product itself" from the definition of "harm to persons or property" for which economic loss is recoverable.

Quicknotes

BREACH OF EXPRESS WARRANTY The breach of an express promise made by one party to a contract on which the other party may rely, relieving that party from the obligation of determining whether the fact is true and indemnifying the other party from liability if that fact is shown to be false.

Ventura v. Ford Motor Corp.

Car owner (P) v. Car manfacturer (D)

N.J. Super. Ct. App. Div., 180 N.J. Super. 45, 433 A.2d 801 (1981).

NATURE OF CASE: Appeal from award of rescission of contract for breach of warranty.

FACT SUMMARY: Ventura (P) bought a new car from Marino Auto Sales, Inc. (D) and then sued for breach of warranty when it turned out to be a lemon.

RULE OF LAW

If a supplier of consumer products provides a written limited warranty with respect to the goods to the consumer, it may not completely disclaim implied warranties.

FACTS: Ventura (P) bought a Mercury Marquis, manufactured by Ford Motor Corp. (Ford) (D), from an authorized dealer, Marino Auto Sales, Inc. (Marino) (D). Paragraph 7 of Marino's (D) sales contract expressly stated that Marino (D) was not making any warranties regarding the car and, instead, passed Ford's (D) written warranty on to the consumer. The same paragraph stated that Marino (D) would be responsible for performing all terms and conditions of Ford's (D) owner service policy. As it turned out, the car hesitated and stalled constantly. When Marino (D) refused to fix it, Ventura (P) sued Marino (D) and Ford (D) for breach of the implied warranties of merchantability and fitness. Marino (D) cross-claimed against Ford (D) for indemnification. The trial court granted Ventura (P) rescission of the contract plus refund of the purchase price less an allowance for use of the car; found in favor of Marino (D) on its cross-claim against Ford (D); and awarded counsel fees to Ventura (P) against Ford (D) under the Magnuson-Moss Warranty Act. Ford (D) and Marino (D) appealed.

ISSUE: Can a supplier completely disclaim implied warranties for a consumer product where it has provided a written limited warranty to the consumer with respect to the goods?

HOLDING AND DECISION: (Botter, J.) No. A supplier may not completely disclaim implied warranties for a consumer product where it has provided a written limited warranty to the consumer with respect to the goods. The Magnuson-Moss Warranty Act § 2304 specifically forbids it. Among other things, paragraph 7 of the sales agreement promised that Marino (D) would perform any remedial action required by Ford's (D) warranty. This is a limited warranty within the meaning of Magnuson-Moss, and Marino's (D) disclaimer of the implied warranty of merchantability and fitness was therefore invalid. As Marino (D) clearly breached these warranties, judgment for Ventura (P) was proper. In addition, the grant of counsel fees to Ventura (P) against Ford (D), even though no judgment was obtained as against Ford (D), was also proper. Although under the Act for such fees to be granted Ford (D) had to have been informed of the defect and given an opportunity to cure the defect, that condition is satisfied here because Ford's (D) representative, Marino (D), was so notified, as was a direct employee of Ford (D), and Marino (D) had multiple opportunities to repair the vehicle. Because nominal damages could have been assessed against Ford (D), and counsel fees attached to that judgment, Ford (D) is not prejudiced by the trial judge's failure to have awarded such nominal damages. Moreover, the grant of counsel fees supports the Act's purpose and there was no abuse of discretion as to the amount of the fees. Affirmed.

ANALYSIS

Title I of the Magnuson-Moss Warranty Act applies to all consumer products covered by a written warranty. 15 U.S.C. § 2301–2312. Magnuson-Moss divides all warranties into two categories: full and limited. Full warranties are those which give consumers the choice to receive a full refund or replacement of a defective product that is beyond repair. Anything else is a limited warranty. Limited warranties cannot disclaim implied warranties or modify them, except to limit them in time. This is a radical departure from previous law, where the warrantor could disclaim almost anything so long as it was done with clear notice, such as a writing given to the consumer.

Quicknotes

IMPLIED WARRANTY OF MERCHANTABILITY An implied promise made by a merchant in a contract for the sale of goods that such goods are suitable for the purpose for which they are purchased.

INDEMNIFICATION Reimbursement for losses sustained or security against anticipated loss or damages.

Colonial Pacific Leasing Corp. v. McNatt Datronic Rental Corp.

Lessor (D) v. Lessee (P)

Ga. Sup. Ct., 268 Ga. 265, 486 S.E.2d 804 (1997).

NATURE OF CASE: Certiorari to review breach of contract.

FACT SUMMARY: **Quick-Trip Printers (P) brought suit against the equipment supplier, manufacturer and lessors (D) of defective computer equipment it leased from Colonial and Datronic (D), seeking rescission of the leases.**

RULE OF LAW

A "hell or high water" clause does not insulate a lessor's assignee from a claim of fraud where an agency relationship can be established between the assignee and the perpetrators of the alleged fraud.

FACTS: The McNatts, sole shareholders and officers of Quick-Trip Printers (Quick-Trip) (P), entered into negotiations with Itex for the acquisition of a computer printing system. They executed a finance agreement with Burnham, which assigned its interests to Colonial and Datronic. Quick-Trip (P) experienced problems with the equipment and delayed payment to Itex. The lessors repossessed the equipment and Quick-Trip (P) filed suit against the equipment supplier, manufacturer and lessors seeking rescission of the leases. Colonial and Datronic (D) filed counterclaims seeking payment on the leases. The trial court granted summary judgment in favor of lessors (D) on the main claims and counterclaims. The court of appeals reversed as to the main claims and counterclaim for unpaid rent, holding that the leases' requirement that the rental payments be made even if the equipment were damaged, defective, or unfit (the "hell or high water" clauses) could not be enforced where it was alleged that the employees of the vendor had fraudulently induced the lessee to acquire the equipment.

ISSUE: Does a "hell or high water" clause insulate a lessor's assignee from a claim of fraud where an agency relationship can be established between the assignee and the perpetrators of the alleged fraud?

HOLDING AND DECISION: (Benham, C.J.) No. A "hell or high-water" clause does not insulate a lessor's assignee from a claim of fraud where an agency relationship can be established between the assignee and the perpetrators of the alleged fraud. In Georgia all lease contracts for goods after 1993 are governed by the Universal Commercial Code (U.C.C.) Article 2A. Under pre-Article 2A law, the conduct of the parties to a lease finance transaction is governed by the terms of the lease and the law favors such bargains so long they are not the product of fraud or violative of public policy. A finance lessor's disclaimers of warranties are not expressly prohibited. A contractual requirement the lessee make its rental payments is also valid in the absence of fraud on the part of the finance lessor. Here the leases clearly exclude warranty and promissory liability of the finance lessor and its assignees to Quick-Trip (P), stating that Quick-Trip (P) agreed to pay the full amount of the rental agreement to assignee/lessors regard of defect, damage or unfitness of the equipment, and that the lessee agreed not to assert against the assignee lessors defenses it could not assert against the original lessor. Thus, the contract precludes the lessee from asserting fraud of the original finance lessor as a defense against the assignee lessor's claim for payment. Here, however, Quick-Trip (P) sued first to rescind its lease contracts on the ground of fraudulent inducement. In order for the alleged fraud of the employees of the equipment supplier to authorize rescission of the finance lease, their actions must somehow be imputed to the assignee lessors through the finance lessor. The record indicates that the requirement supplier's employees acted only as a conduit of information between the lessee and the finance lessor and that there was no evidence that the lease was negotiated pursuant to authorization given to the employees by the lessor (i.e., there is no evidence of a relationship pursuant to which the alleged fraud of the supplier's employers could be imputed to the finance lessor so as to invalidate the contracts.) Thus the "hell or high water" clauses in the lease are viable. Affirmed in part and reversed in part.

ANALYSIS

Whether or not employees of an equipment supplier are agents of the finance lessor depends upon the circumstances of the particular arrangement. While a contractual statement denying the existence of such relationship is not conclusive, the mere submission of a supplier's employee of a business/lessee's credit application to the finance lessor does not make that employee, as a matter of law, an agent of the finance lessor. However, where the supplier's employees were trained with respect to completing the leasing documents and authorized to negotiate such leases, this has been sufficient to support a finding of agency. *Potomac Leasing v. Thrasher*, 181 Ga. App. 833 (1987).

Continued on next page.

Quicknotes

ASSIGNEE A party to whom another party assigns his interest or rights.

FRAUD A false representation of facts with the intent that another will rely on the misrepresentation to his detriment.

CHAPTER 4

Terms of the Contract

Quick Reference Rules of Law

	PAGE
1. *Casserlie v. Shell Oil Co.* When a price that has been left open in a contract is fixed at a price posted by a seller or buyer, and the posted price is both commercially reasonable and nondiscriminatory, the price setter has acted in good faith, and a subjective inquiry into the motives of the price setter is not permitted.	*50*
2. *Cook Specialty Co. v. Schrlock.* Where a contract specifies shipment by a carrier, unless the contract states otherwise, risk of loss passes to the buyer as soon as the goods are delivered to the carrier.	*52*
3. *Rheinberg-Kellerei GmbH v. Vineyard Wine Co.* If a seller is authorized to send goods to the buyer and no particular destination is specified, seller must give prompt notice to buyer of actual shipment so that buyer may protect his interests.	*53*

Casserlie v. Shell Oil Co.

Gasoline dealer/franchisee (P) v. Oil company/franchisor (D)

Ohio Sup. Ct., 121 Ohio St. 3d 25, 902 N.E.2d 1 (2009).

NATURE OF CASE: Appeal from affirmance of summary judgment for defendant in action for bad-faith pricing.

FACT SUMMARY: Gasoline dealers (P) who were under contract to obtain their gasoline from Shell Oil Co. (Shell) (D) at a wholesale price set by Shell (D) at the time of delivery, i.e., at an open price, alleged that Shell (D) had acted in bad faith in setting the open price, and contended that the definition of "good faith" under Uniform Commercial Code (U.C.C.) § 2-305, which incorporates an "honesty in fact" component, requires a subjective inquiry.

RULE OF LAW

When a price that has been left open in a contract is fixed at a price posted by a seller or buyer, and the posted price is both commercially reasonable and nondiscriminatory, the price setter has acted in good faith, and a subjective inquiry into the motives of the price setter is not permitted.

FACTS: Gasoline dealers (P) in Cleveland leased gas stations, including equipment and land, from Shell Oil Co. (Shell) (D) and operated them as franchisees. The parties' contracts obligated the dealers (P) to buy gasoline exclusively from Shell (D) at a wholesale price set by Shell (D) at the time of delivery. This type of term in a contract is known as an open-price term. The price paid by the dealers (P) was referred to as the dealer-tank-wagon (DTW) price because it included the cost of delivery to the stations. Shell (D) charged the dealers a DTW price that was based on market factors including the prices offered by its major competitor and the street price within areas of the city. In each area of the city, called a price administration district (PAD), Shell (D) charged all dealers (P) the same DTW price. Shell (D) also sold gasoline to "jobbers," which were independent companies operating non-Shell-owned gas stations. Jobbers purchased gasoline directly at the oil company's terminal and paid the "rack" price, which was the cost of purchasing gasoline at the oil company's terminal and thus did not include delivery costs. The dealers (P) filed suit against Shell (D), alleging, inter alia, that Shell (D) had engaged in bad faith when it set the DTW price. The dealers alleged that the rack price was often substantially lower than the DTW price, which allowed jobbers to offer wholesale DTW prices that were substantially lower than the DTW price charged to the dealers. The dealers (P) contended that this pricing was unreasonable and was part of a scheme that was designed to drive them out of business. The dealers (P) alleged that Shell's (D) goal was to eliminate them so that it could take over operation of the gas stations, thus profiting from all of the sales, including nonfuel sales, at the stations, and not just from wholesale gasoline sales to and rental income from the dealers. The case was bifurcated and moved forward on the bad-faith issue. The trial court granted summary judgment to Shell (D), finding that it had satisfied the good faith requirement in the state's version of U.C.C. § 2-305 by setting the DTW in a commercially reasonable manner. The dealers (P) appealed, arguing that bad faith may be shown either by evidence of a party's intent, a subjective standard, or by evidence of its commercial unreasonableness, which is an objective standard. The state's intermediate appellate court, adopting a purely objective standard, affirmed. The state's highest court granted review.

ISSUE: When a price that has been left open in a contract is fixed at a price posted by a seller or buyer, and the posted price is both commercially reasonable and nondiscriminatory, has the price setter acted in good faith, and is a subjective inquiry into the motives of the price setter not permitted?

HOLDING AND DECISION: (Moyer, C.J.) Yes. When a price that has been left open in a contract is fixed at a price posted by a seller or buyer, and the posted price is both commercially reasonable and nondiscriminatory, the price setter has acted in good faith, and a subjective inquiry into the motives of the price setter is not permitted. In the case of a merchant, such as Shell (D), good faith means "honesty in fact and the observance of reasonable commercial standards of fair dealing in the trade." The issue is whether there is room for a subjective inquiry within the honesty-in-fact portion of the good-faith definition where a seller has been shown to have set an open price in an objectively reasonable commercial manner. The U.C. does not define the term "honesty in fact," and this state's case law on this issue is sparse or not helpful. However, Official Comment 3 to § 2-305 does provide some guidance. That Comment provides a safe harbor where a "posted price" satisfies good faith in its entirety, and a number of other jurisdictions have adopted this safe harbor when deciding cases presenting facts similar to the case at bar. Those jurisdictions have concluded that a subjective good-faith inquiry injects uncertainty into the law of contracts and undermines one of the U.C.C.'s primary goals of promoting certainty and predictability in commercial transactions. The drafters of the U.C.C., therefore, incorporated the posted-price safe harbor to prevent extensive litigation involving any open-price term, while seeking to avoid discriminatory prices. Some of those courts have concluded that subjective intent is not intended to stand alone as

Continued on next page.

a basis for liability and must also have some basis in objective fact, which at a minimum requires some connection to the commercial realities of the case. On the other hand, some courts that have considered the Comment have concluded that it does not provide a safe harbor where there is subjective bad faith. Those cases contend that the comment is limited to the "normal case," which does not include a situation where the seller is purposefully trying to drive the buyer out of business. However, this latter interpretation would eviscerate the safe harbor in any action in which the plaintiff alleges circumstantial evidence of an improper motive, leading to drawn-out litigation even if the prices ultimately charged were undisputedly within the range of those charged throughout the industry. In other words, if a subjective inquiry could determine bad faith, a seller charging a fair price, even exactly the same price as another, good-faith seller, could be deemed to be acting in bad faith. Therefore, the safe harbor applies where there is a posted-price scenario, but it does not apply when the facts present a "normal case." In the "normal case," subjective intent may be relevant to an analysis of good faith under § 2-305(2). A price that is nondiscriminatory among similarly situated buyers correspondingly qualifies as a "posted price" or the like. A discriminatory price could not be considered a "posted" or "market" price, because, in effect, the seller is not being "honest in fact" about the price that it is charging as a posted price, since it is charging a different price to other buyers. Therefore a price that is both commercially reasonable and nondiscriminatory fits within the limits of the safe harbor and complies with the statute's good-faith requirement. Applying these principles here, the prices set by Shell (D) were both commercially reasonable and nondiscriminatory. Although the prices set were too high for dealers (P) to remain profitable and compete with jobbers in the city, Shell (D) was not required to sell gasoline at a price that was profitable for buyers. The DTW prices set by Shell (D) were within the range set by its competitors, and it was reasonable for Shell (D) to adjust the prices according to competition by PADs. Within and among those PADs, Shell (D) did not discriminate among similarly situated buyers. Moreover, jobbers, who received lower rack prices, were not similarly situated to the dealers (P), since gasoline was not delivered to the jobbers and the jobbers performed additional functions compared to dealers, such as maintaining the properties they owned and bearing the risk of environmental liability. Because jobbers relieved Shell (D) of these obligations, they were charged a lower price. Accordingly, the prices set by Shell (D) were not commercially unreasonable or discriminatory, and the posted-price safe harbor therefore applied. Affirmed.

ANALYSIS

Judge Pfeifer dissented on the grounds that the majority's reliance on the safe-harbor presumption was misplaced because the state's legislature had never adopted Official Comment 3 to § 2-305. Accordingly, he argued that the safe-harbor presumption was not part of the state's law, despite the "majority opinion's insouciant belief to the contrary." He also noted that "good faith" is generally treated as incorporating both subjective and objective standards, and that although § 2-305 deals exclusively with open-price terms, it does not define "good faith" differently from its customary meaning. He also pointed out that many different jurisdictions in many different contexts, including in the context of an open-price term, define "good faith" as requiring both subjective and objective analysis, and he reasoned that since the Comment was not part of the state's law, good faith does not have a different meaning when used with open-price terms than when used in any other context. Thus, cases discussing "good faith" in a variety of contexts were good precedent, and the courts in those cases agreed that it is not possible to determine whether a party acted in "good faith" without a subjective inquiry.

Quicknotes

BAD FAITH Conduct that is intentionally misleading or deceptive.

BIFURCATION At trial, the consideration of issues separately.

GOOD FAITH An honest intention to abstain from taking advantage of another.

Cook Specialty Co. v. Schrlock

Buyer (P) v. Defendant (D)

772 F. Supp. 1532 (E.D. Pa. 1991).

NATURE OF CASE: Cross-motions for summary judgment in action for damages for breach of contract.

FACT SUMMARY: Cook Specialty Co. (P) ordered a press brake from Machinery Systems Inc. (D) which fell from the carrier's truck and broke before delivery.

RULE OF LAW

Where a contract specifies shipment by a carrier, unless the contract states otherwise, risk of loss passes to the buyer as soon as the goods are delivered to the carrier.

FACTS: Machinery Systems Inc. (MSI) (D) sold Cook Specialty Co. (Cook) (P) a hydraulic press brake worth $28,000. The terms were F.O.B. MSI's (D) warehouse, after which a carrier would deliver the brake to Cook (P). When the brake fell off the carrier's truck and broke during transit, Cook (P) was only able to recover $5,000 from the carrier's insurer. Cook (P) sued MSI (D) for the difference, claiming that MSI's (D) delivery to an underinsured carrier was unreasonable, and as the brake was not properly delivered to a carrier, risk of loss never passed to Cook (P). Both parties moved for summary judgment.

ISSUE: Where a contract specifies shipment by a carrier, does risk of loss pass to the buyer as soon as the goods are delivered to the carrier?

HOLDING AND DECISION: (Waldman, J.) Yes. If a contract specifies shipment by a carrier, unless the contract states otherwise, risk of loss passes to the buyer as soon as the goods are delivered to the carrier. Universal Commercial Code (U.C.C.) § 2-504 states that "F.O.B. (name of place)" means that the seller bears the risk of delivering goods to the carrier at that place. Section 2-509 states that as soon as the carrier takes possession, risk of loss shifts to the buyer. The requirement in U.C.C. § 2-504 that transportation must be arranged "as may be reasonable having regard to the nature of the goods" does not require MSI (D) to ensure adequate insurance. It imposes only a duty to choose a mode of transportation that will be suitable to the goods, such as shipping perishables in a refrigerated carrier (U.C.C. § 2-504 Official Comment 3). MSI's (D) delivery was reasonable. MSI's (D) motion for summary judgment granted; Cook's (P) cross-motion for summary judgment therefore denied.

ANALYSIS

Cook relied on the minority case of *LaCasse v. Blaustein*, 403 N.Y.S.2d 440 (Civ. Ct. 1979). In *LaCasse*, a student ordered calculators and authorized the seller to spend up to $50 for shipping and insurance. The seller shipped in two cartons by fourth-class mail; spent only $9.98; insured for only $400 when the calculators were worth in excess of $3,000; misaddressed one carton; and "inscribed a theft-tempting notation on it." Plaintiff student won breach of contract action brought against the seller. As the court noted, the facts in *LaCasse* are exceptionally egregious, and it is the only reported case to hold that the seller's failure to obtain insurance breached U.C.C. § 2-504.

Quicknotes

F.O.B. Free on board; agreement between a seller and buyer pursuant to which the seller agrees to deliver the subject matter of the contract to a particular destination at his own expense and until which time he assumes all liability therefor.

RISK OF LOSS Liability for damage to or loss of property that is the subject matter of a contract for sale.

Rheinberg-Kellerei GmbH v. Vineyard Wine Co.

Wine supplier (P) v. Wine buyer (D)

N.C. Ct. App., 53 N.C. App. 560, 281 S.E.2d 425 (1981).

NATURE OF CASE: Cross-appeals from order dismissing suit for breach of contract.

FACT SUMMARY: Vineyard Wine Co.'s (D) order of German wine was lost at sea while in transit.

RULE OF LAW

If a seller is authorized to send goods to the buyer and no particular destination is specified, seller must give prompt notice to buyer of actual shipment so that buyer may protect his interests.

FACTS: Vineyard Wine Co. (Vineyard) (D) ordered 620 cases of wine from Rheinberg-Kellerei GmbH (Rheinberg) (P), a West German wine company. The order was placed in the United States through Rheinberg's (P) agent and was to be shipped by sea from Germany. Vineyard (D) sent Rheinberg (P) special instructions, stating that Vineyard (D) would cover insurance and requesting notice of arrival of the shipment. Shipment was delayed, and although Vineyard (D) made several inquiries of Rheinberg's (P) agent, it received no information about shipment or arrival dates. When Rheinberg (P) finally shipped the wine, it notified its agent, who failed to pass this information on to Vineyard (D). Approximately one week later, the ship sank, together with all hands and cargo. Vineyard (D) received no information about the shipment until after it had been lost at sea. When Vineyard (D) refused to pay for the wine, Rheinberg (P) sued. When the lower court dismissed Rheinberg's (P) action on the grounds that it had failed to give Vineyard (D) notice of the shipment as required in Universal Commercial Code (U.C.C.) § 2-504(c), both parties appealed. [The casebook excerpt does not include the grounds for Vineyard's (D) appeal.]

ISSUE: If a seller is authorized to send goods to the buyer and no particular destination is specified, must seller give prompt notice to buyer of when shipment is made?

HOLDING AND DECISION: (Wells, J.) Yes. If a seller is authorized to send goods to the buyer and no particular destination is specified, seller must give prompt notice to buyer of when shipment is made. Under U.C.C. § 2-504 risk of loss passes to the buyer upon delivery to the carrier. If buyer does not know that delivery has been made, buyer has no reasonable opportunity to protect against loss. Therefore, U.C.C. § 2-504 also requires that seller "promptly notify buyer of the shipment" so that buyer may act to guard his interests. Rheinberg's (P) failure to give notice of shipment until well after the wine was lost was not prompt notice within the meaning of U.C.C. § 2-504. Plaintiff's appeal affirmed and defendant's appeal dismissed.

ANALYSIS

The U.C.C. states that if the seller is a "merchant" as defined in the code, she retains risk of loss until buyer receives the goods. If she is not a "merchant," risk passes to buyer when she tenders. (See U.C.C. § 2-509.) This approach is a radical departure from prior law, where risk of loss belonged to whichever party had actual title to the goods. U.C.C. § 2-401(1) specifically rejects this approach and takes great pains to allocate the risk of loss according to the various stages of a mercantile transaction. The appropriate party, knowing when risk has passed to or from him, can obtain insurance for the correct time period.

Quicknotes

RISK OF LOSS Liability for damage to or loss of property that is the subject matter of a contract for sale.

CHAPTER 5

Performance of the Contract

Quick Reference Rules of Law

Cherwell-Ralli, Inc. v. Rytman Grain Co.

Seller (P) v. Buyer (D)

Conn. Sup. Ct., 433 A.2d 984, 29 U.C.C. Rep. Serv. 513 (1980).

NATURE OF CASE: Appeal from award of damages for breach of contract.

FACT SUMMARY: Rytman Grain Co. (Rytman) (D) stopped payment on a check sent to Cherwell-Ralli, Inc. (P) to compensate for past deliveries made under an installment contract because an independent contractor truck driver led Rytman (D) to believe that Cherwell-Ralli (P) would be unable to complete the deliveries, while Cherwell-Ralli (P) gave assurances.

RULE OF LAW

A party to a sales contract may not suspend its performance for which it has already received the agreed return without reasonable grounds for insecurity as to the remainder of the other party's performance.

FACTS: Cherwell-Ralli, Inc. (P) entered into an installment contract for the sale of Cherco Meal and C-R-T Meal. Rytman Grain Co. (Rytman) (D), the buyer, became delinquent in payment almost immediately, but Cherwell-Ralli (P) continued to make deliveries. When the price of meal rose, Rytman (D) became concerned that Cherwell-Ralli (P) might not be able to supply all of the meal contracted for, but Cherwell-Ralli (P) assured that it would. However, when a truck driver, who did not work for Cherwell-Ralli (P), told Rytman (D) that this was his last load, Rytman (D) stopped payment on the check it had tendered for payment on previous shipments already received. Cherwell-Ralli (P) refused to make further deliveries and recovered $21,013.60 for payments due and owing. Rytman (D) unsuccessfully pressed a counterclaim for damages for breach of contract due to Cherwell-Ralli's (P) refusal to make the remaining installment deliveries. Rytman (D) appealed.

ISSUE: May a party to a sales contract, suspend its performance for which it has already received the agreed return without reasonable grounds for insecurity as to the remainder of the other party's performance?

HOLDING AND DECISION: (Peters, J.) No. A party to a sales contract may not suspend its performance for which it has already received the agreed return without reasonable grounds for insecurity as to the remainder of the other party's performance. The trial court found that Rytman (D) had no reasonable grounds for doubting Cherwell-Ralli's (P) performance. Furthermore, Rytman (D) showed no accurate evidence to establish the damages it might have sustained because of the failure to deliver. Rytman (D) received all goods it ordered under the contract and could not rely upon its own nonpayments as a basis for such insecurity as would entitle Rytman (D) to demand assurances or resort to any remedy. A party to a sales contract may not suspend its performance for which it has already received the agreed return without reasonable grounds for insecurity as to the remainder of the other party's performance. The insecurity alleged by Rytman (D) was found to be inadequate by the trial court, and the record sustains this finding. Affirmed.

ANALYSIS

Universal Commercial Code (U.C.C.) § 1-609(2) states that the reasonableness of the grounds for insecurity must be determined according to "commercial standards." Note 2 of the Official Comment under that section points out that a reasonable ground for insecurity need not, however, arise from or be directly related to the contract in question. Something more than price fluctuation and a remark by a third party to the contract is required, nonetheless, as this case demonstrates.

Quicknotes

INSTALLMENT CONTRACT A contract pursuant to which the parties are to render performance or payment in periodic intervals.

Wilson v. Scampoli

[Parties not identified.]

D.C. Ct. App., 228 A.2d 848, 4 U.C.C. Rep. Serv. 178 (1967).

NATURE OF CASE: Appeal of rescission of award of contract.

FACT SUMMARY: Kolley (P), who bought a television set which arrived defective, rejected the retailer's (D) offer to repair the set and insisted on a new television.

RULE OF LAW

The seller has the right to cure minor defects through repair rather than replacement.

FACTS: Kolley (P), representing her father, bought a color television set on November 4, 1965, from a retailer (D). The television came with a guarantee of free service for 90 days and replacement of any defective parts for one year. The set was delivered two days later, at which time it did not operate properly. A service representative came two days after that and informed Kolley (P) that the television needed to be taken to a repair shop in order to determine the problem. Kolley (P) refused this offer and insisted upon a new television set. The retailer (D) would not refund the purchase price nor give Kolley (P) a new television. Kolley (P) filed suit, seeking a rescission of the sales contract. The trial court found for Kolley (P), and the retailer (D) appealed. [The title parties were not identified and the retailer's (D) name was not given in the casebook excerpt.]

ISSUE: May a seller cure minor defects by repairing the defective goods rather than replacing the merchandise?

HOLDING AND DECISION: (Myers, J.) Yes. A seller may cure minor defects by repairing the defective goods rather than replacing the merchandise. Universal Commercial Code (U.C.C.) § 2-601 retains the perfect tender rule. However, U.C.C. § 2-508 allows the seller to cure defects in the goods in a reasonable time where the seller believed that the goods were conforming at the time of performance. This cure may be effected through repair of the goods rather than replacement. Here, the retailer (D) reasonably believed that the television would conform to the contract at the time of delivery. Therefore, the retailer (D) was entitled to a reasonable time in which to repair the television so that it would conform to the contract. Kolley (P) denied the retailer (D) this opportunity and thus is not entitled to rescission of the contract. Reversed.

ANALYSIS

The perfect tender rule, as preserved by U.C.C. § 2-601, allows the buyer to reject goods for any nonconformity. It protects the buyer against delivery of flawed goods. It was created for single delivery sales because the buyer does not have the same bargaining position as buyers do in installment sales.

Quicknotes

CURE In a commercial transaction, the seller has a right to correct a delivery of defective goods within the time originally provided for performance as specified in the contract.

RESCISSION The canceling of an agreement and the return of the parties to their positions prior to the formation of the contract.

Ramirez v. Autosport

Buyer (P) v. Seller (D)

N.J. Sup. Ct., 88 N.J. 277, 440 A.2d 1345 (1982).

NATURE OF CASE: Appeal from award of rescission of contract and denial of damages on counterclaim for breach of contract.

FACT SUMMARY: Ramirez (P) bought a camper from Autosport (D) which had minor defects which were not immediately repaired, causing Ramirez (P) to seek rescission of the contract.

RULE OF LAW

Buyers may reject goods which do not completely conform to the contract.

FACTS: The Ramirezes (P) bought a camper from Autosport (D) on July 20, 1978. The camper cost $14,100, from which $4,700 was deducted for the Ramirezes' (P) van, which was traded in to Autosport (D). Delivery of the camper was contracted to take place on August 3, 1978. On that date the camper was discovered to have many small defects, and the Ramirezes (P) chose not to accept it. On August 14, 1978, Autosport (D) told the Ramirezes (P) that the camper was ready, but again several defects were present and the Ramirezes (P) chose not to accept the camper. The next day Autosport (D) transferred title to the Ramirezes (P) without informing them. Autosport (D) and the Ramirezes (P) attempted to negotiate a settlement, but finally the Ramirezes (P) requested that the contract be canceled and their van returned. However, Autosport (D) had already sold their old van to a third party and refused to cancel the contract. The Ramirezes (P) filed suit to rescind the sales contract, and Autosport (D) counterclaimed for breach of contract. At trial, the Ramirezes (P) prevailed, and Autosport (D) appealed.

ISSUE: May buyers reject goods which do not completely conform to the contract?

HOLDING AND DECISION: (Pollock, J.) Yes. Buyers may reject goods which do not completely conform to the contract. Under Universal Commercial Code (U.C.C.) § 2-602, a buyer may reject goods for any nonconformity to the contract and obtain cancellation. This rejection must take place within a reasonable time. The seller must prove conformity or cure the defect within a reasonable time in order to avoid cancellation. The Ramirezes (P) rejected the camper when they refused to accept it on August 14, 1978. Autosport (D) failed to demonstrate that the defects were corrected within a reasonable time. The Ramirezes (P) acted rightfully and were entitled to cancellation of the contract. Since the Ramirezes' (P) trade-in van was sold to a third party, they were also entitled to its fair market value, which the trial court determined was the contract price. It was not necessary under the Code to return the van to them, since a remedy available for one who has rightfully rejected goods is recovery of so much of the purchase price as has been paid, but payment is not defined and does not necessarily have to be made in cash. Affirmed.

ANALYSIS

The definition of acceptance is found in U.C.C. § 2-606. Upon acceptance, the burden of proof on the issue of whether the goods conform to the contract shifts from the seller to the buyer. Under U.C.C. § 2-601, the perfect tender rule is preserved and mandates that the seller prove conformity as of the time of delivery.

Quicknotes

PERFECT TENDER Goods tendered pursuant to a contract for sale, which conform precisely to the contract's requirements.

U.C.C. § 2-602 Provides that a rejection after an opportunity to inspect may be effective unless the buyer manifests acceptance in the manner invited by the offeror.

Plateq Corp. of North Haven v. Machlett Laboratories, Inc.

Tank constructor (P) v. Tank buyer (D)

Conn. Sup. Ct., 189 Conn. 433, 456 A.2d 786 (1983).

NATURE OF CASE: Appeal from award of damages for breach of contract.

FACT SUMMARY: Machlett Laboratories, Inc. (D) contended it never effectively accepted the tanks purchased from Plateq Corp. of North Haven (P) and, therefore, could reject them for nonconformity.

RULE OF LAW

A buyer may be found to have accepted goods despite their known nonconformity and despite the absence of actual delivery.

FACTS: Machlett Laboratories, Inc. (Machlett) (D) contracted to pay Plateq Corp. of North Haven (Plateq) (P) for constructing certain lead covered steel tanks. The tanks were to be designed for the purpose of testing X-ray tubes and thus had to be radiation-proof. Plateq (P) constructed the tanks and while Machlett (D) noted several minor defects, it never indicated that the tanks did not substantially conform to the contract. On the contrary, Machlett (D) communicated its general acquiescence to the construction, and Machlett (D) led Plateq (P) to believe it would pick up the tanks for transport to its premises. No trucks were sent, and Machlett (D) notified Plateq (P) that it was rejecting tender of goods. Plateq (P) sued, contending Machlett (D) had already accepted the goods and that no grounds existed for rejection or repudiation of acceptance. Machlett (D) appealed from a verdict for Plateq (P).

ISSUE: May a buyer be found to have accepted goods despite their known nonconformity and despite the absence of actual delivery?

HOLDING AND DECISION: (Peters, J.) Yes. A buyer may be found to have accepted goods despite their known nonconformity with the contract despite the absence of actual delivery. Under Universal Commercial Code (U.C.C.) § 2-606(1), acceptance occurs where the buyer (a) signifies that he will take the goods after he has inspected them or (b) fails to make an effective rejection. Clearly in this case Machlett (D) signified its willingness to take the goods even though it was aware of the defects and also failed to make an effective rejection, and the trial court's findings to this effect are supported by the record and are not clearly erroneous. Machlett (D) had an opportunity to inspect the goods and indicated it would send trucks to pick up the tanks. Under the circumstances, a post-installation test was intended that would have permitted rejection after acceptance if nonconformity continued. Thus, Machlett (D) signified its willingness to take the tanks. Also, Machlett (D) failed to make effective rejection since its telegram purporting to effect cancellation was insufficiently specific and, in fact, interfered with Plateq's (P) right to cure. Thus, not only was the attempted rejection ineffective, it was also wrongful. Thus, acceptance occurred. As a result Machlett (D) could avoid the contract only by proving acceptance substantially impaired the value of the goods to it. Consequently, no revocation is available. Affirmed.

ANALYSIS

A buyer must have been afforded a reasonable time to inspect and object to the defect in the goods. Thus, if Machlett (D) had had no such opportunity, presumably the "Perfect Tender Rule" would have allowed it to reject the tanks. However, Plateq (P) would have been afforded an opportunity to cure the nonconformity.

Quicknotes

ACCEPTANCE OF GOODS In a contract for the sale of goods, the buyer's taking of possession of the goods that are the subject matter of the offer constitute acceptance by the buyer.

NONCONFORMING GOODS Goods tendered pursuant to a contract for sale that do not conform with the contract's requirements or which are otherwise defective in some way.

PERFECT TENDER Goods tendered pursuant to a contract for sale, which conform precisely to the contract's requirements.

Waddell v. L.V.R.V. Inc.

RV purchaser (P) v. RV dealer (D)

Nev. Sup. Ct., 122 Nev. 15, 125 P.3d 1160 (2006).

NATURE OF CASE: Appeal and cross-appeal from judgment allowing revocation of acceptance of a contract and an order awarding attorney fees and costs.

FACT SUMMARY: L.V.R.V. Inc., D/B/A Wheeler's Las Vegas RV (Wheeler's) (D) contended the Waddells (P), who had bought an RV from Wheeler's (D) that experienced repeated problems that could not be fixed, were not entitled to revoke acceptance of the RV. [Both parties raised other issues that were mentioned, but not treated, in the casebook extract.]

RULE OF LAW

(1) Under Universal Commercial Code (U.C.C.) § 2-608, a purchaser may revoke acceptance of a purchased item where there is evidence that nonconformities substantially impair the value of the item to the purchaser based on his unique subjective needs.

(2) Under U.C.C. § 2-608, revocation of acceptance of a nonconforming item occurs within a reasonable time where the seller has had several opportunities to attempt to cure the defects, but has been unable to, and revocation occurs immediately after these attempts.

FACTS: L.V.R.V. Inc., D/B/A Wheeler's Las Vegas RV (Wheeler's) (D) sold an RV made by Coachmen, along with an extended warranty, to the Waddells (P). The Waddells (P), who led an RV-based lifestyle traveling all over, had come to Wheeler's (D) seeking to upgrade from a prior RV they owned, intending to sell their house and travel in the RV around the country for two to three years. Over the course of 18 months, the Waddells (P) experienced repeated problems with the RV, including engine overheating, heating/cooling problems, battery problems, and others, which Wheeler's (D) repeatedly attempted to fix in good faith but could not. After it became apparent that the problem could not be fixed, and the Waddells (P) sought a refund of the purchase price without success, the Waddells (P) brought suit against Wheeler's (D) for revocation of acceptance and other remedies. The trial court, finding that the RV's nonconformities substantially impaired its value to the Waddells (P), and that the Waddells (P) had brought suit within a reasonable time, allowed them to revoke their acceptance of the RV and ordered Wheeler's (D) to return all of the Waddells' (P) out-of-pocket expenses. Wheeler's (D) had sought indemnification from Coachmen, but the court denied such relief. Although the trial court granted the Waddells (P) their attorneys' fees, it denied interest on those fees, and also denied separate research fees. It denied Wheeler's (D) attorneys' fees. Wheeler's (D) appealed the court's decision regarding revocation of acceptance, indemnification by Coachmen, denial of its attorneys' fees, and some evidentiary issues. The Waddells' (P) cross-appealed the decision denying research fees and interest on attorneys' fees. The state's highest court granted review. [The casebook presents only the part of the appellate court's decision that treats the revocation of acceptance issue.]

ISSUE:

(1) Under U.C.C. § 2-608, may a purchaser revoke acceptance of a purchased item where there is evidence that nonconformities substantially impair the value of the item to the purchaser based on his unique subjective needs?

(2) Under U.C.C. § 2-608, does revocation of acceptance of a nonconforming item occur within a reasonable time where the seller has had several opportunities to attempt to cure the defects, but has been unable to, and revocation occurs immediately after these attempts?

HOLDING AND DECISION: (Gibbons, J.)

(1) Yes. Under U.C.C. § 2-608, a purchaser may revoke acceptance of a purchased item where there is evidence that nonconformities substantially impair the value of the item to the purchaser based on his unique subjective needs. It is an issue of first impression in this jurisdiction as to when a nonconformity substantially impairs the value of a good to the buyer. However, other states that have adopted U.C.C. § 2-608 verbatim have developed a two-prong test comprised of an objective element and a subjective element, and this court adopts that test. The subjective part of the test considers the buyer's particular needs, not those of an average buyer. The objective part of the test considers evidence of whether the nonconformity in fact substantially impairs the value of the goods to the buyer in light of his specific needs. As to the subjective part of the test, the evidence shows that the Waddells' (P) subjective need was for an RV in which they could live and travel around the country for several years and that such an RV constituted the subjective value to them of the RV. Based on the Waddells' (P) subjective need, the objective part of the test asks whether the nonconformities substantially impaired the value of the RV to them. Here there was evidence that especially because of engine overheating problems, the RV spent 7 of the 18 months following purchase in

Continued on next page.

Wheeler's (D) shop. This constitutes sufficient objective evidence of substantial impairment of value since it shows that not only could the Waddells (P) not enjoy the RV and their faith in its reliability was shaken, but it was also objectively unsafe to use it. Affirmed as to this issue.

(2) Yes. Under U.C.C. § 2-608, revocation of acceptance of a nonconforming item occurs within a reasonable time where the seller has had several opportunities to attempt to cure the defects, but has been unable to, and revocation occurs immediately after these attempts. U.C.C. § 2-608 provides that revocation of acceptance must be made within a reasonable time after the purchaser discovers or should have discovered the grounds for such revocation. This jurisdiction has never before ruled on what constitutes a reasonable timeline for revocation of acceptance, but other jurisdictions have ruled that a reasonable timeline depends on the nature, purpose, and circumstances of the transaction; i.e., this is a question of fact. The Waddells (P) brought the RV in for repairs immediately after noticing problems, but Wheeler's (D) could not fix those problems. The parties also were unable to resolve the demand for a refund prior to the litigation. While a seller must be given an opportunity to cure before the buyer may revoke acceptance, the seller may not postpone revocation by continually attempting to cure. There comes a point where the buyer is entitled to say, "That's all," and revoke, notwithstanding the seller's repeated good-faith efforts to cure. Also, the time for revocation is tolled while the seller attempts to cure. Here, the evidence shows that the Waddells (P) were entitled to say "That's all" after Wheeler's (D) repeated unsuccessful attempts to cure all the RV defects over seven months. Therefore, the trial court's determination that revocation was made within a reasonable time is supported by substantial evidence and is not clearly erroneous. Affirmed as to this issue.

ANALYSIS

As to the objective component of the two-part revocation of acceptance test, some courts have held that a nonconformity effects a substantial impairment of value if it "shakes the buyer's faith or undermines his confidence in the reliability and integrity of the purchased item." [See, e.g., *McCullough v. Bill Swad Chrysler-Plymouth,* 449 N.E.2d 1289 at 1294 (Ohio 1983)]. The Supreme Judicial Court of Massachusetts has recognized that "even cosmetic or minor defects that go unrepaired . . . or defects which do not totally prevent the buyer from using the goods, but circumscribe that use . . . can substantially impair the goods' value to the buyer." (*Fortin v. Ox-Bow Marina, Inc.,* 408 Mass. 310, 557 N.E.2d 1157, 1162 (Mass. 1990)). And some courts have even expressed the opinion that a seller's inability to correct defects in motor vehicles creates a major hardship and an unacceptable economic burden on the consumer. [See, e.g., *Milicevic v. Mercedes-Benz USA, LLC,* 256 F. Supp. 2d 1168, 1176 (D. Nev. 2003)].

Quicknotes

NONCONFORMING GOODS Goods tendered pursuant to a contract for sale that do not conform with the contract's requirements or which are otherwise defective in some way.

Jakowski v. Carole Chevrolet, Inc.

Car buyer (P) v. Car dealer (D)

N.J. Super. Ct., 180 N.J. Super. 122, 433 A.2d 841 (1981).

NATURE OF CASE: Plaintiff's motion for summary judgment on action for damages for breach of contract.

FACT SUMMARY: After Carole Chevrolet, Inc. (Carole) (D) neglected to undercoat Jakowski's (P) new car purchased from Carole (D), Jakowski (P) returned the car to Carole's (D) lot for the work, from where it was stolen.

RULE OF LAW

The seller of goods remains liable for the risk of their loss when the buyer receives nonconforming goods without accepting the nonconformity and the seller has not effected cure.

FACTS: Jakowski (P) entered into a contract to purchase from Carole Chevrolet, Inc. (Carole) (D) a new 1980 Chevrolet Camaro. Prior to delivery, Carole (D) was instructed to apply undercoatings and a finish coating. The car was delivered without the coatings, and the next day Jakowski (P) so notified Carole (D), who agreed to cure the defect and add the coatings. The car was in Carole's (D) lot awaiting cure when it was stolen and never recovered. Carole (D) refused demands to replace the car or refund the purchase price paid. Jakowski (P) was still liable on his installment loan for that price. Jakowski (P) then brought this action for damages based on the purchase price.

ISSUE: Does the seller of goods remain liable for the risk of their loss when the buyer receives nonconforming goods without accepting the nonconformity and the seller has not cured?

HOLDING AND DECISION: (Newman, J.) Yes. The seller of goods remains liable for the risk of their loss when the buyer receives nonconforming goods without accepting the nonconformity and the seller has not effected cure. The seller contends that the risk of loss passed to Jakowski (P) under Universal Commercial Code (U.C.C.) § 2-509(3) upon the latter's receipt of the automobile. That section goes on to provide, however, that § 2-510 governs the effect of breach upon the risk of loss. The automobile as delivered failed to conform to the contract and would have given Jakowski (P) the right to reject but for cure provision of that section passing the risk to the buyer after cure. Since no evidence of cure was interposed and no contention was made that cure had been effected, the nonconformity remained and so did Carole's (D) liability for risk of loss. It has been established that receipt of an automobile is not always an "acceptance," and in this case, Jakowski (P) did not accept the nonconforming car because he had no "reasonable opportunity to inspect" it under U.C.C. § 2-606 or to reject the goods in the face of Carole's (D) acknowledgment of the nonconformity and offer of cure. Thus, U.C.C. § 2-510(1) is applicable. The seller of goods remains liable for the risk of their loss when the buyer receives nonconforming goods without accepting the nonconformity and the seller has not cured. Jakowski (P) is entitled here to a refund of as much of the purchase price as has been paid, including the finance charges. Judgment granted.

ANALYSIS

The Official Comment clearly states that the cure by the seller in such cases does not operate to shift the risk of loss from the seller to the buyer until such cure is completed. This is true even where delivered goods are repossessed in contemplation of a new tender after cure.

Quicknotes

NONCONFORMING GOODS Goods tendered pursuant to a contract for sale that do not conform to the contract's requirements or which are otherwise defective in some way.

RISK OF LOSS Liability for damage to or loss of property that is the subject matter of a contract for sale.

Arabian Score v. Lasma Arabian Ltd.

Horse buyer (P) v. Horse seller (D)

814 F.2d 529 (8th Cir. 1987).

NATURE OF CASE: Appeal of grant of motion for summary judgment denying rescission of contract.

FACT SUMMARY: After Arabian Score (Arabian) (P) bought a horse from Lasma Arabian Ltd. (D), who promised to promote the horse for five years, the horse died, and Arabian (P) sought to recover the amount of money which would have been spent promoting the horse.

RULE OF LAW

The occurrence of an event that is a foreseeable risk does not provide the basis for rescinding a contract on the grounds of impossibility of performance.

FACTS: Arabian Score (Arabian) (P) purchased a horse named "Score" from Lasma Arabian Ltd. (Lasma) (D) for $1 million on October 27, 1983. The price included various promotional activities for Score that Lasma (D) was to perform over a period of five years. The agreement purported to disclaim all implied warranties. Arabian (P) obtained life insurance for Score in February 1984. Score died in September 1984. Arabian (P) sought to recover the amount of money that Lasma (D) would have spent promoting Score over the next four years on the grounds of impossibility. Lasma (D) responded that Score's death was a foreseeable risk assumed by Arabian (P). Furthermore, Lasma (D) presented evidence that they often promoted dead horses. Summary judgment was granted in favor of Lasma (D), and Arabian (P) appealed.

ISSUE: Does the occurrence of an event that is a foreseeable risk provide the basis for rescinding a contract on the grounds of impossibility of performance?

HOLDING AND DECISION: (Wollman, J.) No. The occurrence of an event that is a foreseeable risk does not provide the basis for rescinding a contract on the grounds of impossibility of performance. The doctrine of commercial frustration applies where performance under a contract becomes impossible due to the occurrence of enforceable events beyond the control of the parties. The death of Score was a foreseeable event to Arabian (P). This was evidenced by the fact that Arabian (P) obtained life insurance for Score. In addition, despite Score's death, Lasma (D) never indicated any inability or unwillingness to complete their promotional duties, and there was evidence that they regularly promoted deceased horses for a variety of legitimate purposes. Thus, there is no evidence that performance is impossible under these circumstances. Affirmed.

ANALYSIS

Events such as the changing of zoning regulations and price increases are generally ruled foreseeable to the parties and do not provide the basis for the impossibility defense. Events which do qualify as unforeseeable are usually wars, embargoes, or natural catastrophes which affect the parties' ability to perform under the contract.

Quicknotes

FORESEEABILITY A reasonable expectation that an act or omission would result in injury.

IMPOSSIBILITY A doctrine relieving the parties to a contract from liability for nonperformance of their duties thereunder, if the subject matter of the contract ceases to exist, a person essential to the performance of the contract is deceased, or the service or goods contracted for has become illegal.

RESCISSION The canceling of an agreement and the return of the parties to their positions prior to the formation of the contract.

Louisiana Power & Light Co. v. Allegheny Ludlum Industries, Inc.

Buyer (P) v. Seller (D)

517 F. Supp. 1319 (E.D. La. 1981).

NATURE OF CASE: Motion for summary judgment for breach of contract.

FACT SUMMARY: Allegheny Ludlum Industries, Inc. (D) claimed that performance under the contract by which Louisiana Power & Light Co. (P) bought steel tubing for delivery two years after the agreement was made was impracticable when the cost of producing the tubing rose substantially during this period.

RULE OF LAW

Increases in costs do not allow sellers to raise commercial impracticability as a defense to performing under the contract unless they are unreasonable and severe.

FACTS: Louisiana Power & Light Co. (P) contracted with Allegheny Ludlum Industries, Inc. (Allegheny) (D) to buy condenser tubing for use at a nuclear power plant. The contract was executed on February 8, 1974, with delivery to take place during June 1976. In May 1975, Allegheny (D) wrote to Louisiana Power & Light (P) requesting an adjustment in the contract price because the costs of making the tubing had increased substantially, causing Allegheny (D) to lose money on the contract, although the plant producing the tubing would remain slightly profitable overall. Louisiana Power & Light (P) refused, and Allegheny (D) responded that they might not perform under the contract. In February 1976, Allegheny (D) informed Louisiana Power & Light (P) that it would deliver the tubing only at the price which it cost to produce, which was 38 percent higher than at the time of the contract. Louisiana Power & Light (P) refused this offer and contracted with another company to deliver the tubing at a higher price than was provided for in the parties' contract. Louisiana Power & Light (P) filed suit to recover these extra costs due to Allegheny's (D) refusal to perform under the contract. Allegheny (D) defended by claiming that the higher production costs made performance commercially impracticable. Louisiana Power & Light (P) moved for summary judgment.

ISSUE: May sellers raise commercial impracticability as a defense to performing under a contract where the reason for the impracticability is substantially increased production costs?

HOLDING AND DECISION: (Gordon, J.) No. Sellers may not raise commercial impracticability as a defense to performance under a contract where the reason is increased production costs unless they are unreasonable and severe. According to Universal Commercial Code (U.C.C.) § 2-615, commercial impracticability excuses performance of the contract when it is impracticable due to the occurrence of a contingency not contemplated by the parties. In order to show impracticability, the party must show that performance would cause an unreasonable and severe loss. Allegheny's (D) loss would not have been unreasonable because production costs increased only 38 percent from when the contract was executed. Other cases, including *Iowa Electric Light and Power Co. v. Atlas Corp.*, 467 F. Supp. 129 (N.D. Iowa 1978), indicate that cost increases of up to 58 percent do not constitute commercial impracticability. Furthermore, although Allegheny (D) would have lost money on the Louisiana Power & Light (P) contract, the plant producing the tubing remained profitable. Thus, Allegheny (D) could not defend the alleged breach of contract based upon commercial impracticability. Summary judgment granted to Louisiana Power & Light (P).

ANALYSIS

U.C.C. § 2-615 allows impracticability as a defense upon "the occurrence of a contingency the non-occurrence of which was a basic assumption" of the parties at the time of the contract. It was intended to expand the common law defense of impossibility. However, many courts have treated § 2-615 as synonymous with common law impossibility.

Quicknotes

IMPRACTICABILITY A doctrine relieving the parties to a contract from liability for nonperformance of their duties thereunder, if the subject matter of the contract ceases to exist.

CHAPTER 6

Remedies

Quick Reference Rules of Law

Teradyne, Inc. v. Teledyne Industries, Inc.

Buyer (P) v. Seller (D)

676 F.2d 865 (1st Cir. 1982).

NATURE OF CASE: Appeal from award of damages for breach of contract.

FACT SUMMARY: When Teledyne Industries, Inc. (D) breached its contract with Teradyne, Inc. (P) for the purchase of a transistor test system, Teradyne (P) filed suit to recover its lost profits.

RULE OF LAW

The measure of damages for breach of contract by the buyer is the anticipated profit, including reasonable overhead, which the seller would have made but for the breach.

FACTS: After contracting to purchase a transistor test system from Teradyne, Inc. (P), Teledyne Industries, Inc. (D) breached the contract, offering to buy a less expensive machine instead. Teradyne (P) refused this offer. It then dismantled, tested, and reassembled the machine for sale to another purchaser, and filed suit for damages. Teradyne (P) would have made the sale to the second purchaser even if Teledyne Industries (D) had not broken its contract. It was not disputed that Teledyne Industries (D) broke the contract or that Teradyne's (P) right to damages was governed by Universal Commercial Code (U.C.C.) § 2-708(2). What was disputed was the calculation of damages. The master concluded that the appropriate formula for calculating damages was "gross profit" including fixed costs but not costs saved as a result of the breach. The district court adopted the master's report, and this appeal followed.

ISSUE: Is the measure of damages for breach of contract by the buyer the anticipated profit, including reasonable overhead, which the seller would have made but for the breach?

HOLDING AND DECISION: (Wyzanski, J.) Yes. The measure of damages for breach of contract by the buyer is the anticipated profit, including reasonable overhead, which the seller would have made but for the breach. The master's formula made no deductions on account of the wages paid to testers, shippers, installers, and other Teradyne (P) employees who directly handled the machine in preparing it for sale to the subsequent purchaser, or on account of their fringe benefits amounting to 12 percent of wages. The work of those employees entered directly into producing and supplying the machine and should not be regarded as "reasonable overhead" within U.C.C. § 2-708(2). Thus, as a "direct cost," the wages of the testers, etc., should have been deducted from the contract price, and fringe benefits should also have been deducted as direct costs. Vacated and remanded with respect to the omitted direct labor costs specified.

ANALYSIS

Section 2-708(2) applies only if the damages provided by § 2-708(1) are inadequate to put the seller in as good a position as he would have been had there been performance. Under § 2-708(1), the measure of damages is the difference between unpaid contract price and market price. Because the unpaid contract price here was $97,416, due to a discount, and the market price was $98,400, no damages would be recoverable under § 2-708(1). If Teledyne Industries (D) had performed, Teradyne (P) would have had the proceeds from two contracts, both Teledyne Industries' (D) and the subsequent purchaser's. Such losses by a "volume seller" are referred to as "lost volume profits."

Quicknotes

LOST PROFITS The potential value of income earned or goods which are the subject of the contract; may be used in calculating damages where the contract has been breached.

Hughes Communications Galaxy, Inc. v. United States

Satellite manufacturer (P) v. Federal government (D)

271 F.3d 1060 (Fed. Cir. 2001).

NATURE OF CASE: Appeal of breach of contract damages calculation.

FACT SUMMARY: Hughes Communications Galaxy, Inc. (Hughes) (P) had a contract with NASA whereby NASA would use its best efforts to launch 10 Hughes (P) satellites on space shuttles. As the result of the space shuttle Challenger explosion, NASA changed its program and informed Hughes (P) it would not use the space shuttles for launching any satellites. Hughes (P) then used expendable launch vehicles to launch its satellites at greater cost than it would have incurred by using the space shuttle. Hughes (P) sued the United States (D) for breach of contract and was awarded $102,680,625. in contract damages.

RULE OF LAW

(1) In calculating "cover" damages for the cost of substitute services, it is not error for a court to use the cost of what it determines are commercially reasonable substitutes instead of services that are identical to those involved in the contract.

(2) In calculating "cover" damages for the cost of substitute services, it is not error for a court to project what actual performance would have been.

(3) In calculating "cover" damages for the cost of substitute services, it is not error for a court to average actual costs to determine total damages.

(4) In calculating "cover" damages for the cost of substitute services, it is not error for a court not to reduce damages by amounts passed through to customers.

FACTS: Hughes Communications Galaxy, Inc. (Hughes) (P) entered into a Launch Services Agreement (LSA) with NASA that required NASA to use its best efforts to launch 10 Hughes (P) HS-393 satellites on space shuttles before September 30, 1994. In January 1986, the space shuttle Challenger exploded. As a result, by August 1986, NASA decided not to launch commercial satellites on shuttles. After 1986, Hughes (P) launched three of its HS-393s on expendable launch vehicles (ELVs) and also launched similar satellites on expendable launch vehicles (ELVs), including six HS-601s. Hughes (P) incurred more costs by launching satellites on ELVs rather than on shuttles. Hughes (P) sued the United States (Government) (D) for breach of contract. On remand, the Court of Federal Claims granted summary judgment for Hughes (P) for breach of contract, but before holding a trial on damages, that court ruled that the Government (D) could not produce evidence to reduce its damages by the amount Hughes (P) had passed on to its customers in increased prices. Hughes (P) presented two methods for calculating the increased costs. The first method, the Ten HS 393 Satellites Method, compared the costs of launching ten HS 393s on shuttles with the costs of launching ten HS-393s on ELVs. Because Hughes (P) had actually launched only three HS-393s on ELVs, the method based the ELV launch costs on the actual costs of launching the three HS-393s. The second method, the Primary Method, compared Hughes's (P) actual costs of launching ten satellites on ELVs with the costs that Hughes (P) would have incurred by launching ten satellites on shuttles. The ten satellites included the three HS-393s, the six HS-601s, and one HS-376. The Court of Federal Claims used the Ten HS-393 Satellites Method to calculate Hughes's (P) cost of "cover." However, the court modified this method in several important ways: (1) the court found that even using its best efforts, NASA would have only launched five HS-393s under the LSA, so it only awarded Hughes (P) increased costs for five satellites; (2) the court averaged the costs of launching on shuttles the three HS-393s that were actually launched on ELVs and used that average for the fourth and fifth satellites, rather than individually calculating the cost of launching each satellite on a shuttle; (3) in calculating the ELV launch costs for the fourth and fifth satellites, the court escalated the costs using the midpoint between March 1989 and September 1994, rather than the midpoint between March 1989 and December 1995, as Hughes's (P) expert had done; (4) the court refused to award Hughes (P) prejudgment interest on its damages; (5) the court refused to award Hughes (P) reflight insurance costs and increased launch insurance costs for the five satellites. Based on these modifications, the court awarded Hughes (P) $102,680,625. in damages for its increased launch costs. Hughes (P) and the Government (D) both appealed.

ISSUE:

(1) In calculating "cover" damages for the cost of substitute services, is it error for a court to use the cost of what it determines are commercially reasonable substitutes instead of services that are identical to those involved in the contract?

(2) In calculating "cover" damages for the cost of substitute services, is it error for a court to project what actual performance would have been?

(3) In calculating "cover" damages for the cost of substitute services, is it error for a court to average actual costs to determine total damages?

Continued on next page.

(4) In calculating "cover" damages for the cost of substitute services, is it error for a court not to reduce damages by amounts passed through to customers?

HOLDING AND DECISION: (Rader, J.)

(1) No. In calculating "cover" damages for the cost of substitute services, it is not error for a court to use the cost of what it determines are commercially reasonable substitutes instead of services that are identical to those involved in the contract. The Court of Federal Claims awarded Hughes (P) "cover" damages—the difference between the cost of the substitute and the contract price plus other losses. Although the Universal Commercial Code (U.C.C.) does not govern the LSA, it provides useful guidance. Under the U.C.C., substitute goods or services that are used for cover do not have to be identical to those in the contract; they only have to be "commercially usable as reasonable substitutes under the circumstances." Whether cover provides a reasonable substitute is a question of fact. The Government (D) argues that Hughes (P) should be able to recover damages only for the three HS-393s that it actually launched. Although Hughes (P) did not actually launch the fourth and fifth HS-393s that the trial court used to calculate damages, Hughes (P) did incur costs in launching the HS-601s. However, based on the evidence presented, the trial court found that HS-601 launches were reasonable substitutes under the circumstances (the court believed that Hughes (P) would not have developed the HS-601s but for the breach). This was an issue of credibility, a determination of which rarely is subject to reversal for clear error. As the victim of the breach, Hughes (P) was within its rights to obtain commercially reasonable substitute launch services even if the substitute services were not identical to those covered by the LSA. The trial court thus did not clearly err in holding that Hughes (P) successfully covered by launching HS 601s on ELVs. By using increased HS-393 launch costs (comparing the cost of ELV launches to shuttle launches) as a reasonable approximation for increased costs attributable to the substitute HS-601 launches, the trial court did not abuse its discretion. Moreover, these damages were direct because they represented increased launch costs only. In sum, there was no error for awarding damages for increased costs incurred by obtaining substitute launch services for two HS-601s in addition to the three HS-393s.

(2) No. In calculating "cover" damages for the cost of substitute services, it is not error for a court to project what actual performance would have been. The Court of Federal Claims found that NASA could have launched five HS-393s during the LSA contract period using its best efforts. This finding was based on various sources of evidence, including NASA's manifests, expert testimony, and the circumstances surrounding NASA's revised shuttle program. Based on this evidence, the trial court did not clearly err in its finding of what actual performance would have been limited to.

(3) No. In calculating "cover" damages for the cost of substitute services, it is not error for a court to average actual costs to determine total damages. Because Hughes (P) actually launched only three HS 393s, the trial court calculated the average costs of launching those three satellites on shuttles. Then, using the report of Hughes's (P) expert, it applied that average to project the shuttle launch costs of the fourth and fifth satellites. Hughes (P) asserted that the court should have used the shuttle launch costs for each individual satellite shown in the expert's report. However, the trial court's method was symmetrical with its calculation of the costs of ELV launches and was within the court's discretion.

(4) No. In calculating "cover" damages for the cost of substitute services, it is not error for a court not to reduce damages by amounts passed through to customers. The Government (D) wanted the court to reduce damages by the amount Hughes (P) recouped by increasing ("passing through") prices to its customers. As the trial court correctly noted, such mitigation is too remote, and allowing pass-through damages reduction in a breach of contract action would destroy symmetry between reduction and escalation of damages. Moreover, a standard for pass-through reductions would entail extremely difficult burdens for the trial court. Thus, the trial court did not abuse its discretion by disallowing pass-through damages reductions. Affirmed.

ANALYSIS

As this case repeatedly demonstrates, courts have discretion in determining what constitutes reasonable substitutes in determining "cover" damages. Because such a determination is heavily fact-driven, it is difficult to overturn on grounds of abuse of discretion or clear error.

Quicknotes

BREACH OF CONTRACT Unlawful failure by a party to perform its obligations pursuant to contract.

Tongish v. Thomas

Sunflower seed grower (P) v. Buyers (D)

Kan. Ct. App., 16 Kan. App. 2d 809, 829 P.2d 916, *aff'd on opinion below,* Kan. Sup. Ct., 251 Kan. 728, 840 P.2d 471 (1992).

NATURE OF CASE: Appeal from judgment awarding damages for breach of contract.

FACT SUMMARY: The Decatur Coop Association (D), the buyer, contended that damages awarded to it for Tongish's (P) breach of contract should be the market price differential, not lost profits.

RULE OF LAW

When a seller breaches a sales contract, the proper measure of damages is the difference between the contract price and market price.

FACTS: The Decatur Coop Association (Coop) (D) contracted to buy sunflower seeds from Tongish (P). Coop (D) also contracted to sell the seeds to a third party at the same price, plus a set handling fee. Therefore, Coop (D) had no risk on fluctuating market prices in its contract with Tongish (P). By the time the seeds were ready to deliver, the market price of sunflower seeds had risen greatly. Tongish (P) refused to honor the contract and sold to another party, Thomas (D), at a higher price. After Tongish (P) successfully sued Thomas (D) for the sales price, Coop (D) intervened as a third party, alleging that Tongish (P) had breached its contract. The court awarded Coop (D) $455.51, the amount of his handling fee. Coop (D) appealed, contending that the appropriate measure of damages was the difference between the contract and market price.

ISSUE: When a seller breaches a sales contract, is the proper measure of damages the difference between the contract price and market price?

HOLDING AND DECISION: (Walton, J.) Yes. When a seller breaches a sales contract, the proper measure of damages is the difference between the contract price and market price. This is true even if this amount does not accurately reflect the buyer's anticipated profits. Universal Commercial Code (U.C.C.) § 1-106 provides that the proper measure of damages for a breach of contract generally is the aggrieved party's lost profits. Section 2-713, however, prescribes that, when a seller breaches, the proper measure of damages is the difference between contract price and market price. Both sections could be applied here. However, § 1-106 is a general rule; § 2-713 is a specific statute. When a general rule and a specific statute conflict, the specific statute should prevail. Also, § 2-713, to a greater extent than § 1-106, tends to discourage breaches of contract and thus promotes commercial stability. Thus, the trial court should have applied § 2-713, not § 1-106. Reversed and remanded.

ANALYSIS

Coop (D) received more than $5,000 under § 2-713, while its expected profit on the transaction would have only been $455.51. This seems unfair and, as between the parties here, may well have been. However, § 2-713 also serves a general deterrent purpose that was served here.

Quicknotes

LOST PROFITS The potential value of income earned or goods which are the subject of the contract; may be used in calculating damages where the contract has been breached.

U.C.C. § 2-713 Provides that the measure of damages for non-delivery by the seller is the difference between the market price at the time the buyer learned of the breach and the contract price.

Mydlach v. DaimlerChrysler Corp.

Used car purchaser (P) v. Car manufacturer (D)

Ill. Sup. Ct., 226 Ill. 2d 307, 875 N.E.2d 1047 (2007).

NATURE OF CASE: Appeal from reversal of grant of summary judgment to defendant in action for breach of a repair warranty.

FACT SUMMARY: In June 1998, Mydlach (P) purchased a used car made by DaimlerChrysler Corp. (DaimlerChrysler) (D). The car, which was put into service in June 2006, came with a limited warranty, which had around either a year or 10,000 miles left on it. As required by the warranty, starting in July 1998, Mydlach (P) brought the car to authorized dealers for repair of a fluid leak, but they were unable to fix the problem. In May 2001, Mydlach (P) brought suit against DaimlerChrysler (D) under the federal Magnuson-Moss Act (Act), which has no statute of limitations. The parties agreed the Uniform Commercial Code (U.C.C.) should provide the appropriate limitations period. DaimlerChrysler (D) argued that the appropriate period was four years from when the car was put into service. Mydlach (P) contended the appropriate period was four years from when repairs were attempted.

RULE OF LAW

Under U.C.C. § 2-725, the four-year limitations period for an action for the breach of a repair warranty commences when the warrantor fails or refuses to repair the defect, rather than at tender of delivery.

FACTS: In June 1998, Mydlach (P) purchased a used car made by DaimlerChrysler Corp. (DaimlerChrysler) (D) that had around 26,000 miles on it. The car, which was put into service in June 2006, came with a three-year/36,000-mile limited warranty, which provided that DaimlerChrysler (D) would cover the costs of labor and parts needed to repair any item on the vehicle (with a few non-relevant exceptions) that was defective in material, workmanship, or factory preparation. The warranty had around either a year or 10,000 miles left on it, whichever came first. As required by the warranty, starting in July 1998, Mydlach (P) brought the car to authorized dealers for repair of a fluid leak, but they were unable to fix the problem. In May 2001, Mydlach (P) brought suit against Daimler Chrysler (D) for legal and equitable relief under the federal Magnuson-Moss Act (Act), which has no statute of limitations. Where a federal statute fails to specify a limitations period for suits under it, courts apply the most closely analogous statute of limitations under state law. Courts generally consider the U.C.C. to be the most closely analogous statute and have borrowed the limitations provision contained therein. The parties did not dispute that the four-year limitations of U.C.C. § 2-725, titled "Statute of limitations in contracts for sale," should be applied. Section 2-725(2) provides that "A cause of action accrues when the breach occurs, regardless of the aggrieved party's lack of knowledge of the breach. A breach of warranty occurs when tender of delivery is made. . . ." DaimlerChrysler (D) argued that the appropriate period was four years from when the car was put into service (1996), so that Mydlach's (P) suit (2001) was untimely. Mydlach (P) contended the appropriate period was four years from when repairs were attempted (1998), so that her suit (2001) was brought within the limitations period. The trial court granted summary judgment for DaimlerChrysler (D). The state's intermediate appellate court reversed and the state's highest court granted review.

ISSUE: Under U.C.C. § 2-725, does the four-year limitations period for an action for the breach of a repair warranty commence when the warrantor fails or refuses to repair the defect, rather than at tender of delivery?

HOLDING AND DECISION: (Fitzgerald, J.) Yes. Under U.C.C. § 2-725, the four-year limitations period for an action for the breach of a repair warranty commences when the warrantor fails or refuses to repair the defect, rather than at tender of delivery. Contrary to DaimlerChrysler's (D) argument, the analysis of the issue does not begin and end with the "tender of delivery" language. The U.C.C. and the Act, while similar in many respects, are not identical. U.C.C. article 2 addresses warranties that are created by a "seller," whereas the Act addresses warranties from a "supplier" or "warrantor" who may or may not be the immediate seller. The Act speaks of implied warranties and written warranties, the latter of which may be either full or limited, whereas the U.C.C. speaks of express warranties (which may be oral or written), implied warranties, and warranty of title. Although the parties agree that DaimlerChrysler's (D) warranty is a "written warranty" under the Act, they disagree as to whether the warranty is an "express warranty" under the U.C.C. DaimlerChrysler (D) argues that the repair warranty qualifies as an express warranty and that Mydlach's (P) claim is therefore governed by the tender-of-delivery rule. Mydlach (P) argues that the warranty does not qualify as an express warranty and that her claim is not subject to the tender-of-delivery rule. Under U.C.C. § 2-313, an express warranty is related to the quality or description of the goods, and such a warranty is breached if, and at the time that, the seller delivers nonconforming goods. Even if the buyer is unaware that the goods, as delivered, do not conform to the seller's affirmation, promise, description, sample or model, the warranty has been breached. Under this scenario, the pronouncement in § 2-725(2) that "[a] breach of warranty occurs when tender

Continued on next page.

of delivery is made" makes perfect sense, and the four-year limitations period commences at that time. The repair warranty at issue here, however, is not related to the quality or description of the goods at tender. It does not warrant that the vehicle will conform to some affirmation, promise, description, sample or model. Rather, the warranty promises only that the manufacturer will repair or replace defective parts during the warranty period. Accordingly, it is not, for U.C.C. purposes, an express warranty. Notwithstanding that it is a "written warranty" for purposes of the Act, it is not the type of warranty that can be breached on tender of delivery. Nevertheless, the first sentence of § 2-725(2) remains applicable. The first sentence states: "[a] cause of action accrues when the breach occurs, regardless of the aggrieved party's lack of knowledge of the breach." The U.C.C. does not specify when a breach of a repair promise occurs, and, therefore, the general law of contracts may be looked to for guidance on that question. Under the general law of contracts, performance under a vehicle manufacturer's promise to repair or replace defective parts is due not at tender of delivery, but only when, and if, a covered defect arises and repairs are required. In that event, if the promised repairs are refused or unsuccessful, the repair warranty is breached and the cause of action accrues, triggering the four-year limitations period. Such an approach is supported by leading commentators. The correctness of this approach is also seen when considering warranties with warranty periods of greater than four years. If the tender-of-delivery approach is used, any warranty period after four years could be cut off by the limitations period. Statutes of limitations, however, are intended to prevent stale claims, not to preclude claims before they are ripe for adjudication. Because longer warranty periods are not uncommon in the auto industry, adopting a tender-of-delivery approach might invite manufacturers and sellers of automobiles, as well as other goods, to engage in misleading marketing. That is, a manufacturer or seller could use the marketing advantage of a longer repair warranty, yet escape the accompanying obligations of that warranty by pleading the statute of limitations in defense. Moreover, contrary to DaimlerChrysler's (D) argument, commencing the four-year limitations period from the date the warrantor fails or refuses to repair the vehicle does not result in a limitless limitations period; in no event will the warrantor's exposure extend beyond the warranty period, plus four years. Finally, while a fact question may arise as to the date on which a repair warranty was breached which, in turn, would create some uncertainty as to when the four-year limitations period should commence, such fact questions are typically resolved by a trier of fact. Therefore, commencing the limitations period when the warrantor fails or refuses to repair the defect, rather than at tender of delivery, will not create unacceptable uncertainty in the limitations period. Applying these principles here, because the attempted repairs of Mydlach's (P) car occurred in 1998, and because she brought suit in 2001, her suit was timely. Affirmed as to this issue.

ANALYSIS

Those commentators that agree with the approach taken by the court in this case find that the failure to repair or replace is merely a breach of contract and not a breach of warranty, and therefore no cause of action arises until the warrantor has refused to repair or replace the goods. Whereas the delivery of nonconforming goods under an express warranty immediately triggers the breach, even if the buyer is not aware of it, the breach of the repair warranty does not occur until the warrantor has failed or refused to make the repairs or provide a replacement. The buyer has no right to commence an action for damages until such failure or refusal. Therefore, the commentators reason, the action is timely if brought within four years of the warrantor's failure or refusal.

Quicknotes

BREACH OF WARRANTY The breach of a promise made by one party to a contract on which the other party may rely, relieving that party from the obligation of determining whether the fact is true and indemnifying the other party from liability if that fact is shown to be false.

EXPRESS WARRANTY A promise made by one party to a contract that the other party may rely on a fact, relieving that party from the obligation of determining whether the fact is true and indemnifying the other party from liability if that fact is shown to be false.

TENDER OF PERFORMANCE The seller's delivery of conforming goods to the buyer pursuant to the requirements of a sales contract.

Central Washington Refrigeration, Inc. v. Barbee

Refrigeration systems contractor (P) v. Customer (D)

Wash. Sup. Ct., 133 Wash. 2d 509, 946 P.2d 760 (1997).

NATURE OF CASE: Appeal from affirmance of dismissal of a third-party indemnity claim in an action for payment of a debt.

FACT SUMMARY: McCormack Engineering (McCormack), a manufacturer of refrigeration coils used by Central Washington Refrigeration, Inc. (Central) (P) in a refrigeration system it installed in an orchard (D) storage facility, contended that Central (P) was not entitled to bring an indemnity action against it (McCormack) for damages claimed by the orchard (D) as resulting from improper functioning of the refrigeration system. McCormack also contended that even if Central (P) could maintain an indemnity action against McCormack, such action was barred by the Uniform Commercial Code's (U.C.C.'s) four-year statute of limitations.

RULE OF LAW

(1) A buyer of goods may bring an indemnity action against the seller for liability incurred to a third party for a defect in the goods.
(2) In an indemnity action brought by a buyer against the seller for liability incurred to a third party for a defect in the goods, the statute of limitations commences when the buyer pays damages to the third party or the third party obtains judgment against the buyer, whichever is first in time.

FACTS: Central Washington Refrigeration, Inc. (Central) (P), a refrigeration systems contractor, contracted with an orchard (D) to install a cold storage system for the orchard. Central (P) designed special coils for the system, which it had McCormack Engineering (McCormack) manufacture. McCormack delivered the coils in August 1987, at which time Central (P) installed them in the cold storage rooms. From the start, however, the orchard (D) experienced problems with the cold storage rooms. After several repair attempts and an intervening bankruptcy by the orchard (D), the orchard (D) defaulted on payments for the cold storage rooms and Central (P) subsequently sued for payment. In March 1989 the orchard counterclaimed for damages asserting Central (P) misdesigned the cold storage system, used poor workmanship in building it, installed improper components, and failed to repair the system. In May 1992—over four-and-a-half years after McCormack delivered the coils—Central (P) filed a third-party complaint against McCormack alleging the coils were defective and caused all the problems, seeking contribution and/or indemnity from McCormack for any damages due the orchard (D) from Central (P). McCormack contended that Central (P) was not entitled to bring an indemnity action against it, and that even if Central (P) could maintain an indemnity action against it, such action was barred by the U.C.C.'s four-year statute of limitations. The trial court dismissed the indemnity claim, and the state's intermediate appellate court affirmed. The state's highest court granted review.

ISSUE:

(1) May a buyer of goods bring an indemnity action against the seller for liability incurred to a third party for a defect in the goods?
(2) In an indemnity action brought by a buyer against the seller for liability incurred to a third party for a defect in the goods, does the statute of limitations commence when the buyer pays damages to the third party or the third party obtains judgment against the buyer, whichever is first in time?

HOLDING AND DECISION: (Sanders, J.)

(1) Yes. A buyer of goods may bring an indemnity action against the seller for liability incurred to a third party for a defect in the goods. Although indemnity sounds in contract and tort, it is a separate equitable cause of action. The type of indemnity implicated here is known as implied contractual indemnity, also called "implied in fact" indemnity. This type of indemnity arises when one party incurs a liability the other party should discharge by virtue of the nature of the relationship between the two parties. Thus, the question here is whether the contractual relationship between buyer (Central (P)) and seller (McCormack) under the U.C.C. is sufficient to give rise to an implied right of indemnity when a defect in the good causes damage to a third party user (orchard (D)) and such defect constitutes a breach of the seller's warranties. Under a minority view, which deems the relationship to be insufficient to support an indemnity action, the buyer's claim is nothing more than a claim for damages under a sales contract between merchants for breach of implied warranties resulting in consequential damages owed to a third party. Under the U.C.C., breach of contract actions must be commenced within four years of date of delivery of goods regardless of when the buyer discovers the defect. Hence, under the minority view, Central's (P) action against McCormack would be time barred, because it was brought later than four years from delivery of the coils. This was the view adopted by the court below. In contrast to the minority view, the majority view holds that the contractual relationship, with its concomitant implied

Continued on next page.

warranties, between the buyer and seller is sufficient under the U.C.C. to support an implied indemnity claim when the buyer incurs liability to a third party as a result of a defect in the goods which would constitute a breach of the seller's implied or express warranties. This holding recognizes that there is a substantial difference between an instance where a product simply fails as opposed to a situation where the product fails and causes damage to a third party. Reversed as to this issue.

(2) Yes. In an indemnity action brought by a buyer against the seller for liability incurred to a third party for a defect in the goods, the statute of limitations commences when the buyer pays damages to the third party or the third party obtains judgment against the buyer, whichever is first in time. Indemnity actions are distinct, separate causes of action from the underlying wrong and are governed by separate statutes of limitations. It is well settled that indemnity actions accrue when the party seeking indemnity pays or is legally adjudged obligated to pay damages to a third party. The statute of limitations on the indemnity action therefore begins to run at that point. Accordingly, the U.C.C.'s four-year statute of limitations is not applicable. Instead, the statute of limitations on Central's (P) indemnity claim began to run when Central (P) paid the orchard (D) to settle the orchard's (D) claims. Because Central (P) brought suit at the same time it settled, its indemnity action was not time barred. Reversed and remanded.

DISSENT: (Guy, J.) The majority's holding leaves commercial retailers susceptible to indemnity claims indefinitely, and, therefore is inconsistent with the U.C.C.'s purpose of providing predictability and consistency for all commercial sales transactions. The transaction between Central (P) and McCormack was a sale of goods, and, therefore, any claim stemming from this commercial sales transaction, including one for indemnity, must be governed by the U.C.C.'s four-year statute of repose. Contrary to the majority's assertion, there is not a majority view and a minority view of the issue at bar; instead, there is a split of authority. Thus, there exists authority from other jurisdictions to support both sides of the policy debate as to whether all contract-based claims, including those of indemnity, are bound by the U.C.C. As a matter of policy, finding contract-based indemnity claims are governed by the U.C.C. is correct because it creates a policy consistent with the purpose of the U.C.C. The majority finds that fairness is upheld by giving a commercial buyer who pays out-of-pocket damages to a third party a remedy unrestricted by a statute of limitations. However, the law must also recognize commercial realities and practices, and so must recognize the principle of bargained-for risk. Commercial buyers do not purchase items with the notion they are receiving an implied lifetime guarantee. They know products may not last forever. The U.C.C. provides an implied warranty that lasts for four years after delivery, in order to create a balance between fairness and bargained-for risk, and has identified this four-year period, commencing at the time of delivery, as a fair period of time for a commercial buyer to expect guaranteed warrantability and a commercial retailer to expect to be held liable. The U.C.C.'s four-year statute of limitations was adopted in § 2-725 to take sales contracts out of the general laws limiting the time for commencing contractual actions. By allowing a common-law remedy in a commercial sale relationship, the majority contradicts this goal. Moreover, § 2-725 should be viewed as a statute of repose rather than a statute of limitations. A statute of limitation bars plaintiffs from bringing an already accrued claim after a specified period of time; a statute of repose terminates a right of action after a specified time, even if the injury has not yet occurred. Based on § 2-725's clear language, Central's (P) contractual indemnity claim, based on the breach of an implied warranty, was barred when the action was filed in May 1992, since the coils were delivered more than four and a half years earlier. This straight-forward rule forces buyers to sue when evidence is most readily available and allows sellers to continue with their businesses without fear of suit after a reasonable definite period.

ANALYSIS

Problems with the four-year U.C.C. limitation period have been recognized, and various solutions—lying between the majority's position and that of the dissent in this case—have been suggested. For example, it has been recognized that the limitation period may be too short, especially in breach of warranty cases. One suggested revision would be to shorten the limitation period to two years from knowledge of a breach, tempered by an eight-year statute establishing repose. Another revision would also shorten the limitation period to two years from discovery, but would impose no statute of repose. Although these suggested revisions reflect the concern that some claims are not discovered before an individual's right to bring an action expires, the U.C.C.'s four-year time period has not been revised accordingly—presumably because it is viewed as striking the appropriate balance between fairness and bargained-for risk.

Quicknotes

INDEMNITY The duty of a party to compensate another for damages sustained.

STATUTE OF LIMITATIONS A law prescribing the period in which a legal action may be commenced.

STATUTE OF REPOSE A law prescribing the period of time in which an action can be commenced that begins to run upon the delivery of goods or the completion of performance.

CHAPTER 7

Negotiability

Quick Reference Rules of Law

Triffin v. Dillabough

Money order holder (P) v. Order presenter (D)

Pa. Sup. Ct., 552 Pa. 550, 716 A.2d 605 (1998).

NATURE OF CASE: Appeal from judgment in favor of defendant in an action demanding payment on a money order.

FACT SUMMARY: American Express (D) refused to pay on a stolen money order that it issued.

RULE OF LAW

Money orders that contain an unconditional promise to pay on demand are negotiable instruments.

FACTS: American Express (D) issued many money orders that were stolen after they had been signed. Dillabough (D) presented two of these stolen money orders at a check cashing operation and received cash. The check cashing company presented the orders to American Express (D) who refused to pay on them because they had already been listed on a fraud log. The check cashing operation sold the money orders to Triffin (P) who filed suit against Dillabough (D) and American Express (D) to collect on the money orders. The trial court ruled that American Express (D) was not liable because the money orders were not negotiable instruments due to a statement on the back that the money order will not be paid if it has been stolen or forged. Triffin (P) appealed.

ISSUE: Are money orders containing unconditional promises to pay on demand negotiable instruments?

HOLDING AND DECISION: (Newman, J.) Yes. Money orders that contain an unconditional promise to pay on demand are negotiable instruments. The commercial code contains a four part test to determine whether a document qualifies as a negotiable instrument. It must (1) be signed by the maker; (2) contain an unconditional promise to pay; (3) be payable on demand; and (4) be payable to order or to bearer. The only contested issue in the present case is whether American Express's (D) money orders contain an unconditional promise to pay. For purposes of this test, the legend on the back of the money order does not render conditional the money order's otherwise unconditional promise to pay. Rather, the legend is more accurately viewed as a warning that American Express (D) is reserving its statutory defenses. In the instant case, the statutory defenses are not applicable because Triffin (P) is a holder in due course as the assignee of the money order. Accordingly, American Express (D) is liable to Triffin (P) for the face value of the orders. "The Order of the Superior Court is affirmed and this matter is remanded to the trial court for the entry of an order consistent with this Opinion."

DISSENT: (Castille, J.) The express and explicit language on the American Express (D) money orders plainly contains a condition on payment. The majority is unjustified in construing it otherwise.

ANALYSIS

The majority cited a Louisiana appellate court decision as persuasive. The dissent was unimpressed by this decision, especially since Louisiana hadn't adopted the Universal Commercial Code (U.C.C.) at the time of the decision. U.C.C. § 3-106 contains the relevant provision to conditional orders.

Quicknotes

NEGOTIABLE INSTRUMENT A signed writing promising to pay a specific sum of money either on demand or at a specified time.

Woodworth v. The Richmond Indiana Venture

Borrower (P) v. Lender (D)

Ohio Ct. Common Pleas, 13 U.C.C. Rep. Serv. 2d 1149 (1990).

NATURE OF CASE: Appeal from grant of plaintiff's partial motion for summary judgment in an action contesting negotiability of a promissory note.

FACT SUMMARY: When Woodworth (P) defaulted on the payments on his promissory note, he filed this action questioning the note's negotiability, since The Richmond Indiana Venture (D) had previously assigned the note to Signet Bank (D).

RULE OF LAW

To be negotiable, a promissory note must not be cluttered by other promises, orders, obligations, or powers unless otherwise authorized.

FACTS: Woodworth (P) executed a promissory note in which he promised to pay The Richmond Indiana Venture (Richmond) (D), a limited partnership, $655,625. The note also contained a term providing for forfeiture of Woodworth's (P) partnership interest in Richmond (D) should he default on the payments. Woodworth (P) defaulted on the payments after the promissory note was assigned or negotiated to Signet Bank (D), and he filed this action contesting the note's negotiability on the ground that it was cluttered by an additional unnecessary term. Woodworth's (P) motion for partial summary judgment was granted, and Richmond (D) filed a motion for reconsideration.

ISSUE: To be negotiable, must a promissory note not be cluttered by other promises, orders, obligations, or powers unless otherwise authorized?

HOLDING AND DECISION: (Johnson, J.) Yes. To be negotiable, a promissory note must not be cluttered by other promises, orders, obligations, or powers unless otherwise authorized. In order to be negotiable, a promissory note must be a signed, unconditional promise to pay a sum certain in money which is payable on demand or at a definite, stated time. The additional term is clearly a forfeiture provision in addition to other remedies under the partnership agreement. Nothing in the Universal Commercial Code authorizes this forfeiture term. Thus, the negotiability of the promissory note is doubtful. Where there is doubt, the decision should be against negotiability. Since the promissory note is not negotiable, Signet Bank (D) cannot claim the status of a holder in due course and is subject to ordinary contract defenses that Woodworth (P) may assert. As to the motion for reconsideration, it is persuasive that the forfeiture provision may be exercised at the option of the partnership, not the holder of the instrument. Including such provision in the instrument clutters the unconditional promise to pay and makes the commercial viability of this instrument less certain. Plaintiff's motion sustained and defendant's motion denied. Court's decision affirmed in reconsideration.

ANALYSIS

The policy under pre-Code law was that instruments should be as concise as possible and free from collateral engagements. As seen in the rule above, the Code continues this policy. Since the forfeited interest here flowed to the partnership, that interest was not applied to the unpaid balance on the instrument. The court noted that any deleterious effects upon the flow of commercial instruments could be avoided by confining forfeiture provisions such as this one to the partnership agreement.

Quicknotes

PROMISSORY NOTE A written promise to tender a stated amount of money at a designated time and to a designated person.

Note: There are no principal cases in Chapter 8 of the casebook.

CHAPTER 9

Holders in Due Course

Quick Reference Rules of Law

Falls Church Bank v. Wesley Heights Realty, Inc.

Bank (P) v. Check casher (D)

D.C. Ct. App., 256 A.2d 915, 6 U.C.C. Rep. Serv. 1082 (1969).

NATURE OF CASE: Appeal from judgment denying award of damages to a holder in due course.

FACT SUMMARY: When Wesley Heights Realty, Inc. (Wesley Heights) (D) stopped payment on a check it issued to (P) customer of Falls Church Bank (the Bank) after the Bank (P) approved the customer's withdrawal of a portion of the check's value, the Bank (P) sought to collect the withdrawal amount from Wesley Heights (D).

RULE OF LAW

A bank becomes a holder in due course and acquires a security interest in items deposited with it to the extent that the provisional credit given the customer in the item is withdrawn.

FACTS: Wesley Heights Realty, Inc. (Wesley Heights) (D) drew a check payable to the order of a customer of Falls Church Bank (the Bank) (P). After the customer deposited the check in his account, the Bank (P) allowed him to withdraw a small portion of the check prior to learning that Wesley Heights (D) had stopped payment on the check. The customer, who could not be found, left no credit in his account on which to recover the amount withdrawn. When Wesley Heights (D) refused the Bank's (P) demand to pay the amount of the withdrawal, the Bank (P) filed suit. At trial, Wesley Heights (D) moved for summary judgment on the grounds that the Bank (P) "was an agent for collection only, had no security interest, and was not a holder in due course for value." The trial court granted the motion, and the Bank (P) appealed.

ISSUE: Does a bank become a holder in due course and acquire a security interest in items deposited with it to the extent that the provisional credit given the customer in the item is withdrawn?

HOLDING AND DECISION: (Hood, J.) Yes. A bank becomes a holder in due course and acquires a security interest in items deposited with it to the extent that the provisional credit given the customer in the item is withdrawn. As a holder in due course as to the amount withdrawn, the Bank's (P) claim cannot be defeated except by those defenses set out in Universal Commercial Code (U.C.C.) § 3-305(2), none of which were alleged herein. Reversed.

ANALYSIS

Under the U.C.C., a bank will be permitted to recover if it is out of pocket for anything and can prove that it paid value for the check. The crucial point in such instances is whether a bank permitted its customer to withdraw money before the subject check was cleared through the bank upon which it was drawn. A bank is deemed by the U.C.C. to be an agent of its customer and may be a holder in due course while acting as a collecting agent for its customer. *Citizens Bank of Booneville v. National Bank of Commerce*, 334 F.2d 257, 261 (10th Cir. 1964).

Quicknotes

HOLDER IN DUE COURSE A party who takes an instrument in good faith and for consideration without notice of any claims therein.

SECURITY INTEREST An interest in property that may be sold upon a default in payment of the debt.

In re Dixon-Ford

[Parties not identified.]

2011 WL 6749083 (Bankr. D.N.J. 2011).

NATURE OF CASE: Motion for summary judgment in bankruptcy adversary proceeding asserting claims for fraud at common law and under a state's consumer fraud act.

FACT SUMMARY: Dixon-Ford (Debtor) (P), a debtor in bankruptcy, asserted that Weichert Financial Services (D) had committed fraud in connection with her mortgage application, and that U.S. Bank National Association (US Bank) (D), as the trustee of a trust containing securitized mortgages, including hers, knew or should have known of the alleged misrepresentations made in connection with the origination of her mortgage. In its defense, US Bank (D) asserted holder in due course status.

RULE OF LAW

A holder of a negotiable instrument is a holder in due course where the holder has given value for the instrument; the instrument is facially free from any irregularity that could have alerted the holder to the existence of a potential fraud; and the holder has no knowledge of special circumstances that would place it under a duty to investigate whether there might be a defense to the transaction.

FACTS: Dixon-Ford (Debtor) (P) engaged Weichert Realtors (D) to be her realtor in finding a house. After finding a house, Debtor (P) sought to finance the purchase through a mortgage loan with Weichert Financial Services (WFS) (D). Debtor (P) was employed by the Social Security Administration (SSA) as a "telephone service representative" earning approximately $45,000 annually. The type of loan she obtained was a stated income loan, which is based on the borrower's income as stated in the loan application. The lender then performs a Verification of Employment (VOE) directly with the borrower's employer to confirm the borrower's stated income. Debtor (P) apparently executed a loan application indicating she was employed as the "Vice President" of the SSA earning $11,900 monthly ($142,800 annually). A couple of months later, she closed on the property and executed a second loan application that also misstated her employment and income information. Post-closing review revealed the existence of two VOEs. One correctly stated the Debtor's (P) employment while the other incorrectly stated she was the "Vice President" of the SSA. The incorrect VOE was supplied to the WFS (D) underwriter. Debtor's (P) loan was securitized and placed into a trust, with U.S. Bank National Association (US Bank) (D) as trustee. US Bank (D) did not conduct an independent review of the individual mortgages, as it had obtained a warranty from the seller in the transaction that the mortgages were enforceable and underwritten in accordance with its guidelines at the time of their originations. US Bank (D) received the Debtor's (P) mortgage note and the original recorded mortgage. There were no indicia of fraud, alteration, or invalidity on the face of the Debtor's (P) mortgage or note. Further, neither WFS (D) nor the Debtor (P) alerted US Bank (D) to any alleged misrepresentations or other flaw in the origination of the mortgage. Debtor (P), who went into bankruptcy and defaulted on the mortgage, asserted that she had provided documentation that accurately described her employment and overall financial position, including: (1) pay stubs; (2) tax returns; (3) bank statements showing direct deposits of her wages; and (4) a credit report. Nevertheless, the WFS (D) loan officer prepared the loan application containing the incorrect employment information. A WFS (D) officer has spoken with Debtor's (P) supervisor, who had informed the officer of Debtor's (P) correct position and salary. In addition, the officer noted that the VOE containing incorrect information appeared to have been altered and had been faxed from the same area code as where the office where the loan application was completed was located. From this, the Debtor (P) opined that the WFS (D) loan officer altered the VOE in order to qualify the Debtor (P) for a larger loan. The Debtor (P), in a bankruptcy adversary proceeding, brought claims for fraud against, inter alia, US Bank (D), arguing that US Bank (D) knew or should have known of the alleged misrepresentations made in connection with the origination of the Debtor's (P) mortgage. In its defense, US Bank (D) asserted holder-in-due-course status, and it moved for summary judgment.

ISSUE: Is a holder of a negotiable instrument a holder in due course where the holder has given value for the instrument; the instrument is facially free from any irregularity that could have alerted the holder to the existence of a potential fraud; and the holder has no knowledge of special circumstances that would place it under a duty to investigate whether there might be a defense to the transaction?

HOLDING AND DECISION: (Steckroth, J.) Yes. A holder of a negotiable instrument is a holder in due course where the holder has given value for the instrument; the instrument is facially free from any irregularity that could have alerted the holder to the existence of a potential fraud; and the holder has no knowledge of special circumstances that would place it under a duty to investigate whether there might be a defense to the transaction. US Bank (D) bears the burden of establishing that it is a holder in due course. A holder of an instrument becomes a holder in due course when he takes the instrument "for value, in

Continued on next page.

good faith, and without notice of any defense or claim against it." In addition, the instrument, when negotiated to the holder, must not bear such apparent evidence of forgery or alteration or must not otherwise be so irregular or incomplete as to call into question its authenticity. A holder in due course takes an instrument free of any personal defenses the maker may assert against the payee. Here, it is undisputed that US Bank (D) took the mortgage for value. Therefore, the question becomes whether US Bank (D) acted in good faith. Good faith is defined as "honesty in fact and the observance of reasonable commercial standards of fair dealing," and thus concerns both the subjective actions of the holder and the objective elements of the transaction. Ordinarily, where a note appears to be negotiable in form and regular on its face, the holder is under no duty to inquire as to possible defenses. However, if there are special circumstances of which the holder has knowledge that would require further inquiry, the failure to inquire reveals a deliberate desire on the holder's part to evade knowledge because of a belief or fear that investigation would disclose a defense from the transaction. Here, the note was facially free from any irregularity that could have alerted US Bank (D) to the existence of a potential fraud. While US Bank (D) did possess the mortgage file containing the allegedly altered VOE, it was under no duty to inquire under the circumstances. Failure to investigate inconsistencies in the mortgage file regarding the Debtor's (P) income, without more, does not evidence bad faith sufficient to prevent US Bank (D) from a holder in due course status. Moreover, US Bank (D) did not participate in the origination of the mortgage, nor was there evidence of collusion or communication between WFS (D) and US Bank (D) regarding the Debtor's (P) mortgage. In sum, there was nothing that served to apprise US Bank (D) of potential defenses at the time of taking, and there is no evidence to impugn US Bank's (D) good faith. Therefore, it takes the mortgage as a holder in due course. Because the claim at bar is one of fraud in the inducement (Debtor (P) was induced by fraud to negotiate the mortgage), and fraud in the inducement is a personal defense against transferees who have been parties to any fraud or illegality affecting the instrument or transferees who were prior holders with notice of the defenses or claims and not against holders in due course, US Bank (D) is immune to the Debtor's (P) claims. Summary judgment for US Bank (D).

ANALYSIS

This case illustrates how the concepts of good faith and notice are intertwined in the holder in due course analysis. If at the time the holder gives value for the instrument the holder is on notice of a defense the maker has against the payee, the holder does not take the instrument with the good faith expectation that it should be paid notwithstanding the defense. Thus, in this case, because there was no evidence that US Bank (D) had notice of any defenses to the mortgage, such lack of notice supported a finding that US Bank (D) had taken the instrument in good faith, and, therefore, was a holder in due course.

Quicknotes

FRAUD IN THE INDUCEMENT Occurs when a testator is induced to execute a testamentary instrument as a result of the misrepresentation of certain facts existing at the time of its creation that may have effected the manner in which the testator disposed of his property.

GOOD FAITH REQUIREMENT An implied warranty that the parties will deal honestly in the satisfaction of their obligations and without an intent to defraud.

HOLDER IN DUE COURSE A party who takes an instrument in good faith and for consideration without notice of any claims therein.

Any Kind Checks Cashed, Inc. v. Talcott

Corporation/Check holder (P) v. Check drawer (D)

Fla. Dist. Ct. App., 830 So. 2d 160, 48 U.C.C. Rep. Serv. 2d 800 (2002).

NATURE OF CASE: Appeal from a judgment on a check enforcement action.

FACT SUMMARY: Any Kind Checks Cashed, Inc. (Any Kind) (P) filed a two-count suit against John G. Talcott, Jr. (Talcott) (D) to enforce payment on two checks drafted by Talcott (D) and cashed with Any Kind (P) by a third party, on grounds that Any Kind (P) was a holder in due course. Talcott's (D) defense was that Any Kind (P) was not a holder in due course.

RULE OF LAW

To satisfy the good faith requirement to qualify as a holder in due course, a party must objectively observe the reasonable commercial standards of fair dealing.

FACTS: John G. Talcott, Jr. (Talcott) (D) had purchased an "investment" from a financial advisor, D. J. Rivera (Rivera), for approximately $75,000, which had yielded no return. Rivera contacted Talcott (D) and informed him that if he paid an additional $10,000 in travel expenses for him that he would be able to obtain a return on his initial investment. Rivera instructed Talcott (D) to send a $10,000 check to his partner and "broker," Salvatore Guarino (Guarino), by Federal Express. After Talcott (D) sent the check to Guarino, Rivera informed Talcott (D) that he really only needed $5,700 in travel expenses. Talcott (D) then sent a new check in the amount of $5,700 to Guarino and notified his bank to stop payment on the first $10,000 check. Guarino had check cashing privileges with Any Kind Checks Cashed, Inc. (Any Kind) (P). Any Kind (P) had a policy of not cashing checks for amounts greater than $2000 without supervisory approval, but there were no set guidelines for how a supervisor would make decisions for approving checks. Guarino cashed the $10,000 check at Any Kind (P). The supervisor, who was also the teller that day, approved the transaction without contacting Talcott (D), the maker of the check. After receiving the second check for $5,700, Guarino returned to Any Kind (P) and cashed it, but the teller on duty that day, at the direction of the supervisor, would not approve the check without first contacting the maker. Talcott (D) was contacted by Any Kind (P) regarding the second check and he approved of it being cashed, not realizing that Any Kind (P) had cashed the first check. Two days after Guarino had cashed the $5,700 check Rivera contacted Talcott (D) and informed him that Guarino was a thief. Talcott (D) then called his bank and stopped payment on the second check. Talcott's (D) bank returned the checks to Any Kind (P) without payment because of the stop payment orders. There is no dispute that Rivera and Guarino had engaged in a fraudulent scam to induce Talcott (D) to draw the checks. However, Any Kind (P), who had cashed the checks, filed suit against Talcott (D) to enforce payment. The trial court entered judgment in favor of Any Kind (P) on the check for $5,700, but found in favor of Talcott (D) with regard to the $10,000 check. The trial court determined that Any Kind (P) was not a holder in due course of the $10,000 check and that Talcott (D) was not obligated as the drawer to pay on it. Any Kind (P) appealed.

ISSUE: To satisfy the good faith requirement to qualify as a holder in due course, must a party objectively observe the reasonable commercial standards of fair dealing?

HOLDING AND DECISION: (Gross, J.) Yes. To satisfy the good faith requirement to qualify as a holder in due course, a party must objectively observe the reasonable commercial standards of fair dealing. Talcott (D) was the drafter of the checks that were issued to Guarino. See Universal Commercial Code (U.C.C.) §§ 3-103(a)(3) and 3-105(a). Once Guarino negotiated the checks with Any Kind (P), it became the holder with the right of enforcement. See U.C.C. §§ 1-201(2) and 3-301. Talcott's (D) obligation to pay on the check, when his bank refused, required that the holder be a holder in due course. A holder in due course takes or receives the check, or other instrument, where there is no apparent evidence of fraud, forgery, or alteration. To be a holder in due course, the check also must be taken in good faith and without notice of any claims or defenses against the instrument. See U.C.C. § 3-302(a). "Good faith," as defined in U.C.C. § 3-320 means "honesty in fact and the observance of reasonable commercial standards of fair dealing." The Florida regulatory scheme for the check cashing business contemplates that the business will use various types of verification of a check prior to cashing it. See Chapter 560 of the Florida Statutes. Rule 3C of § 560.801 of the Florida Administrative Code even permits the tellers of check cashing businesses to collect the direct costs associated with check verification so there no financial impairment to the verify the check with the drawer prior to cashing it. Given the size of the check involved and Any Kind's (P) own policy of regarding checks in amount greater than $2000 with suspicion, standards of good faith and fair dealing required that Any Kind (P) verify the check with the drawer, Talcott (D), prior to cashing it. Any Kind (P) was not a holder in due course because of its failure to meet the good faith requirement in U.C.C. § 3-320. The decision of the trial court is affirmed.

Continued on next page.

ANALYSIS

Prior to 1992, the version of the U.C.C. adopted by Florida defined "good faith" as being "honesty in fact in the conduct of the transaction concerned." The legislature adopted the new version of U.C.C. § 3-302 in response to a recognized need to protect people from the increased risk of scams being perpetrated by use of check cashing businesses. The immediate distribution of funds provided by these businesses created the exact situation illustrated in this case whereby funds would be paid without verification leaving the drawer of the check subject to being scammed. Any perceived slowing of commerce accompanying the adoption of this objective standard for qualifying as a holder in due course was considered necessary to restore reasonable commercial fairness to an industry that was negotiating checks without question to the detriment of the drawers. It should also be noted that the defendant in this case, Talcott (D), was a 93-year-old gentleman. Given the prevalence of scams perpetrated against the elderly, and given the population demographics of the state of Florida where many elderly people relocate for their retirement, the Florida legislature may have perceived a greater need to regulate the check cashing industry to prevent these types of scams.

Quicknotes

GOOD FAITH REQUIREMENT An implied warranty that the parties will deal honestly in the satisfaction of their obligations and without an intent to defraud.

HOLDER IN DUE COURSE A party who takes an instrument in good faith and for consideration without notice of any claims therein.

Winter & Hirsch, Inc. v. Passarelli

Lender (P) v. Borrower (D)

Ill. App. Ct., 122 Ill. App. 2d 372, 259 N.E.2d 312 (1970).

NATURE OF CASE: Appeal from denial of motion to vacate a judgment by confession.

FACT SUMMARY: Because Winter & Hirsch, Inc. (P) issued a check to Equitable Mortgage & Investment Corporation for purchase of a note before the note was formalized, Winter & Hirsch (P) was deemed to be a co-originator of the loan and on notice of its usurious rate and, thus, not to be a holder in due course.

RULE OF LAW

When an instrument is so incomplete as to call its validity into question, a purchaser of that instrument is on notice of the possibility of a claim against it and, thus, cannot be a holder in due course.

FACTS: In return for a promissory note, Equitable Mortgage & Investment (Equitable) loaned Passarelli (D) $10,000, with repayment totaling $16,260. Ten days prior to the time Passarelli (D) formally executed the note, Winter & Hirsch, Inc. (P), by check, purchased it from Equitable for $11,000. Winter & Hirsch (P) claimed it made an effective purchase of the note from Equitable. Passarelli (D) defaulted on the note, and Winter & Hirsch (P) obtained a judgment by confession. It was uncontested that Equitable charged a usurious rate of interest on the note. Passarelli (D) moved to vacate the judgment, claiming that Winter & Hirsch (P) purchased the note with knowledge of the usurious interest and consequently could not have become a holder in due course. The trial court denied the motion, and this appeal followed.

ISSUE: When an instrument is so incomplete as to call its validity into question, is a purchaser of that instrument on notice of the possibility of a claim against it and is, thus, not a holder in due course?

HOLDING AND DECISION: (McCormick, J.) Yes. When an instrument is so incomplete as to call its validity into question, a purchaser of that instrument is on notice of the possibility of a claim against it and, thus, is not a holder in due course. Winter & Hirsch (P) was a co-originator of the note since it advanced the funds for the usurious loan before the note was formalized, and it thus became charged with the knowledge of the terms of the loan, including the interest rate information. The difference between what Winter & Hirsch (P) paid Equitable and the amount due to be repaid on the note was so great that Winter & Hirsch (P) was on notice of a possible violation of the usury statute. Because the principal sum of the loan extended to Passarelli (D) did not appear on its face, the instrument was "so incomplete" as to call its validity into question after Winter & Hirsch (P) learned that it was able buy it for only $11,000. Winter & Hirsch (P) should have inquired how much money was loaned to Passarelli (D). Thus Winter & Hirsch (P) had "reason to know" there was a good defense against the note. Reversed and remanded.

ANALYSIS

The court declared that parties cannot be permitted to intentionally keep themselves in ignorance of facts which, if known, would defeat their lawful purpose. Where it appears from the facts and circumstances of a particular transaction that a reasonably prudent businessman would have found the purchase suspicious, he should inquire as to the truth. The suspicion is even more compelling when the paper is bought from a broker in the business of selling such paper for profit.

Quicknotes

HOLDER IN DUE COURSE A party who takes an instrument in good faith and for consideration without notice of any claims therein.

Jones v. Approved Bancredit Corp.

Homeowner (D) v. Bank (P)

Del. Sup. Ct., 256 A.2d 739, 6 U.C.C. Rep. Serv. 1001 (1969).

NATURE OF CASE: Appeal from award of foreclosure of mortgage.

FACT SUMMARY: When Jones (D) refused to pay for construction of a home which was never finished and which had to be demolished at her expense, Approved Bancredit Corp. (P), holder of the promissory note and mortgage, sought to foreclose on the mortgage and collect payments for the balance of the contract, as a holder in due course.

RULE OF LAW

The more a holder knows about the underlying transaction that is the source of the paper, or controls or participates in it, the less he fits the role of good-faith purchaser for value that would accord him the protected status of holder in due course.

FACTS: Jones (D), after signing a purchase order contract and credit application, made a deposit to have a house built on her land by Albee Dell Homes, Inc. (Dell). Dell's representative presented a series of documents to sign; the representative immediately endorsed the paper and assigned it to Approved Bancredit Corp. (P). When the builder's employee knocked the partially completed house off its foundations, the builder refused to go forward with the work, and Jones (D) eventually had to pay for demolition of the structure. Bancredit (P) subsequently sought to foreclose on the mortgage and collect the unpaid balance. The trial court entered judgment for Bancredit (P) as a holder in due course, even though Dell and Bancredit (P) were both wholly owned subsidiaries of a holding company, Albee Homes, with Albee Homes and Bancredit (P) having the same officers and directors. Jones (D) appealed.

ISSUE: Does the more a holder knows about the underlying transaction that is the source of the paper, or controls or participates in it, make him less fit the role of good-faith purchaser for value that would accord him the protected status of holder in due course?

HOLDING AND DECISION: (Herrmann, J.) Yes. The more a holder knows about the underlying transaction that is the source of the paper, or controls or participates in it, the less he fits the role of good-faith purchaser for value that would accord him the protected status of holder in due course. Under the circumstances, Bancredit (P) was so involved in the transaction that it may not be treated as a subsequent purchaser for value. By reason of its sister corporation relationship to Dell and the established course of dealing between them, Bancredit (P) was more nearly an original party to the transaction than a subsequent purchaser of the paper and should thus be denied the protected status of holder in due course. Reversed and remanded.

ANALYSIS

The court pointed out that the problem arises in holder-in-due-course cases involving the financing of installment sales. There is a need to balance the interest of the commercial community in the unrestricted negotiability of commercial papers against the interest of installment buyers in the preservation of their normal remedy of withholding payment whenever there has been misrepresentation, failure of consideration, etc. While some jurisdictions protect finance companies from purchaser defenses on the grounds that the free flow of credit is an overriding consideration in assuring easy negotiability of commercial paper, most courts follow a guideline whereby the closer the financial institution is to the underlying transaction, the less likely it will be protected as a holder in due course.

Quicknotes

GOOD-FAITH PURCHASER FOR VALUE A party who purchases property in good faith and for valuable consideration without notice of a defect in title.

HOLDER IN DUE COURSE A party who takes an instrument in good faith and for consideration without notice of any claims therein.

MORTGAGE An interest in land created by a written instrument providing security for the payment of a debt or the performance of a duty.

Sullivan v. United Dealers Corp.

Borrower (D) v. Lender (P)

Ky. Ct. App., 486 S.W.2d 699, 11 U.C.C. Rep. Serv. 810 (1972).

NATURE OF CASE: Appeal from award for breach of promissory note.

FACT SUMMARY: Sullivan (D), who had executed a promissory note that was subsequently purchased by United Dealers Corp. (P), defaulted on the payments, alleging that the house for which he got the construction loan was built in an unworkmanlike manner.

RULE OF LAW

To be effective, notice to a purchaser of a negotiable instrument must be received at such time and in such manner as to give a reasonable opportunity to act on it.

FACTS: Sullivan (D), in contracting for construction of a prefabricated dwelling, executed and delivered a negotiable promissory note to the contractor, who then negotiated the note and assigned it to United Dealers Corp. (United) (P). Sullivan (D) delivered written statements to United (P) that the foundation and framing members of the house had been properly installed in a workmanlike manner. Sullivan (D) then defaulted on the note, and United (P) filed suit. In defense, Sullivan (D) pleaded that United (P) was not a holder in due course because the contractor had constructed the house in an unworkmanlike manner. The trial court found that United (P) was a holder in due course; therefore, the defense was not assertable against it. Sullivan (D) appealed.

ISSUE: To be effective, must notice to a purchaser of a negotiable instrument be received at such time and in such manner as to give a reasonable opportunity to act on it?

HOLDING AND DECISION: (Reed, J.) Yes. To be effective, notice to a purchaser of a negotiable instrument must be received at such time and in such manner as to give a reasonable opportunity to act on it. "Notice" means notice at the time of the taking or at the time the instrument is negotiated and not subsequently. Here, the maker of the note, Sullivan (D), had represented that the contractor was one in compliance with the duties imposed by the contract. The evidence failed to demonstrate any bad faith on the part of United (P) at the time of the negotiation and transfer of the note to it. Indeed, all of the evidence demonstrated a complete lack of notice that would justify a finding that United (P) failed to acquire the status of a holder in due course. Affirmed.

ANALYSIS

The court expressed the thought that the policy of the Universal Commercial Code is to encourage the supplying of credit for the buying of goods by insulating the lender from lawsuits over the quality of the goods. The insulation provided, however, appears intended primarily for finance institutions that act independently to supply credit, rather than to protect a manufacturer who finances his own sales either in his own name or in the name of a subsidiary he controls. Although United (P) and the contractor had a frequent course of dealing between them, the instant case demonstrates the point that knowledge of the underlying transaction is not the same thing as notice of a claim or a defense to a claim arising out of that transaction.

Quicknotes

COURSE OF DEALING Previous conduct between two parties to a contract which may be relied upon to interpret their actions.

NEGOTIABLE INSTRUMENT A signed writing promising to pay a specific sum of money either on demand or at a specified time.

Triffin v. Somerset Valley Bank

Purchaser of dishonored checks (P) v. Bank (D)

N.J. Super. Ct., App. Div., 343 N.J. Super. 73, 777 A.2d 993 (2001).

NATURE OF CASE: Appeal from summary judgment on liability for dishonored checks.

FACT SUMMARY: Triffin (P) purchased dishonored checks from check cashing companies and brought suit against the issuer, Hauser Contracting Co. (D). No proof was presented that the checks on their face indicated forgery, alteration, or other irregularity, and summary judgment was granted for Triffin (P).

RULE OF LAW

A holder in due course is entitled to enforce a negotiable instrument where there is no evidence presented that there is anything on the face of the instrument to indicate that the instrument has been forged or altered or is otherwise irregular.

FACTS: Triffin (P) is in the business of purchasing dishonored negotiable instruments, and he purchased 18 dishonored checks from check cashing companies, totaling $8,826.42. All the instruments on their face were issued by Hauser Contracting Co. (Hauser) (D), and Triffin (P) sued to enforce Hauser's (D) liability on the checks. Although none of the checks had been authorized, they were all signed with a facsimile stamp and otherwise manifested no signs of forgery, alteration, or other irregularities. The trial court, concluding that the checks at issue seemed genuine and that the check cashing companies took them in good faith, granted summary judgment to Triffin (P).

ISSUE: Is a holder in due course entitled to enforce a negotiable instrument where no evidence is presented that there is anything on the face of the instrument to indicate that the instrument has been forged or altered or is otherwise irregular?

HOLDING AND DECISION: (Cuff, J.) Yes. A holder in due course is entitled to enforce a negotiable instrument where there is no evidence presented that there is anything on the face of the instrument to indicate that the instrument has been forged or altered or is otherwise irregular. As a threshold matter, the checks at issue met the definition of a negotiable instrument. Although Hauser (D) claimed that the checks were not negotiable instruments because they had not been authorized, lack of authorization is a separate issue from whether an instrument is negotiable. The issue raised by lack of authorization is whether the checks are unenforceable by holders in due course as a result of the lack of authorization or forgery. Here, the check cashing companies were each holders in due course, a fact Hauser (D) did not dispute. Also, Triffin (P) complied with the Universal Commercial Code's (U.C.C.'s) requirement for check transfers, and, again, Hauser (D) did not dispute this fact. Hauser (D) instead argued that the checks were per se invalid because they were fraudulent and unauthorized. Under the U.C.C., a person is not a holder in due course if the instrument bears "apparent evidence of forgery or alteration" or is otherwise "so irregular. . . ." Here, however, Hauser (D) did not present any evidence, other than conclusory assertions, that it was apparent on the face of the checks that they were forged, altered, or irregular. Thus, the U.C.C.'s presumption that the signature on a check is valid remains unless it is rebutted by a defendant. Here, Hauser Co. (D) did not meet its burden of proof, and, therefore, did not raise any genuine issues of material fact. Affirmed.

ANALYSIS

This case is a clear illustration of the U.C.C.'s shelter rule, codified in § 3-203(b), which gives the transferee of a holder in due course the holder's rights, even though the transferee would otherwise not be entitled to those rights. The business of purchasing dishonored checks and pursuing their issuer's liability would not be possible without this rule.

Quicknotes

COURSE OF DEALING Previous conduct between two parties to a contract that may be relied upon to interpret their actions.

HOLDER IN DUE COURSE A party who takes an instrument in good faith and for consideration without notice of any claims therein.

NEGOTIABLE INSTRUMENT A signed writing promising to pay a specific sum of money either on demand or at a specified time.

Federal Deposit Insurance Corp. v. Culver

Bank (P) v. Borrower (D)

640 F Supp. 725 (D. Kan. 1986).

NATURE OF CASE: Motion for summary judgment in action for breach of promissory note.

FACT SUMMARY: After Culver (D), who had received a loan from the now-insolvent bank and later signed a promissory note which he was told was a receipt and which contained no essential terms, he attempted to assert a defense of fraud in the factum against the Federal Deposit Insurance Corp. (P), which took over as receiver.

RULE OF LAW

A holder in due course takes the instrument free from all defenses of any party to the instrument with whom the holder has not dealt except where misrepresentation has induced the party to sign the instrument with neither the knowledge nor reasonable opportunity to obtain knowledge of its character or its essential terms.

FACTS: After Culver (D) received $30,000 in a wire transfer from the Rexford State Bank, he was approached by an individual who asked him to sign a document which Culver (D) was told was merely a receipt for the money. However, the document was a preprinted promissory note form containing no execution date, no maturity date, no principal amount, and no interest rate. Those were filled in later, with the principal amount shown as $50,000. When the bank became insolvent, the Federal Deposit Insurance Corp. (FDIC) (P) was appointed as its receiver. Culver (D) defaulted on the note, and the FDIC (P) filed this action for payment. Because the FDIC (P) was a holder in due course, Culver (D) sought to assert the "real" defense of fraud in the factum against it. The FDIC (P) moved for summary judgment.

ISSUE: Does a holder in due course take the instrument free from all defenses of any party to the instrument with whom the holder has not dealt except where misrepresentation has induced the party to sign the instrument with neither knowledge nor reasonable opportunity to obtain knowledge of its character or its essential terms?

HOLDING AND DECISION: (O'Connor, J.) Yes. A holder in due course takes the instrument free from all defenses of any party to the instrument with whom the holder has not dealt except where misrepresentation has induced the party to sign the instrument with neither knowledge nor reasonable opportunity to obtain knowledge of its character or its essential terms. The test for the defense of fraud in the factum is that of excusable ignorance of the contents of the writing signed. Being literate in English language, Culver (D) was negligent in relying on another's assurance that the note was only a receipt. He has also failed to show the "excusable ignorance" needed to establish fraud in the factum, since he had a "reasonable opportunity to obtain knowledge of the document's character" before he signed it. As a holder in due course, the FDIC (P) is thus entitled to enforce this note as completed. Motion for summary judgment granted.

ANALYSIS

A prior Kansas Supreme Court ruling held that if a party is in possession of his faculties and able to read, he can know the character of every instrument to which he put his signature. Further, he owes a duty to any party who may be subsequently affected by his act to know what it is he signs. *Ort v. Fowler*, 2 P. 580 (Kan. 1884). Moreover, K.S.A. § 84-3-407 provides, in part, that a subsequent holder in due course may in all cases enforce the instrument according to its original tenor, and when an incomplete instrument has been completed, he may enforce it as completed.

Quicknotes

FRAUD IN THE FACTUM Occurs when a testator is induced to execute a testamentary instrument as a result of a misrepresentation as to the nature of the document or its provisions.

HOLDER IN DUE COURSE A party who takes an instrument in good faith and for consideration without notice of any claims therein.

MISREPRESENTATION A statement or conduct by one party to another that constitutes a false representation of fact.

Sea Air Support, Inc. v. Herrmann

Debt holder (P) v. Gambler (D)

Nev. Sup. Ct., 613 P.2d 413, 29 U.C.C. Rep. Serv. 918 (1980).

NATURE OF CASE: Appeal from dismissal of action to recover on a gaming debt.

FACT SUMMARY: Sea Air Support, Inc. (P) attempted to collect on a dishonored check made payable to a casino by Herrmann (D).

RULE OF LAW

Checks drawn for gambling purposes are void and unenforceable.

FACTS: Herrmann (D) wrote a check for $10,000 payable to a casino to cover the cost of gaming chips he had purchased earlier. After discovering that Herrmann (D) did not have sufficient funds in his account, the casino assigned the debt to Sea Air Support, Inc. (Sea Air) (P), which sued Herrmann (D) to recover the $10,000. The trial court dismissed the action as barred by the Statute of Anne, which provides that all notes drawn for gambling purposes are void. Sea Air (P) appealed, arguing that the court should either enforce the gambling debt or consider Sea Air (P) a holder in due course and, therefore, immune to Statute of Anne defense.

ISSUE: Are checks drawn for gambling purposes void and unenforceable?

HOLDING AND DECISION: (Per curiam) Yes. Checks drawn for gambling purposes are void and unenforceable. Nevada law incorporates the common law of gambling as modified by the Statute of Anne. The Statute of Anne provides that notes drawn for the purpose of reimbursing or repaying any money knowingly advanced for gaming are void and unenforceable. Here, Herrmann's (D) check was clearly drawn for the purpose of repaying money knowingly advanced for gaming. Therefore, it was void and unenforceable. Furthermore, Sea Air (P) was not a holder in due course, defined as one who takes a negotiable instrument (1) for value; (2) in good faith; and (3) without notice of having been dishonored or of any defense against it. A promise to enforce collection in the future—as was made by Sea Air (P) to the casino in exchange for assignment of the debt—is not taking for value. Also, Sea Air (P) had constructive notice of the Statute of Anne defense and actual notice that the check had been dishonored. Affirmed.

ANALYSIS

Although the court concluded that Sea Air (P) was not a holder in due course, a contrary conclusion would have resulted in the same outcome. Although holders in due course are, indeed, immune to most personal defenses, Universal Commercial Code (U.C.C.) § 3-305(2) expressly subjects them to so-called "real" defenses—including the defense of illegality raised by Herrmann (D) in this case. Therefore, even if Sea Air (P) had successfully claimed holder in due course status, it still would not have been able to enforce the check. Three years after *Sea Air Support* was decided, the Nevada legislature modified state law to permit casinos to sue on checks issued to pay gambling debts. Nev. Rev. Stat. § 4 63.368 (1983).

Quicknotes

HOLDER IN DUE COURSE A party who takes an instrument in good faith and for consideration without notice of any claims therein.

Kedzie & 103rd Currency Exchange, Inc. v. Hodge

Bank (P) v. Putative check writer (D)

Ill. Sup. Ct., 156 Ill. 2d 112, 619 N.E.2d 732 (1993).

NATURE OF CASE: Appeal from order dismissing action seeking to collect on a negotiable instrument.

FACT SUMMARY: Hodge (D), drawer of a check, contended that she was not liable to the Currency Exchange, Inc. (P), the holder in due course, because she had drawn the check to pay a plumber who was not licensed as required by state law.

RULE OF LAW

Unless the instrument arising from a contract is itself made void by statute, the illegality defense is not available to bar the claim of a holder in due course.

FACTS: Hodge (D) hired Fentress (D) to perform plumbing services. Fentress (D) was not licensed to perform these services as required by Illinois law. Hodge (D) drew a check for $500, payable to Fentress (D). When Fentress (D) failed to perform, Hodge (D) stopped payment. In the meantime, Fentress (D) negotiated the check to Kedzie & 103rd Currency Exchange, Inc. (Currency Exchange) (P). When Currency Exchange (P) presented the check to the drawee bank, the bank refused to pay. Currency Exchange (P) sued Hodge (D) and Fentress (D). Hodge (D) moved to dismiss, claiming the defense of illegality based on Fentress's (D) unlicensed status. The trial court dismissed, and Currency Exchange (P) appealed.

ISSUE: Is the illegality defense available to bar the claim of a holder in due course if the instrument arises from an obligation that has not been expressly declared void by the legislature?

HOLDING AND DECISION: (Freeman, J.) No. Unless the instrument arising from a contract is itself made void by statute, the illegality defense is not available to bar the claim of a holder in due course. When local law renders an obligation null and void, as opposed to merely voidable, illegality exists as a defense to a claim by one of the contracting parties. But unless the instrument memorializing the obligation is also declared void by the legislature, an innocent third party—i.e., a holder in due course—will be protected and will be permitted to make a claim for payment. For example, an instrument associated with a debt incurred by illegal gambling is void by law no matter who possesses it, and illegality could be raised as a defense in that case. In contrast, an obligation to an unlicensed contractor is merely voidable at the option of the obligor. In this case, the transaction between Hodge (D) and Fentress (D) was voidable by Hodge (D), but the instrument itself was not void under Illinois law. Therefore, the illegality defense is unavailable to Hodge (D). Reversed and remanded.

DISSENT: (Bilandic, J.) Universal Commercial Code (U.C.C.) § 3-305 makes it clear that where a transaction's illegality renders the maker's obligation a nullity, the illegality defense is available. The legislature need not declare the instrument void too, as the majority contends. Since the contract at issue here was illegal and void, the action against Hodge (D) should be dismissed.

ANALYSIS

The holder in due course concept represents an exercise in choosing the lesser of evils. Commercial practice requires that negotiable instruments be exchangeable with a high degree of certainty. Therefore, a holder can be reasonably sure he can negotiate such instruments, and the occasional injustice to a maker, such as Hodge (D) here, will not change this. However, as the dissent noted, free negotiability is not absolute. Certain transactions such as those involving duress, illegality, or misrepresentation are disfavored on public policy grounds.

Quicknotes

HOLDER IN DUE COURSE A party who takes an instrument in good faith and for consideration without notice of any claims therein.

Virginia National Bank v. Holt

Bank (P) v. Putative note signer (D)

Va. Sup. Ct., 216 Va. 500, 219 S.E.2d 881 (1975).

NATURE OF CASE: Appeal from denial of award of damages in action to recover on a promissory note.

FACT SUMMARY: Virginia National Bank (P) sued Holt (D) on a promissory note that Holt (D) claimed she had not signed.

RULE OF LAW

The party seeking recovery on an instrument is not required to prove that any signature is genuine until the defendant introduces evidence which would support a finding that the signature is forged.

FACTS: Virginia National Bank (the Bank) (P) filed suit against Holt (D), seeking recovery on a promissory note allegedly bearing her signature. In her pleadings, Holt (D) denied that she had signed the note. Holt (D) did not testify at trial, but her denial was admitted in the form of a statement from her discovery deposition. The only other evidence offered in her behalf were admissions from the Bank's (P) witnesses that they did not see Holt (D) sign the note. The Bank (P) moved for summary judgment, contending that Holt (D) had failed to overcome the presumption that her signature was genuine. After the judge denied the motion, the case was submitted to the jury, which returned a verdict in Holt's (D) favor. The Bank (P) appealed.

ISSUE: Is the party seeking recovery on an instrument required to prove that the instrument's signature is genuine if the defendant has not introduced evidence which would support a finding that the signature is forged?

HOLDING AND DECISION: (Compton, J.) No. The party seeking recovery on an instrument is not required to prove that the signature on the instrument is genuine until the defendant introduces evidence which would support a finding that the signature is forged. Motivated by the rarity of forged or unauthorized signatures, Universal Commercial Code (U.C.C.) § 3-307 established a presumption that a signature on an instrument is genuine or authorized. Under § 3-307, each signature on an instrument is admitted, unless the party denying the validating of the signature is able to introduce sufficient evidence to establish grounds for her denial. If she can, then the burden of establishing the genuineness of the signature shifts to the party who is claiming under the signature. In this case, Holt (D) initially put the genuineness of the signature on the promissory note in issue by denying that she signed the note. Pursuant to § 3-307, the signature was presumed to be genuine. But, merely presenting one statement from a deposition is not sufficient to make a showing supporting a finding that she did not in fact write her name on the note. Therefore, the § 3-307 presumption required the trial judge to make a finding that the signature on the instrument was genuine and effective, rather than submit the case to the jury. The Bank (P) was entitled to recover on the note. Reversed.

ANALYSIS

If, at the very least, Holt (D) had testified on her own behalf that the signature on the note was not hers, she may have been able to overcome the § 3-307 presumption that her signature was genuine. Even an equivocal denial of genuineness by a purported signer has been held sufficient to overcome the presumption and to raise a factual issue for the jury to decide. The burden of establishing the effectiveness of Holt's (D) signature by a preponderance of the evidence would then have been on the Bank (P). See, e.g., *Metropolitan Mortgage Fund v. Basiliko*, 407 A.2d 773 (1979).

Quicknotes

PRESUMPTION A rule of law requiring the court to presume certain facts to be true based on the existence of other facts, thereby shifting the burden of proof to the party against whom the presumption is asserted to rebut.

Herzog Contracting Corp. v. McGowen Corp.

Corporation (P) v. Corporation (D)

976 F.2d 1062 (7th Cir. 1992).

NATURE OF CASE: Appeal from summary judgment in a diversity suit to enforce two promissory notes.

FACT SUMMARY: McGowen Corp.'s (D) evidence offered to prove that promissory notes it had given Herzog Contracting Corp. (P) had in fact been a sham to disguise a sales installment payment in order to minimize tax liability was ruled inadmissible.

RULE OF LAW

One otherwise liable on an instrument may, as against a nonholder in due course, present evidence that the instrument was never intended to be binding.

FACTS: Herzog Contracting Corp. (Herzog) (P) purchased certain assets from McGowen Corp. (D) for five annual installments of $500,000. That same year, McGowen (D) gave Herzog (P) two notes totaling $400,000 in exchange for that amount from Herzog (P). When the notes became due, Herzog (P), whose relations with McGowen (D) had soured, sued for payment. McGowen (D) admitted receiving the $400,000 but contended that the "loan" had actually been a disguised prepayment by Herzog (P) for the second installment and that the notes had only been designed to make the transaction look like a loan in order to lessen tax liability. The district court held evidence of the purported purpose to be inadmissible and entered summary judgment against McGowen (D), which appealed.

ISSUE: May one otherwise liable on an instrument, as against a nonholder in due course, present evidence that the instrument was never intended to be binding?

HOLDING AND DECISION: (Posner, J.) Yes. One otherwise liable on an instrument, as against a nonholder in due course, may present evidence that the instrument was never intended to be binding. Per Universal Commercial Code (U.C.C.) § 3-305(b), one other than a holder in due course takes an instrument subject to all defenses thereto. It is well settled that a document or contract that was never meant to be binding will not be so held. At common law, courts were reluctant to allow parol evidence in actions based on negotiable instruments (as opposed to contracts in general) for any reason other than showing mistake or fraud in formation. However, the trend for well over a century has been to allow parol evidence to show any "special purpose" behind an instrument that may not be apparent on its face. The parol evidence rule now applies to instruments as much as it does to contracts: it may not be used as evidence of additional or different terms, but may be used to explain the terms themselves. Here, McGowen (D) was not trying to change the terms in the promissory notes but was only trying to show that they were intended to fool the IRS, rather than to create a legally enforceable obligation. It should have been allowed to do so. Reversed and remanded.

ANALYSIS

This case illustrates the wide protections that a holder in due course enjoys that a party to an instrument does not. Of course, like Herzog (P), one may sue on an instrument whether or not one is a holder in due course. In fact, under some circumstances, one need not even be a holder in order to enforce the instrument—the true owner of a lost instrument, for example, enjoys this right. A holder's due course status only becomes significant once a defense to an instrument is raised.

Quicknotes

HOLDER IN DUE COURSE A party who takes an instrument in good faith and for consideration without notice of any claims therein.

PAROL EVIDENCE RULE Doctrine precluding parties to an agreement from introducing evidence of prior or contemporaneous agreements in order to repudiate or alter the terms of a written contract.

CHAPTER 10

The Nature of Liability

Quick Reference Rules of Law

Fifth Third Bank v. Jones

Deed of trust holder (P) v. Debtor (D)

Colo. Ct. App., 168 P.3d 1, 64 U.C.C. Rep. Serv. 2d 187 (2007).

NATURE OF CASE: Appeal from judgment for debtor in action to foreclose on a deed of trust.

FACT SUMMARY: Fifth Third Bank (the Bank) (P), the holder of a deed of trust securing a mortgage on Jones's (the Debtor's) (D) house, received a check from a third party, which was forwarded by the Bank's (P) employee to the Bank's (P) payoff department. The check was lost en route, and the Bank (P) sought to foreclose on the deed of trust. The Debtor (D) contended that the check had been a cashier's check that paid off the entire debt, and the trial court agreed. The Bank (P) argued that the trial had erred as a matter of law because the Bank (P) could not have taken the missing check for an obligation while its internal administrative procedures were pending.

RULE OF LAW

A bank takes for an obligation a certified check, cashier's check, or teller's check without regard to the bank's internal administrative procedures.

FACTS: Jones (the Debtor) (D) executed a promissory note in favor of a mortgage company that was secured by a deed of trust on her home. Sometime thereafter, Fifth Third Bank (the Bank) (P) became the holder of the note. The Debtor (D) then defaulted in the payment of the note, and, subsequently, the Bank (P) and the Debtor (D) entered into a modification of the note, which raised the note's balance. The debtor again defaulted on the note. A few months later, the Bank (P) received a check from a third party as payment on the debtor's account. The Bank's (P) representative working on the Debtor's (D) account noted receipt of the check in the bank records and forwarded it to the payoff department. Approximately one week later, it was noted in the Bank's (P) records that the check had been lost without having been posted to the Debtor's (D) account or submitted for payment. The Bank (P) notified the Debtor (D) of the loss, and both parties searched, without success, for a copy of the lost check or evidence of the identity of its maker, drawee bank, or amount. The Bank (P) then commenced a foreclosure of the deed of trust. The debtor (D) claimed that the note had been paid in full by a cashier's check issued by an out-of-state bank at the request of a deceased aunt. The evidence showed that that if the Bank (P) had received a personal check instead of certified funds, a notation would have been made in the Debtor's (D) record, but no such notation was made. Also, the Bank (P) would not have accepted a personal check as a payoff, but would have accepted a certified check, certified funds, teller's check, etc. as payoff. The bank representative accordingly entered a note on the Debtor's (D) account which stated that the Bank (P) had received a "payoff," and forwarded the payment down to the "payoff department." The bank representative also testified that she assumed the check was a payoff because it was for a large amount. The bank representative had worked with the Debtor's (D) account prior to receiving the check and appeared to be familiar with the account. Based on this evidence, the trial court found that the check "was either a cashier's check or certified funds or a certified check" and that the check was "for the full amount of a payoff." Accordingly, the trial court held that the promissory note was paid in full. The Bank (P) appealed, arguing that the trial court findings were unsupported and that the trial court erred as a matter of law in its holding because the missing check was not "taken for an obligation" by the bank within the meaning of the pertinent statute. The state's intermediate court of appeals granted review.

ISSUE: Does a bank take for an obligation a certified check, cashier's check, or teller's check without regard to the bank's internal administrative procedures?

HOLDING AND DECISION: (Roy, J.) Yes. A bank takes for an obligation a certified check, cashier's check, or teller's check without regard to the bank's internal administrative procedures. As a threshold matter, the evidence—in the form of the bank representative's testimony and documentary evidence—was sufficient to support the trial court's finding that the check was either a cashier's check or certified funds or a certified check, and that the check was for the full amount of a payoff. Moreover, any uncertainty in ascertaining the amount of the check was caused by the Bank's (P) own actions. As to whether the missing check was "taken for an obligation," the pertinent statute states in pertinent part: "Unless otherwise agreed, if a certified check, cashier's check, or teller's check is taken for an obligation, the obligation is discharged to the same extent discharge would result if an amount of money equal to the amount of the instrument were taken in payment of the obligation." Contrary to the Bank's (P) argument that a check is not "taken for an obligation" while internal administrative actions are pending, the check here was "taken for" the Debtor's (D) obligation without regard to the Bank's (P) internal procedures. This conclusion is supported by the statute's plain language, as well as by comments to that statute, and case law. The official comment indicates that the drafters intended that the taking for an obligation occurs simultaneously with the giving of the payment. This interpretation corresponds with the plain meaning of the verb "take." Also, the Bank's (P) interpretation of "taken for an

Continued on next page.

obligation" would render meaningless the next part of the statute, which provides that "if a note or an uncertified check is taken for an obligation, the obligation is suspended to the same extent the obligation would be discharged if an amount of money equal to the amount of the instrument were taken" until the check is paid, certified, or dishonored. Further, as used in the Uniform Commercial Code (U.C.C.), certified or bank checks are the equivalent of cash in satisfying the underlying obligation, and there is no case law to support the proposition that a bank has not taken cash when internal administrative actions are pending or that the risk of loss of cash lies with the payor. Finally, title to a cashier's check, money order, or currency passes with delivery to the person who receives it in good faith and for valuable consideration, and when a commercial paper is made payable directly and originally to the bank at which it is deposited, the legal title is vested in the bank upon its receipt of the instrument. For these reasons, the Bank (P) took the check for the Debtor's (D) obligation. Affirmed.

ANALYSIS

The statute at issue in this case was the state's version of U.C.C. § 3-310, which addresses the effect of an instrument on the obligation for which the instrument is taken. Section 3-310(b) codifies the common law doctrine of merger, which provides that once an instrument is offered and accepted in satisfaction of an underlying obligation, the obligation merges with the instrument, and, until the instrument is dishonored, the obligation is suspended. Once the instrument is actually paid, the obligation is discharged and is no longer in suspension. However, if the instrument is dishonored, under § 3-310(b)(3) the obligation is separated from the instrument, and separate actions then exist for both.

Quicknotes

DEED OF TRUST A legal document that acts as a mortgage, placing a security interest in the deeded property with a trustee to insure the payment of a debt.

FORECLOSURE An action to recover the amount due on a mortgage of real property where the owner has failed to meet the mortgage obligations, terminating the owner's interest in the property which must then be sold to satisfy the debt.

OBLIGATION A debt; a duty that a person is legally or morally bound to perform; an action or forbearance that a party promises to do or refrain from doing.

Ward v. Federal Kemper Insurance Co.

Insured (P) v. Insurance company (D)

Md. Ct. App., 62 Md. App. 351, 489 A.2d 91 (1985).

NATURE OF CASE: Appeal from denial of declaratory judgment in insurance claim.

FACT SUMMARY: After Federal Kemper Insurance Co. (D) overpaid Ward (P) with a refund check that Ward (P) never negotiated, it canceled his insurance policy when he failed to return the difference.

RULE OF LAW

Until a check is presented and honored, no one is directly liable on the check itself, and the underlying obligation represented by the check is suspended.

FACTS: Federal Kemper Insurance Co. (Federal Kemper) (D) sent Ward (P) a $12 check representing a refund of an overpaid premium, only to discover that the proper refund should have been $4.50. Ward (P) received the check but never negotiated it. Federal Kemper (D) billed Ward (P) for the $7.50 difference. When Ward (P) failed to pay, Federal Kemper (D) canceled his insurance policy. Ward (P) subsequently had a car accident, but Federal Kemper (D) refused to provide coverage, contending that its cancellation was a proper response to Ward's (P) failure to pay the premium due balance included in the unnegotiated $12 check. The trial court agreed and ruled in Federal Kemper's (D) favor. Ward (P) appealed.

ISSUE: Is direct liability on a check suspended, along with the underlying obligation represented by the check, until a check is presented and honored?

HOLDING AND DECISION: (Adkins, J.) Yes. Until a check is presented and honored, no one is directly liable on the check itself, and the underlying obligation represented by the check is suspended. The drawer does not own the funds it has on deposit with the drawee. The drawee owns them. When the drawer draws a check on the drawee and delivers the check to the payee, the check is regarded as only a conditional payment on the underlying obligation, the conditions being presentment and dishonor. Until those conditions are met, the check does not itself operate as an assignment of any funds in the hands of the drawee. In this case, Ward (P) received the check, but the funds it represented were never transferred to Ward (P) because he never presented the check to the bank (the drawee). Thus, Federal Kemper (D) never became liable directly on the check and its underlying obligation (to refund $4.50 to Ward) (P) was never actually discharged. Since Ward (P) did not owe any premium to Federal Kemper (D), Federal Kemper (D) could not lawfully cancel Ward's (P) policy for nonpayment of a premium. Reversed and remanded.

ANALYSIS

Ward is an exception to the typical check case where the suspension of the underlying obligation has little practical significance because the parties expect the check to be presented promptly. Compare the situation in which a party gives the other a note due in 90 days. Now the suspension of the underlying obligation is more meaningful since the payee gives up a valuable right to insist on immediate payment and the maker acquires valuable time to get more money together. At the other end of the spectrum, transferring a cashier's check extinguishes the underlying obligation completely since the bank is both the drawer and the drawee, and there is no recourse on the instrument against the transferor.

Quicknotes

DECLARATORY JUDGMENT A judgment of the rights between opposing parties that is binding, but does not grant coercive relief (i.e., damages).

Floor v. Melvin

Holder of note (P) v. Decedent's estate (D)

Ill. App. Ct., 5 Ill. App. 3d 463, 283 N.E.2d 303 (1972).

NATURE OF CASE: Appeal from dismissal of action to recover on a promissory note.

FACT SUMMARY: Melvin's estate (D) argued that, as a guarantor against "loss" rather that nonpayment, its decedent was only secondarily liable on a promissory note issued to Floor (P).

RULE OF LAW

A guarantee as against "loss" is a guarantee of collection rather than payment.

FACTS: Melcro, Inc. issued a $12,000 promissory note payable to the order of Floor (P). The back of the note contained the statement: "[W]e irrevocably guarantee Floor (P) against loss by reason of nonpayment of this note." It also contained the signature of Melvin's (D) decedent. Melcro, Inc. failed to pay when the note became due, and Floor (P) sued Melvin's estate (D) to recover the $12,000. Melvin's estate (D) moved to dismiss for failure to state a cause of action, arguing that its decedent was not liable because Floor (P) had not yet prosecuted her claim against the maker of the note. The trial court agreed and dismissed the case. Floor (P) appealed.

ISSUE: Is a guarantee against "loss" a guarantee of collection rather than payment?

HOLDING AND DECISION: (Alloy, J.) Yes. A guarantee against "loss" is a guarantee of collection rather than payment. Universal Commercial Code (U.C.C) § 3-416 declares that contracts of guaranty of negotiable instruments are of two kinds: (1) contracts guaranteeing the collection of the notes and (2) contracts guaranteeing the payment of the notes. A contract guaranteeing the collection of a note is conditional, in that the guarantor agrees to pay the debt if the owner of the note first attempts to collect payment from the maker but is unable to do so. On the other hand, a contract guaranteeing the payment of a note is an absolute contract; if the note is not paid upon maturity, the guarantor may be sued immediately. In this case, the terms of the guarantee were made conditional upon collection of the note. Although Melvin's decedent (D) did not actually use the word "collection," the guarantee against "loss" was, in effect, a guarantee of collection and not of payment. Since Floor (P) neither alleged that she prosecuted an unsatisfied claim against Melco, Inc., the maker of the note, nor that Melco became insolvent, she failed to comply with U.C.C. § 3-416(2), and dismissal of her action was proper. Affirmed.

ANALYSIS

Under U.C.C. § 3-416(5), the liability of an endorser who adds "payment guaranteed" to his signature is virtually indistinguishable from that of a co-maker. One who adds "collection guaranteed," on the other hand, forestalls liability until the holder has a judgment and unsatisfied execution against the principal debtor. Note, however, that under § 416(2), the holder may fulfill this requirement by showing that proceeding to judgment and execution would be a useless act.

Quicknotes

GUARANTOR A party who agrees to be liable for the debt or default of another.

Chemical Bank v. Pic Motors Corp.

Bank (P) v. Car dealership (D)

N.Y. App. Div., 87 A.D.2d 447, 452 N.Y.S.2d 41, *aff'd on the opinion below,* 58 N.Y.2d 1023, 448 N.E.2d 1349 (1982).

NATURE OF CASE: Appeal from summary judgment awarding recovery on a loan.

FACT SUMMARY: Siegel (D) claimed that Chemical Bank's (P) failure to keep track of Pic Motors Corp.'s (D) inventory of cars discharged his obligations as a guarantor.

RULE OF LAW

Where the collateral is in the possession of the debtor, inaction by the creditor, negligent or otherwise, does not release a guarantor who has waived the creditor's obligation to protect and preserve the collateral.

FACTS: Chemical Bank (P) agreed to periodically loan funds to Pic Motors Corp. (Pic) (D), using Pic's (D) inventory of automobiles as collateral. Chemical Bank (P) verified Pic's (D) sales by periodic inspections. Siegel (D), Pic's (D) director, personally guaranteed the loans "absolutely and unconditionally." When Pic (D) was unable to account for 50 percent of its inventory, Chemical Bank (P) demanded repayment of its loan and instituted suit against Pic (D) and Siegel (D). Siegel (D) denied liability, arguing that Chemical Bank (P) had impaired the collateral by failing to regularly inspect the inventory and, furthermore, that its employees had submitted false inventory reports and approved loans on nonexistent cars. Concluding that Siegel (D) was an unconditional guarantor, the lower court granted Chemical Bank's (P) motion for summary judgment. Siegel (D) appealed.

ISSUE: Where the collateral is in the possession of the debtor, does inaction by the creditor, release a guarantor who has waived the creditor's obligation to protect and preserve the collateral?

HOLDING AND DECISION: (Fein, J.) No. Where the collateral is in the possession of the debtor, inaction by the creditor, negligent or otherwise, does not release a guarantor who has waived the creditor's obligation to protect and preserve the collateral. A surety may waive any obligation of a creditor, including an obligation not to impair the security. Here, Chemical Bank (P) was not obligated by either its agreement with Pic (D) or by the guaranty to conduct inspections or to preserve or protect the collateral. Also, the terms of the guaranty allowed Chemical Bank (P) to release or surrender the collateral or extend further credit without notifying or discharging Siegel (D). Therefore, the alleged actions by Chemical Bank's (P) employees did not serve to discharge Siegel (D). Affirmed.

DISSENT: (Milonas, J.) A waiver of a creditor's obligation to protect the collateral should not be enforced to bind a guarantor on the underlying obligation where the creditor has engaged in negligent, fraudulent, or tortious conduct. Enabling a creditor to shield itself by inserting a waiver clause is contrary to the spirit of the Universal Commercial Code (U.C.C.) and to public policy.

ANALYSIS

Sureties like Siegel (D) have an interest in how the creditor handles the collateral because, once the principal debtor defaults and the surety pays off the creditor, thereby acquiring the debt, the surety is entitled to the collateral. The creditor's conduct regarding the collateral (in the absence of a waiver) is measured by a "reasonable care" standard. See Comment 5 to U.C.C. § 3-606.

Quicknotes

COLLATERAL Property that secures the payment of a debt.

GUARANTOR A party who agrees to be liable for the debt or default of another.

NEGLIGENCE Conduct falling below the standard of care that a reasonable person would demonstrate under similar conditions.

London Leasing Corp. v. Interfina, Inc.

Corporation (P) v. Corporation (D)

N.Y. Sup. Ct., 53 Misc. 2d 657, 279 N.Y.S.2d 209 (1967).

NATURE OF CASE: Motion for summary judgment in action to recover on promissory note.

FACT SUMMARY: Evans (D) argued that he should not be personally liable on a note that he executed in his corporate capacity as well as endorsed in his personal capacity since he did not personally consent to an agreement extending the time for payment of the note.

RULE OF LAW

Consent to alter a suretyship contract need not be expressed but may be implied from the surrounding circumstances or from the surety's conduct.

FACTS: Interfina, Inc. (D) made and delivered to London Leasing Corp. (P) a promissory note in the amount of $52,000, signed by Evans (D), as president of Interfina (D), and also personally endorsed by him. Then, acting solely in his corporate capacity, he sought, negotiated, and signed an agreement with London Leasing (P), extending the time for payment of the note. When Interfina (D) defaulted on the note, London Leasing (P) sued Interfina (D) and Evans (D). Evans (D) contended that the extension agreement discharged him from personal liability on the note because he had not consented personally to the extension London Leasing (P) moved for summary judgment.

ISSUE: May consent to alter a suretyship contract be implied from the surety's conduct?

HOLDING AND DECISION: (Crawford, J.) Yes. Consent to alter a suretyship contract need not be expressed but may be implied from the surrounding circumstances or from the surety's conduct. Parties to a contract may always alter the contract by mutual agreement. However, under Universal Commercial Code (U.C.C.) § 3-606, the holder discharges any party to the instrument to the extent that the holder agrees to suspend the right to enforce the instrument without such party's consent. However, if the surety does consent to a modification of the contract between the principal creditor and the debtor, he will not be discharged from liability. Although the U.C.C. does not define consent, Stearns *Law of Suretyship* (5th ed., § 6.13) states that consent by a surety need not be expressly given but may be implied from the surrounding circumstances or from his conduct. In this case, Evans (D) applied for, negotiated, and received the agreements extending the time for payment and then signed them in his corporate capacity. Evans's (D) conduct exceeded mere knowledge or acquiescence in the extension agreements and, under the circumstances, constituted consent. Motion for summary judgment granted.

ANALYSIS

Under U.C.C. § 3-606(2), if a creditor wants to grant a debtor an extension of time to make payments, but the surety refuses to consent, the creditor may still prevent a surety's claim to discharge by "expressly reserving" his rights against the surety. Theoretically, the surety is not harmed by the creditor's express reservation of rights because the surety can immediately pay the instrument and then exercise his right of recourse against the principal debtor. Note, however, that § 3-606 does not require the creditor to notify the surety when he expressly reserves his rights against him, and the surety can hardly exercise his option to pay and sue if he has no knowledge of the creditor's actions.

Quicknotes

SURETYSHIP A situation in which one party guarantees payment of the debt of another party to a creditor.

Messing v. Bank of America, N.A.

Non-account check holder (P) v. Bank (D)

Md. Ct. Spec. App., 143 Md. App. 1, 792 A.2d 312 (2002), *aff'd*, Md. Ct. App., 373 Md. 672, 821 A.2d 22 (2003).

NATURE OF CASE: Appeal from summary judgment dismissing action against a bank's thumbprint signature requirement for non-account holders.

FACT SUMMARY: Messing (P) attempted to cash a check drawn on a Bank of America, N.A. (the Bank) (D) customer account at a Bank of America (the Bank) branch. The Bank (D) required a thumbprint signature from all non-account holders before cashing a check drawn on one of its customer's accounts. When Messing (P) refused to provide his thumbprint, the Bank (D) refused to cash the check. Messing (P) sued, claiming the thumbprint requirement was unlawful.

RULE OF LAW

A thumbprint signature is a form of reasonable identification that may be requested by a bank of a non-account holder wishing to cash a check drawn on a bank's customer account.

FACTS: Messing (P) attempted to cash a $976 check at a Bank of America, N.A. (the Bank) (D) branch. The check was made out to Messing (P) and was drawn on a Bank of America customer's checking account. The teller asked for identification, and Messing (P) presented his driver's license and a major credit card. The teller then asked Messing (P) if he was a Bank of America customer. When Messing (P) replied he was not, the teller asked him to place his thumbprint signature on the check by applying his thumb to an inkless fingerprinting device that is neither messy nor time consuming. This was in accordance with the Bank's (D) policy relating to non-account holders, which was posted at every teller station. When Messing (P) refused, the teller put away the cash she had counted out. The branch manager confirmed that the Bank's (D) policy did not permit cashing the check without Messing's (P) thumbprint signature, and that this policy was pursuant to an agreement with the Bank's (D) customers. Messing (P) sued, claiming the Bank's (D) policy was unlawful. He also claimed that the Bank (D) unlawfully dishonored his check. The trial court granted the Bank's (D) motion for summary judgment and dismissed with prejudice.

ISSUE: Is a thumbprint signature a form of reasonable identification that may be requested by a bank of a non-account holder wishing to cash a check drawn on a bank's customer account?

HOLDING AND DECISION: (Krauser, J.) Yes. A thumbprint signature is a form of reasonable identification that may be requested by a bank of a non-account holder wishing to cash a check drawn on a bank's customer account. The Bank's (D) thumbprint requirement is a form of "reasonable identification" under the Universal Commercial Code (U.C.C.) for several reasons. First, this form of identification has been accepted by drafters of the Maryland U.C.C. as an effective, reliable, and accurate way to authenticate a writing on a negotiable instrument, i.e., a signature may be a thumbprint. Second, the process that a non-account holder goes through to provide a thumbprint signature is unobtrusive and is not unreasonably inconvenient. Third, this procedure is a reasonable and necessary response to the growing incidence of check fraud, and has been endorsed by numerous bank groups for that purpose. Finally, although a thumbprint cannot confirm the true identity of a non-account holder at the time of presentment, it nevertheless serves the purpose of reasonable identification. Messing (P) also claimed that the trial court had erred in holding that the Bank (D) had not dishonored the check. His argument rested on the assumption that the Bank (D) had accepted the check, but in fact, the Bank (D) had not accepted the check. In that situation, there is no dishonor if presentment fails to comply with an agreement of the parties. The Bank (D) had the authority to refuse payment in accordance with the deposit agreement it had with each account holder, which gave it authority to refuse payment unless "reasonable identification" was presented. Messing's (P) failure to provide his thumbprint rendered the presentment ineffective. Reversed and remanded.

ANALYSIS

Although the court in the instant case concludes that a thumbprint signature is a form of "reasonable identification," it does not expressly address the question that the plaintiff seemed to be raising, which is why his proffer of his driver's license and/or a major credit card, which are also recognized as forms of "reasonable identification," was not enough to satisfy the reasonable identification requirement. The decision seems to imply that those non-physical forms of identification are not as sound as the thumbprint in combating fraud, but the court never comes out and explicitly says so.

Makel Textiles, Inc. v. Dolly Originals, Inc.

Corporation (P) v. Corporation (D)

N.Y. Sup. Ct., 4 U.C.C. Rep. Serv. 95 (1967).

NATURE OF CASE: Determination of individual liability of endorsers in action to recover on promissory notes made on behalf of a corporation.

FACT SUMMARY: Goldberg (D), Dolly Originals, Inc.'s (D) principal officer and president, contended that he was not individually liable on promissory notes payable to the order of Makel Textiles, Inc. (P) that he endorsed on behalf of Dolly Originals (D), as well as in his individual capacity, because the notes had not been presented for payment. Kushner (D), who was merely an endorser on the notes, claimed he was not personally liable on the notes because no notice of presentment or dishonor had been made.

RULE OF LAW

Formal notice of presentment and dishonor may be excused if defendant's rights will not be injured or prejudiced in any way.

FACTS: Goldberg (D), president and principal officer of Dolly Originals, Inc. (D), executed two promissory notes payable to the order of Makel Textiles, Inc. (Makel) (P) and, together with Kushner (D), endorsed them on the back. Goldberg (D) endorsed both on behalf of Dolly Originals (D) and in his individual capacity. Lewis's (D) signatures were purportedly also on the notes. These notes were given to Makel (P) as repayment on a loan. Several checks given to Makel (P) by Dolly Originals (D) to pay off the notes went unpaid. There was no evidence that Makel (P) had complied with requirements for presentment and dishonor. When Dolly Originals (D) defaulted on the notes, Makel (P) sued Goldberg (D), Kushner (D), and Lewis (D) in addition to Dolly Originals (D). The trial court determined that Lewis's (D) signature had been forged and dismissed him from the suit. Judgment was rendered against Dolly Originals (D), but it made no answer. Thus, the trial court moved to the issue of Goldberg's (D) and Kushner's (D) individual liability. Goldberg (D) and Kushner (D) moved for a dismissal, contending that the promissory notes had never been presented for payment and thus their obligation was discharged.

ISSUE: May formal notice of presentment and dishonor be excused if defendant's rights will not be injured or prejudiced in any way?

HOLDING AND DECISION: (Spiegel, J.) Yes. Formal notice of presentment and dishonor may be excused if defendant's rights will not be injured or prejudiced in any way. Here, the usual obligation of presentment and notice of dishonor was unnecessary as to Goldberg (D) because Goldberg (D) was an active participant in Dolly Originals' (D) affairs and knew that the notes he had executed and endorsed could not be paid from corporate funds. Therefore, giving him notice of presentment or dishonor would not inform him of anything he did not already know, so that not providing him with formal notice of presentment and dishonor would not prejudice him. On the other hand, there was no evidence of any corporate activity or participation by Kushner (D), so that presentment and notice of dishonor were required to hold him liable. Judgment for Makel (P) against Goldberg (D); complaint dismissed as to Kushner (D).

ANALYSIS

Universal Commercial Code § 3-511(2) specifies when the formality of presentment and notice of dishonor will be excused. For example, an endorser may expressly waive his right to have the instrument presented by including a waiver either in the body or on the back of the instrument. Presentment and notice of dishonor will also be excused when an endorser has played an active role in causing an instrument to be dishonored. An endorser's mere knowledge of the maker's insolvency, however, is not sufficient to excuse the technical requirements.

Quicknotes

PRESENTMENT AND NOTICE OF DISHONOR A demand for payment or acceptance, accompanied by notice of liability for such payment.

Norton v. Knapp

Seller (P) v. Buyer (D)

Iowa Sup. Ct., 64 Iowa 112, 19 N.W. 867 (1884).

NATURE OF CASE: Action for payment on a sight draft.

FACT SUMMARY: When Knapp (D) received a sight draft for the price of a mill delivered to him by Norton (P), he wrote "Kiss my foot" on the back of the draft and signed it.

RULE OF LAW

If a bill is presented to a drawee for his acceptance, he will be considered an acceptor if he does anything to it or with it which does not clearly indicate that he will not accept it.

FACTS: Norton (P) delivered a flaxseed-cleaner mill, priced at $80, to Knapp (D). When Knapp (D) did not pay the $80, Norton (P) drew a draft on Knapp (D), payable on sight. When Knapp (D) received the sight draft, he wrote "Kiss my foot" on the back and signed his name. Claiming that Knapp's (D) writing and signature constituted a valid acceptance, Norton (P) sued for the unpaid draft.

ISSUE: If a bill is presented to a drawee for his acceptance, will he be considered an acceptor if he does anything to it or with it which does not clearly indicate that he will not accept it?

HOLDING AND DECISION: (Seevers, J.) Yes. If a bill is presented to a drawee for his acceptance, he will be considered an acceptor if he does anything to it or with it which does not clearly indicate that he will not accept it. If the drawee writes anything on the bill which does not clearly negative an intention to accept, he can be charged as an acceptor. The term "kiss my foot" may be vulgar, but, when used in reply to a request, it is understood to signify one thing only: refusal. In this case, drawee Knapp's (D) use of the term "kiss my foot" was clearly meant to emphasize his intention not to accept the sight draft or, for that matter, to have anything to do with it or with Norton (P). Therefore, Knapp's (D) signature accompanied by the words "kiss my foot" was not a legal or valid acceptance.

ANALYSIS

When a drawee "accepts" a draft other than a check, he becomes primarily liable upon the instrument. Comment 4 to Universal Commercial Code (U.C.C.) § 3-410 specifies the formalities required for accepting an instrument. Customarily the signature is written vertically across the face of the instrument, but a drawee's signature anywhere on the instrument is sufficient to manifest acceptance. Comment 4 states that nothing in § 3-410 is intended to change such decisions as *Knapp*. Thus, although a signature need not be accompanied by such words as "accepted," an instrument must not bear any words indicating an intent to refuse to honor the bill.

Quicknotes

SIGHT DRAFT An instrument demanding payment, payable when presented.

Galyen Petroleum Co. v. Hixson

Corporation (P) v. Account holder (D)

Neb. Sup. Ct., 213 Neb. 683, 331 N.W.2d 1 (1983).

NATURE OF CASE: Appeal from summary judgment in suit to recover on three checks.

FACT SUMMARY: Drawee Commercial Bank (D) refused payment on three checks drawn by Hixson (D) presented by Galyen Petroleum Co. (P) despite sufficient funds in the account to pay some of the checks.

RULE OF LAW

A check is not an assignment of the drawer's funds in the hands of the drawee and creates no lien on the money which the holder can enforce against the bank.

FACTS: On November 12, Galyen Petroleum Co. (Galyen) (P) personally presented three checks totaling $6,883, drawn by Hixson (D) to drawee Commercial Bank (D). Commercial Bank (D) unconditionally refused payment of all three checks, although Hixson's (D) account had a credit balance of approximately half that amount. Later that same day, Commercial Bank (D) set off Hixson's (D) account against payment of two notes made payable to it, virtually depleting the account, although the credited notes were not due at that time. Galyen (P) filed suit against Commercial Bank (D) for unlawfully refusing payment of the checks on presentment. Summary judgment was granted in favor of Commercial Bank (D), and Galyen (P) appealed.

ISSUE: Is a check an assignment of the drawer's funds in the hands of the drawee (the bank), creating a lien on the money which the holder can enforce against the bank?

HOLDING AND DECISION: (Colwell, J.) No. A check is not an assignment of the drawer's funds in the hands of the drawee and creates no lien on the money which the holder can enforce against the drawee bank. Absent special circumstances, a check gives the holder of the check no right of action against the drawee and no valid claim to the fund of the drawer in its hands, even though the drawer has on deposit sufficient funds to pay the check. There were no special circumstances in this case that would warrant a different result. Galyen (P) had no standing or cause of action against Commercial Bank (D), based on its refusal to honor the three checks. Affirmed.

ANALYSIS

Although, in general, the drawer's writing of a check does not create any immediate rights in the checking account funds, there are special circumstances when a drawee bank may become liable to the holder prior to acceptance. Liability may arise apart from the instrument itself. Universal Commercial Code § 3-409(2) states: "Nothing in this section shall affect any liability in contract, tort or otherwise arising from any letter of credit or other obligation or representation which is not an acceptance." This provision preserves the common law rule that allows the drawer, by special agreement, to immediately assign bank-held funds in order to give the holder of the check a claim against the drawee bank prior to acceptance.

Quicknotes

ASSIGNMENT A transaction in which a party conveys his or her entire interest in property to another.

LIEN A claim against the property of another in order to secure the payment of a debt.

Mundaca Investment Corp. v. Febba

Receiver (P) v. Trustees (D)

N.H. Sup. Ct., 727 A.2d 990, 38 U.C.C. Rep. Serv. 2d 464 (1999).

NATURE OF CASE: Appeal from summary judgment holding defendants liable on two promissory notes.

FACT SUMMARY: Mundaca Investment Corp. (P) brought suit against the trustees (D) of L.T.D. Trust, seeking to hold them personally liable for amounts due on two promissory notes executed by the trustees (D) for the purchase of two condominium units.

RULE OF LAW

A representative may be held personally liable to a holder in due course on a promissory note that does not unambiguously show that the representative's signature is made on behalf of a represented person identified in the instrument where the holder takes the instrument without notice that the representative did not intend to be personally liable, and the representative may be liable to any other person unless the representative proves the original parties did not intend the representative to be personally liable.

FACTS: Trustees (D) of L.T.D. Trust purchased two condominium units for trust. To finance the purchase, they executed two promissory notes secured by two mortgages, payable to Dartmouth Savings Bank. The notes identified trustees (D) as the "borrowers," but the trust was not identified. Mundaca Investment Corp. (Mundaca) (P) acquired the notes as receiver for the bank and notified the trustees (D) they were in default. Mundaca (P) foreclosed on the condominiums and filed suit against the trustees (D) individually for the remaining amount due. Both parties moved for summary judgment and the trial court ruled in favor of Mundaca (P) on the basis that the trustees' (D) signatures did not clearly show that they were acting in a representative capacity. Trustees (D) appealed, arguing that reading the mortgages and notes together unambiguously showed that they were acting in a representative capacity and that there was a genuine issue if material fact as to whether the original parties intended the trustees (D) to be personally liable.

ISSUE: May a representative be held personally liable to a holder in due course on a promissory note that does not unambiguously show that the representative's signature is made on behalf of a represented person identified in the instrument where the holder takes the instrument without notice that the defendant did not intend to be personally liable and to any other person unless the defendants prove the original parties did not intend them to be personally liable?

HOLDING AND DECISION: (Brock, C.J.) Yes. A representative may be held personally liable to a holder in due course on a promissory note that does not unambiguously show that the representative's signature is made on behalf of a represented person identified in the instrument where the holder takes the instrument without notice that the representative did not intend to be personally liable, and the representative may be liable to any other person unless the representative proves the original parties did not intend the representative to be personally liable. Because here the represented person, the trust, was not identified in the instrument as required by state law, the case falls under RSA 382-A:3-402(b)(2), which states that the trustees (D) could be personally liable in two situations: (1) to a holder in due course who takes the instrument without notice that the defendants did not intend to be held personally liable; and (2) to any other party unless the defendants prove the original parties did not intend to hold them personally liable. The trustees (D) argued that summary judgment was inappropriate because there was a genuine issue of material fact as to the intent of the original parties. This court agrees. The record contains conflicting evidence regarding the intent of the original parties. Since the court did not address the issue of whether Mundaca (P) was a holder in due course without notice that the defendants did not intend to be held personally liable, this issue is to be resolved by the trial court on remand. Reversed and remanded.

ANALYSIS

The trustees (D) also argued that the mortgages served as a defense to their personal liability on the promissory notes. This argument was erroneous. They only provided a defense to the extent the mortgages modified, supplemented or nullified the trustees' (D) liability on the notes, which they did not do here. While the mortgages were issued as collateral for the notes, both instruments failed to clearly identify the borrower.

Quicknotes

FORECLOSURE An action to recover the amount due on a mortgage of real property where the owner has failed to meet the mortgage obligations, terminating the owner's interest in the property which must then be sold to satisfy the debt.

HOLDER IN DUE COURSE A party who takes an instrument in good faith and for consideration without notice of any claims therein.

Continued on next page.

PERSONAL LIABILITY An obligation pursuant to which the personal assets of an individual may be required for payment.

PROMISSORY NOTE A written promise to tender a stated amount of money at a designated time and to a designated person.

Nichols v. Seale

Business owner (D) v. Check holder (P)

Tex. Ct. Civ. App., 493 S.W.2d 589, 12 U.C.C. Rep. Serv. 711 (1973).

NATURE OF CASE: Appeal from summary judgment awarding recovery on a promissory note.

FACT SUMMARY: Nichols (D) argued that a note that contained his corporation's assumed name and his signature was sufficiently ambiguous to allow parol evidence to show that he signed in his corporate capacity only.

RULE OF LAW

When a corporation is named on a note by use of its assumed name, extrinsic evidence is allowed to show that the signer was not personally obligated.

FACTS: Nichols (D) signed a note on behalf of his corporation, Mr. Carls Fashion, Inc., doing business as (dba) The Fashion Beauty Salon. Only the dba name appeared on the note. Seale (P), the payee, sued on the note, and the trial court upheld its motion for summary judgment against Nichols (D), concluding that Nichols (D) was personally liable on the note because the note neither named the corporation nor showed that Nichols (D) signed in his individual capacity. Nichols (D) appealed.

ISSUE: When a corporation is named on a note by use of its assumed name, is extrinsic evidence allowed to show that the signer was not personally obligated?

HOLDING AND DECISION: (Guittard, J.) Yes. When a corporation is named on a note by use of its assumed name, extrinsic evidence is allowed to show that the signer was not personally obligated. Under Universal Commercial Code (U.C.C.) § 3-403, a representative who signs his own name to an instrument is personally obligated if the instrument neither names the person represented (here, the corporation) nor shows that he signed in a representative capacity. In this case, Nichols's (D) use of an assumed name did "name the person represented" within the meaning of the U.C.C., which expressly authorizes use of an assumed name in a negotiable instrument under § 3-401(2). Furthermore, corporations are expressly permitted to use assumed names under state law. When a corporation is "named" by use of its assumed name, § 3-403(2) does not forbid extrinsic evidence to show that, as between the original parties, the signer was not personally obligated. Such proof is admissible to explain an ambiguity with respect to the capacity of the signer. Therefore, summary judgment in this case was not appropriate. Reversed and remanded.

ANALYSIS

The Texas Supreme Court reversed on appeal. Apparently Nichols's (D) affidavit stated that he signed the note as president of the corporation, indicating his subjective intent to sign as an agent, but he did not state that he had ever disclosed his intent to Seale (P). Texas law provides that in order for an agent to avoid liability for his signature on a contract, he must communicate his intent to sign as a representative to the other contracting party. Consequently, Nichols (D) did not raise an issue of fact, and Seale's (P) motion was properly granted by the trial court. *Seale v. Nichols*, 505 S.W.2d 251 (Tex. 1974).

Quicknotes

EXTRINSIC EVIDENCE Evidence that is not contained within the text of a document or contract, but which is derived from the parties' statements or the circumstances under which the agreement was made.

PAROL EVIDENCE Evidence given verbally; extraneous evidence.

PERSONAL LIABILITY An obligation pursuant to which the personal assets of an individual may be required for payment.

CHAPTER 11

Banks and Their Customers

Quick Reference Rules of Law

Cincinnati Ins. Co. v. Wachovia Bank, N.A.

Subrogee of bank customer (P) v. Bank (D)

2010 WL 2777478, 72 U.C.C. Rep. Serv. 2d 744 (D. Minn. 2010).

NATURE OF CASE: Motion for summary judgment in subrogation action to recover amounts paid as a result of check fraud.

FACT SUMMARY: Cincinnati Insurance Company (Cincinnati) (P), as subrogee of Schultz Foods, contended that Wachovia Bank, N.A. (Wachovia) (D) was liable for the amount of a check from Schultz Foods's account that had been altered by thieves, and that Wachovia (D) had paid. Wachovia (D) contended that, under its deposit agreement with Schultz Foods, Schultz Foods (or its subrogee) was liable for the amount of the altered check because Schultz Foods had declined to implement a fraud-detection program called Positive Pay offered by Wachovia (D)—a program that would have prevented the loss.

RULE OF LAW

A bank may contractually avoid liability under Uniform Commercial Code (U.C.C.) § 4-401(a) for charging a customer's account for a check that is not properly payable by obtaining a release from the customer that is objectively reasonable under the circumstances.

FACTS: Schultz Foods issued a check in the amount of $153,856.46 to Amerada Hess Corporation. Thieves stole the check, changed the name of the payee to "Kenneth Payton," and induced Payton (an unwitting accomplice) to deposit the check into his account at TCF Bank (TCF). TCF presented the check for payment to Schultz Foods's bank, Wachovia Bank (Wachovia) (D), and Wachovia charged the amount of the check against Schultz Foods's account. By the time that Schultz Foods discovered the fraud, Payton had wired the funds to an overseas bank account, and the thieves had disappeared with the money. Under the deposit agreement between Schultz Foods and Wachovia (D), Schultz Foods was required to bear the loss because Schultz Foods failed to implement a fraud-detection program called Positive Pay offered by Wachovia (D)—a program that would have prevented the loss. The cost of Positive Pay involved modest monthly and per-check fees, and a one-time cost of around $500 to make Schultz Foods's computer system compatible with the program. Wachovia (D) refused to re-credit Schultz Foods's account, and Schultz Foods filed a claim with its insurer, Cincinnati Insurance Company (Cincinnati) (P). Cincinnati (P) paid the claim and then filed a subrogation action in federal district court against Wachovia (D). Cincinnati (P) contended that, when Wachovia (D) deducted the amount of the altered check from Schultz Foods's account, Wachovia (D) violated U.C.C. § 4-401(a). Wachovia (D) responded that, under the terms of the deposit agreement between Schultz Foods and Wachovia (D), Schultz Foods's failure to implement Positive Pay made Schultz Foods, and not Wachovia (D), liable for the loss.

ISSUE: May a bank contractually avoid liability under U.C.C. § 4-401(a) for charging a customer's account for a check that is not properly payable by obtaining a release from the customer that is objectively reasonable under the circumstances?

HOLDING AND DECISION: (Schiltz, J.) Yes. A bank may contractually avoid liability under U.C.C. § 4-401(a) for charging a customer's account for a check that is not properly payable by obtaining a release from the customer that is objectively reasonable under the circumstances. Section 4-401(a) of the U.C.C. provides that "[a] bank may charge against the account of a customer an item that is properly payable from that account. . . . An item is properly payable if it is authorized by the customer and is in accordance with any agreement between the customer and the bank." Ordinarily, if a bank charges a customer's account for a check that is not properly payable—as Wachovia (D) did here—the bank will be liable to the customer for the loss under § 4-401(a). However, this is merely a default rule, and § 4-103(a) permits banks and their customers to agree to a different rule, except that an agreement between a bank and a customer "cannot disclaim the responsibility of a bank for its lack of good faith or failure to exercise ordinary care." Thus, the question is whether the deposit agreement between Wachovia (D) and Schultz Foods succeeded in altering the default rule of § 4-401(a). Section 12 of the deposit agreement contained a conditional release, which provided that if a customer failed to implement a fraud-detection program offered by Wachovia (D), the customer would be "precluded from asserting any claims against [Wachovia (D)] for paying any unauthorized, altered, counterfeit or other fraudulent item that such product, service, or precaution was designed to detect or deter, and we will not be required to re-credit your account or otherwise have any liability for paying such items." Cincinnati (P) contends that the release is invalid on several grounds. First, Cincinnati (P) argues that a bank and a customer may not enter an agreement that absolves the bank of this strict liability provided in § 4-401(a). This argument is incorrect, since under § 4-103, a bank and its customer may, within certain limits, vary the effect of § 4-401. Cincinnati (P) also argues that

Continued on next page.

the release is not valid because it purports to excuse Wachovia (D) from exercising ordinary care. Although it is true that the release could protect Wachovia (D) from liability for paying an unauthorized check even if Wachovia (D) failed to exercise ordinary care in some cases, there is no allegation in this case that Wachovia (D) in fact failed to exercise ordinary care in paying the unauthorized check to Payton. Thus, notwithstanding the release is generally overbroad, it can still be enforced in the case at bar. The release would be invalid if it protected Wachovia (D) in a case where Wachovia (D) failed to exercise ordinary care. However, given that the deposit agreement contains a severability clause, the release could be severed in such a case with invalidating the entire agreement. Another issue is whether the release was reasonable. Section 4-103 imposes a couple of "reasonableness" requirements on the attempts of parties to use contracts to vary the provisions of Article 4 of the U.C.C., including § 4-401. First, § 4-103 (a) allows parties to agree to the standards by which a bank's responsibility to exercise ordinary care will be measured, as long as the agreed-upon standards are not "manifestly unreasonable." Second, § 4-103(d) permits parties to agree to "procedures" that vary from those provided in Article 4, as long as the agreed-upon procedures are "reasonable under the circumstances." Here, the provisions of the deposit agreement relating to the implementation of Positive Pay, and the consequences for failing to implement that program, were not "manifestly unreasonable" for purposes of § 4-103(a) and were "reasonable under the circumstances" for purposes of § 4-103(d). Reasonableness under either standard is a function of (1) the technical feasibility of implementing Positive Pay and (2) the cost of installing and participating in the program. It is undisputed that it was technically feasible for Schultz Foods to implement Positive Pay. However, Cincinnati (P) argues that requiring Schultz Foods to implement Positive Pay was because Schultz Foods mistakenly believed—as a subjective matter—that the cost of implementation would be thousands of dollars and was unreasonable. There is no authority for the principle that under § 4-103, the reasonableness of standards or procedures imposed under an agreement is to be judged based on the subjective beliefs of the parties to that agreement. Because a subjective standard would be unworkable, an objective standard is to be used in measuring the agreement's reasonableness. Under such a standard, the Positive Pay obligation imposed by the deposit agreement was unquestionably reasonable Summary judgment is granted to Wachovia (D) and Cincinnati's (P) claims are dismissed with prejudice.

ANALYSIS

While it is indeed true that, under § 4-401(a) ordinarily a bank is strictly liable for charging a customer's account with an amount that the customer had not authorized the bank to pay, as this case underscores, such strict liability is subject to releases and other contractual modifications that are objectively reasonable. Banks also have other defenses to such strict liability, including customer negligence and subrogation.

Quicknotes

SUBROGATION The substitution of one party for another in assuming the first party's rights or obligations.

Twin City Bank v. Isaacs

Bank (D) v. Account holders (P)

Ark. Sup. Ct., 263 Ark. 127, 672 S.W.2d 651 (1984).

NATURE OF CASE: Appeal from denial of defense motion for new trial upon award of damages for wrongful dishonor.

FACT SUMMARY: After the Isaacs (P) were awarded damages for mental anguish they suffered when Twin City Bank (Twin City) (D) wrongfully dishonored their checks and wrongfully withheld their funds, Twin City (D) appealed the denial of its motion for a new trial on the basis that damages were speculative.

RULE OF LAW

Damages resulting from mental anguish are recoverable, even though they cannot be determined with exactness.

FACTS: After discovering their checkbook missing, the Isaacs (P) reported the loss to Twin City Bank (Twin City) (D). They later learned that two forged checks totaling $2,050 had been written on their account and honored by Twin City (D) before they realized the checkbook was missing. Nevertheless, Twin City (D), believing the Isaacs (P) were somehow involved with the forged checks, issued a hold order on the account, leaving the balance at approximately $2,000. As a result, the Isaacs (P) sued for wrongful dishonor of their checks and wrongful withholding of their funds, and the jury, finding substantial evidence of mental anxiety, awarded them compensatory and punitive damages. Twin City (D) moved for a new trial, contending that damages awarded on the basis of mental anguish were speculative. The district court denied its motion, and Twin City (D) appealed.

ISSUE: Although they cannot be determined with exactness, are damages resulting from mental anguish recoverable?

HOLDING AND DECISION: (Hays, J.) Yes. Damages resulting from mental anguish are recoverable, even though they cannot be determined with exactness. This rule is based in Uniform Commercial Code § 4-402. Although this section appears to circumscribe the old common law rule that damages may not be had where they are speculative, a majority of courts addressing this issue have allowed recovery. (See esp. *Wasp Oil v. Arkansas Oil & Gas*, 280 Ark. 420, 658 S.W.2d 397 (1983).) In the instant case, there was substantial evidence establishing mental anxiety on the part of the Isaacs (P) occasioned by their financial strain. The district court did not err in denying Twin City's (D) motion for a new trial after the jury found it liable to the Isaacs (P) for compensatory and punitive damages awarded on the basis of their mental anguish. Affirmed.

ANALYSIS

The court above awarded punitive damages, stating that they were not excessive since Twin City (D) was in a favorable financial condition. Interestingly enough, however, these damages are usually awarded in the case of mental anguish where the defendant intended to engage in wrongful activity that naturally brings about such anguish on the part of the plaintiff. Punitive damages can also be awarded where the defendant's conduct is not intentional, but unreasonable under the circumstances. The degree of unreasonableness of the defendant's conduct will naturally influence the amount of punitive damages awarded.

Quicknotes

PUNITIVE DAMAGES Damages exceeding the actual injury suffered for the purposes of punishment of the defendant, deterrence of the wrongful behavior or comfort to the plaintiff.

Walter v. National City Bank of Cleveland

Creditor (P) v. Bank (D)

Ohio Sup. Ct., 42 Ohio St. 2d 524, 330 N.E.2d 425 (1975).

NATURE OF CASE: Appeal from grant of summary judgment awarding recovery for conversion.

FACT SUMMARY: Walter (P) successfully sued National City Bank of Cleveland (National) (D) for conversion, thereby receiving a priority of right to funds owed him by Ritzer, whose account at National (D) he had garnished after National (D) withheld the sum Ritzer owed it before paying Walter (P).

RULE OF LAW

Absent insolvency, a bank does not have a priority of right in equity where it seeks to set off an unmatured indebtedness.

FACTS: After Ritzer opened a commercial account with National City Bank of Cleveland (National) (D), National (D) made a loan to Ritzer, against collateral of an unmatured 90-day promissory note for $3,600, despite knowing that Ritzer was insolvent. Subsequently, when Walter (P) recovered a judgment against Ritzer for $6,831.95, he served National (D) by mail as garnishee with an order in aid of execution. At the time of service, Ritzer had on deposit with National (D) the sum of $3,651.75 and the unmatured debt on National's (D) promissory note, which then totaled $3,626.25, interest included. After National (D) set off the amount of its loan, leaving a balance of $25.50, it mailed this amount to Walter (P) to satisfy his judgment. Consequently, Walter (P) sued National (D) for conversion, claiming a priority of right to the funds in Ritzer's account. At trial, both sides moved for summary judgment, and the district court granted Walter's (P) motion, which was affirmed on appeal. National (D) appealed.

ISSUE: Absent insolvency, does a bank have a priority of right in equity where it seeks to set off an unmatured indebtedness?

HOLDING AND DECISION: (Stern, J.) No. Absent insolvency, a bank does not have a priority of right in equity where it seeks to set off an unmatured indebtedness. This rule represents the general principle courts have applied to unmatured indebtedness, which is in stark contrast to the principle followed when the indebtedness is matured. An unmatured debt is not presently due or collectible and is not available for setoff since setoff would alter the contract made by the parties. In the case of insolvency, however, a bank may set off an unmatured indebtedness where equitable principles dictate. In the instant case, since National (D) voluntarily granted Ritzer a loan on a 90-day promissory note, which had not matured, despite knowing that Ritzer was insolvent, the later, specific terms of this note controlled over the general language of National's (D) rules and regulations that would allow it to apply the balance of the commercial account to the note. Under these circumstances, the lower courts did not err in granting and upholding summary judgment in Walter's (P) favor. Affirmed.

ANALYSIS

According to § 362(a)(7) of the Bankruptcy Code, the filing of a petition in bankruptcy creates an automatic stay against creditor collection activity, specifically including the exercise of the right of setoff. Individuals injured by a violation of the automatic stay may sue under Bankruptcy Code § 362(h) and recover "actual damages, including costs and attorney fees, and, in appropriate circumstances, may recover punitive damages."

Quicknotes

CONVERSION The act of depriving an owner of his property without permission or justification.

INSOLVENT One's liabilities exceed one's assets; inability to pay one's debts.

Parr v. Security National Bank

Checking account holder (P) v. Bank (D)

Okla. Ct. App., 680 P.2d 648, 38 U.C.C. Rep. Serv. 275 (1984).

NATURE OF CASE: Appeal from denial of recovery of stop payment amount.

FACT SUMMARY: Parr (P) appealed from a decision denying her the right to recover the amount of a check paid by Security National Bank (the Bank) (D), upon which she had requested a stop payment, contending a single-digit error in the amount made in the stop payment order did not deprive the Bank (D) of a reasonable opportunity to stop payment.

RULE OF LAW

A single-digit error in the amount of a check in a stop payment order does not deprive a bank of a reasonable opportunity to act on the stop payment order.

FACTS: Parr (P) wrote a check to Champlin, mailing it on September 14, 1981. During the next two days, Parr (P), both by phone and in person, ordered payment stopped on the check. Both orders were accurate in their descriptions of the check except that a $0.50 error was made in identifying the amount of the check. The Security National Bank's (the Bank's) (D) computer keyed in the amount of the check, and, as a result, the Bank (D) paid the check on September 17, 1981. Parr (P) sued to recover the amount of the check, plus interest and attorney fees. The Bank (D) argued that Parr's (P) error as to the amount of the check relieved it from liability, as its computer was programmed to stop payment only if the amount of the check as reported was correct. The Bank (D) prevailed, and Parr (P) appealed, contending the error in the check amount did not deprive the Bank (D) of a reasonable opportunity to stop payment.

ISSUE: Will a single-digit error in the amount of a check in a stop payment order deprive a bank of a reasonable opportunity to act on the stop payment order?

HOLDING AND DECISION: (Reynolds, J.) No. A single-digit error in the amount of a check in a stop payment order does not deprive a bank of a reasonable opportunity to act on the stop payment order. Parr's (P) stop payment order was accurate in all respects except as to the reported check amount. The Universal Commercial Code (U.C.C.) contains the applicable law as to stop payment orders and makes clear the policy that losses through failure to stop payment should be borne by the banks. Most cases have held that a single-digit error in the reported check amount still provides the banks with notice of sufficient accuracy so as to allow the bank to stop payment. In those cases where a different result is reached, the bank has informed the customer of the importance of an accurate check amount. It is not contended that the Bank (D) informed Parr (P) that any discrepancy in check amount would prevent compliance with the stop payment order. With the check described with sufficient accuracy in other respects, and U.C.C. policy being clear, the Bank (D) should bear the responsibility for failing to have effected the stop payment order. Reversed and remanded.

ANALYSIS

Many states have amended the U.C.C. language so as to require more specificity in a stop payment order, somewhat relieving the bank of liability for failure to stop payment. These amendments are in part a response to the failure of the U.C.C. to keep pace with the advances associated with modern computerized banking techniques.

Quicknotes

STOP PAYMENT ORDER The demand by a customer that his bank not honor a check issued from the customer's account.

Canty v. Vermont National Bank

Account holder (P) v. Bank (D)

Vt. Super. Ct., 25 U.C.C. Rep. Serv. 2d 1184 (1994).

NATURE OF CASE: Motion for summary judgment in a suit to recover improperly paid funds.

FACT SUMMARY: The Internal Revenue Service (IRS) redeposited checks which had already been paid and received payment a second time.

RULE OF LAW

Where a bank has improperly paid on checks redeposited a second time, but the payment was to the IRS, a rebuttable presumption will be raised in favor of the bank that no harm has come to the depositor.

FACTS: Canty (P) had a checking account with Vermont National Bank (D). The Internal Revenue Service (IRS) asked Canty (P) for cancelled checks to verify that he had paid obligations owing to the IRS. The IRS then redeposited the cancelled checks, which Vermont National Bank (D) paid a second time. Canty (P) sued to recover the funds improperly paid twice.

ISSUE: If a bank improperly paid on checks redeposited a second time, but the payment was to the IRS, will it be presumed that no harm has accrued to the depositor?

HOLDING AND DECISION: (Katz, J.) Yes. Where a bank has improperly paid on checks redeposited a second time, but the payment was to the IRS, a rebuttable presumption will be raised in favor of the bank that no harm has come to the depositor. A depositor with a bank has a valid expectation that drafts drawn on his account will be paid out only once. However, a problem arises when a draft is paid on twice. If the twice-paid check satisfies some obligation, a recrediting of the account by the bank will unjustly enrich the depositor. The depositor will have both paid on an obligation and received a recredit. In this case, the problem is particularly clear. By recrediting Canty's (P) account, he would have both paid a future tax bill and received the funds back. Such an unjust enrichment cannot be proper. Since the IRS was the entity paid twice, it is presumed, as a matter of law, that Vermont National Bank (D) has raised a presumption that no actual loss has occurred. Canty's (P) motion for summary judgment is denied; unless he can show actual loss, his claims will be dismissed. His motion for punitive damages is also dismissed because Vermont National Bank (D) has raised meritorious defenses and because Canty (P) must win on the underlying claim before being able to raise a claim of wrongful litigation that would support such punitive damages.

ANALYSIS

This particular rule of law favors the bank at the expense of the depositor. Unjust enrichment could also be avoided if the bank was forced to recredit, but was given a right to recover, the funds improperly paid. The court's reasoning in this case is flawed. A depositor is harmed whenever funds are paid out in an unplanned fashion. Interest on the money is lost, but the harm may merely be the outrage at paying on an obligation sooner than was planned.

Quicknotes

OBLIGATION A debt; a duty that a person is legally or morally bound to perform; an action or forbearance that a party promises to do or refrain from doing.

REBUTTABLE PRESUMPTION A rule of law, inferred from the existence of a particular set of facts that is conclusive in the absence of contrary evidence.

UNJUST ENRICHMENT The unlawful acquisition of money or property of another for which both law and equity require restitution to be made.

Patriot Bank v. Navy Federal Credit Union

Certified check holder (P) v. Drawer/drawee certified check (D)

Va. Cir. Ct., 2002 WL 481129, 47 U.C.C. Rep. Serv. 2d 662 (2002).

NATURE OF CASE: Check enforcement action on a certified check.

FACT SUMMARY: Patriot Bank (Patriot) (P) brought a check enforcement action against Navy Federal Credit Union (NFCU) (D) for refusing to honor a cashier's check that NFCU (D) had issued.

RULE OF LAW

A bank that issues a cashier's check is obligated to pay on it according to terms at the time it was issued, unless it has a recognized defense.

FACTS: Thomas Peeso, a member of Navy Federal Credit Union (NFCU) (D), obtained a cashier's check from NFCU (D) in the amount of $7,000 to use for the purchase of an automobile. He delivered the check to Nation's Auto Loan Center (Nation's) in exchange for the vehicle and endorsed the check with his signature made payable to Nation's. Nation's, in turn, endorsed the check with its account number and deposited the check with Patriot Bank (Patriot) (P) who credited the $7,000 to Nation's account and then submitted the cashier's check to NFCU (D) for payment. NFCU (D) denied reimbursement because it questioned Nation's endorsement on the check and returned it to Patriot (P) demanding Patriot (P) guarantee the endorsement made by its customer, Nation's, prior to paying on the cashier's check. In the meantime, Peeso had received a call from Nation's informing him that NFCU (D) had refused payment because the check was defective in some manner. Consequently, Peeso requested NFCU (D) to stop payment on the cashier's check and issue him a new one. NFCU (D), knowing that demand for payment had been made on the first check, issued the second cashier's check to Peeso who again presented it to Nation's. This time Nation's negotiated the second check with a different institution and NFCU (D) honored that check. Patriot (P), after having the first check returned to it by NFCU (D), attempted to reverse the credit it gave Nation's only to discover that Nation's account was overdrawn and that Nation's had ceased doing business. Patriot (P) filed suit against NFCU (D) for refusal to honor the check. While suit was pending, Patriot (P) again attempted to negotiate the check with NFCU (D) noting it was to be negotiated according to the payee's instructions absent a guaranteed endorsement, and this time NFCU (D) refused, stating it was honoring Peeso's stop payment request.

ISSUE: Is a bank that issues a cashier's check obligated to pay on it according to terms at the time it was issued, unless it has a recognized defense?

HOLDING AND DECISION: (Roush, J.) Yes. A bank that issues a cashier's check is obligated to pay on it according to terms at the time it was issued, unless it has a recognized defense. (Universal Commercial Code (U.C.C.) § 8.3A-412.) A cashier's or certified check is a draft where the drawer and drawee are the same. (U.C.C. § 8.3A-04(g)). When a bank issues a cashier's check it is the same as assuming liability on a promissory note. The customer purchases the check. As such, a customer has no authority to stop payment because it is not the equivalent of a check drawn on a customer's account. (U.C.C. § 8.4-403, Official Comment 4.) Nation's used its account number as its endorsement on the cashier's check. This bank account number satisfies the U.C.C.'s definition of an endorsement which can be "any symbol executed or adopted by a party with the present intention to authenticate a writing. (U.C.C. § 8.1-201(39)). Because the cashier's check was properly endorsed, and because Peeso had no authority to stop payment on the check, NFCU (D) was obligated to pay Patriot (P) when it presented the check to NFCU (D), absent a defense NFCU (D) might have, such as the customer's refusal to pay for the check. In this instance, NFCU (D) has no defense of its own and it cannot raise any defenses that the remitter, or purchaser of the check, might have. (U.C.C. § 8.3A-411, Official Comment 2.) U.C.C. § 8.3A 411(b) provides that if an obligated bank wrongfully refuses to pay on a cashier's or certified check, that the person entitled to cash the check is entitled to compensation, the cost of recovery and lost interest, and to consequential damages if the obligated bank had received notice of the circumstances giving rise to those damages. NFCU (D) wrongfully refused payment to Patriot (P) on the cashier's check. The court entered judgment in favor of Patriot (P) in the amount of $7,000 plus interest, attorney's fees of $5,700, and costs of $186.26.

ANALYSIS

Once a bank certifies a check, the bank as payor becomes the primary obligor on the instrument. As such, the person who is essentially purchasing the check from the bank has no right to stop payment or require the bank to breach the contract that is formed when the bank becomes the primary obligor. The instrument is treated similarly to a promissory note and the bank is obligated to pay on the note when presented by a proper holder. The same is true for cashier's checks, where the bank is both drawer and drawee; and with teller's checks, where a check is drawn

Continued on next page.

by one bank on another. Because the customer has no right to stop payment on these types of checks, the drafters of the U.C.C. proposed an addition to solve the problem that results if these types of instruments are lost or stolen. The new provision, U.C.C. § 3-312, allows the person who lost the check to file a declaration of loss with the issuing bank. If the check is not presented to the bank by an entity entitled to enforce it within 90 days, then the amount of the check is paid to the person filing the declaration of loss.

Quicknotes

STOP PAYMENT ORDER The demand by a customer that his bank not honor a check issued from the customer's account.

Rock Island Auction Sales, Inc. v. Empire Packing Co.

Seller (P) v. Buyer (D)

Ill. Sup. Ct., 32 Ill. 2d 269, 204 N.E.2d 721 (1965).

NATURE OF CASE: Appeal from award of damages for breach of the "midnight deadline."

FACT SUMMARY: Illinois National Bank (D), the payor bank of a check, held it past the statutory deadline for dishonoring a check.

RULE OF LAW

A payor bank which holds a check past the dishonoring deadline is liable when a party is damaged thereby.

FACTS: Rock Island Auction Sales, Inc. (Rock Island) (P) sold certain cattle to Empire Packing Co. (Empire) (D). Empire (D) paid with a check drawn from Illinois National Bank (Illinois National) (D). Rock Island (P) deposited the check, and it was sent by the depository bank to Illinois National (D) on September 27, 1962. Illinois held it until October 2 before dishonoring it due to insufficient funds and returning it. Empire (D) later declared bankruptcy. Rock Island (P) brought an action against Illinois National (D) for damages it suffered as a result of the delay in dishonoring the check. The trial court awarded Rock Island (P) the amount of the check, and Illinois National (D) appealed.

ISSUE: Is a payor bank which holds a check past the dishonoring deadline liable when a party is damaged thereby?

HOLDING AND DECISION: (Schaffer, J.) Yes. A payor bank which holds a check past the dishonoring deadline is liable when a party is damaged thereby, Universal Commercial Code § 4-302 provides that a payor bank is accountable for the amount of a check if it does not honor or dishonor the check by midnight of the banking day it is received. In the context of this statute, "accountable" is synonymous with "liable," Illinois National's (D) protestations to the contrary notwithstanding. The disparate treatment between depository and payor banks does not violate equal protection because the legislature could rationally conclude that they are in materially different positions in the check-processing chain. Here, since Illinois National (D) held the check for well past the statutory deadline, it is liable therefor. Affirmed.

ANALYSIS

Federal legislation has, since this case was decided, marginally affected § 4-302. The Expedited Funds Availability Act allows a bank to miss the midnight deadline, so long as the check gets back to the presenting bank the next day. In practice, the difference is minimal, and the effect is the same.

First National Bank of Chicago v. Standard Bank & Trust

Bank (P) v. Bank (D)

172 F.3d 472 (7th Cir. 1999).

NATURE OF CASE: Action for declaratory judgment.

FACT SUMMARY: First National Bank of Chicago (NBD at the time of the suit) (P) brought suit seeking declaratory judgment alleging that Standard Bank & Trust (D) failed to return some $4 million in checks to NBD (P) in a timely fashion as required by federal law.

RULE OF LAW

The Universal Commercial Code's (U.C.C.'s) "midnight deadline" does not apply with respect to checks returned in order to avoid a check-kiting scheme.

FACTS: An individual presented checks to both First National Bank of Chicago (NBD at the time of the suit) (P) and Standard Bank & Trust (Standard) (D) for approximately $4 million. NBD (P) opted not to honor the checks and Standard (D) also attempted to dishonor the checks. NBD (P) brought suit alleging that Standard (D) failed to return the checks in a timely fashion under the Expedited Funds Availability Act. The district court granted summary judgment to Standard (D) and awarded Standard (D) prejudgment interest on the returned checks. Standard (D) claimed it was entitled to the prime rate, but the court used the three-month Treasury Bill rate compounded quarterly. Both parties appealed.

ISSUE: Does the U.C.C.'s "midnight deadline" apply with respect to checks returned in order to avoid a check-kiting scheme?

HOLDING AND DECISION: (Flaum, J.) No. The U.C.C.'s "midnight deadline" does not apply with respect to checks returned in order to avoid a check-kiting scheme. The issue here is whether Standard's (D) return of the checks complies with Federal Reserve Board Regulation CC sec. 229.30(c)(1), which extends the U.C.C.'s "midnight deadline." NBD (P) argued the extension did not apply here since the legislative history of the regulation indicates the extension was intended to be limited to banks regularly using courier services to return checks. First, the plain language of the regulation must be considered before resorting to legislative history. The regulation's plain language extends the U.C.C. deadline when a paying bank expedites delivery of a returned check. Moreover, the use of the singular "check" indicates that the regulation was intended to apply to one-time singular check transactions. This reading is further substantiated by the second clause of the regulation, which allows a bank to extend the deadline when it "uses a means of delivery that would ordinarily result in the returned check being received by the bank to which it is sent on or before the receiving bank's next business day following the otherwise applicable deadline." Furthermore, the board issued a clarifying amendment to remove any doubt as to whether the midnight deadline applies to checks returned to avoid a kiting scheme. The district court's finding that NBD (P) should have honored the checks was correct. Judgment on pleadings in favor of Standard (D) affirmed. Grant of prejudgment interest vacated and remanded to enter an award consistent with the average prime rate for the applicable period.

ANALYSIS

The U.C.C.'s "midnight deadline" permits a paying bank to dishonor or revoke payment on a check before midnight in the following business day after receiving the check. The purpose of the U.C.C. provision is to expeditiously deal with dishonored checks; however, the regulation in issue here extends the requirement that the return process be commenced by midnight on the basis that it might have the indirect effect of slowing the process since many banks would elect to return the checks by mail rather than wait until the following day to dispatch a courier service.

Quicknotes

DECLARATORY JUDGMENT A judgment of the court establishing the rights of the parties.

Valley Bank of Ronan v. Hughes

Bank (P) v. Depositor (D)

Mont. Sup. Ct., 334 Mont. 335, 147 P.3d 185 (2006).

NATURE OF CASE: Appeal from summary judgment for plaintiff/counterclaim defendant and from exclusion of evidence in action for foreclosure on a promissory note.

FACT SUMMARY: **Hughes (D) claimed that the Universal Commercial Code (U.C.C.) did not preempt his common law and equitable counterclaims arising from alleged misrepresentations the personnel at Valley Bank of Ronan (Valley Bank) (P) made to him in connection with the check settlement process used by the bank, so that summary judgment should not have been granted to Valley Bank (P) in its action to foreclose on a promissory note Hughes (D) had given to the bank. [Hughes (D) raised other issues that were mentioned, but not treated, in the casebook extract.]**

RULE OF LAW

The U.C.C. does not preempt common law and equitable claims relating to misrepresentations made by a bank's personnel regarding the settlement process.

FACTS: Hughes (D) was taken in by a scam that involved him advancing fees, some of which were wire transferred from his accounts at Valley Bank of Ronan (Valley Bank) (P). As part of the scam, Hughes (D) received four checks totaling $1.632 million from the con artists, two that were purportedly "official" and two that were personal. Prior to depositing the checks, Hughes (D) requested that a cashier and officer verify the validity of the official checks, and she allegedly informed him that they were the same as cash and just like cashier's checks. Four days later, Hughes (D) delivered a written transfer order to Valley Bank (P) to wire $800,000 to a bank in Jordan, and the transfer was effected around 1:51 p.m. that day. The funds were promptly withdrawn (and never to be seen again) from the Jordanian bank. About ten minutes later, Hughes (D) and Valley Bank (P) learned that one of the personal checks was returned for insufficient funds, and later it became clear the "official" checks were counterfeit. Hughes (D) immediately requested that the wire transfer be reversed, but this effort failed, resulting in Hughes's (D) account being overdrawn by $800,000. Valley Bank (P) exercised its right to charge back the account and collect the funds from Hughes (D). Ultimately, Hughes (D) defaulted on a promissory note he had given to the bank to secure repayment of the charge-back, and Valley Bank (P) brought suit for judicial foreclosure. Hughes (D) asserted various counterclaims, including negligence, negligent misrepresentation, constructive fraud, unjust enrichment, breach of contract, breach of the implied covenant of good faith and fair dealing, promissory estoppel, and intentional infliction of emotional distress (which was later abandoned). The trial court granted summary judgment to Valley Bank (P) on its claims and against Hughes (D) on his counterclaims, as well as ruling to exclude an expert for Hughes (D). The state's highest court granted review. [The casebook presents only the part of the appellate court's decision that treats the issue of whether the U.C.C. preempted Hughes's (D) common law and equitable claims.]

ISSUE: Does the U.C.C. preempt common law and equitable claims relating to misrepresentations made by a bank's personnel regarding the settlement process?

HOLDING AND DECISION: (Rice, J.) No. The U.C.C. does not preempt common law and equitable claims relating to misrepresentations made by a bank's personnel regarding the settlement process. Part of the typical settlement process that is encouraged by the U.C.C. is "provisional settlement" whereby a bank credits a deposited check to the depositor's account before the bank has received payment from the drawee bank (i.e., before "final settlement"). The U.C.C. supports this by providing that if the drawee bank dishonors the check, the bank may charge back the amount it has credited to the depositor's account. Hughes (D) argues that preemption of his common law and equitable claims (based on the representations made to him by the bank personnel regarding the official checks) does not occur because there are no regulations or U.C.C. provisions that expressly regulate promises and representations that bank personnel make to their customers. The trial court correctly noted that the U.C.C. provides that where there is no express U.C.C. provision, common law and equity principles supplement its provisions, but do not supplant the U.C.C. provisions where doing so would be in direct conflict with them. Under the U.C.C., a bank must use "ordinary care" (follow reasonable commercial standards) to settle checks. Here, there were two actions by Valley Bank (P): (1) the settlement of the deposited checks and (2) the alleged representations about the settlement process. The trial court failed to distinguish the application of "ordinary care" to these two actions. The U.C.C. expressly provides that a bank does not have a duty to examine instruments such as checks to meet the ordinary care standard. Therefore, the trial court was correct in concluding that to the extent that Hughes's (D) common law claims related to Valley Bank's (P) processing of the checks, they were

Continued on next page.

preempted by the U.C.C. In fact, the U.C.C. also expressly provides that charge-back is permitted even where nonpayment occurs as a result of the depositary bank's own negligence, so that whether Valley Bank (P) exercised ordinary care is irrelevant to Hughes's (D) claims relating to check processing. However, as to his claims about the bank's communications to him regarding the check processing, the U.C.C. does not have express provisions governing that situation, so that common law and equity principles supplement the U.C.C. in that regard. For this reason, the trial court erred by concluding that the U.C.C. preempted common law and equitable principles with respect to the alleged misrepresentations. Thus, while Hughes (D) must repay Valley Bank (P) to satisfy its charge-back rights it nevertheless is possible for Hughes (D) to obtain a judgment to compensate him for the charge-back debt. Cases from other states, which the trial court erroneously determined supported preemption, in fact support the opposite result. In each of those cases, although the defendant bank was granted summary judgment, the decisions intimated that common law and equity principles may supplement the U.C.C. where the bank breaches a duty to its depositor by misrepresenting the status of the check settlement process. Affirmed in part, reversed in part, and remanded.

ANALYSIS

Under the holding of this case, it seems that while UCC § 4-212(4) will not hold liable for charge-back a bank whose employee inadvertently in some remark misleads a customer as to the precise likelihood that an item will clear, the bank may be liable for an affirmative representation that the bank has made final settlement on an account when in fact it has not and the depositor relies on that representation.

Quicknotes

BREACH OF CONTRACT Unlawful failure by a party to perform its obligations pursuant to contract.

CONSTRUCTIVE FRAUD Breach of a duty at law or in equity that tends to deceive another to whom the duty is owed, resulting in damages.

IMPLIED COVENANT OF GOOD FAITH AND FAIR DEALING An implied warranty that the parties will deal honestly in the satisfaction of their obligations and without an intent to defraud.

INTENTIONAL INFLICTION OF EMOTIONAL DISTRESS Intentional and extreme behavior on the part of the wrongdoer with the intent to cause the victim to suffer from severe emotional distress, or with reckless indifference, resulting in the victim's suffering from severe emotional distress.

NEGLIGENCE Conduct falling below the standard of care that a reasonable person would demonstrate under similar conditions.

NEGLIGENT MISREPRESENTATION A misrepresentation that is made pursuant to a business relationship, in violation of an obligation owed, upon which the plaintiff relies to his detriment.

PROMISSORY ESTOPPEL A promise that is enforceable if the promisor should reasonably expect that it will induce action or forbearance on the part of the promisee, and does in fact cause such action or forbearance, and it is the only means of avoiding injustice.

PROMISSORY NOTE A written promise to tender a stated amount of money at a designated time and to a designated person.

UNJUST ENRICHMENT Principle that one should not be unjustly enriched at the expense of another.

CHAPTER 12

Wrongdoing and Error

Quick Reference Rules of Law

Leeds v. Chase Manhattan Bank, N.A.

Payee on check (P) v. Bank (D)

N.J. Sup. Ct. App. Div., 752 A.2d 332, 42 U.C.C. Rep. Serv. 2d 195 (2000).

NATURE OF CASE: Appeal from summary judgment dismissing strict liability for conversion for payment on an altered check by the depository bank and the drawer/drawee/payor bank.

FACT SUMMARY: A Summit Bank teller's check made payable to William Leeds, Carol Leeds (mother and son, hereinafter "Leeds") (P) and Isabel Gibbs was altered by Leeds's attorney to be made payable to the attorney. The attorney deposited the altered check in an account with Chase Manhattan Bank, N.A. (Chase) (D) and Summit Bank (Summit) (D) honored the check. The attorney paid monies owing to Leeds (P) out of an account the attorney held at Trust Company of New Jersey (Trustco) by using monies that rightfully belonged to Shrewsbury State Bank (Shrewsbury). Trustco sought repayment of the monies traceable to the attorney's fraud from the attorney, as well as from Leeds (P). Leeds (P) then brought suit alleging strict liability for conversion for payment on the altered check against both Chase (D) and Summit (D).

RULE OF LAW

(1) Where a payee's agent wrongfully alters an instrument so that it is payable to the agent, a depository bank is strictly liable for conversion of the altered instrument.

(2) Where a payee's agent wrongfully alters an instrument so that it is payable to the agent, a drawer/drawee/payor bank is not strictly liable for conversion of the altered instrument.

FACTS: Leeds (P) hired Egnasko, an attorney, for his representation in a real estate transaction. Egnasko accepted a settlement check for $87,293.56 on Leeds's (P) behalf. The check was made payable to Leeds (P) and was a Summit Bank (Summit) (D) teller's check. Unbeknownst to Leeds (P), Egnasko altered the check by making it payable to himself as attorney for Leeds (P). Egnasko then deposited the check into his attorney trust account with Chase Manahattan Bank, N.A. (Chase) (D). Summit (D) honored its own check upon presentment. Then Egnasko drew a check for $92,050 payable to Leeds (P) from another attorney trust account he had at Trust Company of New Jersey (Trustco). However, the funds in that account came from Egansko's alteration of a check payable to Shrewsbury State Bank (Shrewsbury). Facing a claim of conversion from Shrewsbury, Trustco filed suit against Egnasko and Leeds (P) in New York, seeking repayment of the monies traceable to Egnasko's fraud. Leeds (P) contested liability in that action and then filed an action alleging strict liability for conversion against Chase (D), as the depository bank, including damages related to the cost of defending the New York action, and Summit (D), as the drawer/drawee/payor bank. The defendants moved for summary judgment, which the trial court granted. Leeds (P) appealed.

ISSUE:

(1) Where a payee's agent wrongfully alters an instrument so that it is payable to the agent, is a depository bank strictly liable for conversion of the altered instrument?

(2) Where a payee's agent wrongfully alters an instrument so that it is payable to the agent, is a drawer/drawee/payor bank strictly liable for conversion of the altered instrument?

HOLDING AND DECISION: (Wecker, J.)

(1) Yes. Where a payee's agent wrongfully alters an instrument so that it is payable to the agent, a depository bank is strictly liable for conversion of the altered instrument. The check was not delivered to Leeds (P); it was delivered to Egnasko as Leeds's (P) attorney. Therefore, Leeds (P) is entitled to bring the action for conversion against Chase (D) as one who received delivery of the instrument through delivery to an agent. Section 3-420a of the Universal Commercial Code (U.C.C.) makes it clear that Egnasko was a person, who by virtue of his altering the check, was not entitled to enforce the check or receive payment on it—his actions constituted forgery. By crediting Egnasko's account, Chase (D) paid a person not entitled to receive payment. Under the U.C.C., a depository bank is strictly liable for conversion on a forged instrument. Therefore, Chase (D) is strictly liable on Leeds's (P) claim for conversion. Chase (D) had argued in favor of its summary judgment motion that Leeds (P) had been paid and therefore suffered no damages. This defense of payment is not persuasive in light of Leeds's (P) continuing exposure to the New York action, and Chase (D) is not entitled to summary judgment. Reversed and remanded.

(2) No. Where a payee's agent wrongfully alters an instrument so that it is payable to the agent, a drawer/drawee/payor bank is not strictly liable for conversion of the altered instrument. A drawee bank, like Summit (D), is strictly liable for conversion when it pays on a forged endorsement. However, U.C.C. § 3-420a limits damages for conversion where the actions by such a party have been made in good faith. Here, there were no

Continued on next page.

allegations that Summit (D) acted in bad faith, and, therefore, it cannot be liable to Leeds (P) for conversion. Summary judgment is, therefore, affirmed in favor of Summit (D).

ANALYSIS

Although Leeds's (P) strict liability action against Summit (D) failed, Leeds (P) could have brought an action against Summit (D) for negligence. Because Summit (D) was the drawer of the check, Leeds (P) would likely have had a strong case that Summit (D) was negligent in failing to detect the alteration on its own teller's check.

Quicknotes

CONVERSION The act of depriving an owner of his property without permission or justification.

FRAUD A false representation of facts with the intent that another will rely on the misrepresentation to his detriment.

STRICT LIABILITY Liability for all injuries proximately caused by a party's conducting of certain inherently dangerous activities without regard to negligence or fault.

Price v. Neal

Lender (P) v. Borrower (D)

K.B., 3 Burr. 1354, 97 Eng. Rep. 871 (1762).

NATURE OF CASE: Action seeking recovery on a draft with a forged drawer's signature.

FACT SUMMARY: Price (P) accepted as payment of a debt a pair of drafts endorsed by Neal (D) which had been forged prior to Neal's (D) possession of them.

RULE OF LAW

A drawee accepting a draft has no recourse against a good-faith endorser where the drawer's signature has been forged.

FACTS: Neal (D) owed £80 to Price (P). Neal (D) endorsed a pair of £40 drafts that had come into his possession, supposedly having been drawn on one Sutton. In fact, they had been forged and were worthless. Price (P) accepted the drafts as payment for the debt. When they were found to be forgeries, Price (P) sued Neal (D) for the debt.

ISSUE: Does a drawee accepting a draft have recourse against a good-faith endorser where the drawer's signature has been forged?

HOLDING AND DECISION: (L. Mansfield, J.) No. A drawee accepting a draft has no recourse against a good-faith endorser where the drawer's signature has been forged. Neal (D) acted innocently and in good faith. It is also true that Price (P) has no recourse against the forger and is also an innocent victim. In a situation such as this, it is incumbent on the drawee to inquire as to the genuineness of the drawer's signature, but not incumbent on the endorser. Therefore, if there is any neglect here, it is on Price's (P) part. Even if neither party had been negligent, since both parties were equally blameless, it would not be appropriate for the law to shift the loss from one innocent party to the other. Rather, the parties must be left as they were, with Price (P) bearing the loss.

ANALYSIS

The rule stated here still has much vitality. Essentially, a drawee accepting a negotiable instrument cannot pass off the risk of forgery. Uniform Commercial Code § 3-418 to some extent codifies this rule.

Quicknotes

GOOD FAITH REQUIREMENT An implied warranty that the parties will deal honestly in the satisfaction of their obligations and without an intent to defraud.

Decibel Credit Union v. Pueblo Bank & Trust Co.

Drawee bank (P) v. Presenting bank (D)

Colo. Ct. App., 996 P.2d 784, 43 U.C.C. Rep. Serv. 2d 941 (2000).

NATURE OF CASE: Appeal from summary judgment on breach of warranty of presentment and transfer claims.

FACT SUMMARY: Checks belonging to a customer of Decibel Credit Union (Decibel) (P) were stolen, the drawer's name was forged, and the checks were cashed at Pueblo Bank & Trust Co. (Pueblo Bank) (D) during a 40-day period. As soon as the forgeries were discovered, Decibel (P) notified Pueblo Bank (D) and demanded reimbursement from it. Pueblo Bank (D) declined, and Decibel (P) sued.

RULE OF LAW

Presentment and transfer warranties are not made to a drawee bank when a presenting bank submits for payment to the drawee bank a check that has on it a forged drawer's name.

FACTS: A thief stole blank checks furnished by Decibel Credit Union (Decibel) (P) to one of its customers. The thief forged the customer's signature on 14 checks totaling $2,350 and during a 40-day period cashed the forged checks at Pueblo Bank & Trust Co. (Pueblo Bank) (D) where the thief had an account. Pueblo Bank (D) processed all the forged checks through the Federal Reserve System to Decibel (P), and Decibel (P) paid the checks. When the customer discovered the forgeries upon receipt of his bank statement, the customer immediately notified Decibel (P), which in turn immediately notified Pueblo Bank (D). Decibel (P) made demand on Pueblo Bank (D) for reimbursement, and when Pueblo Bank (D) declined, Decibel (P) sued. The trial court granted summary judgment for Decibel (P) on the ground that Pueblo Bank (D) had triggered its presentment and transfer warranties when it submitted the checks to Decibel (P) for payment. Pueblo Bank (D) appealed.

ISSUE: Are presentment and transfer warranties made to a drawee bank when a presenting bank submits for payment to the drawee bank a check that has on it a forged drawer's name?

HOLDING AND DECISION: (Ruland, J.) No. Presentment and transfer warranties are not made to a drawee bank when a presenting bank submits for payment to the drawee bank a check that has on it a forged drawer's name. For purposes of the Universal Commercial Code (U.C.C.), Decibel (P) was the drawee bank and Pueblo Bank (D) was the presenting bank. With regard to the presentment warranty in § 4-208(a), subsection (a)(1) provides only a warranty that there are no unauthorized or missing endorsements on the check. Other subsections do not apply because the checks were not altered and because Pueblo Bank (D) had no knowledge of the forged signatures. If a bank in the position of Pueblo Bank (D) had to warrant that all signatures were genuine, the U.C.C.'s final payment doctrine, which creates certainty as to which bank must bear a loss, would be rendered meaningless. Therefore, Pueblo Bank (D) did not extend any presentment warranties to Decibel (P) when it presented the checks for payment. As to the transfer warranty, assuming there was a transfer here, it is well settled that a transfer warranty as to the genuineness of the drawer's signature does not apply for the benefit of the drawer bank. Therefore, Pueblo Bank (D) did not extend any transfer warranties to Decibel (P). Reversed and remanded.

ANALYSIS

The result in this case rests on the distinction between forgeries of the drawer's name and forgeries of endorsements. The reviewing court had the straightforward task of applying well established principles under the Code that the presentment and transfer warranties apply to forgeries of endorsements (unless there is knowledge on the part of the presenting bank of the forged drawer's name).

Quicknotes

WARRANTY An assurance by one party that another may rely on a certain representation of fact.

Wachovia Bank, N.A. v. Foster Bancshares, Inc.

Bank (P) v. Bank (D)

457 F.3d 619 (7th Cir. 2006).

NATURE OF CASE: Appeal from summary judgment for plaintiff in declaratory judgment action in diversity.

FACT SUMMARY: Foster Bancshares, Inc. (D), contended that it should not be liable for an altered or forged check presented to it and paid by Wachovia Bank, N.A. (Wachovia) (P) where Wachovia (P) had destroyed the paper check so that it was impossible to determine whether the check had in fact been altered or forged.

RULE OF LAW

Where a drawee bank has destroyed a paper check that has either been forged or altered, and consequently it is impossible to determine whether forgery or alteration is responsible for the lack of genuineness, liability does not rest with the drawee bank as opposed to the presenting bank.

FACTS: Choi, who had an account with Foster Bancshares, Inc. (Foster) (D), deposited a check payable to her in her Foster (D) account. The check had been drawn on Wachovia Bank, N.A. (Wachovia) (P) by MediaEdge. Foster (D) presented the check to Wachovia (P) for payment, and Wachovia (P) paid Foster (D) and debited MediaEdge's account. It was discovered, however, that the check had not been originally issued to Choi, who had withdrawn the money and vanished, but to a different party. Pursuant to normal and legally accepted practices, Wachovia (P) had destroyed the paper check and retained only a digital image of it. Consequently, it was not possible to determine if the check was an altered original or a forgery. MediaEdge sued Wachovia (P) for the amount of the check, and Wachovia (P) brought an action in federal district court for a declaratory judgment that, should MediaEdge prevail in its suit, Foster (D) would be required to indemnify Wachovia (P). Wachovia's (P) suit was based on the Universal Commercial Code's (U.C.C.'s) "presentment warranty," which provides that when a depositary bank (such as Foster (D) in this case), presents a check for payment by the bank that issued the check, it warrants that the check "has not been altered." The district court granted summary judgment to Wachovia (P). The court of appeals granted review.

ISSUE: Where a drawee bank has destroyed a paper check that has either been forged or altered, and consequently it is impossible to determine whether forgery or alteration is responsible for the lack of genuineness, does liability rest with the drawee bank as opposed to the presenting bank?

HOLDING AND DECISION: (Posner, J.) No. Where a drawee bank has destroyed a paper check that has either been forged or altered, and consequently it is impossible to determine whether forgery or alteration is responsible for the lack of genuineness, liability does not rest with the drawee bank as opposed to the presenting bank. The "presentment warranty" rule under the U.C.C. is that the depositary bank warrants that a check has not been altered, whereas the drawee bank warrants that the check has not been forged (U.C.C. 3-418(c)). These rules made sense in days prior to the availability of sophisticated digital copying technology by allocating loss to the party that was in the best position to avoid the loss at lowest cost. With the advent of such technology, while having a paper copy of the check might reveal whether the check has been altered or forged, there is no guaranty that such a determination can be made. Thus, both Foster (D) and Wachovia (P) are in a "tie" situation. The question is thus whether in cases of doubt forgery should be assumed [in which case Foster (D) wins] or alteration should be assumed (in which case Wachovia (P) wins). In such cases, under current law, the tie should go to the drawee bank. Both banks can take measures to help prevent fraud. The drawee bank, for example, can take measures to mark checks in a way that a forger could not discover and therefore duplicate. The depository bank, on the other hand, could adopt red flag rules for atypical deposits that would permit a delay of the deposit and further investigation. Foster (D), however, has not made a showing that retention of paper checks would in fact be a reasonable way to determine whether the drawee bank or the presenting bank should be liable for the loss. Foster (D) also did not present evidence that forgery of an entire check, versus alteration of an original, has become a prevalent practice, nor did it present evidence that banks have been contracting around the provisions of the U.C.C. relating to the warranties of drawee and presenting banks in cases such as this. But even if it had made these showings, the question of which bank would be the "cheaper cost avoider" would still be open. Therefore, in the face of such uncertainty, it does not make sense for a court to change well-settled law. If change is needed to appropriately respond to modern copying technology, that change should be left to the Uniform State Commissioners. Affirmed.

ANALYSIS

The reality of bank practice, given check truncation and electronic presentment, is that many payor banks do not recapture their drawers' checks and have no opportunity

Continued on next page.

to compare drawers' signatures with the signature cards. Some banks also engage in a practice called "bulk filing," in which the banks do not physically examine the checks at all if they are below a certain amount but simply file them away in bulk. If a check proves forged and the forger cannot be found, these banks recredit the drawers' accounts and look to their forgery insurance. A dwindling number of banks still examine all checks and return those with forged drawers' signatures before final payment occurs. These practices, of course, are economically driven.

Quicknotes

DRAWEE A person who is requested to pay a bill or draft.

DRAWER A person who requests another to pay a bill or draft by making or executing an instrument.

Hutzler v. Hertz Corp.

Claimant (P) v. Corporation (D)

N.Y. Ct. App., 39 N.Y.2d 209, 347 N.E.2d 627 (1976).

NATURE OF CASE: Appeal from award of damages for negligence.

FACT SUMMARY: After her attorney converted the proceeds of a settlement from Hertz Corp. (D) by forging her signature in the endorsement area on the back of a check, Hutzler (P) sued Hertz (D) for negligence.

RULE OF LAW

A party whose attorney forges an endorsement on a settlement check may not recover her converted funds from the tortfeasor.

FACTS: Hertz Corp. (D), as settlement of a tort claim against it by Hutzler (P), executed a check in the amount of $10,929, payable to her and Yudow, her attorney. To make it appear that Hutzler (P) endorsed the check, Yudow forged her signature, took the funds, and disappeared from the scene. Hutzler (P), upon learning of this, sued Hertz (D) for negligence and the drawee bank for conversion. The trial court granted summary judgment in favor of Hutzler (P), which the appellate division modified slightly. Hertz (D) appealed.

ISSUE: May a party whose attorney forges an endorsement on a settlement check recover her converted funds from the tortfeasor?

HOLDING AND DECISION: (Jasen, J.) No. A party whose attorney forges an endorsement on a settlement check may not recover her converted funds from the tortfeasor. An attorney retained to collect a debt is an agent and has at least apparent authority to receive payment from a settlor or judgment-debtor. From this relationship it has long been the rule that a debtor's liability is discharged when a check payable to the creditor is wrongfully endorsed by the creditor's agent and paid by the drawee bank. This is true in the attorney-client relationship. To hold otherwise would inject unhealthy uncertainty into legal transactions. It is true that Universal Commercial Code § 3-401(1) states that an unauthorized signature is inoperative against the person whose name is signed. However, under the aforementioned agency principles, a client in a situation such as Hutzler (P) is estopped from denying as unauthorized the signature of her agent. Reversed.

ANALYSIS

The rule stated here would appear to comport with the majority of jurisdictions in this country. It is embodied in the Restatement (Second) of Agency, at § 178. The view is that, between a blameless client and blameless tortfeasor, the client, who made the unwise attorney selection, should bear the loss.

Quicknotes

AGENT An individual who has the authority to act on behalf of another.

FORGERY The false preparation or modification of a written document with an intent to defraud another.

Auto-Owners Ins. Co. v. Bank One

Employer/fraud victim (P) v. Bank of employee (D)

Ind. Sup. Ct., 879 N.E.2d 1086, 64 U.C.C. Rep. Serv. 2d 1027 (2008).

NATURE OF CASE: Appeal from affirmance of summary judgment for defendant in action under § 3-405 of the Uniform Commercial Code (U.C.C.), asserting that a bank failed to exercise ordinary care in opening a bank account.

FACT SUMMARY: Auto-Owners Ins. Co. (Auto-Owners) (P) contended that Bank One (D) violated U.C.C. § 3-405 by not exercising ordinary care when it opened a personal account for Auto-Owners's (P) employee, Wulf, in the name of "Auto-Owners, Kenneth B. Wulf," without requiring any documentation or inquiring whether the account was for a business.

RULE OF LAW

A bank cannot violate U.C.C. § 3-405 merely through the manner in which it opens a new account.

FACTS: Wulf was an employee of Auto-Owners Ins. Co. (Auto-Owners) (P), an insurance company. Wulf worked as an adjustor, handling the file for each of his cases and the checks that Auto-Owners (P) received for subrogation and salvage. When a check arrived, clerical staff would open it and attach it to the relevant file before passing the check and file on to the adjustor. No other record was kept of such checks. It was the adjuster's responsibility to forward the checks back to clerical staff, who would then send the checks to Auto-Owners's (P) main office. It was Auto-Owners's (P) policy for all files to be reviewed by a manager every six months. Three years after starting to work for Auto-Owners (P), Wulf opened a personal account Bank One (D) in the name of "Auto-Owners, Kenneth B. Wulf." Wulf used a post office box as the address for the account. Bank One (D) did not request, nor did Wulf provide, any documents to confirm his authorization to open and use the account on behalf of Auto-Owners (P). The tax identification number obtained for the account was Wulf's social security number, rather than a number appropriate for a business entity. Wulf used a stamp that said "Auto Owners Insurance Deposit Only" to endorse checks made out to Auto-Owners and deposit them into his account. Wulf deposited a total of $546,000 meant for Auto-Owners (P) into his account over the course of almost eight year, until his fraud was discovered and his employment was terminated. Auto-Owners (P) brought suit against Bank One (D), alleging that Bank One (D) had failed to exercise ordinary care, as required by U.C.C. § 3-405, in its opening of Wulf's account, that this failure substantially contributed to Auto-Owners's (P) losses, and that Bank One (D) was liable for Auto-Owners's losses up to the moment of discovery, regardless of any statute of limitations. Bank One (D) denied that it had failed to exercise ordinary care at any time and contended that, in any event, a three-year statute of limitations precluded recovery for any checks paid three years before the fraud's discovery. The trial court granted Bank One's (D) motion for summary judgment and the state's intermediate appellate court affirmed. The state's highest court granted review.

ISSUE: Can a bank violate U.C.C. § 3-405 merely through the manner in which it opens a new account?

HOLDING AND DECISION: (Sullivan, J.) No. A bank cannot violate U.C.C. § 3-405 merely through the manner in which it opens a new account. The section requires ordinary care from a bank in the "paying" or "taking" of an instrument, and says nothing about opening a new account. Procedures in place to be applied during the opening of an account are often there for the protection of the bank, not a particular customer. In addition, in the absence of a bank's negligence, the statute shifts the burden for monitoring possibly wayward employees away from a bank and onto the employer. The rationale for this responsibility shift is that an employer is in a better position to select and supervise its employees than an outside bank, and an employer is also better able to put in place measures to prevent fraud among its employees. It is possible that the circumstances of opening an account could play a role in whether a bank has used ordinary care in paying or taking a check, but such circumstances would be among all the facts relating to the bank's conduct with respect to the bank's collection or payment of a check; the manner of opening an account, by itself, is not a focus of the rule. Under the circumstances of this case, the opening of the account does not bear on whether Bank One (D) exercised ordinary care in handling the checks deposited by Wulf. The opening of the account happened many years before any checks at issue were deposited (given the three-year limitations period) and all the checks deposited were for relatively small sums. Accordingly, the connection between Bank One's (D) handling of the checks and its opening of the account is minimal. In sum, Bank One (D) exercised ordinary care in taking and paying the checks proffered by Wulf. Moreover, even if Bank One (D) did not demonstrate ordinary care in its acceptance of the checks proffered by Wulf, Auto-Owners (P) must still show that such a lack of ordinary care "substantially contributed" to its losses. To determine whether conduct has substantially contributed to a loss, it must be determined whether the opening of the bank account was (1) a contributing factor to Auto-Owners's (P) loss and (2) whether the opening of

Continued on next page.

the bank account was a substantial factor in bringing the loss about—when viewing Bank One's (D) conduct in its entirety. Other than failing to use stringent procedures in opening the bank account, Bank One (D) seems to have followed required protocol in depositing checks from Wulf. Even if assuming that Bank One's (D) conduct in opening the account was a contributing factor to Auto-Owners's (P) loss, and meets the first part of the "substantially contributed" test, Bank One's (D) conduct was not a substantial factor in bringing that loss about under the second part of the test. In other words, when viewed in its entirety, Bank One's (D) conduct does not meet the "substantially contributed" test. Indeed, it appears that Auto Owners (P) was the substantial contributor to its own losses, given its less than rigorous monitoring of its files and incoming checks. Affirmed.

DISSENT IN PART: (Boehm, J.) Summary judgment was inappropriately granted because there are genuine issues of material fact as to whether Bank One (D) exercised ordinary care when it opened the account for Wulf. The tax identification number obtained for the account was Wulf's social security number, rather than a number appropriate for a business entity. More importantly, opening a bank account for a legal entity, such as a business corporation or insurance company, ordinarily requires proof of identity and authority in the form of tax identification numbers and corporate resolutions. Given the lack of corporate documentation, from Bank One's (D) point of view, the only owner the account could have was Wulf himself, as an individual perhaps using "Auto-Owners Insurance" as his assumed business name. If so, it was Bank One's (D) practice, and the practice throughout the industry, to obtain an assumed business name certificate to open such an account. All of this adds up to a genuine issue of material fact as to the Bank One's (D) exercise of ordinary care in opening the account. Additionally, the majority errs in limiting Bank One's (D) failure to exercise ordinary care to opening the account. When it came time to deposit checks into this account, Wulf showed up with checks payable to "Auto-Owners Insurance Company" and similar names. That payee would ordinarily be taken to be an insurance company, most of which are organized as corporations. Thus, it seems there is at least a jury question whether acceptance of such a check deposited into an individual's account with no authorizing documentation whatever constitutes failure to exercise "ordinary care" as that term is used in U.C.C. § 3-405(b). Thus, the opening of the account cannot be separated from Bank One's (D) taking and paying checks presented by Wulf. Whether acceptance of some or all of these deposits also constituted failure to exercise ordinary care is not resolvable on the evidence in the record. A comment to U.C.C. § 3-405 recognizes that the circumstances of opening an account may be relevant to whether ordinary care is exercised in subsequently accepting deposits into the account. Here, there is acceptance of checks payable to an insurance company, endorsed by a variant of the company's name, and deposited into an individual account created with none of the paperwork associated with a corporate account or an assumed business name. While the majority suggests that any requirements for opening an account in a corporate name are for the benefit of the bank, not the general public, U.C.C. § 3-405 provides for the bank's potential liability if it fails to exercise ordinary care, so that ordinary banking procedures, including those related to the opening of the account, are evidence relevant to that determination. Finally, as to the "substantial contribution" issue, even if the majority is correct that the evidence establishes that Auto-Owners (P) contributed substantially to its own loss, this does not warrant summary judgment for Bank One (D). That is because U.C.C. § 3-405 sets up a "pure" comparative negligence exercise. In such a regime, the plaintiff's negligence proportionally reduces, but does not eliminate, the right to recover, even if the plaintiff's negligence is greater than the defendant's. Bank One's (D) acceptance of the many checks deposited by Wulf over a period of years substantially contributed to Auto-Owners's (P) loss. The "extent" of that contribution compared to the lack of oversight attributable to Auto-Owners (P) is a jury question not resolvable on summary judgment.

ANALYSIS

U.C.C. § 3-405 is addressed to fraudulent endorsements made by an employee with respect to instruments with respect to which the employer has given responsibility to the employee. It covers two categories of fraudulent endorsements: Endorsements made in the name of the employer to instruments payable to the employer and endorsements made in the name of payees of instruments issued by the employer. This section applies to instruments generally but normally the instrument will be a check. Section 3-405 adopts the principle that the risk of loss for fraudulent endorsements by employees who are entrusted with responsibility with respect to checks should fall on the employer rather than the bank that takes the check or pays it, if the bank was not negligent in the transaction. Section 3-405 is based on the belief that the employer is in a far better position to avoid the loss by care in choosing employees, in supervising them, and in adopting other measures to prevent forged endorsements on instruments payable to the employer or fraud in the issuance of instruments in the name of the employer. As this case note, if the bank failed to exercise ordinary care, subsection (b) allows the employer to shift loss to the bank to the extent the bank's failure to exercise ordinary care contributed to the loss. "Ordinary care" is defined in § 3-103(a)(7). The provision applies regardless of whether the employer is negligent.

Continued on next page.

Quicknotes

ORDINARY CARE The degree of care exercised by a reasonable person when conducting everyday activities or under similar circumstances; synonymous with due care.

The Bank/First Citizens Bank v. Citizens and Associates

Depository bank (P) v. Drawer (D)

Tenn. Sup. Ct., 82 S.W.3d 259, 48 U.C.C. Rep. Serv. 2d 26 (2002).

NATURE OF CASE: Appeal from affirmance of judgment in declaratory action allocating loss of forged checks between the drawer and depository bank.

FACT SUMMARY: Citizens and Associates (D), the endorsement of whose three checks made payable to Allied Mortgage Capital Company (Allied Mortgage) were forged and deposited into the personal account of Allied Mortgage's branch manager, Gray, contended that Gray's depository bank, The Bank/First Citizens Bank ("First Citizens Bank" or "the bank") (P), could not assert under Uniform Commercial Code (U.C.C.) § 3-406 that Citizens and Associates (D) was precluded from asserting the forgery against First Citizens Bank (P), because First Citizens Bank (P) did not show that any failure by Citizens and Associates (D) to exercise ordinary care substantially contributed to the making of the forged endorsements.

RULE OF LAW

Where the endorsement on a drawer's check has been forged, a depository bank may not assert U.C.C. § 3-406 against the drawer absent a showing that the drawer's failure to exercise ordinary care substantially contributed to the making of the forged endorsement and the forger's posing as the intended payee.

FACTS: Gray, the branch manager of Allied Mortgage Capital Company (Allied Mortgage), convinced Citizens and Associates (D) to invest in Allied Mortgage as a franchisee—even though in reality Allied Mortgage was not seeking investors. Citizens and Associates (D) did not verify with Allied Mortgage whether it was seeking investors, but proceeded over a month to give three checks to Gray totaling around $50,000. Gray did not forward the checks to the main office. Instead, she forged the endorsements on the checks in the name of the corporation and deposited them into her personal account with The Bank/First Citizens Bank (First Citizens Bank) (P). Citizens and Associates (D) soon discovered the fraud and confirmed that Allied Mortgage did not license franchises and that Gray was not authorized to negotiate franchise agreements—even though she was authorized to accept documents and checks on Allied Mortgage's behalf. Citizens and Associates (D) then contacted First Citizens Bank (P) and demanded repayment of the face amounts of the checks, but First Citizens Bank (P) denied any liability on the instruments. First Citizens Bank (P) then filed suit seeking a declaration that it possessed no liability on the three checks. Citizens and Associates (D) counterclaimed against First Citizens Bank (P), alleging that the bank (P) failed to exercise ordinary care in taking the instruments and was liable under U.C.C. § 3-406. The trial court found that First Citizens Bank (P) failed to exercise ordinary care in taking the checks by permitting the deposit of checks made payable to a corporation into a personal account, especially when the corporation itself did not have an account with the bank. The court also found that Citizens and Associates (D) was negligent in delivering the checks to Gray without first confirming the transaction with Allied Mortgage. The trial court then allocated the loss of the instruments, as required by § 3-406(c), as 80 percent to Citizens and Associates (D) and 20 percent to First Citizens Bank (P). The state's intermediate appellate court affirmed, and the state's highest court granted review.

ISSUE: Where the endorsement on a drawer's check has been forged, may a depository bank assert U.C.C. § 3-406 against the drawer absent a showing that the drawer's failure to exercise ordinary care substantially contributed to the making of the forged endorsement and the forger's posing as the intended payee?

HOLDING AND DECISION: (Barker, J.) No. Where the endorsement on a drawer's check has been forged, a depository bank may not assert U.C.C. § 3-406 against the drawer absent a showing that the drawer's failure to exercise ordinary care substantially contributed to the making of the forged endorsement and the forger's posing as the intended payee. Under § 3-406, First Citizens Bank (P) may assert that Citizens and Associates (D) is precluded from asserting the forgery against the bank (P) by showing (1) that it took the instruments in good faith; (2) that Citizens and Associates (D) failed to exercise ordinary care; and (3) that this failure by Citizens and Associates "substantially contributed" to making of Gray's forged signatures. If the bank (P) cannot show even one of these elements, it will bear the entire loss. First Citizens Bank (P) has met its burden on the first element, because it took the instruments in good faith, with honesty in fact. Even though there is some evidence that the state's legislature intended to include in § 3-406 an objective element of good faith, which is shown by adherence to "reasonable commercial standards of fair dealing," the state's version of the U.C.C. ultimately failed to include this objective standard for Articles 3 and 4 (in which § 3-406 is found). Therefore, the general U.C.C. definition of good faith, meaning "honesty in fact in the conduct or transaction involved," is the one to be applied. Under this standard,

Continued on next page.

First Citizens Bank (D) took the instruments in good faith because it took the checks with an absence of a "knowing or reckless disregard of a customer's rights." While First Citizens Bank (P) was negligent in permitting the deposit of a check made payable to a corporation into an individual account, no evidence showed that it knowingly disregarded the rights of anyone, nor was there evidence support a finding that the bank acted recklessly in this regard. As to the second and third elements, the bank (P) has not met its burden. The requirements of "ordinary care" or "substantial contribution" as they relate to the conduct of a drawer are issues of first impression in this state. The U.C.C.'s official comments indicate that conduct is a substantial contribution to a forged signature if the conduct is a "contributing cause" of the signature and is "a substantial factor in bringing it about." The comment also notes that the "substantial contribution" standard "is meant to be less stringent than a 'direct and proximate cause' test." Relying on this comment, the intermediate court of appeals held that a drawer can be precluded under § 3-406 if the drawer negligently issues an instrument to a third party for delivery to the payee. Other courts, however, have held that only negligence which proximately relates or contributes to the forgery, and not merely to the issuance of the checks, would relieve a collecting bank of liability for improper payment of a fraudulently endorsed check. One court has gone even so far as holding, as a matter of law, that the drawer's negligence in issuing the instrument, without more, cannot substantially contribute to the forgery within the contemplation of § 3-406. This last view best comports with the language of the section, which speaks only of the drawer's negligence being a substantial contribution "to the making of a forged signature." Thus, a drawer's negligence leading to the unwarranted issuance of checks will not generally suffice to establish a defense under § 3-406. Rather, the party asserting the preclusion must show some causal relationship between the lack of ordinary care and the actual making of the forged signature, such that the drawer's negligence can be said to have substantially contributed to the ability of the unauthorized person to forge the payee's name and to pose as the intended payee. Here, Citizens and Associates' (D) negligence increased the possibility that Gray would forge the endorsement of Allied Mortgage and pose as the payee of the instruments to her bank. Citizens and Associates (D) only delivered these checks to an acknowledged agent of the payee that, according to testimony by an employee of Allied Mortgage, possessed the actual authority to receive checks on behalf of the payee. Without something more, this conduct alone simply cannot be said to have substantially contributed to the making of the forged endorsements. Reversed.

ANALYSIS

The court's holding in this case might have been different had Citizens and Associates' (D) negligence substantially contributed to the making of the forged endorsements, if, for example, it had left blank the name of the payees in the various checks or made the checks payable to Gray as an agent of Allied Mortgage. It should be noted that § 3-406 does not make the negligent party liable in tort for damages resulting from the forgery or alteration. If the negligent party is estopped from asserting the alteration or forgery, the person taking the instrument is fully protected because the taker can treat the instrument as having been issued in the altered/forged form.

Quicknotes

FORGERY The false preparation or modification of a written document with an intent to defraud another.

GOOD FAITH REQUIREMENT An implied warranty that the parties will deal honestly in the satisfaction of their obligations and without an intent to defraud.

ORDINARY CARE The degree of care exercised by a reasonable person when conducting everyday activities or under similar circumstances; synonymous with due care.

Peters v. Riggs Natl. Bank, N.A.

Representative of depositor's estate (P) v. Bank (D)

D.C. Ct. App., 942 A.2d 1163 (2008).

NATURE OF CASE: Appeal from grant of summary judgment to defendant in action for negligence, breach of contract, and violations of the Electronic Funds Transfer Act.

FACT SUMMARY: Peters (P), as the representative of his mother's estate, discovered that there had been what he suspected were unauthorized withdrawals from his mother's account with Riggs Bank (the Bank) (D), most of which occurred while she was incapacitated or deceased. He contended that notwithstanding that neither he nor his mother had notified the Bank (D) of any unauthorized transactions within 60 days, as required by the Bank's Rules and Regulations, his claims were not time-barred because the 60-day notification period was invalid, or, if the period was valid, because equitable considerations should toll the period.

RULE OF LAW

Failure to comply with a 60-day notice period for notifying a bank of unauthorized signatures or alterations will absolutely bar a bank customer's claim against the bank based on such unauthorized signatures or alterations, regardless of equitable considerations.

FACTS: Peter's (P) mother, Graves, had checking and savings accounts with Riggs Bank (the Bank) (D). When she opened the accounts, she entered into a customer agreement that included adoption of the Bank's Rules and Regulations, and executed a signature card. The Rules and Regulations provided that the Bank (D) would not be liable "for payments made and charged to your account . . . unless you notify us of an error, including . . . unauthorized payment or other irregularity within (a) sixty (60) calendar days . . . of the mailing date of the earliest statement describing the charge or deposit to your account." In June 2002, many years after she had opened the accounts, Graves had an incapacitating stroke, and around five months later, she died. Between May and December of 2002, someone withdrew money from her accounts through the writing of checks, phone transfers, and ATM withdrawals. Peters (P), who was appointed the personal representative of Graves's estate, discovered that these withdrawals totaled $131,278.61, and he suspected they had been unauthorized, although he could not be sure. He did, however, discover that the signature on some of the checks did not match that of his mother. In November 2003, Peters (P) communicated to the Bank (D) his suspicion that the Bank (D) may have improperly permitted the payment on unauthorized checks and allowed unauthorized ATM cash withdrawals. In August 2004, Peters (P) filed suit against the Bank (D) for negligence, breach of contract, and violations of the Electronic Funds Transfer Act (EFTA). The Bank (D) moved for summary judgment, claiming, inter alia, that the claims were time-barred. The trial court accepted the representations of the Bank (D) that it had sent monthly account statements to Graves, and that neither she nor Peters (P) had notified the Bank (D) of any unauthorized transactions in a timely manner. Accordingly, the court granted summary judgment to the Bank (D). The jurisdiction's intermediate appellate court granted review.

ISSUE: Will failure to comply with a 60-day notice period for notifying a bank of unauthorized signatures or alterations absolutely bar a bank customer's claim against the bank based on such unauthorized signatures or alterations, regardless of equitable considerations?

HOLDING AND DECISION: (Washington, C.J.) Yes. Failure to comply with a 60-day notice period for notifying a bank of unauthorized signatures or alterations will absolutely bar a bank customer's claim against the bank based on such unauthorized signatures or alterations, regardless of equitable considerations. The issue is governed by the jurisdiction's version of Uniform Commercial Code (U.C.C.) § 4-406(f), which imposes upon bank customers a duty to discover and report unauthorized signatures or alterations to the bank, and which provides for a one-year notification period. It is well-established in other jurisdictions that this period is not a statute of limitations, but, rather, a statutory prerequisite of notice, i.e., a statute of repose. Some courts have noted that the provision constitutes a condition precedent to the customer's right to file claims against a bank. In this jurisdiction, a statute of repose establishes an absolute time period within which legal proceedings must be initiated, regardless of when a cause of action accrues. Here, § 4-406(f) is a statute of repose, so that a customer who does not discover and report an unauthorized signature or alteration is precluded from asserting against the bank the unauthorized signature or alteration. Therefore, the next question is whether Riggs Bank (D) permissibly shortened the length of the statute of repose from one year to a period of 60 days. The U.C.C. itself permits contracting parties, within certain limits, to vary the U.C.C.'s terms, and the relationship between a bank and a depositor is a contractual relationship that is governed by the written agreement between the parties. Peters (P) contends that 60 days is too

Continued on next page.

short a period of time for a person to discover and report problems in their account. However, other jurisdictions that have considered this question have consistently upheld the contractual shortening of the notice provision to periods of 60 days or shorter. Such a contractual shortening does not alter a bank's duty to exercise ordinary care or good faith, but merely varies the U.C.C.'s contractual notice provision. A reasonable contraction of the discovery and notice period encourages due diligence by the customer in inspecting account statements, and it also promotes the U.C.C.'s goal of finality. For these reasons, contracting parties may shorten the notice period to 60 days. Notwithstanding the validity of the shortened notice period, Peters (P) contends that the notice provision should be tolled in this case because of Graves's incapacitation and subsequent death and because Peters (P) did not discover the unauthorized transactions until months after his mother's death. In essence, he requests equitable tolling of a statute of repose. Such a position, however, is untenable: equitable tolling cannot apply to statutes of repose. A statute of repose establishes an absolute time period within which legal proceedings must be initiated, regardless of when a cause of action accrues, i.e., regardless of when the plaintiff knew or should have known about the injury. Courts have applied this statutory bar even in cases where the result is harsh, and even where a customer has not actually received bank statements—even where the statements were intercepted by a forger. The bar is absolute, regardless of incapacity, mental competence, or other equitable considerations. This is because the certainty that the U.C.C. seeks to achieve in respect to commercial transactions would quickly dissipate if ad hoc exceptions to its commands were too eagerly crafted to accommodate the occasional "hard case." The rule upholds the underlying policies of the U.C.C. by encouraging the efficiency and finality of transactions through a uniform and predictable application of the law. For these reasons, § 4-406(f) is not subject to equitable tolling, and, because it is undisputed that neither Graves nor Peters (P) timely notified the Bank (D) of the unauthorized transactions, Peters's (P) claims are barred. Affirmed.

ANALYSIS

Peters (P) urged the court to adopt an exception to the rule carved out by a California appellate court. In *Mac v. Bank of Am.*, 76 Cal. App. 4th 562, 90 Cal. Rptr. 2d 476 (Cal. Ct. App. 1999), the court found that § 4-406 (f) did not apply and did not bar the claim of a personal representative to recover for unauthorized transactions that cleared after the account holder's death because § 4-406 (a) requires that statements be "made available to the customer," and in that case, there was no customer because the customer had died. The court in this case declined to adopt *Mac,* reasoning that it functionally imposes a discovery rule inconsistent with the principles underlying statutes of repose, as well as the policies of uniformity and predictability espoused by the U.C.C. The court also concluded that such an exception would create the type of ad hoc exception that other jurisdictions have avoided. Further, it would impose upon banks the duty of ensuring actual receipt—a logistical problem whose extra costs would undoubtedly be passed on to the consumer.

Quicknotes

STATUTE OF REPOSE A law prescribing the period of time in which an action can be commenced that begins to run upon the delivery of goods or the completion of performance.

Falk v. Northern Trust Co.

Account holder (P) v. Bank (D)

Ill. App. Ct., 763 N.E.2d 380, 46 U.C.C. Rep. Serv. 2d 302 (2001).

NATURE OF CASE: Appeal from dismissal of damages and accounting action as time-barred.

FACT SUMMARY: Falk's (P) personal assistant and bookkeeper misappropriated over $2 million from his accounts at The Northern Trust Co. (the Bank) (D) over the course of four years. He (P) sued the Bank (D) for damages and an accounting. His suit was dismissed as time-barred by § 4-406(f) of the Universal Commercial Code (U.C.C.)

RULE OF LAW

Section 4-406(f) of the U.C.C. does not bar suits brought beyond the time limitation set forth in that section where plaintiff-customer alleges that the bank acted in bad faith in paying items that are the subject of suit.

FACTS: Falk (P) employed Podmokly as his personal assistant and bookkeeper for over 13 years. In 1984, she was made a signatory on his accounts at The Northern Trust Co. (the Bank) (D) and held a position of a fiduciary with respect to Falk (P), a fact known to the Bank (D). In 1993, Podmokly began misappropriating funds from Falk's (P) accounts at the Bank (D) for her own benefit. Over the next four years, she misappropriated over $2 million from Falk (P). Podmokly maintained her own account at the Bank (D). Falk (P) sued the Bank (D) for damages and an accounting, claiming that the Bank (D) had been placed on notice of Podmokly's misappropriations because of the number of changes and irregularities in Falk's (P) accounts and by virtue of knowing her personal information—the Bank (D) was aware that her income was insufficient to support the account and loan activity she was generating. The Bank (D) moved to dismiss under U.C.C. § 4-406(f), which requires that a bank's customer notify the bank of any irregularities within one year after receiving his bank statements. The trial court granted the motion and dismissed. Falk (P) appealed.

ISSUE: Does § 4-406(f) of the U.C.C. bar suits brought beyond the time limitation set forth in that section where plaintiff-customer alleges that the bank acted in bad faith in paying items that are the subject of suit?

HOLDING AND DECISION: (Hall, J.) No. Section 4-406(f) of the U.C.C. does not bar suits brought beyond the time limitation set forth in that section where plaintiff-customer alleges that the bank acted in bad faith in paying items that are the subject of suit. An amendment to § 4-406 eliminated the requirement that the bank pay items in "good faith" in order for the customer to have to report unauthorized signatures or alterations to the bank within one year of receiving the items and a bank statement relating to those items. Prior to the amendment, the Seventh Circuit in *Appley v. West*, 832 F.2d 1021 (7th Cir. 1987), held that the time limitation did not apply where the plaintiff alleged that the bank acted in bad faith in allowing the plaintiff's fiduciary to misappropriate funds from plaintiff's accounts. The Bank (D) maintains that *Appley* is no longer controlling, given that the requirement the bank pay items in good faith was eliminated. However, *Appley* is persuasive precedent, unlike the cases the Bank (D) relies on, because it encompasses a scenario in which the Bank acted in bad faith in paying an item. The issue, then, is whether the amendment to § 4-406 requires a result different from that in *Appley*. As a matter of statutory construction, § 4-406(f) does not bar suits brought beyond the one-year time limitation where bad faith on the part of the bank is alleged. That is because the other subsections of § 4-406 now require the bank and the customer to share the loss where the bank did not use ordinary care in paying an item and because new § 4-406 now allows customers to avoid preclusion altogether if they can prove the bank did not pay an item in good faith. Moreover, the U.C.C. requires good faith in the performance of every duty or obligation. Therefore, the Bank (D) was required to pay the items in good faith in order to claim the protection of the one-year notice requirement in § 4-406(f)—the public policy behind that protection is not served where "the bank is a party, either actively or passively, to a scheme to defraud the customer." However, the customer must allege sufficient facts to establish "bad faith." Here, Falk (P) alleged sufficient facts to show that the Bank (D) was on notice that Podmokly was acting in breach of her fiduciary duties to Falk (P). Given the number of years and the number of transactions involved, the Bank's (D) failure to investigate was more than a lack of care. Thus, Falk (P) alleged sufficient facts to establish that the Bank (D) acted in bad faith. Reversed and remanded.

DISSENT: (Cerda, J.) Because the legislature did not insert a "good faith" requirement into § 4-406(f), the Bank (D) should not be required to have paid the items in dispute in good faith for the statute's one-year period to apply.

ANALYSIS

The definition of "bad faith" in the instant case does not have to do with dishonesty, but rather with whether it is

Continued on next page.

commercially unjustifiable for the payee to disregard and refuse to learn facts that are readily available. It is remaining passive, in the light of obvious circumstances, that constitutes "bad faith."

Quicknotes

BAD FAITH Conduct that is intentionally misleading or deceptive.

CHAPTER 13

Electronic Banking

Quick Reference Rules of Law

	PAGE
1. *Azur v. Chase Bank, USA.* (1) Section 1643 of the Truth in Lending Act does not provide a credit cardholder with a right to reimbursement for fraudulent charges made with the card. (2) A credit cardholder vests an agent with apparent authority to use the card sufficient to preclude claims brought under the Truth in Lending Act for the agent's fraudulent use of the card where the cardholder enables the continuous payment of the credit card charges over a period of time by failing to exercise oversight over the agent, failing to review his financial statements, and otherwise failing to separate the approval and payment functions within his cash disbursement process.	*142*
2. *Grain Traders, Inc. v. Citibank, N.A.* In the funds transfer context, the originator of the funds transfer is the party who bears the risk of loss.	*144*
3. *Corfan Banco Asuncion Paraguay v. Ocean Bank.* Acceptance of a wire transfer by the recipient bank is precluded where the name, bank account or other identifying information of the beneficiary is nonexistent or unidentifiable.	*146*
4. *Bank of America N.T.S.A. v. Sanati.* A bank is entitled to restitution from the beneficiaries for the amount of an unauthorized transfer despite its own negligence, unless the beneficiaries have, in good faith, applied the overpayment to a pre-existing debt owed by the originator.	*147*
5. *Experi-Metal, Inc. v. Comerica Bank.* Under U.C.C. § 4A-202, unauthorized wire transfer orders from a customer's account are not, as a matter of law, effective as orders of the customer where there are genuine issues of material fact as to whether the bank accepted the payment orders in good faith and in compliance with its security procedure and any written agreement or instruction of the customer restricting acceptance of payment orders issued in the name of the customer.	*148*

Azur v. Chase Bank, USA

Credit cardholder (P) v. Credit card issuer (D)

601 F.3d 212 (3d Cir. 2010).

NATURE OF CASE: Appeal from summary judgment for defendant in action under the Truth in Lending Act.

FACT SUMMARY: After Azur's (P) personal assistant, Vanek, misappropriated over $1 million from Azur (P) through the fraudulent use over the course of seven years of a credit card issued to Azur (P) by Chase Bank, USA (Chase) (D), Azur (P) claimed that Chase (D) was liable, inter alia, under §§ 1643 and 1666 of the Truth in Lending Act (TILA), and contended that § 1643 of TILA provided him with a right to reimbursement, and that his claims were not precluded because he had not vested Vanek with apparent authority to use the Chase (D) credit card.

RULE OF LAW

(1) Section 1643 of the Truth in Lending Act does not provide a credit cardholder with a right to reimbursement for fraudulent charges made with the card.

(2) A credit cardholder vests an agent with apparent authority to use the card sufficient to preclude claims brought under the Truth in Lending Act for the agent's fraudulent use of the card where the cardholder enables the continuous payment of the credit card charges over a period of time by failing to exercise oversight over the agent, failing to review his financial statements, and otherwise failing to separate the approval and payment functions within his cash disbursement process.

FACTS: Azur's (P) personal assistant, Vanek, misappropriated over $1 million from Azur (P) through the fraudulent use over the course of seven years of a credit card issued to Azur (P) by Chase Bank, USA (Chase) (D). Vanek's responsibilities consisted of picking up Azur's (P) personal bills, including his credit card bills, from a post office box; opening the bills; preparing and presenting checks for Azur (P) to sign; mailing the payments; and balancing Azur's (P) checking and savings accounts at Dollar Bank. It was Vanek's job alone to review Azur's (P) credit card and bank statements and contact the credit card company to discuss any odd charges. Azur (P) also provided Vanek with access to his credit card number to enable her to make purchases at his request. Azur (P) forgot that he had the Chase (D) credit card. In her position, Vanek was able to withdraw without authorization cash advances of between $200 and $700, typically twice a day, from the credit card account. Each fraudulent transaction included a fee and a finance charge. The fraudulent charges were reflected on at least 65 monthly billing statements sent by Chase (D) to Azur (P), and Vanek paid the bills by either writing checks or making on-line payments from Azur's (P) Dollar Bank checking account. When writing checks, Vanek forged Azur's (P) signature. On occasion, the transactions triggered Chase's (D) fraud detection strategies, but whenever Chase called to confirm the charges at the number it had on file, Vanek was able to verify the account's security questions and validate the card activity. When Azur (P) finally discovered the fraud, he immediately terminated Vanek, and the next day he notified Chase (D) by telephone of the fraudulent use of the Chase (D) account and closed the account. He subsequently sent written correspondence disputing his responsibility for unpaid charges as well as all prior fraudulent transactions on the account, and affirming the unauthorized use of the account. He then filed suit against Chase (D) under §§ 1643 and 1666 of the Truth in Lending Act, 15 U.S.C. §§ 1601 et seq. (2006), and common law negligence. Chase (D) moved for summary judgment, which the district court granted it. The court of appeals granted review.

ISSUE:

(1) Does § 1643 of the Truth in Lending Act provide a credit cardholder with a right to reimbursement for fraudulent charges made with the card?

(2) Does a credit cardholder vest an agent with apparent authority to use the card sufficient to preclude claims brought under the Truth in Lending Act for the agent's fraudulent use of the card where the cardholder enables the continuous payment of the credit card charges over a period of time by failing to exercise oversight over the agent, failing to review his financial statements, and otherwise failing to separate the approval and payment functions within his cash disbursement process?

HOLDING AND DECISION: (Fisher, J.)

(1) No. Section 1643 of the Truth in Lending Act does not provide a credit cardholder with a right to reimbursement for fraudulent charges made with the card. Therefore, Azur (P) cannot recover under § 1643 the moneys already paid to Chase (D). The statute's plain meaning places a ceiling on a cardholder's obligations under the law and thus limits a card issuer's ability to sue a cardholder to recover fraudulent purchases. The language of § 1643 does not, however, enlarge a card issuer's liability or give the cardholder a right to reimbursement. The section does not impose any obligation on issuers of credit cards to pay the costs associated with unauthorized or fraudulent use of credit cards. It simply limits the liability of cardholders, under certain circumstances,

Continued on next page.

to a maximum of $50 for unauthorized charges Indeed, § 1643 does not address, nor is it even concerned with, the liability of a card issuer or any party other than the cardholder for unauthorized charges on a credit card; it imposes liability only upon the cardholder. Affirmed as to this issue.

(2) Yes. A credit cardholder vests an agent with apparent authority to use the card sufficient to preclude claims brought under the Truth in Lending Act for the agent's fraudulent use of the card where the cardholder enables the continuous payment of the credit card charges over a period of time by failing to exercise oversight over the agent, failing to review his financial statements, and otherwise failing to separate the approval and payment functions within his cash disbursement process. Section 1643 provides that a cardholder is liable for the unauthorized use of a credit card in certain circumstances. The term "unauthorized use" is defined as the "use of a credit card by a person other than the cardholder who does not have actual, implied, or apparent authority for such use and from which the cardholder receives no benefit." Relatedly, § 1666(a) sets forth the procedures a creditor must follow to resolve alleged billing errors. Like the phrase "unauthorized use," the phrase "billing error" includes "[a] reflection on or with a periodic statement of an extension of credit that is not made to the consumer or to a person who has actual implied, or apparent authority to use the consumer's credit card or open-end credit plan." State law determines whether an agent has apparent authority. Under state law, apparent authority is power to bind a principal which the principal has not actually granted but which he leads persons with whom his agent deals to believe that he has granted. The test for determining whether an agent possesses apparent authority is whether a man of ordinary prudence, diligence and discretion would have a right to believe and would actually believe that the agent possessed the authority he purported to exercise. Other circuits have found apparent authority under circumstances similar to those presented here. The key to the finding of apparent authority in those circuits was that the cardholder's negligent omissions furthered the fraud or theft of by the unauthorized card user. In one case, a firm's failure to examine any of the credit card or bank statements created, as a matter of law, 'apparent authority for [the assistant's] continuing use of the cards, especially because it enabled [the assistant] to pay all of the American Express statements with forged checks, thereby fortifying American Express's continuing impression that nothing was amiss with the Corporate and Platinum Accounts." In another case, rather than fault the cardholder for merely failing to inspect monthly credit card statements, the court focused on the cardholder's continuous payment of the fraudulent charges without complaint—which stemmed from its failure to separate the approval and payment functions within its cash disbursement process. In that case, the court held that, as a matter of law, no reasonable juror could disagree that at some point the cardholder led the card issuer reasonably to believe that the fraudulent user had authority to use its card. The latter, more nuanced approach is the correct approach to take. Thus, a cardholder may, in certain circumstances, vest a fraudulent user with the apparent authority to use a credit card by enabling the continuous payment of the credit card charges over a period of time. By identifying apparent authority as a limitation on the cardholder's protections under § 1643, Congress recognized that the cardholder is oftentimes in the best position to identify fraud committed by its employees. Here, Azur's (P) negligent omissions led Chase (D) to reasonably believe that the fraudulent charges were authorized. Although Azur (P) may not have been aware that Vanek was using the Chase (D) credit card, or even that the Chase (D) credit card account existed, Azur (P) knew that he had a Dollar Bank checking account, and he did not review his Dollar Bank statements or exercise any other oversight over Vanek. Thus, he failed to separate the approval and payment functions within his cash disbursement process. Had he occasionally reviewed his statements, he would have likely noticed that checks had been written to Chase (D). Accordingly, Azur (P) vested Vanek with apparent authority to use the Chase (D) credit card, thus barring his §§ 1643 and 1666 claims. Affirmed as to this issue.

ANALYSIS

The courts have differentiated between the acquisition and use of a credit card obtained through fraud or theft. While the courts accept the proposition that the acquisition of a credit card through fraud or theft cannot be said to occur under the apparent authority of the cardholder, such acquisition does not preclude a finding of apparent authority for the subsequent use of a credit card so obtained. Thus, a cardholder would not be barred from bringing a claim under Truth in Lending Act where an unauthorized party, such as an employee or personal assistant, applies for and obtains an additional card to the account in that party's own name without the cardholder's knowledge.

Quicknotes

AGENT An individual who has the authority to act on behalf of another.

APPARENT AUTHORITY The authority granted to an agent to act on behalf of the principal in order to effectuate the principal's objective, which may not be expressly granted, but which is inferred from the conduct of the principal and the agent.

Grain Traders, Inc. v. Citibank, N.A.

Bank (P) v. Bank (D)

960 F. Supp. 784 (S.D.N.Y. 1997).

NATURE OF CASE: Diversity action seeking recovery of funds lost in an electronic funds transfer.

FACT SUMMARY: Grain Traders, Inc. (P) brought suit against Citibank, N.A. (D) seeking the refund of money it allegedly lost in the process of an electronic funds transfer.

RULE OF LAW

In the funds transfer context, the originator of the funds transfer is the party who bears the risk of loss.

FACTS: Grain Traders, Inc. (P) initiated a funds transfer designed to move $310,000 from Grain Traders (P) to Kraemer in one day. The transfer was to proceed as follows: (1) Grain Traders' (P) account at Banco de Credito Nacional (BCN) was to be debited $310,000; (2) the funds would be transferred to Banque Du Credit Et Investissement Ltd. (BCI) at Citibank, N.A. (D) by means of a debit to BCN's Citibank (D) account and a corresponding credit to BCI's Citibank (D) account; (3) the funds were in turn to be transferred from BCI to Banco Extrader, S.A.; and (4) the funds finally transferred to Kraemer's account at Extrader. Just before BCI's account at Citibank (D) was credited it was placed on a "hold for funds" status. Since BCI's account with Citibank (D) was overdrawn by more than $12 million, BCI was prevented from making further withdrawals from the account. Kraemer never received a credit to his account for the $310,000. Grain Traders (P) brought suit against Citibank (D) seeking a refund under Universal Commercial Code (U.C.C.) § 4-A-402, for a refund as well as reasonable expenses and attorney's fees under U.C.C. §§ 4-A-209, 4-A-301, and 4-A-305, for breach of the obligation to deal in good faith under § 1-203 and for conversion under the common law.

ISSUE: In the funds transfer context, is the originator of the funds transfer the party who bears the risk of loss?

HOLDING AND DECISION: (Chin, J.) Yes. In the funds transfer context, the originator of the funds transfer is the party who bears the risk of loss. In the first cause of action, Grain Traders (P) claims it is entitled to a refund under the "money back guarantee" of § 4-A-402. Citibank (D) argued that under that provision a party to a funds transfer may only recover against the next party or bank in line; thus Grain Traders (P) may only seek a refund from BCN. This court agrees. First the plain language of § 4-A-402 and other provisions of Article 4-A clearly states that a party to a fund transfer may only recover a refund from the specific party to whom it made payment. Moreover, § 4-A-402(5) makes clear that there is no right to a refund between the originator and an intermediary bank. The official comments to the section also state that when the originator chooses an intermediary bank that is financially unable to complete its part of the funds transfer, the originator bears the risk of loss. In addition, § 4-A-305(2) provides that a receiving bank is liable to the originator for interest and expenses under certain circumstances. This section shows that when the drafters of Article 4-A wanted to give the originator the right to bring a cause of action against any bank in the funds transfer chain, they knew how to make that clear. They failed to do so with respect to an intermediary bank. Thus summary judgment is granted for Citibank (D) as to the first claim for relief. Grain Traders (P) also alleged that since Citibank (D) intended to use the funds as a set-off to the debt owed by BCI, it did not intend to carry out the payment order received by BCN and thus did not constitute "execution" or "acceptance" under §§ 4-A-209 and 4-A-301. The record, however, shows that Citibank (D) properly executed the payment order it received, thereby satisfying its obligation to issue a payment order intended to carry out the payment order received by the sender. Thus the second claim for relief is dismissed. Grain Traders (P) also asserted Citibank's (D) conduct violated § 1-203, which imposes an obligation of good faith and fair dealing on a party's performance of or enforcement of any contract or duty within the scope of the U.C.C., seeking damages. Section 1-203 only imposes an obligation of good faith and fair dealing on the performance of a contract or duty. Here, no contract is alleged to have existed between Citibank (D) and Grain Traders (P). There is also no statutory duty since Grain Traders (P) failed to state a claim under Article 4-A. Since there is no contractual or statutory duty this claim is dismissed as well. Last, Grain Traders (P) asserted a claim for relief based on the common law torts of "conversion" and "money had and received." These claims must be dismissed as well since Grain Traders (P) failed to present evidence in support of either of these claims.

ANALYSIS

A funds (or wire) transfer is a method of payment by which the originator (the person making the payment) transmits an instruction to a bank to make payment to a beneficiary or to instruct another bank to make the payment to the beneficiary. It consists of several such orders and is accomplished via a series of debits and credits to bank accounts.

Continued on next page.

Quicknotes

DIVERSITY ACTION An action commenced by a citizen of one state against a citizen of another state or against an alien, involving an amount in controversy set by statute, over which the federal court has jurisdiction.

Corfan Banco Asuncion Paraguay v. Ocean Bank

Transnational bank (P) v. Florida bank (D)

Fla. Dist. Ct. App., 715 So. 2d 967, 35 U.C.C. Rep. Serv. 2d 1320 (1998).

NATURE OF CASE: Appeal from summary judgment for defendant on causes of action for violation of the Universal Commercial Code (U.C.C.) and common law negligence.

FACT SUMMARY: Corfan Banco Asuncion Paraguay (P) erroneously sent two wire transfers to the same person and brought suit against Ocean Bank (D) for repayment of one.

RULE OF LAW

Acceptance of a wire transfer by the recipient bank is precluded where the name, bank account or other identifying information of the beneficiary is nonexistent or unidentifiable.

FACTS: Corfan Banco Asuncion Paraguay (Corfan) (P) originated a wire transfer of $72,972 via its intermediary Swiss Bank to the account of Silva in Ocean Bank (Ocean) (D). Ocean (D) noticed a discrepancy in the account numbers and did not inform Corfan (P) or Swiss Bank of the error. Once the correct account number was confirmed by Silva, Ocean (D) accepted the wire transfer and credited his account. Corfan (P) became aware of the discrepancy and issued a second wire transfer of $72,972 to Silva's correct account number at Ocean (D). The second transfer did not indicate that it was a correction or replacement of the first transfer. The transfer was automatically credited to Silva's account. Several days later Corfan (P) inquired regarding the transfers indicating that only one was intended. Silva had already withdrawn both transfers from the account. When Ocean (D) refused to repay $72,972 to Corfan (P), Corfan (P) brought suit under the U.C.C. and for common law negligence. The trial court granted Ocean's (D) motion for summary judgment as to the U.C.C. count and dismissed the negligence count.

ISSUE: Is acceptance of a wire transfer by the recipient bank precluded where the name, bank account or other identifying information of the beneficiary is nonexistent or unidentifiable?

HOLDING AND DECISION: (Sorondo, J.) Yes. Acceptance of a wire transfer by the recipient bank is precluded where the name, bank account or other identifying information of the beneficiary is nonexistent or unidentifiable. The plain language of Florida Statutes § 670.207(1) states that "if, in a payment order received by the beneficiary's bank, the name, bank account number, or other identification of the beneficiary refers to a nonexistent or unidentifiable person or account, no person has rights as a beneficiary of the order and acceptance cannot occur." Here, the payment order referred to a nonexistent bank account number. Thus, under the clear and unambiguous terms of the statute, acceptance of the order could not have occurred. The trial court dismissed the negligence count on the basis that the statutory scheme preempted any common law negligence claim. Since the duty claimed to have been breached by Ocean (D) in the negligence claim (the duty of care to follow the accepted banking practice of the community and to return the funds from the first transfer upon receipt due to a nonexistent account number) is exactly the same duty now governed by statute, the statutory scheme preempts the negligence claim and the dismissal of the claim is affirmed. Reversed in part, affirmed in part, and remanded.

DISSENT: (Nesbitt, J.) Corfan (P) was negligent in handling the wire transaction by incorrectly listing Silva's account number on the first wire transfer and then by compounding that error by sending the second wire transfer with no indication that it constituted a correction of the first, resulting in Corfan's (P) loss. Moreover, Ocean's (D) actions here were not precluded by the statute since reading the statutory scheme in its entirety shows that the receiving bank is permitted to look to other identification in accepting the wire transfer.

ANALYSIS

It is common practice with respect to wire transfers for the recipient bank to ignore the name of the beneficiary and look only to the account number specified. U.C.C. § 4A-207 deals with this issue and allows the recipient bank to ignore the name identified as the beneficiary and to only look to the account number.

Quicknotes

ACCEPTANCE Assent to the specified terms of an offer resulting in the formation of a binding agreement.

Bank of America N.T.S.A. v. Sanati

Bank (P) v. Account holder (D)

Cal. Ct. App., 14 Cal. Rptr. 2d 615, 19 U.C.C. Rep. Serv. 2d 531 (1992).

NATURE OF CASE: Appeal from judgment granting plaintiff's motion for summary judgment in an action for unjust enrichment.

FACT SUMMARY: After Mr. Sanati (D) left the United States, having arranged for monthly interest payments from an account held solely in his name to be made to his wife (D) and two children in California, the Bank of America (P) erroneously transferred the principal of the account as well as the interest to his wife (D).

RULE OF LAW

A bank is entitled to restitution from the beneficiaries for the amount of an unauthorized transfer despite its own negligence, unless the beneficiaries have, in good faith, applied the overpayment to a pre-existing debt owed by the originator.

FACTS: When Mr. Sanati (D) permanently left the United States, he arranged for monthly interest payments to be made to Mrs. Sanati (D) and their two children in California from a London account held in Mr. Sanati's (D) name only. The Bank of America (the Bank) (P) later erroneously transferred the principal as well as the interest—a total of $203,750—to the California account. Mrs. Sanati (D) withdrew the principal, depositing it into bank accounts she and her children controlled, and refused the Bank's (P) request for restitution. The Bank (P) then filed an action for unjust enrichment. Mrs. Sanati (D) argued that the Uniform Commercial Code (U.C.C.) controlled and that she had a quasi-community property interest in the London account. Applying the common law, the trial court granted the Bank's (P) motion for summary judgment. Sanati (D) appealed.

ISSUE: Is a bank entitled to restitution from the beneficiaries for the amount of an unauthorized transfer despite its own negligence?

HOLDING AND DECISION: (Johnson, J.) Yes. A bank is entitled to restitution from the beneficiaries for the amount of an unauthorized transfer despite its own negligence, unless the beneficiaries have, in good faith, applied the overpayment to a pre-existing debt owed by the originator. The general common law and equitable principles applied at the time of the fund transfer in this case. However, even if the U.C.C. did apply, the Bank (P) would be entitled to restitution, unless Mrs. Sanati (D) had detrimentally relied on the payment without notice of the mistake or unless she had, in good faith, applied the erroneous payment to a pre-existing debt or lien owed to her by Mr. Sanati (D). While Mrs. Sanati (D) raises a reasonable inference of a potential quasi community property interest in the funds, this does constitute a pre-existing debt or lien at the time of the transfer. Moreover, she and her children do not contend that they changed their position to their detriment in reliance on the erroneously transmitted funds. The Bank (P) is entitled to restitution. Affirmed.

ANALYSIS

In recognizing a reasonable inference of a pre-existing debt or lien, courts have applied the "discharge for value" rule. The Restatement of Restitution describes the rule as applying to debts that are liquidated, concrete, and pre-existing, not merely probable and undetermined. This case would raise entirely different issues if there had been a pre-existing judgment dividing the couple's assets, but Mrs. Sanati (D) did not file for dissolution until several months after the erroneous fund transfer.

Quicknotes

RESTITUTION The return or restoration of what the defendant has gained in a transaction to prevent the unjust enrichment of the defendant.

UNJUST ENRICHMENT The unlawful acquisition of money or property of another for which both law and equity require restitution to be made.

Experi-Metal, Inc. v. Comerica Bank

Bank customer (P) v. Bank (D)

2010 WL 2720914, 72 U.C.C. Rep. Serv. 2d 666 (E.D. Mich. 2010).

NATURE OF CASE: Motion for summary judgment in action under a state's version of Uniform Commercial Code (U.C.C.) §§ 4A-202 and 4A-203 to recover funds stolen by unauthorized wire transfer.

FACT SUMMARY: Experi-Metal, Inc. (P) contended that Comerica Bank (Comerica) (D) was liable for amounts charged to Experi-Metal's (P) account based on numerous unauthorized wire transfers made by thieves through Comerica's (D) online wire transfer service, contending the wire transfers from its account were not effective as payment orders of the company under the state's version of U.C.C. §§ 4A-202 and 4A-203. Comerica (D) sought summary judgment.

RULE OF LAW

Under U.C.C. § 4A-202, unauthorized wire transfer orders from a customer's account are not, as a matter of law, effective as orders of the customer where there are genuine issues of material fact as to whether the bank accepted the payment orders in good faith and in compliance with its security procedure and any written agreement or instruction of the customer restricting acceptance of payment orders issued in the name of the customer.

FACTS: Experi-Metal (P) did its business banking with Comerica Bank (Comerica) (D), and it entered into agreements with Comerica (D) to permit Experi-Metal (P) to access its bank accounts via the internet using Comerica's (D) online banking system. One of these was "to send payment order[s] or receive incoming funds transfers." Experi-Metal (P) designated Allison, its president, and Maslowski, its controller, as authorized users to initiate monetary transfers through Comerica's (D) wire transfer service. This service was initially known as NetVision Wire Transfer Service (NetVision) but later became known as TM Connect Web, even though the actual service did not change. The account could be set up to require the approval of one or two individuals for each wire transfer or wire transfers above a specified dollar amount, but Experi-Metal (P) did not request this feature. Initially, Comerica (D) employed a security process known as "digital certificates" for its wire transfer service. Users had to routinely "renew" these "digital certificates" in order to initiate monetary transfers for their accounts. Comerica (D) sent e-mails to the users, requiring the users to click on a link specified in the e-mail. Once on the linked website, users were required to log in and enter certain information to obtain the renewal of the digital certificate. Subsequently, Comerica (D) switched from digital certificates to "secure token technology." Under this system, a user accesses the Comerica's (D) website by entering his or her user ID, his or her confidential 4-digit PIN, and a six-digit code from a secure token. The code displayed on the secure token is a randomly generated number that changes every 60 seconds. Comerica (D) listed Maslowski as an authorized user of the TM Connect Web service and provided a secure token for his use. Although Experi-Metal (P) had wanted Maslowski removed as an authorized user, it never communicated that to Comerica (D), despite being given the opportunity to do so. Several months after Comerica (D) initiated the secure token system, Maslowski received an e-mail that purported to be from Comerica (D). According to Maslowski, the e-mail was similar to previous e-mails that he had received from Comerica (D) when it utilized digital certificate technology, prompting him to renew Experi-Metal's (P) digital certificates. Like those previous e-mails, Maslowski was directed to click on a link specified in the e-mail. After clicking on the link, Maslowski was diverted to a website that appeared to be a Comerica (D) website. He was then prompted to log in and enter his confidential customer ID number and password and Experi-Metal's (P) confidential customer ID number and password. When he did this, Maslowski unknowingly gave an unauthorized third party access to Experi-Metal's (P) account through Comerica's wire transfer service from which this third party began transferring funds out of Experi-Metal's (P) account to various accounts in Russia, Estonia, Scotland, Finland, and China, as well as domestic accounts. Forty-seven wire transfers were initiated from Experi-Metal's (P) account between 7:30 a.m. and 10:50 a.m. that day. Comerica's (D) employee, Ling, became suspicious of the activity in Experi-Metal's (P) account—Experi-Metal (P) had made only two wire transfers in the prior two years, with those transfers being made at the beginning of the two-year period—and called Allison at 12:05 p.m. Allison informed Ling that Experi-Metal (P) had not made any wire transfers that day and instructed that Comerica (D) should not honor any requested wire transfers or other transfers until further notice. However, between 10:53 a.m. and 2:02 p.m., 46 additional wire transfers were initiated from Experi-Metal's (P) account. All wire transfer activity was stopped shortly thereafter. In total, $1,901,269 was wire transferred, and Comerica (D) was able to recover all but $560,000, which amount was charged to Experi-Metal's (P) account. Experi-Metal (P) filed suit to recover the amount it was charged, contending that the wire transfers from its account were not effective as payment orders of the

Continued on next page.

company under the state's version of U.C.C. §§ 4A-202 and 4A-203 in that Comerica (D) did not act in compliance with the written agreements between it and Experi-Metal (P) and/or Allison's instructions when contacted by Ling that Comerica (D) should not honor any further wire transfer requests. Pursuant to § 4A-202, wire transfer orders are effective as orders of the customer, even though the customer did not authorize the payment orders, if: (1) the bank and customer agreed that the authenticity of payment orders would be verified pursuant to a security procedure; (2) the security procedure is commercially reasonable; and (3) the bank proves that it accepted the orders in good faith and in compliance with the security procedure and any written agreement or instruction of the customer. Under § 4A-203, the risk of loss nevertheless may shift to the bank if the person committing the fraud did not obtain the confidential information facilitating the breach of the security procedure from an agent or former agent of the customer or from a source controlled by the customer source. Comerica (D) moved for summary judgment.

ISSUE: Under U.C.C. § 4A-202, are unauthorized wire transfer orders from a customer's account, as a matter of law, effective as orders of the customer where there are genuine issues of material fact as to whether the bank accepted the payment orders in good faith and in compliance with its security procedure and any written agreement or instruction of the customer restricting acceptance of payment orders issued in the name of the customer?

HOLDING AND DECISION: [Judge not identified in casebook extract.] No. Under U.C.C. § 4A-202, unauthorized wire transfer orders from a customer's account are not, as a matter of law, effective as orders of the customer where there are genuine issues of material fact as to whether the bank accepted the payment orders in good faith and in compliance with its security procedure and any written agreement or instruction of the customer restricting acceptance of payment orders issued in the name of the customer. As a threshold matter, § 4A-203 does not shift the risk of loss to Comerica (D) here because it cannot be disputed that the thieves obtained Experi-Metal's (P) confidential information from Maslowski, Experi-Metal's (P) agent. Section 4A-202 therefore is determinative of which party is responsible for the loss at issue in this case. Under § 4A-202, whether the security procedure that Comerica (D) employed for its wire transfer service was commercially reasonable is a question of law. Based on the plain and unambiguous terms of the agreements between the parties, Comerica's (D) secure token technology was commercially reasonable, as a matter of law, because the parties so agreed. However, unauthorized wire transfer orders from Experi-Metal's (P) account are not effective as orders of Experi-Metal (P) unless Comerica (D) proves that it accepted the payment order in good faith and in compliance with the security procedure and any written agreement or instruction of Experi-Metal (P) restricting acceptance of payment orders issued in Experi-Metal's (P) name. First, there is a genuine issue of fact with regard to whether Maslowski was authorized to initiate wire transfer orders using Comerica's (D) online service on the date that the unauthorized transfers occurred. For this reason, there is a genuine issue of fact with respect to whether Comerica (D) complied with the security procedure when it accepted the wire transfer orders initiated with Maslowski's user information. There is also a genuine issue of material fact with respect to whether Comerica (D) acted in "good faith." Article 4A of the U.C.C. defines "good faith" as "honesty in fact and the observance of reasonable commercial standards of fair dealing." Neither the state's courts, nor the federal courts sitting in this jurisdiction, have elaborated on the meaning of the phrase "the observance of reasonable commercial standards of fair dealing." Other courts that have considered this meaning have framed the issue as whether the conduct comported with industry or commercial standards applicable to the transactions and whether those standards were reasonable standards intended to result in fair dealing. Experi-Metal (P) argues that reasonable commercial standards of fair dealing would not entail allowing 47 fraudulent wire transfers to be initiated from its bank account, particularly since it had made only two wire transfers in the prior two years, with those transfers being made two years ago. Experi-Metal (P) further argues that Comerica (D) did not engage in reasonable commercial standards of fair dealing when it allowed the initiation of 46 additional fraudulent wire transfers after the activity in Experi-Metal's (P) account was detected, Ling contacted Allison, and Allison instructed Ling that Comerica (D) should not honor any further transfers. Comerica (D) has the burden on this issue, but it has adduced no evidence to rebut Experi-Metal's (P) claim that the bank should have questioned the transfer orders more quickly in light of Experi-Metal's (P) minimal prior wire transfer activity and the destinations of the payments. As to the additional wire transfers that occurred after Ling's initial detection, the U.C.C. provides that a bank must be given a "reasonable opportunity to act" in response to a customer's instruction. Nevertheless, Comerica (D) has failed to present evidence that it could not reasonably have stopped the transfers before it did. For these reasons, there is a genuine issue of material fact with respect to whether Comerica (D) accepted the wire transfer orders in Experi-Metal's (P) name in good faith. Summary judgment is denied.

ANALYSIS

Here, the court emphasizes that there is an issue of fact as to whether Comerica (D) engaged in reasonable commercial standards of fair dealing. It should be noted that under U.C.C. § 1-201, although fair dealing is a broad term that must be defined in context, it is clear that it is concerned

Continued on next page.

with the fairness of conduct rather than the care with which an act is performed. Failure to exercise ordinary care in conducting a transaction is an entirely different concept than failure to deal fairly in conducting the transaction. Presumably, therefore, at trial, Comerica (D) would have to show that it did more than just exercise ordinary care in the transaction to show that it acted in good faith. In a subsequent decision (2011 U.S. Dist. LEXIS 62677), after trial, the court found that Maslowski was authorized to initiate wire transfer orders through Comerica's (D) online service on the date of the unauthorized transfers, and that Comerica (D) complied with its security procedures when it accepted the wire transfer orders initiated with his user information on that date. However, based on the volume and frequency of the payment orders and the book transfers that enabled the criminal to fund orders; the $5 million overdraft created by those book transfers in what is regularly a zero balance account; Experi-Metal's (P) limited prior wire activity; the destinations and beneficiaries of the funds; and Comerica's (D) knowledge of prior and the current phishing attempts, the court concluded that a bank dealing fairly with its customer, under these circumstances, would have detected and/or stopped the fraudulent wire activity earlier, and, therefore, Comerica (D) failed to present evidence that it acted in good faith.

Quicknotes

GOOD FAITH COMPLIANCE A sincere or unequivocal intention to fulfill an obligation or to comply with specifically requested conduct.

CHAPTER 14

Investment Securities

Quick Reference Rules of Law

First American National Bank v. Christian Foundation Life Insurance Co.

Bank (P) v. Church (D)

Ark. Sup. Ct., 242 Ark. 678, 420 S.W.2d 912 (1967).

NATURE OF CASE: Appeal from declaratory judgment holding denying validity to duplicate.

FACT SUMMARY: An employee of a bond issuer's agent fraudulently sold bonds that were duplicates of bonds previously used as collateral for a loan.

RULE OF LAW

When duplicate bonds are issued due to the malfeasance of an agent of the issuer, the issuer is obligated to pay on the duplicate bonds.

FACTS: First Methodist Church of Mena (Mena) (D) authorized a $90,000 bond issue. The fiscal agent for the issue was Institutional Finance Co. (D). Unbeknownst to anyone, Hayes, the president of Institutional Finance (D), had an extra $25,000 worth of bonds printed, which he used as collateral to obtain a loan. The other bonds were sold to investors. The situation came to Mena's (D) attention when duplicate bond holders presented interest coupons for payment. Mena (D) refused to pay until the validity of the bonds was established. First American National Bank (First American) (P), which had made the loan to the now-deceased Hayes, brought an action for a declaratory judgment that its bonds (the bonds it held as collateral for the loan it made to Hayes) were valid. The trial court held they were invalid, and First American (P) appealed.

ISSUE: When duplicate bonds are issued due to the malfeasance of an agent of the issuer, is the issuer obligated to pay on the duplicate bonds?

HOLDING AND DECISION: (Smith, J.) Yes. When duplicate bonds are issued due to the malfeasance of an agent of the issuer, the issuer is obligated to pay on the duplicate bonds. Universal Commercial Code (U.C.C.) § 8-205 provides that an unauthorized security is valid if held by a bona fide purchaser for value and was signed or otherwise authenticated by an authenticating agent. This is precisely what occurred here. Hayes, employee of issuer agent Institutional Finance (D), authorized the duplicate bonds. They therefore were effective against the issuer. Reversed and remanded.

DISSENT: (Jones, J.) Section 8-202(3) provides that lack of genuineness of a security is a complete defense for the issuer. A forged security is not genuine. Therefore, the bonds should not be effective.

ANALYSIS

A theme running through the U.C.C. is that a loss should fall on the party who is in the best position to prevent such a loss. Section 8-205 is an example of this. An issuer is in a better position to guarantee the fidelity of its agent than is the investor. Thus, a loss occurring because of the agent's dishonesty should fall of the issuer.

Quicknotes

FORGERY The false preparation or modification of a written document with an intent to defraud another.

Jennie Clarkson Home for Children v. Missouri, Kansas & Texas Railway

Bond holder (P) v. Bond issuer (D)

N.Y. Ct. App., 182 N.Y. 47, 74 N.E. 571 (1905).

NATURE OF CASE: Appeal from award of interest on fraudulently registered bonds.

FACT SUMMARY: An agent of the Missouri, Kansas & Texas Railway (D) registered bonds it had previously issued when he accepted forged documents presented by the treasurer of Jennie Clarkson Home for Children (P), the bondholder, and reregistered them in the forger's name.

RULE OF LAW

When an agent of an issuer of registered bonds accepts forged documents and reregisters them, the holder of the bonds is still entitled to his interest therein.

FACTS: Jennie Clarkson Home for Children (Jennie) (P) held certain long-term bonds issued by Missouri, Kansas & Texas Railway (Railway) (D). At one point Jennie's (P) treasurer converted them to his own use. To do this, he had to forge a resolution by Jennie's (P) board of directors authorizing the transfer because the bonds were registered to Jennie (P). The treasurer had been told of this necessity by Gibson, an employee of the brokerage firm employed by Railway (D) to handle its securities. Jennie (P) sued Railway (D) for interest due on the bonds. The trial court granted such relief, and the appellate division affirmed. The court of appeals granted review.

ISSUE: When an agent of an issuer of registered bonds accepts forged documents and reregisters them, is the holder of the bonds still entitled to his interest therein?

HOLDING AND DECISION: (Haight, J.) Yes. When an agent of an issuer of registered bonds accepts forged documents and reregisters them, the holder of the bonds is still entitled to his interest therein. When an agent of an issuer of bonds is instrumental in the false transfer thereof, the defrauded former holder retains the right to assert his interest in the bonds. In addition, New York Stock Exchange rules provide that an endorsement by a member of the exchange on a security is considered a guaranty of its correctness. Here, Gibson, an agent of Railway (D) and an Exchange member, so endorsed the transfer. He also was instrumental in the fraudulent transfer in that he (inadvertently) advised the defrauder on how to effect his theft. Gibson had the opportunity to check on the treasurer's good faith but failed to do so. Therefore, Railway (D), as Gibson's principal, must bear the loss. Affirmed.

ANALYSIS

The present case predates the Universal Commercial Code by many years. However, its rule remains vital under the Code. Section 8-311 provides that an unauthorized endorsement is ineffective against the issuer. This would appear to apply to the facts of this case.

Quicknotes

FORGERY The false preparation or modification of a written document with an intent to defraud another.

REGISTERED BOND A bond registered in the buyer's name on the books of the company that issued it.

Powers v. American Express Financial Advisors, Inc.

Entitlement holder (P) v. Securities intermediary (D)

238 F.3d 414 (4th Cir. 2000).

NATURE OF CASE: Appeal from summary judgment awarding damages to an entitlement holder

FACT SUMMARY: Powers (P) and D'Ambrosia had a joint investment account with American Express Financial Advisors, Inc. (American Express) (D). The signature of both owners was required for transfers of $50,000 or more. On the instructions of D'Ambrosia alone, American Express (D) transferred all the funds (over $86,000) to a joint account that D'Ambrosia then liquidated. Powers (P) sued to recover the money.

RULE OF LAW

Where an investment agreement requires more than one entitlement holder signature to authorize a transfer, an entitlement order made by only one entitlement holder is ineffective.

FACTS: Powers (P) and D'Ambrosia had a joint investment account with American Express Financial Advisors, Inc. (American Express) (D). Section C of the investment application required the signature of both owners for redemption requests of $50,000 or more. In a memo signed only by D'Ambrosia that he faxed to American Express (D), D'Ambrosia instructed American Express (D) to close the couple's account and transfer all the funds (over $86,000) to a joint bank account held by Powers (P) and D'Ambrosia, which American Express (D) did. D'Ambrosia then absconded with the money. Powers (P) sued to recover the money and moved for summary judgment, claiming that American Express's (D) transfer had been ineffective. The district court granted summary judgment in favor of Powers (P), and American Express (D) appealed.

ISSUE: Where an investment agreement requires more than one entitlement holder signature to authorize a transfer, is an entitlement order made by only one entitlement holder ineffective?

HOLDING AND DECISION: (Per curiam) Yes. Where an investment agreement requires more than one entitlement holder signature to authorize a transfer, an entitlement order made by only one entitlement holder is ineffective. The reasoning of the district court was correct and was as follows. Under Universal Commercial Code (U.C.C.) § 8-507(b), a securities intermediary, like American Express (D), which transfers funds pursuant to an "ineffective entitlement order," is liable to an entitlement holder for any damages caused by the improper transfer. Although D'Ambrosia was an "appropriate person" to give an entitlement order to American Express (D), when an intermediary has agreed [as American Express (D) did in the investment application] that the "appropriate person" to make an order is both owners of a joint account, both owners must make the order for it to be effective. Because Powers (P) did not ratify the transfer of the funds ordered by D'Ambrosia, the transfer was ineffective. The district court was also correct in rejecting American Express's (D) contention that the $50,000 threshold only applied to transfers from a single mutual fund account (the couple had four), because the plain language of the investment application applied to redemption requests generally, not to redemption requests out of individual funds. The district court was also correct that Powers (P) was not barred under § 8-115 from seeking damages. Under that section, a securities intermediary is not liable to an individual who has an adverse claim to an asset that the intermediary transfers at the direction of a customer—Powers (P) was not an adverse claimant because she was one of two entitlement holders on the account. Finally, the district court was correct that American Express (D) did not have standing to seek a constructive trust on behalf of D'Ambrosia's former employer, from whom D'Ambrosia had been embezzling money. Affirmed.

ANALYSIS

Under § 8-507(a)(2), when an "appropriate person" gives an entitlement order to a securities intermediary, the intermediary has a duty to execute the order. Although the district court acknowledged that D'Ambrosia was an "appropriate person," it was able to restrict the literal meaning of that subsection by looking to § 1-103 of the Code, which states that principles of law and equity shall supplement the Code. Thus, the outcome in this case was the result, ultimately, of the application of general principles and not a strict adherence to the Code itself.

Quicknotes

CONSTRUCTIVE TRUST A trust that arises by operation of law whereby the court imposes a trust upon property lawfully held by one party for the benefit of another, as a result of some wrongdoing by the party in possession so as to avoid unjust enrichment.

EMBEZZLEMENT The fraudulent appropriation of property lawfully in one's possession.

CHAPTER **15**

Documents of Title

Quick Reference Rules of Law

Procter & Gamble Distributing Co. v. Lawrence American Field Warehouse Corp.

Bailor (P) v. Bailee (D)

N.Y. Ct. App., 16 N.Y.2d 344, 213 N.E.2d 897 (1965).

NATURE OF CASE: Appeal from award of damages for breach of a bailment.

FACT SUMMARY: Certain merchandise bailed by Procter & Gamble Distributing Co. (P) to Lawrence American Field Warehouse Corp. (D) for storage disappeared without explanation.

RULE OF LAW

When bailed goods disappear without explanation, the bailee is liable.

FACTS: Procter & Gamble Distributing Co. (P & G) (P), bailor, placed in the custody of Lawrence American Field Warehouse Corp. (Lawrence) (D), bailee, a large amount of soybean oil. It was converted by unknown persons and never traced. P & G (P) sued for the value of the merchandise. The trial court awarded damages in the amount of the value of the oil upon Lawrence's (D) failure to explain the loss. The appellate division affirmed, and Lawrence (D) appealed.

ISSUE: When bailed goods disappear without explanation, is the bailee liable therefor?

HOLDING AND DECISION: (Van Voorhis, J.) Yes. When bailed goods disappear without explanation, the bailee is liable therefor. Section 7-403 of the Universal Commercial Code (U.C.C.), along with other provisions of New York's General Business Law, provides that a bailee is liable for the loss of bailed goods absent the exercise of due care. As the bailee is in a much better position than the bailor to account for a loss of bailed goods, it is incumbent upon the bailee to prove due care, not the bailor to prove otherwise. When goods mysteriously disappear, the bailee cannot escape liability by placing the burden on the bailor to demonstrate why possessions in the control of the bailee are missing. The bailee, having taken possession of the goods, must account for them or compensate the bailor. Such is the case here. [The court affirmed with the modification that the value of the oil was to be determined by reference to the highest value between time of delivery and time of P & G's (P) notification of the loss.]

ANALYSIS

Normally, in a bailment loss, the value of the lost goods is measured by reference to market value at the time of loss. Here, the time of loss was unknown. To have measured the value as of the time of P & G's (P) notification would have allowed Lawrence (D) to have control over the measure of damages, a result the court considered unfair.

Quicknotes

DUE CARE The degree of care that can be expected from a reasonably prudent person under similar circumstances; synonymous with ordinary care.

Admiralty Island Fisheries, Inc. v. Millard Refrigerated Services, Inc.

Seafood company (P) v. Cold storage company (D)

2007 WL 4051649 (D. Neb. 2007).

NATURE OF CASE: Cross-motions for partial summary judgment in action to impose liability on a warehouse for goods stolen by its employees.

FACT SUMMARY: Admiralty Island Fisheries, Inc. (P), a seafood company, other seafood companies, and their insurers (collectively, Plaintiffs) (P) claimed that provisions in warehouse receipts issued by Millard Refrigerated Services, Inc. (Millard) (D) limiting Millard's (D) liability to 50 cents per pound of missing seafood were unenforceable, so that Millard (D) was liable for $455,000, rather than $47,000, for more than 94,000 pounds of seafood allegedly stolen by Millard's (D) employees.

RULE OF LAW

(1) Under Uniform Commercial Code (U.C.C.) § 7-204, a warehouse's limitation of liability provision will apply to a warehouse's liability for conversion where the conversion was not for the warehouse's "own use" or benefit.

(2) Under U.C.C. § 7-204, a warehouse's limitation of liability provision will not be enforceable where the degree of care exercised by the warehouse in preventing theft of deposited goods constitutes gross negligence.

FACTS: Various seafood companies (P), including Admiralty Island Fisheries, Inc. (P), stored their seafood throughout the country in cold storage warehouses operated by Millard Refrigerated Services, Inc. (Millard) (D). When the seafood was delivered, Millard (D) issued a warehouse receipt that contained the parties' agreement regarding the storage of the seafood product. Millard (D) discovered that some of its employees had stolen small quantities of seafood, and fired those employees. The seafood companies (P) and their insurers (P) (collectively "Plaintiffs") brought suit in federal district court, contending that Millard's (D) former employees stole more than 94,000 pounds of seafood with a fair market value of $455,000. Millard (D) contended that its liability for the loss was limited to 50 cents per pound, or $47,000, as specified in the limitation of liability clause included on the front of the warehouse receipts, as well as on the back. Moreover, the Plaintiffs (P) had the opportunity under the warehouse receipts, to negotiate a higher value for their product, and incur a higher storage charge, but chose not to. The parties cross-moved for partial summary.

ISSUE:

(1) Under U.C.C. § 7-204, will a warehouse's limitation of liability provision apply to a warehouse's liability for conversion where the conversion was not for the warehouse's "own use" or benefit?

(2) Under U.C.C. § 7-204, will a warehouse's limitation of liability provision be enforceable where the degree of care exercised by the warehouse in preventing theft of deposited goods constitutes gross negligence?

HOLDING AND DECISION: (Camp, J.)

(1) Yes. Under U.C.C. § 7-204, a warehouse's limitation of liability provision will apply to a warehouse's liability for conversion where the conversion was not for the warehouse's "own use" or benefit. As to the Plaintiffs' (P) motion for partial summary judgment, requesting the court to find as a matter of law that the limitation of liability provisions in Millard's (D) warehouse receipt were inapplicable, Uniform Commercial Code (U.C.C.) § 7-204, which deals with a warehouse's duty of care and contractual limitations on a warehouse's liability, applies to the facts presented. Under that section, a warehouse operator cannot be liable at all absent a failure of due care. Therefore, for purposes of the partial summary judgment motions only, it is assumed that Millard (D) was negligent in failing to prevent the former employees' theft of the Plaintiffs' (P) property. Once Millard (D) is assumed (or ultimately found) to be liable for its negligence, only then does the limitation of liability provision come into play. Assuming Millard's (D) liability arising out ordinary negligence under § 7-204(a), the limitation of liability provision applies according to § 7-204(b), unless the warehouse operator's liability arises out of a conversion "for its own use." Under state law, "conversion for its own use" as used in § 7-204(a), must mean something more and different than simple conversion. Thus, the limitation of liability provision will apply in the presence of ordinary negligence unless there is proof that the former employees' theft was for the purpose of advancing Millard's (D) interests, and Millard (D) bears the burden of proof on this issue. Here, Millard (D) has presented evidence that the conversion was not for its own use, and that Millard (D) did not benefit therefrom. To the contrary, the Plaintiffs (P) have not adduced evidence to create a genuine issue of material fact regarding whether the conversion was for Millard's (D) own use. Merely because the employees who engaged in the conversion did so while employed at Millard (D) and used Millard's (D) equipment and facilities to further the conversion, does not transform the conversion

Continued on next page.

into one that was for Millard's (D) benefit. Accordingly, the Plaintiffs' (P) motion for partial summary judgment is denied.

(2) No. Under U.C.C. § 7-204, a warehouse's limitation of liability provision will not be enforceable where the degree of care exercised by the warehouse in preventing theft of deposited goods constitutes gross negligence. As to Millard's (D) motion for partial summary judgment, asking the court to confirm the enforceability of the limitation of liability clauses in its warehouse receipts, the motion must be denied because there are genuine issues of material fact as to the degree of Millard's (D) negligence. The starting point for the analysis is that the clauses are enforceable, since the parties were of equal bargaining power, and there is a strong policy favoring the enforceability of commercial contracts where ordinary commercial relationships exist. The Plaintiffs (P) had an opportunity to negotiate for a higher price per pound to be paid under the limitation of liability clause in the event of loss, but they did not. As a result, they were not obligated to pay the higher storage costs that likely would have come with a limitation of liability clause that was more advantageous to them. Rather, the parties agreed that the risk of loss greater than 50 cents per pound would be borne by the Plaintiffs (P). However, in opposition to Millard's (D) motion, the Plaintiffs (P) argue that the limitation of liability clause should not be enforced as against public policy, asserting that they will show at trial that Millard (D) acted with gross negligence—not just ordinary negligence—in failing to prevent the theft. If the Plaintiffs (P) can prove that Millard (D) acted with gross negligence, then enforcement of the limitation of liability clause may be contrary to public policy. Both the Plaintiffs (P) and Millard (D) have offered evidence relative to the degree of care exercised by Millard (D) in connection with the seafood. There is some evidence that Millard (D) knew of the thefts or should have known of them several months before it did anything about it. Because there are genuine issues of fact regarding the reasonableness of the security steps Millard (D) took and did not take, whether Millard's (D) conduct rises to the level of gross negligence is an issue for the jury. Millard's (D) motion for partial summary judgment is therefore denied.

ANALYSIS

The court in this case concluded that the burden of proof should be on the warehouse operator to demonstrate that the conversion of the bailor's property was not for its own use. In reaching this legal conclusion, the court acknowledged its rejection of Millard's (D) attempt to place the burden on the Plaintiffs (P) as stated in the warehouse receipts' provisions. The court reasoned that to place the burden of proof on the Plaintiffs (P), as bailors, would ignore the policy arguments that support the enforcement of limitation of liability provisions in commercial contracts. Some reasons supporting this apportionment of the burden of proof are that the warehouse operator is in the best position to explain the loss because the operator has taken control of the goods and has determined the manner in which they are stored; placing the burden on the warehouse operator to show that it acted with due care will encourage warehouse operators to act with care and caution in the handling and storage of bailed goods and to maintain adequate tracking systems that will withstand judicial scrutiny; placing the burden on operators will also have a beneficial effect on the industry because those warehouses that are unable to establish that their storage practices are reasonable will incur increased operating costs, eventually forcing poorly-run facilities out of business; and placing the burden on the warehouses will give the operators incentive to procure insurance on all bailed goods entrusted to them which the operators can procure, presumably at a lower cost than would be incurred if each bailor had to procure its own insurance. See "A Warehouse's Burden of Proof," Ralph Anzivino, *UCC Law Journal* (Spring 2004).

Quicknotes

CONVERSION The act of depriving an owner of his property without permission or justification.

GROSS NEGLIGENCE The intentional failure to perform a duty with reckless disregard of the consequences.

G.A.C. Commercial Corp. v. Wilson

Lender (P) v. Defendant (D)

271 F. Supp. 242 (S.D.N.Y. 1967).

NATURE OF CASE: Motion to dismiss action for damages for fraud.

FACT SUMMARY: G.A.C. Commercial Corp. (P) sued Norwood Railroad (D), a carrier, after it loaned money to St. Lawrence Pulp, secured by straight bills of lading which turned out to be fraudulent.

RULE OF LAW

A creditor who loans money secured by a straight bill of lading has no recourse against the carrier for inaccuracies in the bill.

FACTS: G.A.C. Commercial Corp. (G.A.C.) (P) loaned money to St. Lawrence Pulp & Paper Corp. (St. Lawrence) and took as collateral straight bills of lading, both interstate and intrastate. The carrier was Norwood Railroad (Norwood) (D). After St. Lawrence went bankrupt, the freight cars covered by the bills turned out to be empty. The "loading" had been effected by St. Lawrence, which had also filled out the bills. G.A.C. (P) sued Norwood (D) for $254,173.42, the amount it had loaned. Norwood (D) moved to dismiss, arguing that it was not liable to G.A.C. (P) under the Federal Bills of Lading Act.

ISSUE: Does a creditor who loans money secured by a straight bill of lading have recourse against the carrier for inaccuracies in the bill?

HOLDING AND DECISION: (Bryan, J.) No. A creditor who loans money secured by a straight bill of lading has no recourse against the carrier for inaccuracies in the bill. The Federal Bills of Lading Act, 48 U.S.C. § 81 et seq., controls interstate shipments. This section allows recovery under a straight bill of lading against a carrier only by an owner of goods described in the bill. In a situation where the goods described in the bill don't exist, there can be no owner thereof; therefore, no recovery is possible. As to the intrastate goods, Universal Commercial Code (U.C.C.) § 7-301 gives a remedy only to a "consignee," i.e., the party to whom the goods were destined. A bank which loans money secured by such goods is rarely the consignee. Therefore, except in that unusual situation, a lender will have no recourse. Motion granted.

ANALYSIS

Bills of lading come in two basic types: order and straight. An order of bill is considered a negotiable instrument; a straight bill is not. The former variety contains certain requirements not shared by straight bills and is treated differently under both the Bills of Lading Act and the U.C.C.

Quicknotes

BILL OF LADING A receipt or other documentation given to a shipper by a carrier evidencing the contract to transport such goods and that the shipper possessed title to the goods shipped.

Cleveland v. McNabb

Landlord (P) v. Tenant (D)

312 F. Supp. 155 (W.D. Tenn. 1970).

NATURE OF CASE: Action to enforce lien on chattel.

FACT SUMMARY: Cleveland (P), landlord of farmer McNabb (D), sought to assert a lien on crops grown by McNabb (D) when he fell in arrears on the rent.

RULE OF LAW

A purchaser of crops who does not inquire as to the existence of a landlord's lien thereon is subject to the lien.

FACTS: Cleveland (P) leased certain lands to McNabb (D), who grew cotton thereon. He sold it to, among others, the federal Government (D), through the Commodity Credit Corporation (D). No inquiry was made as to the source of the cotton or whether it was free of any liens. When McNabb (D) fell in rental arrears, Cleveland (P) filed an action to foreclose on a lien which state law gave to a landlord upon a tenant's crops. The Government (D) contended that it acquired title, as a bona fide purchaser, free of the lien.

ISSUE: Is a purchaser of crops who does not inquire as to the existence of a landlord's lien thereon subject to the lien?

HOLDING AND DECISION: (Brown, C.J.) Yes. A purchaser of crops who does not inquire as to the existence of a landlord's lien is subject to the lien. Universal Commercial Code (U.C.C.) § 7-502 provides that the holder of a duly negotiated document of title who takes such document without knowledge of prior interests thereon takes the document, and the chattel it embodies, free of that interest. The Government (D) claimed such status. However, U.C.C. § 1-201 provides that a person has notice of a fact when he has reason to know it exists. Here, the evidence shows that the Government's (D) standard practice is to make an injury regarding the existence of liens. Sensible business practice would also demand such inquiry. As the Government (D) did not make such inquiry, it is not entitled to the protections of § 7-502. Judgment for Cleveland (P).

ANALYSIS

A standard axiom in the law is that a transferor can give a transferee no greater rights that he himself possessed. This is, in fact, not always true. By U.C.C. § 7-502, which codified prior law, a transferee can take an instrument free of defenses thereto which would have been valid against the transferor.

Quicknotes

LIEN A claim against the property of another in order to secure the payment of a debt.

Agricredit Acceptance, LLC v. Hendrix

Lender (P) v. Borrower (D)

82 F. Supp. 2d 1379 (S.D. Ga. 2000).

NATURE OF CASE: Motion for summary judgment on priority of security interest.

FACT SUMMARY: Agricredit Acceptance Corp. (AAC) (P) financed Hendrix's (D) cotton crop with a loan properly perfected and secured by the crop. Sea Island Cotton Trading (Sea Island), the selling agent, sold large quantities of cotton, including the Hendrix (D) cotton, to many cotton merchants (D), who paid Sea Island and received electronic warehouse receipts (EWRs) in their names. Sea Island never paid either AAC (P) or Hendrix (D) as it was obligated to do, and AAC (P) filed suit against the merchants (D) and others to foreclose on its security interest in the Hendrix (D) cotton.

RULE OF LAW

(1) Where there are genuine issues of fact as to whether a document of title has been duly negotiated and as to whether a secured party has acquiesced in the procurement of that document, those questions are for a trier of fact.

(2) A secured party may not entrust goods that it does not own.

FACTS: Agricredit Acceptance Corp. (AAC) (P) financed Hendrix's (D) 1997 cotton crop with a loan properly perfected and secured by the crop. Sea Island Cotton Trading (Sea Island) was designated as the selling agent, through which the crop would be sold. Hendrix's (D) crop was stored in various warehouses, which issued electronic warehouse receipts (EWRs) for the cotton in a central filing system. In 1997 and 1998, various cotton merchants (D) bought large quantities of cotton from Sea Island, including many bales from Hendrix's (D) crop. The merchants paid Sea Island for these bales, and the EWRs representing the bales were transferred into the names of the merchants (D). However, Sea Island never paid either AAC (P) or Hendrix (D) as it was obligated to do. Consequently, AAC (P) filed suit against the merchants (D) and others to foreclose on its security interest in the Hendrix (D) cotton. The merchants (D) argued that because the EWRs were duly negotiated to them by Sea Island and because AAC (P) entrusted the cotton to Hendrix (D) with apparent authority to sell it, the cotton was no longer subject to AAC's (P) security interest. The merchants (D) moved for summary judgment.

ISSUE:

(1) Where there are genuine issues of fact as to whether a document of title has been duly negotiated and as to whether a secured party has acquiesced in the procurement of that document, are those questions for a trier of fact?

(2) May a secured party entrust goods that it does not own?

HOLDING AND DECISION: (Nangle, J.)

(1) Yes. Where there are genuine issues of fact as to whether a document of title has been duly negotiated and as to whether a secured party has acquiesced in the procurement of that document, those questions are for a trier of fact. Under the Universal Commercial Code (U.C.C.), in § 9-309, the rights of a holder to whom a negotiable document of title has been duly negotiated take priority over an earlier, perfected, security interest. A warehouse receipt, such as the EWRs involved here, is a negotiable document of title. To be duly negotiated, a document of title must be negotiated to a holder who (1) purchases in good faith (2) without any notice of any defense against it or claim to it and (3) for value. One of defendants' theories on which they base summary judgment is that the EWRs were duly negotiated to the merchants (D), and, therefore, the merchants' (D) interest in the cotton has priority over AAC's (P) interest. Here, it is undisputed that they purchased the EWRs for value. Here, too, the merchants (D) purchased in good faith—with honesty in fact. AAC (P) is incorrect that good faith requires the merchants (D) to perform a lien check on the cotton prior to purchase. The last hurdle for the merchants (D) to prove the EWRs were duly negotiated is for them to prove that they were purchasers without notice of defenses or claims. AAC (P) argues that their experience with the cotton industry and its willful ignorance as to the existence of liens on the cotton constitutes "reason to know" of AAC's (P) defense to the EWRs. Here, there is a genuine issue of fact whether the merchants (D) had notice of AAC's (P) claims to the cotton. On the one hand, they do not perform lien searches on cotton brought from merchants or gins. On the other hand, when buying directly from the producer or in a state with a central lien filing system, they do perform lien searches. This shows that they knew of the possibility of liens. However, whether failure to search for liens resulted from deliberate indifference or ignorance to their existence is an issue for a jury. Even if the court were to find that the merchants (D) had no notice of AAC's (P) claims, and that the EWRs had been duly negotiated, that determination alone would not

Continued on next page.

automatically provide priority to the merchants' (D) rights over AAC's (P) secured interest. The Code in § 7-503 provides priority to the holder of a duly negotiated document of title as against a holder of a perfected security interest in the goods underlying that document of title only where the holder of the security interest has neither entrusted the goods to the bailor nor acquiesced in the procurement by the bailor of the document of title. Here, the merchants (D) argue that AAC (P) waived the priority of its security interest by entrusting the cotton to Hendrix (D). The Code does not define "acquiesce." Here, AAC (P) may have acquiesced in the procurement of the EWRs. When a bank knows that a farmer is trying to sell his collateral, and it acquiesces in his procurement of documents of title to that collateral, the bank has waived its security interest in that collateral. Here, the evidence is insufficient for the court to rule on this issue as a matter of law, and the question of AAC's (P) acquiescence is best left for a jury.

(2) No. A secured party may not entrust goods that it does not own. With regard to whether AAC (P) entrusted the cotton to Hendrix (D), "entrusted" is only defined in Article 2 (not in Article 1 or 7) of the Code. The courts of this state have interpreted that definition to apply only to owners of goods, because one cannot entrust goods one does not own. As a matter of statutory construction, the court must use that definition here. Therefore, because AAC (P) was not the owner of the cotton, it could not, as a matter of law, have entrusted it to Hendrix (D). Motion for summary judgment denied.

ANALYSIS

As the court observes, § 9-309 (which is now § 9-331) applies when the negotiable document holder and the secured party are both claiming an interest in the document of title (the EWR), whereas § 7-503 covers disputes between competing interests in the underlying goods. Here, the court read those two provisions together to arrive at its decision.

Quicknotes

LIEN A claim against the property of another in order to secure the payment of a debt.

SECURITY INTEREST An interest in property that may be sold upon a default in payment of the debt.

Rheinberg Kellerei GmbH v. Brooksfield National Bank of Commerce

Winemaker (P) v. Bank (D)

901 F.2d 481 (5th Cir. 1990).

NATURE OF CASE: Appeal from denial of award of damages for negligence.

FACT SUMMARY: Brooksfield National Bank of Commerce (D), the collecting bank in an international transaction, failed to inform Rheinberg Kellerei GmbH (P), vendor, of vendee J & J Wine's (D) failure to pay an invoice.

RULE OF LAW

A collecting bank in an international transaction may be liable to the vendor for failing to notify it of the vendee's failure to pay an invoice.

FACTS: J & J Wine (D), an American wine importer, placed an order for wine from winemaker Rheinberg Kellerei GmbH (Rheinberg) (P), a German corporation. Payment was to be made through a letter of collection to be sent from a German bank to Brooksfield National Bank of Commerce (the Bank) (D). Payment was to be due upon arrival of the wine in Houston. On March 27, 1986, the collection letter was forwarded to J & J Wine (D). J & J Wine (D) did not pay but asked for an extension. The wine arrived in port on March 31, and the Bank (D) was never informed of the arrival. J & J Wine (D) never paid and eventually went out of business. The Bank (D) never informed Rheinberg (P) of J & J Wine's (D) failure to pay. Meanwhile, the wine deteriorated to an undrinkable condition. Rheinberg (P) sued the Bank (D) for negligence. The district court entered judgment for the Bank (D) because it never had been informed of the event triggering the payment obligation, the wine's arrival. Rheinberg (P) appealed.

ISSUE: May a collecting bank in an international transaction be liable to the vendor for failing to notify it of the vendee's failure to pay an invoice?

HOLDING AND DECISION: (Garza, J.) Yes. A collecting bank in an international transaction may be liable to the vendor for failing to notify it of the vendee's failure to pay an invoice. Article 20(iii)(cc) of the International Rules for collection provides that a collecting bank must send without delay advice on nonpayment or advice of nonacceptance to the bank from which a collecting order was received. The question to be answered in this case is "what constitutes nonpayment," a term not defined in the Rules. However, the Universal Commercial Code contains analogous concepts. Under § 4-502, a collecting bank need not present collection documents prior to payment being due, but if it elects to do so, it must notify the sender of the documents. This court believes this to be a sensible rule, which it finds applicable to the situation in this case. Here, had the Bank (D) informed Rheinberg (P) or its agent of J & J Wine's (D) non-payment, the loss of the merchandise could have been avoided. It was the Bank (D) that caused the loss. Reversed and remanded.

ANALYSIS

U.C.C. § 4-502 gives collecting banks a good deal of discretion. When collecting documents require presentment "on arrival," and the arrival date is uncertain, the bank can assume arrival in a reasonable time frame, based on its knowledge and experience. In the present case, the Bank (D) did not exercise any such discretion.

Quicknotes

NEGLIGENCE Conduct falling below the standard of care that a reasonable person would demonstrate under similar conditions.

CHAPTER 16

Letters of Credit

Quick Reference Rules of Law

PAGE

1. *Voest-Alpine Trading Co. v. Bank of China.* (1) A notice of refusal of a letter of credit is deficient where by its own terms it does not plainly state that the issuer is actually rejecting the beneficiary's documents or refusing to honor the letter of credit. (2) Discrepancies between a letter of credit and presentation documents that are technical or typographical in nature do not warrant the rejection of the documents where the whole of the documents obviously relate to the transaction on their face. *166*

2. *Sztejn v. J. Henry Schroder Bank Corp.* A court can enjoin payment of drafts under a letter of credit where the caller's fraud has been called to the issuing bank's attention before the drafts and documents have been presented for payment. *168*

3. *Intrinsic Values Corp. v. Superintendencia de Administracion Tributaria.* An injunction against payment of an irrevocable letter of credit is properly entered where presentment would facilitate a material fraud by the beneficiary on the issuer or applicant and where comity militates in favor of such an injunction. *169*

Voest-Alpine Trading Co. v. Bank of China

Beneficiary of credit (P) v. Issuer (D)

167 F. Supp. 2d 940 (S.D. Tex. 2000).

NATURE OF CASE: Action for payment on letter of credit.

FACT SUMMARY: Bank of China (D) issued a letter of credit for the benefit of Voest-Alpine Trading Co. (Voest-Alpine) (P). On the basis of several discrepancies between the letter of credit and documents submitted by Voest-Alpine (P), the Bank of China (D) refused to honor the letter of credit. Voest-Alpine (P) claimed that Bank of China (D) had not provided adequate notice of refusal and that the discrepancies were technical and typographical in nature and did not warrant dishonor.

RULE OF LAW

(1) A notice of refusal of a letter of credit is deficient where by its own terms it does not plainly state that the issuer is actually rejecting the beneficiary's documents or refusing to honor the letter of credit.

(2) Discrepancies between a letter of credit and presentation documents that are technical or typographical in nature do not warrant the rejection of the documents where the whole of the documents obviously relate to the transaction on their face.

FACTS: Voest-Alpine Trading Co. (Voest-Alpine) (P) entered into a contract with Jiangyin Foreign Trade Corp. (JFTC) to sell to JFTC styrene monomer for $1.2 million. JFTC applied for a letter of credit for the benefit of Voest-Alpine (P) from the Bank of China (D). The letter of credit provided for payment once the goods had arrived at Zhangjiagang, China, and Voest-Alpine (P) had presented the documents called for in the letter of credit. The letter of credit had numerous typographical errors in it, including that "Trading USA" in Voest-Alpine's (P) name was inverted and the destination port's name omitted the final "a." The letter of credit clearly stated that it was subject to the 1993 Uniform Customs and Practice, International Chamber of Commerce Publication Number 500 (UCP 500). The goods shipped on July 18, 1995, and on August 1, 1995, Voest-Alpine (P) presented the required documents to Texas Commerce Bank, the presenting bank, which found the discrepancies and alerted Voest-Alpine (P). Voest-Alpine (P) decided the discrepancies did not warrant refusal to pay, and the documents were sent on August 3, 1995, and received by Bank of China (D) on August 9, 1995. On August 11, 1995, Bank of China (D) sent a telex to Texas Commerce Bank that informed of seven discrepancies and that indicated that Bank of China (D) would contact the applicant about the discrepancies. On August 15, 1995, Texas Commerce Bank faxed Bank of China (D) indicating that the discrepancies were not an adequate basis to refuse to pay the letter of credit and requesting honor and payment. Finally, on August 19, 1995, Bank of China (D) sent a telex to Texas Commerce Bank indicating that the discrepancies "may have us refuse to take up the documents. . . ." Bank of China (D) returned the document and did not honor the letter of credit. Voest-Alpine (P) sued for payment.

ISSUE:

(1) Is a notice of refusal of a letter of credit deficient where by its own terms it does not plainly state that the issuer is actually rejecting the beneficiary's documents or refusing to honor the letter of credit?

(2) Do discrepancies between a letter of credit and presentation documents that are technical or typographical in nature warrant the rejection of the documents where the whole of the documents obviously relate to the transaction on their face?

HOLDING AND DECISION: (Gilmore, J.)

(1) Yes. A notice of refusal of a letter of credit is deficient where by its own terms it does not plainly state that the issuer is actually rejecting the beneficiary's documents or refusing to honor the letter of credit. Bank of China (D) claims that under UCP 500, its August 11, 1995, telex to Texas Commerce Bank constituted notice of refusal. Voest-Alpine (P) argues that the telex did not constitute notice of refusal because there was no clear statement of refusal and because the statement in the telex that Bank of China (D) would contact the applicant led to ambiguity. Article 14(d) of the UCP 500 provides that if the issuer elects not to honor the presentation documents, it must provide a notice of refusal within seven banking days of receipt of the documents and must list all discrepancies, the disposition of the rejected documents, and, where it is rejecting the documents, "must give notice to that effect." Here, Bank of China's (D) notice was deficient because nowhere did it state that it was actually rejecting the documents or refusing to honor the letter of credit. Thus, by its own terms, it did not convey refusal. This omission is only compounded by the statement that Bank of China (D) would contact JFTC, because this additional piece of information held open the possibility of acceptance upon waiver of the discrepancies by JFTC. Although Bank of China's (D) August 19, 1995, telex used the

Continued on next page.

word "refuse," this telex, even if it constituted a notice of refusal, came too late, as the expiration of the refusal period would have come on August 18, 1995. Therefore, Bank of China (D) failed to formally refuse the documents before the deadline and is precluded from claiming that the documents were not in compliance with the terms and conditions of the letter of credit.

(2) No. Discrepancies between a letter of credit and presentation documents that are technical or typographical in nature do not warrant the rejection of the documents where the whole of the documents obviously relate to the transaction on their face. Voest-Alpine (P) claims the discrepancies were technical and typographical in nature that do not warrant the rejection of the documents and urges that a "functional standard" of compliance be used to measure the discrepancies. Although there is a wide range of standards that are used to examine presentation documents for compliance—from strict compliance, to strict compliance where there is risk to the issuer, to strict compliance where there is risk to the applicant, to a mirror image approach—the UCP 500 itself contains a moderate standard that requires "consistency" between the letter of credit and the documents. This standard requires that "the whole of the documents must obviously relate to the same transaction . . . on its face." This is a commonsense, case-by-case approach that permits minor typographical deviations because the standard is whether the documents bear a rational link to one another. Here, the discrepancies pointed to by Bank of China (D) do not warrant rejection of the documents. Six of the seven discrepancies are at issue. The first, the inversion of "Trading USA" in Voest-Alpine's (P) name, was not a complete misspelling or an omission, and did not signify a different corporate entity, and thus bore an obvious link to the documents. The second, the stamping of the set of originals of the bill of lading as "original," "duplicate," and "triplicate" instead of "original," also did not warrant rejection because it was clear from the face of these documents that they were all originals. Third, the failure to stamp the packing list documents as "original" was also insufficient to reject these documents because they, too, were clearly originals on their face. Fourth, the date of the survey report was after the bill of lading, but it was clear from the plain language of the report that the survey was conducted before the ship departed. Fifth, the letter of credit number had an extra numeral in it on the beneficiary's certified copy of fax. However, adding the letter of credit number to this document was gratuitous and the document checker could have looked to any other document to verify the letter of credit number or looked to the balance of the information in the document and found that, as a whole, it bore an obvious relationship to the transaction. Finally, the fact that the destination port was misspelled by omitting its last "a" also did not warrant rejection of the documents because it was an obvious misspelling (there are no ports in China with the misspelled name) and the other information contained in the document demonstrated linkage to the transaction on its face. Judgment for the plaintiff.

ANALYSIS

The Universal Commercial Code's (U.C.C.'s) standard for examining presentation documents is strict compliance. This requires an issuer to honor a presentation that "appear on its face strictly to comply with the terms and conditions of the letter of credit." Thus, application of the U.C.C. standard in the instant case could have led to a different result.

Quicknotes

LETTER OF CREDIT An agreement by a bank or other party that it will honor a customer's demand for payment upon the satisfaction of specified conditions.

Sztejn v. J. Henry Schroder Bank Corp.

Buyer (P) v. Bank (D)

N.Y. Sup. Ct., 177 Misc. 719, 31 N.Y.S.2d 631 (1941).

NATURE OF CASE: Motion to dismiss action to have a letter of credit declared void and enjoin payment of drafts thereunder.

FACT SUMMARY: Sztejn (P) sought to restrain the payment of drafts under a letter of credit on the grounds that the party who was its beneficiary had procured bills of lading and invoices stating he had shipped the bristles Sztejn (P) had contracted to buy when, in fact, only garbage was in the crates.

RULE OF LAW

A court can enjoin payment of drafts under a letter of credit where the caller's fraud has been called to the issuing bank's attention before the drafts and documents have been presented for payment.

FACTS: Sztejn (P) was to purchase a quantity of bristles from Transea (D). To pay for them, Sztejn (P) had Henry Schroder Bank Corp. (Henry Schroder) (D) issue an irrevocable letter of credit to Transea (D) that provided drafts by Transea (D) for a specified portion of the purchase price that would be paid under the letter upon shipment of the merchandise and presentation of an invoice and bill of lading. Transea (D) filled crates with rubbish but procured bills of landing and invoices indicating bristles had been shipped. Transea (D) then presented the documents and drew drafts that were presented to and paid by Chartered Bank. Sztejn (P) sought to have the court declare the letter of credit and drafts null and void and to enjoin the payment or presentment for payment of the drafts. As the party who would be presenting the drafts for payment to Henry Schroder (D), Chartered Bank (D) moved to dismiss the complaint, alleging no cause of action existed because the only requirement was that the documents conform on their face to the requirements of the letter of credit.

ISSUE: If the seller's fraud has been called to the issuing bank's attention before there has been a presentment for payment, can payment of drafts under a letter of credit be enjoined?

HOLDING AND DECISION: (Shientag, J.) Yes. A court can enjoin payment of drafts under a letter of credit where the seller's fraud has been called to the issuing bank's attention before the drafts and documents have been presented for payment. Language to the effect that a letter of credit is independent of the primary contract between the buyer and seller has been used by the courts, but in cases concerning alleged breaches of warranty and not in those involving active fraud on the part of the seller. Motion to dismiss denied.

ANALYSIS

Had Chartered Bank (D) been deemed a holder in due course, its claim against the issuing bank would not have been defeated despite the seller's fraud. Universal Commercial Code § 5-114(2) has codified the rule of this case by specifying that where there is "fraud in the transaction," the issuer must honor the draft or demand if honor is demanded by a holder in due course but that a court may enjoin honor by the issuer in all other cases.

Quicknotes

BILL OF LADING A receipt or other documentation given to a shipper by a carrier evidencing the contract to transport such goods and that the shipper possessed title to the goods shipped.

FRAUD A false representation of facts with the intent that another will rely on the misrepresentation to his detriment.

Intrinsic Values Corp. v. Superintendencia de Administracion Tributaria

Beneficiary of credit (D) v. Applicant of credit (P)

Fla. Ct. App., 806 So. 2d 616, 46 U.C.C. Rep. Serv. 2d 1092 (2002).

NATURE OF CASE: Appeal from denial of motion to dissolve a temporary injunction to stop payment on irrevocable letters of credit.

FACT SUMMARY: Superintendencia de Administracion Tributaria (Superintendencia) (P), the tax administration agency of Guatemala, had irrevocable letters of credit issued by Banco de Guatemela for the benefit of Intrinsic Values Corp. (Intrinsic) (D). First Union National Bank and Barclays Bank, PLC, were the confirming banks. When Intrinsic (D) failed to perform on a contract with Superintendencia (P), Superintendencia (P) obtained an injunction in Guatemala that barred Banco de Guatemala from paying on the letters of credit and sought a similar injunction in Florida against payment by the confirming banks.

RULE OF LAW

An injunction against payment of an irrevocable letter of credit is properly entered where presentment would facilitate a material fraud by the beneficiary on the issuer or applicant and where comity militates in favor of such an injunction.

FACTS: Superintendencia de Administracion Tributaria (Superintendencia) (P), the tax administration agency of Guatemala, entered into a contract with Intrinsic Values Corp. (Intrinsic) (D), a Panamanian corporation, for the purchase of various goods. Superintendencia (P) had irrevocable letters of credit issued by Banco de Guatemela for the benefit of Intrinsic (D), with First Union National Bank and Barclays Bank, PLC, as the confirming banks. When Intrinsic (D) failed to perform on the contract, Superintendencia (P) canceled the contract and obtained an injunction in Guatemala that barred Banco de Guatemala from paying on the letters of credit. Superintendencia (P) then brought an action in Florida to enjoin First Union National Bank and Barclays Bank, PLC, from honoring the letters of credit. The lower court granted a temporary injunction. When Intrinsic (D) presented the letters of credit, it learned of the injunction, intervened, and moved to dissolve it. The lower court denied the motion.

ISSUE: Is an injunction against payment of an irrevocable letter of credit properly entered where presentment would facilitate a material fraud by the beneficiary on the issuer or applicant and where comity militates in favor of such an injunction?

HOLDING AND DECISION: (Shevin, J.) Yes. An injunction against payment of an irrevocable letter of credit is properly entered where presentment would facilitate a material fraud by the beneficiary on the issuer or applicant and where comity militates in favor of such an injunction. Universal Commercial Code § 5-109 provides that where honor of a presentation of a letter of credit would facilitate a material fraud by the beneficiary on the issuer or applicant, a court of competent jurisdiction may temporarily or permanently enjoin the issuer from honoring the presentation. Here, Superintendencia (P) demonstrated that honoring a presentation would facilitate such a material fraud by Intrinsic (D), that based on the fact that Intrinsic (D) did not perform on the contract, the contract was canceled, and that Intrinsic (D) had notice of the cancellation. Superintendencia (P) also demonstrated, more likely than not, that it would succeed on a material fraud claim. Under these circumstances, Intrinsic (D) had no basis in fact for making a demand for payment, and permitting it to obtain payment of the money would be unjust. In addition, a foreign decree is entitled to comity where the proceeding that resulted in the decree meets due process and jurisdiction requirements. Here, the Guatemala court's proceedings met those requirements, so the Guatemala injunction is entitled to comity. As a result, the lower court properly enjoined payment by the confirming banks to render effective the Guatemala injunction. Affirmed.

ANALYSIS

The purpose of the temporary injunction in the instant case was to preserve the status quo pending a final decree by the Guatemala court, presumably on breach of contract or other claims.

Quicknotes

COMITY A rule pursuant to which courts in one state give deference to the statutes and judicial decisions of the court of another state.

INJUNCTION A court order requiring a person to do, or prohibiting that person from doing, a specific act.

LETTER OF CREDIT An agreement by a bank or other party that it will honor a customer's demand for payment upon the satisfaction of specified conditions.

CHAPTER 17

Introduction to Secured Transactions

Quick Reference Rules of Law

PAGE

1. *Benedict v. Ratner.* When a bankrupt gives a lien on accounts to a creditor but retains all indicia of ownership thereof, the lien is voidable in bankruptcy. *172*

Benedict v. Ratner

Bankruptcy trustee (P) v. Lender (D)

268 U.S. 353 (1925).

NATURE OF CASE: Appeal from denial of order invalidating a lien.

FACT SUMMARY: Benedict (P), trustee of bankrupt Hub Carpet, sought to invalidate a lien on accounts given by the bankrupt to Ratner (D) wherein all indicia of title to the accounts were retained by the bankrupt.

RULE OF LAW

When a bankrupt gives a lien on accounts to a creditor but retains all indicia of ownership thereof, the lien is voidable in bankruptcy.

FACTS: Hub Carpet (Hub) received certain loan moneys from Ratner (D). In return, Ratner (D) received a lien on all past and future accounts receivable. Unless the lien was foreclosed upon, all indicia of ownership in the accounts were retained by Hub. No recordation of the lien of any sort was made. Hub soon thereafter filed for bankruptcy. Benedict (P), the bankruptcy trustee, filed an action to void the lien as a preferential transfer. The district court upheld the validity of the lien, and the court of appeals affirmed. The Supreme Court granted review.

ISSUE: When a bankrupt gives a lien on accounts to a creditor but retains all indicia of ownership thereof, is the lien voidable in bankruptcy?

HOLDING AND DECISION: (Brandeis, J.) Yes. When a bankrupt gives a lien on accounts to a creditor but retains all indicia of ownership thereof, the lien is voidable in bankruptcy. The Bankruptcy Code allows a trustee to void prefiling fraudulent transfers. What constitutes such a transfer is determined by state law. Here, state law declares as fraudulent a lien on or other security interest in property which is unrecorded, the transferor retaining apparent possession. Ratner (D) contended that this rule should not require delivery, as does transfer of a chattel. However, it is not delivery that matters but rather dominion. When a transferor retains the indicia of dominion over any kind of property, a secret transfer of title can work a fraud on the transferor's future creditors and is, therefore, a fraudulent transfer. Such was the case here. Reversed.

ANALYSIS

The Bankruptcy Code has long allowed a trustee to void prefiling transfers of interest. These are called "preferential transfers." The fear here is that a soon-to-be bankrupt may attempt to favor certain creditors over others by releasing property prior to filing. Code policy favors equal treatment of creditors, so such transfers are voidable.

Quicknotes

BANKRUPTCY A legal proceeding whereby a debtor, who is unable to pay his debts as they become due, is relieved of his obligation to pay his creditors either by liquidation and distribution of his remaining assets or through reorganization and payment from future.

LIEN A claim against the property of another in order to secure the payment of a debt.

PREFERENTIAL TRANSFER A transfer made by the insolvent debtor to a creditor prior to filing the bankruptcy petition, giving a priority to one creditor over others with respect to the debtor's assets.

CHAPTER 18

The Scope of Article 9

Quick Reference Rules of Law

PAGE

1. *In re Fabers, Inc.* A consignor of goods to a bankrupt may be unable to reclaim them upon the consignee's bankruptcy. 174

2. *Gibraltar Financial Corp. v. Prestige Equipment Corp.* (1) Under Uniform Commercial Code (U.C.C.) § 1-203(b), a transaction that purports to be a lease will not be deemed a transaction that creates a secured interest where compliance with the lease requires the lessee to pay more than nominal consideration to become the owner of the leased property. (2) Under U.C.C. § 1-203, notwithstanding that a secured interest has not been created per se by a transaction purporting to be lease, the characterization of the transaction as a lease or as a transaction creating a secured interest will depend on the economic realities of the transaction, including factors such as the leased property's useful life, the total amount of rent, whether the lessee acquired equity or any pecuniary interest in the goods, the practical limitations on the lessee's ability to remove and return the leased goods, the ability of the lessor to market the equipment, and the expectations of the parties concerning the projected value of the equipment at the time they entered into the agreement. 175

3. *Philko Aviation, Inc. v. Shacket.* One who purchases an airplane but does not record the sale with the Federal Aviation Administration will have inferior title to a subsequent purchaser. 178

In re Fabers, Inc.

Carpet dealer (P) v. Carpet retailer (D)

12 U.C.C. Rep. Serv. 126 (Bankr. D. Conn. 1972).

NATURE OF CASE: Petition to reclaim goods from a bankrupt estate.

FACT SUMMARY: Mehdi Dilmaghani & Co. (P) delivered certain carpets to be sold on consignment by Fabers, Inc. (D), which subsequently declared bankruptcy.

RULE OF LAW

A consignor of goods to a bankrupt may be unable to reclaim them upon the consignee's bankruptcy.

FACTS: Mehdi Dilmaghani & Co. (Mehdi) (P), a dealer in Oriental carpets, delivered certain carpets to Fabers, Inc. (D), a carpet retailer in Connecticut. The agreement provided the carpets remain the property of Mehdi (P) until sale, and that the funds received from any sale remain the property of Mehdi (P). It was essentially a consignment. While the carpets were in Fabers's (D) possession, Fabers (D) filed for bankruptcy. Mehdi (P) then petitioned to reclaim the goods from the bankrupt estate.

ISSUE: May a consignor of goods to a bankrupt be unable to reclaim them upon the consignor's bankruptcy?

HOLDING AND DECISION: (Seidman, Ref. Bankr.) Yes. A consignor of goods to a bankrupt may be unable to reclaim them upon the consignee's bankruptcy. Under Universal Commercial Code (U.C.C.) § 2-326, adopted in Connecticut, goods delivered for resale are subject to the claims of the possessors creditors unless (1) the seller is generally known by his creditors to sell goods on consignment, or (2) the deliverer of the goods (the consignor) complies with Article 9 filing provisos. Here, Mehdi (P) admittedly did not file any type of Article 9 financing statement. In addition, there is no evidence that Fabers (D) was known by its creditors to sell goods on consignment. Therefore, the carpets were subject to the claims of Fabers's (D) creditors, and therefore beyond the reach of Mehdi (P) to reclaim them. Petition for reclamation denied.

ANALYSIS

U.C.C. § 2-326 exists to prevent fraud from being perpetrated upon a consignee's creditors. If goods are in a consignee's possession, the consignee's creditors are entitled to believe that any monies loaned or advanced may be secured by the consignee's inventory. Section 2-326 prevents a secret consignment agreement from defeating this reasonable expectation.

Quicknotes

CONSIGNEE A person to whom goods are shipped or delivered.

CONSIGNMENT An agreement whereby one party is to deliver goods to another party who will pay the first party for those goods that the second party sells and will return any of the items that he does not sell.

CONSIGNOR A party who is to deliver goods to another party.

RECLAIM To demand the return of a thing.

Gibraltar Financial Corp. v. Prestige Equipment Corp.

Holder of perfected security interest in defunct company's property (P) v. Possessor of a punch press (D)

Ind. Sup. Ct., 949 N.E.2d 314 (2011).

NATURE OF CASE: Appeal from affirmance of summary judgment for defendants in action to determine whether property was subject to a security interest.

FACT SUMMARY: Gibraltar Financial Corp. (Gibraltar) (P), which held a perfected security interest in now-defunct Vitco Industries, Inc.'s (Vitco's) property, contended that its security interest covered a punch press used by Vitco, which was currently in the possession of Prestige Equipment Co. (Prestige) (D), because Vitco used the press pursuant to a sale subject to a security interest, rather than a true lease of the equipment.

RULE OF LAW

(1) Under Uniform Commercial Code (U.C.C.) § 1-203(b), a transaction that purports to be a lease will not be deemed a transaction that creates a secured interest where compliance with the lease requires the lessee to pay more than nominal consideration to become the owner of the leased property.

(2) Under U.C.C. § 1-203, notwithstanding that a secured interest has not been created per se by a transaction purporting to be lease, the characterization of the transaction as a lease or as a transaction creating a secured interest will depend on the economic realities of the transaction, including factors such as the leased property's useful life, the total amount of rent, whether the lessee acquired equity or any pecuniary interest in the goods, the practical limitations on the lessee's ability to remove and return the leased goods, the ability of the lessor to market the equipment, and the expectations of the parties concerning the projected value of the equipment at the time they entered into the agreement.

FACTS: Vitco Industries, Inc. (Vitco) purchased a punch press for $243,000 to use in its manufacturing business. A few months later, Vitco entered into a transaction with Key Equipment Finance, Inc. (Finance), in which Finance paid Vitco $243,000, and Finance and Vitco executed a contract under which Vitco was entitled to use the punch press in exchange for monthly payments. Finance and Vitco called this contract a "Master Lease Agreement" (Lease). Consistent with the lease nomenclature, Finance did not file a financing statement in connection with the transaction. The six-year Lease specified the amount of monthly rent; that Vitco was required to maintain insurance, pay all personal property taxes, bear all risk of loss, and perform all repairs and maintenance with regard to the press; that Vitco was entitled to buy the press after five years for a little over $78,000 ("Early Buyout Option" or "EBO"); and that, at the end of the lease term, Vitco had the option, if it had not already exercised the EBO, to either purchase the press at fair market value, renew the Lease, pay month-to-month, or return the press, at Vitco's expense, to Finance. Within three years, however, Vitco defaulted on the Lease and became defunct. In the meantime, Gibraltar Financial Corp. (Gibraltar) (P), which held a perfected security interest in virtually all of Vitco's tangible and intangible property, including its equipment, judicially was awarded possession of the collateral in which it had a perfected security interest, including Vitco's equipment. The same month that Gibraltar (P) was awarded such possession, Finance repossessed the press and sold for $160,000 to National Machinery Exchange, Inc. (NME), in a joint venture with Prestige Equipment Corp. (Prestige) (D). Not even a year later, Gibraltar (P) filed suit against Prestige (D) to recover the value of the press, alleging that Prestige (D) had acquired the press subject to Gibraltar's (P) security interest. The parties agreed that the dispute turned on whether the Lease was a true lease (as argued by Prestige (D)) or a sale subject to a security interest (as argued by Gibraltar (P)). The trial court granted summary judgment in favor of Prestige (D) after concluding that the Lease was a true lease. The state's intermediate appellate court affirmed, and the state's highest court granted review.

ISSUE:

(1) Under U.C.C. § 1-203(b), will a transaction that purports to be a lease be deemed a transaction that creates a secured interest where compliance with the lease requires the lessee to pay more than nominal consideration to become the owner of the leased property?

(2) Under U.C.C. § 1-203, notwithstanding that a secured interest has not been created per se by a transaction purporting to be lease, will the characterization of the transaction as a lease or as a transaction creating a secured interest depend on the economic realities of the transaction, including factors such as the leased property's useful life, the total amount of rent, whether the lessee acquired equity or any pecuniary interest in the goods, the practical limitations on the lessee's ability to remove and return the leased goods, the ability of the lessor to market the equipment, and the expectations of the parties concerning the projected value of the equipment at the time they entered into the agreement?

Continued on next page.

HOLDING AND DECISION: (Sullivan, J.)

(1) No. Under U.C.C. § 1-203(b), a transaction that purports to be a lease will not be deemed a transaction that creates a secured interest where compliance with the lease requires the lessee to pay more than nominal consideration to become the owner of the leased property. Under the applicable state's law, the state's version of U.C.C. § 1-203, which sets forth rules for distinguishing a transaction creating a lease and a transaction retaining or creating a security interest, is determinative of whether Gibraltar (P) had a security interest in the press. Although § 1-203(a) provides that "[w]hether a transaction in the form of a lease creates a lease or security interest is determined by the facts of each case," § 1-203(b) dictates that if its specifications are met, the transaction will be deemed to have created a security interest, i.e., if the bright-line test is met, the issue is decided—the transaction has created a security interest and no further inquiry is required. The first of § 1-203(b)'s two prongs is satisfied "if the consideration that the lessee is to pay the lessor for the right to possession and use of the goods is an obligation for the term of the lease and is not subject to termination by the lessee." Here, the first prong of the bright-line test is met because the consideration Vitco was obligated to pay was an obligation for the term of the lease and was not subject to termination by Vitco, notwithstanding the EBO clause. The second prong of the bright-line test is satisfied if, inter alia, the lease provides the lessee with "an option to become the owner of the goods for no additional consideration or for nominal additional consideration upon compliance with the [lease]." The Lease gave Vitco two opportunities to become the owner of the punch press—at the end of the Lease and upon exercise of the EBO. At the end of the Lease, Vitco had the right to purchase the press for its "fair market value." Section 1-203(d)(2), however, provides that "[a]dditional consideration is not nominal if: . . . the price is stated to be the fair market value of the goods determined at the time the option is to be performed." Therefore, because the Lease specified purchase at termination for fair market value, the consideration cannot be deemed to be nominal. As to the purchase under the EBO provision, a specific price was set (around $78,000). There was no evidence demonstrating that the $78,000 price constituted the expectations of Vitco and Finance at the time the transaction was entered into as to what the fair market value of the punch press would be on the EBO date. Such evidence would be necessary to satisfy § 1-203(d)(2)—which requires the fair market value of the goods must be determined at the time the option is to be performed—and to satisfy § 1-203(e)—which requires that " 'reasonably predictable' . . . fair market value . . . shall be determined with reference to the facts and circumstances at the time the transaction is entered into." Other evidence, however, showed that the EBO price was significantly less than fair market value, and such evidence is enough to cast doubt on the Lease's recitation that the EBO price was at fair market value. Therefore, Finance failed to establish that the $78,000 EBO price is not nominal. Nevertheless, the evidence shows that that Vitco did not have an option to become the owner of the punch press for only nominal additional consideration upon compliance with the EBO option. If Vitco declined to exercise the EBO option, it would have been required to pay an additional approximately $43,000 in rent, and the estimated cost to return the punch press would have been approximately $19,500. The $78,000 EBO price is not less than even the sum of these two amounts and, therefore, not nominal within the meaning of § 1-203(d). Accordingly, the Lease did not create a security interest per se.

(2) Yes. Under U.C.C. § 1-203, notwithstanding that a secured interest has not been created per se by a transaction purporting to be lease, the characterization of the transaction as a lease or as a transaction creating a secured interest will depend on the economic realities of the transaction, including factors such as the leased property's useful life, the total amount of rent, whether the lessee acquired equity or any pecuniary interest in the goods, the practical limitations on the lessee's ability to remove and return the leased goods, the ability of the lessor to market the equipment, and the expectations of the parties concerning the projected value of the equipment at the time they entered into the agreement. Even though under the bright-line test of § 1-203(b), the Lease did not create a security interest per se, § 1-203(a) provides that "[w]hether a transaction . . . creates a lease or security interest is determined by the facts of each case." Thus, the facts of this case may nevertheless dictate that the Lease did create a security interest. If a court finds that a transaction did not create a security interest per se, it must then consider the economic reality of the transaction to determine whether the transaction is more fairly characterized as a lease or a secured financing arrangement. There is no single accepted test or methodology for making this determination. Some courts have considered whether the lessor has retained a meaningful reversionary interest in the goods, but this test is flawed, since the U.C.C. does not provide for assessing whether a lessor has retained a meaningful reversionary interest, and, in any event, the test is circular, and there is no consistent set of factors for identifying a lessor's residual interest. The court below concluded that the Prestige (D) was entitled to summary judgment because Finance had retained a meaningful reversionary interest in the punch press, based on the court's conclusion that the equipment would still have had significant value had Vitco decided to return it at the end of the six-year

Continued on next page.

Lease, given that the useful life of the punch press was apparently 15 to 20 years. Such an inference is proper, however, only where the evidence shows a plausible intent by the transferor to repossess the goods. Although it would not have been prohibitively expensive for Finance to repossess the press, the punch press's useful life extending beyond the term of the Lease does not by itself establish that the transaction was a true lease. The focus must be on the economics of the transaction, not just on whether the transferor retained a reversionary interest. In this case, the fact that Vitco already owned the punch press when it entered into the Lease with Finance weighs in favor of finding a transaction creating a security interest. Weighing in favor of the transaction creating a lease are the useful life of the punch press, the absence of limitations on its removal, and the ability of Finance to market it. What cannot be determined without a trial, however, is whether the payment provisions of the Lease are more indicative of a lease or of a secured financing arrangement. The economics of the transaction can be cast to demonstrate a lease, in that the parties agreed that Vitco would lease the punch press for 72 months at $3,592 per month with an option to buy at fair market value at the end. On the other hand, the economics could also be cast to demonstrate a sale subject to a security interest: Vitco agreed to buy the punch press for $294,000 with 60 monthly payments of $3,592 plus a balloon payment of $78,000. Under this approach, the language regarding the sixth year was mere surplus; paying the $78,000 would have been the only economically sensible course for Vitco to take. Thus, there are genuine issues of material fact as to the economic realities of the transaction. Additional evidence needed to resolve these remaining issues of fact would include evidence of the expectations of Vitco and Finance at the time the transaction was entered into as to such factors as the value of the punch press on the EBO and lease expiration dates, the discount rate, and whether the only economically sensible course for Vitco would have been to exercise the EBO. Accordingly, summary judgment was inappropriate. Reversed and remanded.

ANALYSIS

Court decisions, treatises, and articles on commercial law are replete with declarations of the difficulty in distinguishing between "true" leases and sales subject to security agreements, and whether a transaction in the form of a lease is characterized as a lease or a sale subject to a security interest is one of the most frequently litigated issues under the U.C.C. Much of the difficulty arose under the pre-1987 version of the U.C.C. which emphasized the subjective intent of the parties entering into a lease agreement at the time the agreement was made. In discovering intent, courts relied upon factors that were thought to be more consistent with sales or loans than leases. Most of these criteria, however, were as applicable to true leases as to security interests. Accordingly, the 1987 revision of the U.C.C. contained no reference to the parties' intent. While this decoupling of the parties' intent from the lease-security interest determination has reduced the difficulty in arriving at a definitive determination, as this case illustrates, that determination still can be fraught with uncertainty and a plethora of formulations and approaches.

Quicknotes

LEASE An agreement or contract that creates a relationship between a landlord and tenant (real property) or lessor and lessee (real or personal property).

SECURITY INTEREST An interest in property that may be sold upon a default in payment of the debt.

Philko Aviation, Inc. v. Shacket

Airplane manufacturer (D) v. Buyer (P)

462 U.S. 406 (1983).

NATURE OF CASE: Review of declaratory relief action adjudicating rights to chattel.

FACT SUMMARY: The Shackets (P), who had purchased an airplane but not recorded the transaction with the Federal Aviation Administration (FAA), contended that a subsequent sale by their vendor to a third party was void.

RULE OF LAW

One who purchases an airplane but does not record the sale with the Federal Aviation Administration will have inferior title to a subsequent purchaser.

FACTS: The Shackets (P) purchased an airplane from Smith. On Smith's assurances that he would handle the paperwork, the Shackets (P) did not record their purchase with the Federal Aviation Administration (FAA). Smith subsequently entered a fraudulent transaction wherein he sold the aircraft to Philko Aviation, Inc. (Philko) (D). When the Shackets (P) became aware of Philko's (D) claim on the aircraft, they filed a declaratory relief action, seeking title to the plane. The district court and court of appeals held the plane to belong to the Shackets (P), and the United States Supreme Court granted review.

ISSUE: Will one who purchases an airplane but does not record the sale with the FAA have inferior title to a subsequent purchaser?

HOLDING AND DECISION: (White, J.) Yes. One who purchases an airplane but does not record the sale with the FAA will have inferior title to a subsequent purchaser. Under 49 U.S.C. § 1403(C), all transfers of aircraft must be registered with the FAA to have priority over subsequent purchasers for value. It is clear, both from the language of the section and from attendant legislative history, that Congress intended that the FAA serve as a central clearinghouse for all transactions involving transfers of aircraft and that all state regulations to the contrary in this field be preempted. Here, the Shackets (P) did not record their transaction with the FAA. Philko (D), as a subsequent purchaser, therefore had higher title to the aircraft than did the Shackets (P). It, therefore, gained title to the aircraft. Reversed and remanded.

ANALYSIS

As is often the case, § 1403(C) exists to resolve the unhappy situation where both claimants are blameless. Just as with Article 9 of the Universal Commercial Code, many situations implicating § 1403(C) will involve wrongdoers long gone. Here, neither the Shackets (P) nor Philko (D) was blameworthy, but someone had to prevail. Section 1403(C) provided a means for resolving such situations.

Quicknotes

DECLARATORY JUDGMENT An adjudication by the courts which grants not relief but is binding over the legal status of the parties involved in the dispute.

RECORDATION The recording of a document in the public record.

CHAPTER 19

The Creation of a Security Interest

Quick Reference Rules of Law

In re Troupe

[Parties not identified.]

340 B.R. 86, 2006 WL 689515 (Bankr. W.D. Okla. 2006).

NATURE OF CASE: Cross-motions for summary judgment in Chapter 7 bankruptcy adversary proceeding to avoid a security interest.

FACT SUMMARY: The trustee (trustee) (P) in a Chapter 7 bankruptcy contended that Deere's (D) purchase money security interest in a tractor could be avoided because the tractor was non-consumer goods and Deere (D) failed to file a financing statement, so that its interest was unperfected. Deere (D) contended that the tractor was consumer goods under Article 9 of the Universal Commercial Code, so that its security interest was perfected despite its failure to file the financing statement.

RULE OF LAW

A debtor who makes representations in a security agreement regarding the intended use of the collateral is bound by those representations, even where the actual use changes thereafter.

FACTS: The Troupes (debtors) purchased a tractor from Deere (D). On their credit application, the debtors indicated that they were both employed full-time by others. They indicated to Deere's (D) agents that they intended to use the tractor on their 10-acre property, where they raised some livestock. As part of the transaction, the Troupes gave Deere (D) a purchase money security interest in the tractor. On the security agreement, the box marked "Personal" was checked and the box marked "Commercial" was left blank. There were other indications on the agreement that the transaction was a consumer transaction and that the tractor was for personal use only. The Troupes (D) went bankrupt and filed under Chapter 7. The Chapter 7 trustee (trustee) (P) brought suit to avoid Deere's (D) purchase money security interest, claiming that the tractor's use was commercial, not personal. To support this contention, the Troupes averred that their actual use and intended use of the tractor was for the business purpose of farming and ranching, but at deposition they testified that the use was 90 percent personal and 10 percent business. Their tax returns also showed that they had depreciated the tractor for business purposes. The parties agreed that a purchase money security interest in consumer goods is perfected upon attachment, without filing a financing statement. Conversely, they agreed that with respect to non-consumer goods, the filing of a financing statement is required for perfection of a non-possessory purchase money security interest. Thus, the issue came down to whether the tractor was consumer goods or non-consumer goods.

ISSUE: Is a debtor who makes representations in a security agreement regarding the intended use of the collateral bound by those representations, even where the actual use changes thereafter?

HOLDING AND DECISION: (Weaver, C.J.) Yes. A debtor who makes representations in a security agreement regarding the intended use of the collateral is bound by those representations, even where the actual use changes thereafter. Here, the trustee (P) has the rights of a hypothetical lien holder, and his rights are governed by state law. The holder of an unperfected security interest is subordinate to the rights of one who became a lien creditor, including a bankruptcy trustee, before the security interest was perfected. Thus, Deere (D) must have a perfected security interest to prevail over the trustee (P). If the tractor is consumer goods, Deere (D) is perfected; if the tractor is not consumer goods, Deere (D) is unperfected. Consumer goods are goods used primarily for personal purposes, whereas equipment (the other possible classification of the tractor) is defined as "goods other than inventory, farm products or consumer goods." The classification of collateral is made at the time the security interest is created; here, that was when the security agreement was executed, and this classification does not change based on subsequent changes in use. Even if all the evidence presented is accepted as true, it nonetheless shows that the Troupes engaged in ranching and farming activities only after the security interest agreement was entered into. The agreement itself had several indications that the tractor was for personal use, and the Troupes never indicated to Deere (D) that the type of use had changed. The law is clear that where a debtor makes an affirmative representation in loan documents that he or she intends to use goods primarily for personal, family or household purposes, the creditor is protected even if the representation turns out to be erroneous. Since the classification of the tractor is to be made at the time the security interest in it was created, and since the Troupes are bound by their representations in the security agreement, the tractor is consumer goods. Accordingly, Deere (D) had a perfected purchase money security interest in the tractor at the time the interest attached, though it did not file a financing statement, and it prevails over the trustee (P). Summary judgment for Deere (D).

ANALYSIS

This decision is consistent with the long-established principle that it is the debtor's announced use of the collateral that governs how the collateral will be classified. Otherwise, if actual use governed, creditors would con-

Continued on next page.

stantly have to monitor how their collateral was being used, and this would be prohibitive economically.

Quicknotes

CHAPTER 7 BANKRUPTCY A legal proceeding whereby a debtor, who is unable to pay his debts as they become due, is relieved of his obligation to pay his creditors by liquidation and distribution of his remaining assets.

COLLATERAL Property that secures the payment of a debt.

PURCHASE MONEY SECURITY INTEREST Security interest taken by a seller of the collateral to secure its purchase price.

SECURITY INTEREST An interest in property that may be sold upon a default in payment of the debt.

Morgan County Feeders, Inc. v. McCormick

Creditor (P) v. Cattle seller (D)

Colo. Ct. App., 836 P.2d 1051, 180 U.C.C. Rep. Serv. 2d 632 (1992).

NATURE OF CASE: Appeal from a judgment in an action to determine the classification of collateral.

FACT SUMMARY: After Allen sold some cattle to McCormick (D), but before McCormick (D) took delivery, Morgan County Feeders, Inc. (Morgan) (P), holder of a perfected security interest in the cattle, seized them, alleging that they were equipment and thus were subject to Morgan's (P) security interest.

RULE OF LAW

Goods in a business are equipment when they are fixed assets or have, as identifiable units, a relatively long period of use.

FACTS: Allen owned longhorn cattle, which he had acquired to use principally for recreational cattle drives in his recreational business. He entered into an agreement to sell fifty-six head of cattle to McCormick (D). Morgan County Feeders, Inc. (Morgan) (P), holder of a perfected security interest in the cattle, seized them before they were delivered to McCormick (D). In the ensuing trial, the trial court concluded that the cattle purchased by Allen were equipment, rather than inventory, and thus were subject to Morgan's (P) security interest. McCormick (D) appealed.

ISSUE: Are goods in a business, equipment when they are fixed assets or have, as identifiable units, a relatively long period of use?

HOLDING AND DECISION: (Rothenberg, J.) Yes. Goods in a business are equipment when they are fixed assets or have, as identifiable units, a relatively long period of use. Under the Uniform Commercial Code (U.C.C.), "goods" are classified as consumer goods, equipment, farm products, and inventory. The parties agree that the cattle constitute "goods" under the U.C.C. They further agree that the cattle are not "farm products." The remaining issue is whether they are inventory or equipment. Goods are inventory, even though not held for sale, if they are used up or consumed in a short period of time in the production of some end product. Allen did not acquire the cattle for the principal purpose of immediate or ultimate sale or lease but to use for recreational cattle drives. Thus, the trial court was justified in finding that, under these circumstances, the cattle should be classified as "equipment." Affirmed.

ANALYSIS

The distinction between inventory and equipment is important because buyers of inventory in the ordinary course of business take free of perfected security interests. Under the U.C.C., "goods" are defined as "all things which are movable at the time the security interest attaches." The four major types of goods classifications noted by the court are mutually exclusive.

Quicknotes

SECURITY INTEREST An interest in property that may be sold upon a default in payment of the debt.

In re John's Bean Farm of Homestead, Inc.

[Parties not identified.]

378 B.R. 385 (Bankr. S.D. Fla. 2007).

NATURE OF CASE: Motion for summary judgment in bankruptcy action to determine whether a financing statement is seriously misleading, and, therefore, ineffective to perfect a creditor's asserted security interest. [The complete procedural posture of the case is not presented in the casebook extract.]

FACT SUMMARY: The Trustee (P) in bankruptcy contended that Klein's (D) financing statement was "seriously misleading," and, therefore, ineffective to perfect Klein's (D) asserted security interest in the debtor's property because the financing statement was filed under the name "John Bean Farms, Inc." instead of "John's Bean Farm of Homestead, Inc." [The complete factual and procedural posture of the case is not presented in the casebook extract.]

RULE OF LAW

Under Uniform Commercial Code (U.C.C.) § 9-506, a financing statement is "seriously misleading" where the name used for the debtor does not appear on the first page of the search results returned using that name.

FACTS: The Trustee (P) in bankruptcy contended that under revised U.C.C. § 9-506, Klein's (D) financing statement was "seriously misleading," and, therefore, ineffective to perfect Klein's (D) asserted security interest in the debtor's property because the financing statement was filed under the name "John Bean Farms, Inc." instead of "John's Bean Farm of Homestead, Inc.," the latter being the debtor's legal name. When a search is conducted in the state's secured transaction registry, a listing of debtors' names is produced. The listing is an alphabetical listing, and 20 names are displayed. If the debtor's actual name is produced, it is at the top of the list. If the debtor's name is not found, the next succeeding name on the alphabetical list is at the top of the list. To see the next preceding name on the alphabetical list, the searcher must use the "Previous" command on the screen. In fact, at the top of the list is the statement: "Use the Previous and Next buttons to display additional search results." This statement directs the searcher to use the "Previous" command to see the immediately preceding names on the alphabetical list. The Trustee (P) conducted a search of the relevant registry's online database. Using the debtor's correct name, the Trustee's (P) search yielded no matches. When the debtor's correct name was inputted as the search term, the listing of 20 names on the initial search result screen did not disclose the Klein (D) financing statement. Klein's (D) financing statement was only found by striking the "previous" command 60 times. The Trustee (P), relying on precedent, *In re Summit Staffing Polk County, Inc.*, 305 B.R. 347 (Bankr. M.D. Fla. 2003), argued that only the initial search result screen generated when the debtor's correct name is input counts as the search result, and, since Klein's (D) financing statement did not appear on the initial page displayed, the financing statement was seriously misleading. Klein (D) countered that based on the same precedent, where the disputed financing statement did not appear on the initial page displayed, but rather the page displayed when the searcher pushed the "previous" command once, and where the court held that the debtor's name was not seriously misleading, the results of "standard search logic" in the state means something other than the initial result screen and can include a result no matter how far removed from the first page. The issue was one of first impression in the jurisdiction. The Trustee (P) moved for summary judgment. [The complete factual and procedural posture of the case is not presented in the casebook extract.]

ISSUE: Under U.C.C. § 9-506, is a financing statement "seriously misleading" where the name used for the debtor does not appear on the first page of the search results returned using that name?

HOLDING AND DECISION: (Isicoff, J.) Yes. Under U.C.C. § 9-506, a financing statement is "seriously misleading" where the name used for the debtor does not appear on the first page of the search results returned using that name. The current, revised version of U.C.C. § 9-506 was intended to replace the former reasonableness standard with a clearer standard based on the computerized search logic of the filing office. Thus, the accuracy of the debtor's name has become of paramount importance, with even the slightest errors in or differences from the correct name resulting in the name used being deemed seriously misleading. The goal of current § 9-506 is to simplify the filing system as a whole, and to shift the responsibility to the filer by requiring the not too heavy burden of using the legal name of the debtor, thereby relieving the searcher from conducting numerous searches using every conceivable name variation of the debtor. Under the statute, what debtor misnomer is "seriously misleading" is statutorily defined as that which would not be discovered using the state's standard search logic. Thus, under a safe harbor provision, the discoverability of a financing statement expressly delimits permissible error. A financing statement is effective if a computer search run under the debtor's correct name produces the financing statement with the incorrect name. If it does not, then the financing statement

Continued on next page.

is ineffective as a matter of law. The court has no discretion to determine that the incorrect name is "close enough." In the *Summit Staffing* case, on which both the Trustee (P) and Klein (D) rely, the financing statement identified the debtor as "Summit Staffing, Inc." rather than by the debtor's correct name of "Summit Staffing of Polk County, Inc." The court held that this error was not seriously misleading because, although using the standard search logic for the state did not produce a page on which the financing statement appeared, the searcher only had to push the "previous" button one time and the financing statement was listed. The court thus held that a "reasonably diligent searcher" standard survived to some degree, but also concluded that a searcher's responsibility to check the immediately preceding names as well as the immediately succeeding names on an alphabetical list if there is not an exact match of the debtor's correct name is not limitless, and is subject to a "reasonableness" standard. The Trustee (P) argues that to require a secured creditor to search through numerous pages of names would defeat the salutary purpose of revised Article 9 and set dangerous precedent. Klein (D) counters that since the plain language of the statute has no reasonableness requirement the court cannot impose a requirement that the statute does not provide. "According to Klein's (D) interpretation, any financing statement filed, no matter how far it may appear from the proper listing, would be sufficient so long as the statement could be found at some point in the pages preceding or following the initial displayed page. Under this interpretation, absent any reasonableness as to the distance between a proper and improper listing, a searcher would have to look through every page of the online database to determine whether or not a financing statement exists." The crux of the dispute, therefore, is what constitutes the search result using the state's standard search logic. The only "search logic" used in the registry is statutorily defined as a search by the debtor's name or document number. The registry itself explains that a "result" of inputting that search logic is the information on the initial page displayed. The registry does not mention the use of the "previous" or "next" page key in connection with conducting a search using the search criteria. Since it is undisputed that Klein's (D) financing statement did not appear in the search result when the debtor's correct name was input, the financing statement is seriously misleading and summary judgment in the Trustee's (P) favor is appropriate. Although this holding disposes of this case, it is worthwhile addressing Klein's (D) incredible argument that revised § 9-506 unambiguously requires a searcher to scroll through the pages of the search until the nonconforming financing statement is located. The statute is unambiguous, and contains no implicit or explicit obligation of a searcher to go beyond the search result. However, even assuming, arguendo, that Klein (D) is correct that the "search result" means something other than the page displayed when the required data is input, it does not follow that the statute requires a limitless search through the registry database. Notwithstanding that the statute is unambiguous, when applying the plain and ordinary meaning of statutory language produces a result that is not just unwise but is clearly absurd, the statutory language should not be applied literally if doing so would produce an absurd result. Applying Klein's (D) interpretation would yield an absurd result that would eviscerate the purpose of the statute: to create a framework for the perfection of security interests that is less arbitrary, that includes statutory guidance for simplifying the search, while allowing for "minor" errors. Accordingly, even if a search result includes more than the initial page displayed, there is a reasonable limit to the search, which is no more than one page "previous" or "next" from the initial result screen. Even under such an interpretation, Klein's (D) statement was seriously misleading. Summary judgment for Trustee (P).

ANALYSIS

Absent a statutory definition, such as the one in revised U.C.C. § 9-506, of what constitutes "seriously misleading" many courts around the country implemented "reasonably diligent searcher" standard, which required the reviewing court to determine, on a case-by-case basis, whether a hypothetical reasonable searcher would have been able to discover the non-conforming financing statement despite the error in a debtor's name. This allowed judges to second-guess what searchers should or should not have been able to discover had they tried hard enough, and the standard created extensive litigation and fragmented or contradictory decisions. Accordingly, the revision of § 9-506 was "designed to discourage the fanatical and impossibly refined reading of statutory requirements in which courts occasionally have indulged themselves." The revision has seemed, in large part, to have had its intended effect, and the majority of cases decided under revised Article 9 are unforgiving of even minimal errors. For example, "Tyringham Holdings" was seriously misleading because it omitted "Inc." in "Tyringham Holdings, Inc."; "Roger House" instead of the legal name "Rodger House," with a "d," was also held seriously misleading; as was "K W M Electronics Corporation" instead of "K.W.M. Electronics Corporation." As these results, and this decision, underscore, a creditor must use the debtor's correct, legal name, or, most likely face a financing statement being held seriously misleading and ineffective.

Quicknotes

SECURITY INTEREST An interest in property that may be sold upon a default in payment of the debt.

In re Grabowski

Lien creditor (P) v. Secured creditor (D)

277 B.R. 388 (Bankr. S.D. Ill. 2002).

NATURE OF CASE: Complaint filed by Chapter 11 debtors to determine the validity, priority, and extent of liens on their farm equipment.

FACT SUMMARY: Bank of America (D) and South Pointe Bank (South Pointe) (P) both claimed security interests in three items of farm equipment owned by the bankruptcy debtors. South Pointe (P) contended that Bank of America's (D) financing statement (although prior in time) which indicated that Bank of America (D) had a lien on property consisting of "all inventory, chattel paper, accounts, equipment, and general intangibles," was insufficient under the Universal Commercial Code (U.C.C.) to perfect Bank of America's (D) security interest in the farm equipment.

RULE OF LAW

A bank's financing statement that indicates the bank has a lien on property consisting of "all inventory, chattel paper, accounts, equipment, and general intangibles" is sufficient to perfect its security interest in a Chapter 11 debtor's property.

FACTS: Debtors Ronald and Trenna Grabowski filed a Chapter 11 proceeding to reorganize their farming operation. Their schedules included a list of items of equipment used in their farming operation. There were three items of farm machinery as to which a dispute remained between the creditors Bank of America (D) and South Pointe Bank (South Pointe) (P): a John Deere 925 flex platform, a John Deere 4630 tractor, and a John Deere 630 disk. Bank of America (D) claimed a prior security interest in this equipment by virtue of a security agreement signed by the debtors. The Bank of America's (D) financing statement identified the debtors as "Ronald and Trenna Grabowski" and listed their address as "12047 State Highway #37, Benton, Illinois 62812." The financing statement described Bank of America's (D) collateral as: All Inventory, Chattel Paper, Accounts, Equipment and General Intangibles. South Pointe (P) subsequently obtained a lien on the debtors' equipment. South Pointe's (P) financing statement identified the debtors as "Ronald and Trenna Grabowski" at "P.O. Box 38, Dubois, Illinois 62831" and described South Pointe's (P) collateral as: JD 1995 9600 combine . . . , JD 925 FLEX PLATFORM . . . , JD 4630 TRACTOR . . . , JD 630 DISK 28, 1998. South Pointe (P) asserted that Bank of America's (D) financing statement, although prior in time, was insufficient to perfect Bank of America's (D) interest because it failed to place other lenders on notice of Bank of America's (D) interest in the subject equipment. Specifically, South Pointe (P) noted that Bank of America's (D) financing statement contained the address of the debtors' farm equipment business rather than that of the debtors' home where their farming operation was located and, further, that it failed to mention any specific items of equipment or even make reference to "farm equipment" or "farm machinery." South Pointe (P) maintained, therefore, that Bank of America's (D) financing statement did not reasonably identify Bank of America's (D) collateral as required to fulfill the notice function of a financing statement under the U.C.C. The debtors filed a complaint to determine the validity, priority, and extent of the liens held by the various lenders in this equipment.

ISSUE: Is a bank's financing statement that indicates the bank has a lien on property consisting of "all inventory, chattel paper, accounts, equipment, and general intangibles," sufficient to perfect its security interest in a Chapter 11 debtor's property?

HOLDING AND DECISION: (Meyers, J.) Yes. A bank's financing statement that indicates the bank has a lien on property consisting of "all inventory, chattel paper, accounts, equipment, and general intangibles," is sufficient to perfect its security interest in a Chapter 11 debtor's property. The U.C.C. sets forth the requirements for a creditor to obtain and perfect a security interest in personal property of the debtor. Section 9-203 governs the attachment and enforcement of security interests through the parties' execution of a security agreement, while § 9-502 relates to the requisites of a financing statement filed to perfect the creditor's interest against the interests of third parties. Both sections call for a description of the debtor's property. However, the degree of specificity required of such description depends on the nature of the document involved (whether it is a security agreement or a financing statement) and the purpose to be fulfilled by such document. While a security agreement defines and limits the collateral subject to the creditor's security interest, a financing statement puts third parties on notice that the creditor may have a lien on the property described and that further inquiry into the extent of the security interest is prudent. U.C.C. § 9-108 sets forth the test for sufficiency of a description under the U.C.C., stating that a description of personal property is sufficient, whether or not it is specific, if it reasonably identifies what is described. While § 9-108 provides a flexible standard for determining the sufficiency of a description in a security agreement, U.C.C. § 9-504 provides an even broader standard with regard to a financing statement. This section states that a financing statement

Continued on next page.

sufficiently indicates the collateral that it covers if the financing statement provides a description of the collateral or an indication that the financing statement covers all assets or all personal property. Thus, in the case of a financing statement, a creditor may either describe its collateral by "type" or "category" as set forth in § 9-108 or may simply indicate its lien on "all assets" of the debtor. This exceedingly general standard for describing collateral in a financing statement is consistent with the "inquiry notice" function of a financing statement. A financing statement need not specify the property encumbered by a secured party's lien, but need merely notify subsequent creditors that a lien may exist and that further inquiry is necessary "to disclose the complete state of affairs." Here, Bank of America's (D) financing statement was sufficient to perfect its security interest in the farm equipment and Bank of America's (D) interest, being prior in time, was superior to that of South Pointe (P). Accordingly, the court finds in favor of Bank of America (D) and against South Pointe (P) on the debtors' complaint to determine the validity, priority, and extent of liens in the debtors' farm equipment.

ANALYSIS

In the *Grabowski* bankruptcy, the court noted that while a subsequent creditor should not be required to be a "super-detective" in investigating prior secured transactions, the debtors' address in this case was an accurate and ready means of contacting the debtors. Furthermore, even though the mailing address on the bank's financing statement was that of the debtors' business, the debtors' names were listed as "Ronald and Trenna Grabowski," not "Grabowski Tractor-Benton, Inc.," the name of the debtors' business. Accordingly, the court found that a reasonably prudent lender would not be misled into believing that the collateral listed was property of the debtors' business, rather than that of the debtors individually.

Quicknotes

CHAPTER 11 BANKRUPTCY A legal proceeding whereby a debtor, who is unable to pay his debts as they become due, is relieved of his obligation to pay his creditors through reorganization and payment from future income.

COLLATERAL Property that secures the payment of a debt.

FINANCIAL STATEMENT A document demonstrating a creditor's security interest in property.

SECURITY INTEREST An interest in property that may be sold upon a default in payment of the debt.

Border State Bank of Greenbush v. Bagley Livestock Exchange, Inc.

Creditor bank (P) v. Alleged converter of security interest (D)

Minn. Ct. App., 690 N.W.2d 326, 55 U.C.C. Rep. Serv. 2d 397 (2004).

NATURE OF CASE: Appeal from directed verdict and jury verdict in action for conversion of security interest and third-party claim of indemnification and counterclaim thereto.

FACT SUMMARY: Border State Bank of Greenbush (Border State) (P) contended that the cattle-sharing agreement between Johnson (D) and Anderson had to be analyzed to determine whether Anderson had any rights in calves short of full ownership to which Border State's (P) security interest could attach. [Other issues were mentioned, but not treated, in the casebook extract.]

RULE OF LAW

An enforceable security interest attaches when the debtor has signed a security agreement that describes the collateral, value has been given, and the debtor has rights in the collateral, even though those rights may be short of full ownership.

FACTS: Anderson and Johnson (D) had a cattle-sharing contract whereby Anderson would care for and breed cattle owned by Johnson (D). Johnson (D) was to receive a guaranteed percentage of the calf crop, the calves would be sold under Johnson's (D) farm's name, Johnson (D) and Anderson would agree as to when the calves would be sold, and Anderson would receive the balance [after payment to Johnson (D) of the guaranteed percentage] of the proceeds. This agreement was subsequently amended orally. Anderson asserted that the percentage split between the two parties was 40/60, and Johnson (D) would provide feed, including beet tailings, and increased pasture. Johnson (D) conceded that he agrees to provide beet tailings if Anderson would pay for their shipping, but denied agreeing to provide other feed, and he denied agreeing to increased pasture. He also denied changing the terms relating to his "guaranteed" percentage. About half a year after the contract amendment, Anderson borrowed around $155,000 from Border State Bank of Greenbush (Border State) (P). To secure the loans, he granted Border State (P) a security interest in, among other things, all of Anderson's "rights, title and interest" in all "livestock" then owned or thereafter acquired. In the meantime, Johnson (D), after the contract modification, sent beet tailings, and then sent $55,000 for feed, but around a year later, because Anderson experienced difficulty in caring for the cattle for lack of feed, Johnson (D) reclaimed his cattle. Anderson, however, retained 289 calves for sale, and these were sold at Bagley Livestock Exchange, Inc. (Bagley) (D). Bagley (D) knew of Border State's (P) security interest in Anderson's livestock but, after discussing the agreement with Johnson (D), determined the security interest did not attach to the calves. Bagley (D) paid Johnson (D) $119,403. Thereafter, Johnson (D) paid Anderson $19,404, representing Anderson's share of the sale proceeds, less $55,000 that Johnson (D) claimed as repayment for money advanced to Anderson to purchase feed. Border State (P) sued Bagley (D) and Johnson (D), claiming they had converted its perfected security interest in the calves. Johnson (D) brought a third-party complaint against Anderson for indemnity in case Bagley (D) prevailed, and Anderson counterclaimed for breach of contract. The trial court granted Bagley (D) and Johnson (D) a directed verdict on the basis that Johnson (D) had not granted to Anderson an ownership interest in the calves. However, a jury found for Anderson on his breach of contract counterclaim and the trial court denied review of that verdict. The state's intermediate appellate court granted review. [The casebook extract focuses on the part of the appellate court's decision that treats the issue of whether the trial court erroneously applied a legal standard for attachment of a security interest that requires ownership.]

ISSUE: Does an enforceable security interest attach when the debtor has signed a security agreement that describes the collateral, value has been given, and the debtor has rights in the collateral, even though those rights may be short of full ownership.

HOLDING AND DECISION: (Lansing, J.) Yes. An enforceable security interest attaches when the debtor has signed a security agreement that describes the collateral, value has been given, and the debtor has rights in the collateral, even though those rights may be short of full ownership. One of Universal Commercial Code (U.C.C.) Article 9's requirements for the attachment of a security interest is that the debtor "has rights in the collateral or the power to transfer rights." It is not disputed that the calves constituted a part of the collateral at issue here or that they were adequately described. Instead, the trial court issued the directed verdict based on its understanding that Anderson had to own the calves before Border State's (P) security interest could attach. This understanding was erroneous, because the rights referred to by Article 9 may be short of full ownership rights. In other words, the debtor does not have to own the collateral. Instead, the security interest attaches only to the extent of the debtor's rights. This view is supported by other jurisdictions. The trial court's decision, based on its understanding of the incorrect legal

Continued on next page.

standard, precluded a review of the underlying cattle-sharing agreement to determine if Anderson had other rights short of ownership that would have provided a basis for attachment of the security interest. Therefore, the directed verdict must be set aside and the matter reviewed by the trial court in light of the correct legal standard. Thus, on remand, the trial court must determine whether the cattle-sharing agreement was ambiguous, and, if so, what Anderson's rights were under that agreement. Reversed and remanded as to this issue. [The court also affirmed the denial of judgment notwithstanding the verdict to Johnson (D) based on its finding that the verdict was supported by competent evidence.]

ANALYSIS

Article 9 of the U.C.C. provides that a security interest attaches to collateral, and is enforceable against the debtor or third parties, when (1) value has been given; (2) the debtor "has rights in the collateral or the power to transfer rights"; and (3) the debtor has signed a security agreement that contains a description of the collateral. To perfect the security interest, both the security agreement and financing statement must contain an adequate description of the collateral. Attachment refers to the point at which the creditor's security interest becomes effective against the debtor; perfection refers to the point at which the creditor's security interest becomes effective against the rest of the world.

Quicknotes

DIRECTED VERDICT A verdict ordered by the court in a jury trial.

PERFECTED SECURITY INTEREST A security interest that is safeguarded against other claims to the collateral; perfection is generally accomplished by legal steps necessary to give other creditors notice of the interest.

SECURITY INTEREST An interest in property that may be sold upon a default in payment of the debt.

In re Howell Enterprises, Inc.

[Parties not identified.]

934 F.2d 969 (8th Cir. 1991).

NATURE OF CASE: Appeal from bankruptcy court order establishing priority to an item in a bankrupt estate.

FACT SUMMARY: After Howell Enterprises, Inc. mistakenly listed a letter of credit as an account receivable, a lender having a security interest in such accounts sought to claim it.

RULE OF LAW

A party having a security interest in accounts receivable may not be able to claim an item therein when it is incorrectly entered as such an account.

FACTS: Tradax, Inc. and Howell Enterprises devised a plan wherein Tradax would sell rice it milled to a third party in Howell's name. The buyer purchased through a letter of credit made out to Howell but intended to be passed on to Tradax. Through sloppy bookkeeping, the letter of credit was listed on Howell's books as an account receivable. Howell filed for bankruptcy before the letter of credit matured. First National Bank, which had a perfected security interest in Howell's accounts receivable, claimed the right to the letter's proceeds. Tradax made a similar claim. The bankruptcy court held the Bank to have priority, and Tradax appealed.

ISSUE: May a party having a security interest in accounts receivable be able to claim an item therein when it is incorrectly entered as such an account?

HOLDING AND DECISION: (Rosenbaum, J.) No. A party having a security interest in accounts receivable may not be able to claim an item therein when it is incorrectly entered as such an account. A security interest cannot attach unless the debtor giving the interest has rights in the collateral. When the debtor has no such rights, no security interest attaches. When a debtor incorrectly enters an item as an account receivable when in fact it has no interest in such an item, a party having a security interest in such accounts obtains no rights to this item, as the interest never attached. Here, Howell never had any rights in the letter of credit, so no security interest favoring the Bank ever attached to it. Reversed and remanded.

ANALYSIS

A letter of credit is a form of commercial paper that can facilitate a transaction. When a seller is hesitant to extend credit to a buyer, a third party (usually a bank) may guarantee payment through a letter of credit, in which the bank promises to back up the buyer. The bank profits by charging a fee.

Quicknotes

ACCOUNTS RECEIVABLE Amounts that are owed pursuant to an open account and that arise in the normal course of business dealings.

LETTER OF CREDIT An agreement by a bank or other party that it will honor a customer's demand for payment upon the satisfaction of specified conditions.

SECURITY INTEREST An interest in property that may be sold upon a default in payment of the debt.

CHAPTER 20

Perfection of the Security Interest

Quick Reference Rules of Law

In re Short

Bankrupt householder (P) v. Finance company (D)

170 B.R. 128 (Bankr. S.D. Ill. 1994).

NATURE OF CASE: Motion to avoid a lien on household goods in a bankruptcy proceeding.

FACT SUMMARY: Creditor American General Finance (D) argued that its purchase money lien survived after being consolidated with another obligation by debtor Short (P).

RULE OF LAW

A purchase money security interest retains its character when the debt is consolidated with other obligations and thus is not subject to avoidance under Bankruptcy Code § 522(f).

FACTS: Short (P) entered into a retail installment contract to buy bedroom furniture. The entire balance was due in one year. The contract to pay the debt, which granted a security interest in the furniture, was assigned to American General Finance (American) (D) on the date of signing. One year later, Short (P) executed a note with American (D) which consolidated the furniture debt with other debts. The note allowed monthly payments, and it listed the collateral as a continued purchase money interest in the bedroom furniture as well as some other household items owned by Short (P). There was no indication that American (D) had a purchase money security interest in these other items. Short (P) then filed bankruptcy and moved to avoid American's (D) lien on all the furniture, contending that the refinancing destroyed the purchase money character of the lien and therefore the lien should be exempt from creditor process pursuant to Bankruptcy Code § 522(f).

ISSUE: Does a purchase money security interest retain its character when the debt is consolidated with other obligations, thereby escaping unavoidability under Bankruptcy Code § 522(f)?

HOLDING AND DECISION: (Meyers, J.) Yes. A purchase money security interest retains its character when the debt is consolidated with other obligations and thus is not subject to avoidance under Bankruptcy Code § 522(f). Section 522 (f) allows a debtor to avoid the fixing of a lien on property that would otherwise be exempt if such a lien is a nonpossessory, nonpurchase money security interest. The various circuits have split on whether a purchase money security interest is extinguished when the loan is refinanced through consolidation with other debt. The best approach seems to be the "dual status" approach. In other words, if collateral secures both a purchase money security interest and nonpurchase money security interest, so long as the interests can be separated, a consolidation should not destroy the initial character of the interests. In this case, the consolidated loan was in part a purchase money security interest and in part a nonpurchase money security interest. Therefore, American's (D) lien remains on the bedroom furniture to the extent that purchase money debt remains, but the motion to avoid is granted for the nonpurchase money lien.

ANALYSIS

The theory behind automatic perfection of liens on consumer goods is that it is unlikely that the goods will be used to secure other debts. Furthermore, since filing costs money, many consumer purchases would be too small to make filing by the seller financially viable. Under Universal Commercial Code § 9-301(1)(d), the merchant who sells consumer goods by extending credit holds a superior interest in the collateral as compared to other creditors, without the need to file a financing statement.

Quicknotes

PURCHASE MONEY SECURITY INTEREST Security interest taken by a seller of the collateral to secure its purchase price.

General Electric Capital Commercial Automotive Finance, Inc. v. Spartan Motors, Ltd.

Secured creditor (P) v. Debtor (D)

N.Y. App. Div., 246 App. Div. 2d 41, 675 N.Y.S.2d 626 (1998).

NATURE OF CASE: Appeal from grant of summary judgment to plaintiff in action to enforce a security interest in collateral against a secondary creditor.

FACT SUMMARY: General Electric Capital Commercial Automotive Finance, Inc. (P) sought to enforce its security interest in Spartan Motors, Ltd.'s (D) collateral against General Motors Acceptance Corporation and others.

RULE OF LAW

A purchase money security interest may be obtained under Universal Commercial Code (U.C.C.) § 9-107 even where the debtor first obtains the property and is later reimbursed by the purported purchase money security interest creditor.

FACTS: A predecessor of General Electric Capital Commercial Automotive Finance, Inc. (GECC) (P) entered into an "Inventory Security Agreement" with Spartan Motors, Ltd. (Spartan) (D) in connection with its floor plan financing of the dealership's inventory. By assignment of the agreement, GECC (P) obtained a blanket or "dragnet" lien on Spartan's (D) inventory to secure a debt in excess of $1 million. The security agreement was filed with the county clerk and Secretary of State. Spartan (D) subsequently signed a new wholesale security agreement with General Motors Acceptance (GMAC) in which GMAC agreed to finance Spartan's (D) inventory, which was duly filed. GMAC notified GECC (P) of its competing security interest. GECC (P) commenced suit against Spartan (D) seeking $1,180,999.98, representing money then due to GECC (P) under its agreement with Spartan (D). Spartan (D) subsequently filed a bankruptcy petition and ceased doing business. GECC (P), GMAC and MBNA took possession of and liquidated their respective collateral. GECC (P) settled all of its claims against all the defendants except GMAC, which it accused of converting two Mercedes-Benz vehicles in violation of its security interest. The court granted GECC's (P) motion for summary judgment. GMAC appealed.

ISSUE: May a purchase money security interest be obtained under U.C.C. § 9-107 even where the debtor first obtains the property and is later reimbursed by the purported purchase money security interest creditor?

HOLDING AND DECISION: (Friedmann, J.) Yes. A purchase money security interest may be obtained under U.C.C. § 9-107 even where the debtor first obtains the property and is later reimbursed by the purported purchase money security interest creditor. A perfected purchase money security interest is an exception to the general first-in-time, first-in-right rule of competing security interests and has priority over a prior security interest in the same property. The purchase money security interest must meet the U.C.C.'s definition found in § 9-107 of a security interest: "(a) taken or retained by the seller of the collateral to secure all or part of its price; or (b) taken by a person who by making advances or incurring an obligation gives value to enable the debtor to acquire rights in or the use of such collateral if such value is in fact so used." The issue here is whether GMAC's payment to Spartan (D) as reimbursement after it had acquired two Mercedes-Benz automobiles constituted an "advance" or "obligation" granting GMAC a purchase money security interest in the cars. There are two arguments against such a finding: (1) courts have been reluctant to find a purchase money security interest where, as in this case, title to and possession of the merchandise has already passed to the debtor before the loan was advanced; and (2) the express wording of the agreement between GMAC and Spartan (D) seems to accord GMAC purchase money secured status only if GMAC pays the manufacturer, distributor or other seller directly. Prior to the enactment of the U.C.C., the sequence of such transfers was dispositive. U.C.C. § 9-107 was intended to liberalize the rigid transactional rules. The courts have since considered temporal proximity between the debtor's acquisition of the property and value given as one factor to be considered in the determination. The critical inquiry, however, is the intent of the parties, as evidenced by the language of the agreement and the attendant circumstances. Here, GMAC's reimbursements to Spartan (D) were made six and two days after the respective purchases, and such post-purchase reimbursement was common both in the trade and in Spartan's (D) dealings with its financers. With respect to the express language of the agreement between GMAC and Spartan (D), the express terms of an agreement and a different course of performance should be construed as consistent whenever reasonable. When such construction is unreasonable, the express terms of the agreement control. Moreover, a written contract may be modified by the parties' post-agreement course of performance. Here, there was no dispute that it was the custom in the trade and in Spartan's (D) dealings with its financers to reimburse the debtor following delivery of the merchandise and title. The N.Y. Supreme Court erred when it found that GMAC did not acquire a purchase money security

Continued on next page.

interest in the vehicles under § 9-107. GMAC is entitled to retain the proceeds of the sale and to summary judgment. Reversed.

ANALYSIS

Courts have also considered passage of title to be an important factor in determining whether a purchase money security interest exists. The court rejects this rule on the basis that there are many circumstances in which passing of title would be irrelevant to the intentions of the parties.

Quicknotes

PERFECTED SECURITY INTEREST A security interest that is safeguarded against other claims to the collateral; perfection is generally accomplished by legal steps necessary to give other creditors notice of the interest.

PURCHASE MONEY SECURITY INTEREST Security interest taken by a seller of the collateral to secure its purchase price.

In re Wood

Lending attorney (P) v. Borrowing attorney (D)

67 Bankr. 321 (W.D.N.Y. 1986).

NATURE OF CASE: Appeal from order holding security interest invalid.

FACT SUMMARY: Larkin (P), who had loaned money to Wood (D) and taken a security interest in certain accounts receivable but had filed no financing statement, was denied secured-creditor status on account of his alleged status as a sophisticated lender.

RULE OF LAW

That a person is a sophisticated lender does not impact his ability to claim a security interest in accounts receivable.

FACTS: Larkin (P), an attorney, loaned Wood (D), another attorney, $10,000. Larkin (P) later took as security a lien on Wood's (D) contingency interest in two cases Wood (D) was handling. Larkin (P) had otherwise no experience in using accounts receivable as security interests. Wood (D) later filed for bankruptcy. Larkin (P) brought an action seeking to enforce his security interest. The bankruptcy court held the lien invalid, and Larkin (P) appealed.

ISSUE: Will the fact that a person is a sophisticated lender impact his ability to claim a security interest in accounts receivable?

HOLDING AND DECISION: (Telesca, J.) No. That a person is a sophisticated lender does not impact his ability to claim a security interest in accounts receivable. Universal Commercial Code § 9-302 exempts from the general requirement of the filing of financing statements to perfect security interests in accounts receivable those situations where the assignment of such accounts do not constitute a significant part of the accounts of the assignor. This is meant to cover isolated or casual assignments, where neither party may be aware of or have reason to suspect the applicability of Article 9. The tests which have been developed in this area look to the percentage of the assignor's accounts that are given for security and the regularity, or lack thereof, of such assignments. Here, the Bankruptcy Court found, quite properly, that the assignment fell within § 302's exemption. However, the court concluded that, because Larkin (P) was an attorney and therefore a sophisticated lender, he was not entitled to invoke the exception. This was incorrect; as the section makes no reference to lender sophistication, this should not be considered in assessing the section's applicability. Reversed and remanded.

ANALYSIS

The test announced here is subjective in nature. The factors are: whether a "significant part" of the assignor's accounts are secured or whether the transaction is "casual or isolated." It is foreseeable that one situation can exist without the other. The courts are split on which is the more determinative criterion.

Quicknotes

ACCOUNTS RECEIVABLE Amounts that are owed pursuant to an open account and that arise in the normal course of business dealings.

SECURITY INTEREST An interest in property that may be sold upon a default in payment of the debt.

CHAPTER 21

Multistate Transactions

Quick Reference Rules of Law

PAGE

1. *Metzger v. Americredit Financial Services, Inc.* Where a state statute provides that a good faith, non-dealer purchaser of a motor vehicle obtains a vehicle by giving value for it and receiving a certificate of title that does not indicate the existence of a security interest that has previously been perfected in another jurisdiction, the good faith purchaser takes the vehicle free of the security interest even though other statutory provisions may be inconsistent with such an outcome. *198*

Metzger v. Americredit Financial Services, Inc.

Good faith vehicle purchaser (P) v. Secured interest holder (D)

Ga. Ct. App., 273 Ga. App. 453, 615 S.E.2d 120 (2005).

NATURE OF CASE: Appeal from partial grant of summary judgment for defendant in action for conversion.

FACT SUMMARY: Metzger (P) contended that as a good faith purchaser of her car, she came under an exception provided by the special good faith purchaser rule for goods covered by a certificate of title, so that she took the car free of Americredit Financial Services, Inc.'s (Americredit's) (D) security interest in it.

RULE OF LAW

Where a state statute provides that a good faith, non-dealer purchaser of a motor vehicle obtains a vehicle by giving value for it and receiving a certificate of title that does not indicate the existence of a security interest that has previously been perfected in another jurisdiction, the good faith purchaser takes the vehicle free of the security interest even though other statutory provisions may be inconsistent with such an outcome.

FACTS: Metzger (P) purchased a used car from a dealership in Georgia, not knowing that Americredit Financial Services, Inc. (Americredit) (D) had a security interest in it, which it had obtained four years earlier from Strong, who had recorded the lien on his title in New York. When Strong moved from New York to Georgia, he gave up his New York title to Georgia's Department of Motor Vehicles (DMV), but through clerical error, the lien did not transfer onto Strong's new title. Title was transferred several times afterward, each time without the lien. Over half a year after Metzger (P) purchased the car, Americredit (D) repossessed it without warning and sold it along with her personal possessions therein. Metzger (P) sued for, among other things, conversion, and moved for partial summary judgment on this claim. Americredit (D) moved for summary judgment on all the claims, and the trial court granted summary judgment to Americredit (D) on this claim because it found that Americredit (D) had a perfected security interest in the vehicle that it could enforce against Metzger (P). The state's intermediate court granted review.

ISSUE: Where a state statute provides that a good faith, non-dealer purchaser of a motor vehicle obtains a vehicle by giving value for it and receiving a certificate of title that does not indicate the existence of a security interest that has previously been perfected in another jurisdiction, does the good faith purchaser take the vehicle free of the security interest even though other statutory provisions may be inconsistent with such an outcome?

HOLDING AND DECISION: (Bernes, J.) Yes. Where a state statute provides that a good faith, non-dealer purchaser of a motor vehicle obtains a vehicle by giving value for it and receiving a certificate of title that does not indicate the existence of a security interest that has previously been perfected in another jurisdiction, the good faith purchaser takes the vehicle free of the security interest even though other statutory provisions may be inconsistent with such an outcome. The key issue here is whether Metzger (P) had the exclusive right of possession to the car, making Americredit's (D) seizure unlawful, or whether Americredit's (D) security interest entitled it to repossess the car. State law provides the exclusive procedure for perfecting a security interest in a motor vehicle in the state. This law provides that perfection occurs when the application documents properly reflect the security interest and are delivered to the DMV. Such perfection is not affected by the DMV's failure to reflect the security interest on the title instruments that it issues, since compliance with the filing requirements has the effect of imputing constructive notice to all who may subsequently acquire an interest in or lien against the property. Under these provisions, it is clear that Americredit (D) had a perfected security interest. However, the statute has three exceptions. One of these is for a good faith purchaser who is not a dealer and who obtains a certificate of title that neither shows that the goods are subject to a security interest that has been perfected in another state nor contains a statement that they may be subject to security interests not shown on the certificate. Under this section, a buyer can take free of, and the holder of a conflicting security interest can acquire priority over, a security interest that is perfected by any method under the law of another jurisdiction. All elements of the exception are satisfied here, since Americredit (D) first perfected its interest in New York, Metzger (P) was not a car dealer, Metzger (P) gave value and received a title issued by the state that did not show the security interest, and Metzger (P) did not have any knowledge of the security interest. Therefore, Metzger (P) took free of Americredit's (D) security interest. To this, Americredit (D) argues that once Strong submitted the application documents, its security interest was no longer perfected under New York law, but was perfected in Georgia, so that the statutory exception cannot apply, given that it requires the erroneous certificate of title to be issued "while" the security interest in the vehicle is perfected "under the law of another jurisdiction." This argument is rejected. Although the laws of the jurisdiction that issues the title govern perfection and priority, and here

Continued on next page.

Georgia law applied because its title covered the car, the security interest perfected in New York nevertheless remained perfected under the laws of that jurisdiction. Reading the statutes governing this area together, and construing them to harmonize the legislative intent behind them, it can be seen that although Americredit's (D) security interest in the car remained perfected at the time that Metzger (P) purchased it, that security interest could not be enforced as against Metzger (P), a good faith purchaser, since the security interest was not properly reflected on the Georgia certificate of title. Moreover, a more specific statute prevails over a more general statute where they are inconsistent. Here, the statute providing the exception is more specific than the general statutory provisions addressing continued perfection of an out-of-state security interest once goods become covered by a Georgia certificate of title. Therefore, any inconsistency is resolved in favor of the provision containing the exception. Reversed and remanded.

ANALYSIS

As can be seen from this case, Universal Commercial Code (U.C.C.) § 9-337 [which provides the special good faith purchaser rule in subsection (1)], the U.C.C. favors non-business buyers, so that a car dealer in Metzger's (P) position would not benefit from the special rule. Also, the U.C.C. choice of law rules governing perfection, provide a general rule that the law of perfection (and priority) will be the law of the debtor's location. The debtor's location for a debtor created by registration in a state is the state of registration. However, for security interests in fixtures perfected by filing, timber to be cut, and perfection attained by the secured party taking possession of the collateral, the perfection is governed by the law of the jurisdiction in which the collateral is located.

Quicknotes

COLLATERAL Property that secures the payment of a debt.

CONVERSION The act of depriving an owner of his property without permission or justification.

GOOD FAITH PURCHASER A party who purchases property in good faith and for valuable consideration without notice of a defect in title.

LIEN A claim against the property of another in order to secure the payment of a debt.

PERFECTED SECURITY INTEREST A security interest that is safeguarded against other claims to the collateral; perfection is generally accomplished by legal steps necessary to give other creditors notice of the interest.

SECURITY INTEREST An interest in property that may be sold upon a default in payment of the debt.

CHAPTER 22

Priority

Quick Reference Rules of Law

In re Zaochney

[Parties not identified.]

2011 WL 6148727, 76 U.C.C. Rep. Serv. 2d 340 (Bankr. D. Alaska 2011).

NATURE OF CASE: Motion in chapter 7 bankruptcy proceedings to value a security interest.

FACT SUMMARY: Alaska USA Federal Credit Union (Alaska USA) (D), the debtor's (P) creditor, asserted that the debtor's (P) 2008 Chevrolet Impala, valued at $12,950, pursuant to dragnet, cross-collateralization clauses found in its loan documentation, could be used to secure both the debtor's (P) car loan (loan balance of $11,097.87) and her credit line loan (up to $1,852.13 of the outstanding balance). The debtor (P) contended that the dragnet clauses were unenforceable.

RULE OF LAW

In the absence of bad faith, overreaching or unconscionability, dragnet cross-collateralization clauses in consumer loan agreements are enforceable under Uniform Commercial Code (U.C.C.) § 9-204.

FACTS: The debtor (P) in bankruptcy filed a motion to value the security interest of Alaska USA Federal Credit Union (Alaska USA) (D) in a 2008 Chevrolet Impala. Alaska USA contended that the Impala was encumbered not only by a purchase money lien, but also by sums due on a credit line, through dragnet clauses found in its loan documentation. The debtor (P) signed a credit line loan agreement with Alaska USA (D), which contained a clause titled "Cross-Collateralization," and which provided that "Collateral pledged as security for other loans I have now or in the future with Credit Union will also be security for this agreement." Ten days after receiving the credit line, the debtor (P) purchased the Impala, financing the purchase through Alaska USA (D). On the front page of the sale contract, a provision stated, "As permitted by law the goods or Property Being Purchased secures other obligations now or hereafter owed by you to the Creditor and other Collateral held by the Creditor, including funds on deposit with the Creditor, secures this Contract." The reverse side of the sales contract contained a paragraph that stated, "As provided by law, the Collateral for this contract secures other obligations you owe now or later to the Creditor, and other Collateral the Creditor presently holds or later obtains, also secures this contract." The dragnet provisions were not embedded in fine print or written in inscrutable language. The debtor (P) subsequently filed for chapter 7 bankruptcy, listing, in addition to her debts to Alaska USA (D) secured by her house and the Impala, two unsecured debts owed to the credit union: a deficiency balance of $4,836.22 on a repossessed 2005 Chevrolet Trailblazer and $5,000.00 for her credit line. The debtor (P) sought to reaffirm her car loan. Alaska USA (D) placed a value of $12,950.00 on the vehicle, which the debtor did not dispute. Alaska USA (D) contended the vehicle, through the dragnet clauses, secured not only the balance due on the Impala, $11,097.87, but also roughly $1,852.13 of the outstanding balance on the credit line. The debtor (P) disagreed, contending that the dragnet clauses were unenforceable and, therefore, the Impala was collateral only for the vehicle loan.

ISSUE: In the absence of bad faith, overreaching or unconscionability, are dragnet cross-collateralization clauses in consumer loan agreements enforceable under U.C.C. § 9-204?

HOLDING AND DECISION: (MacDonald, J.) Yes. In the absence of bad faith, overreaching or unconscionability, dragnet cross-collateralization clauses in consumer loan agreements are enforceable under U.C.C. § 9-204. Case law decided before § 9-204 was amended in 2001 is inapplicable here. Those decisions held that dragnet clauses deserved strict scrutiny. Because § 9-204 permits a security agreement to "provide that collateral secures . . . future advances or other value, whether or not the advances or value are given pursuant to the commitment," the rationale of decisions decided before the statute was amended is no longer applicable. Under the statute, parties are free to agree that a security interest secures any obligations whatsoever, and determining the obligations secured by collateral is solely a matter of construing the parties' agreement under applicable law. Accordingly, the debtor's (P) reliance on pre-2001 cases is misplaced. In the few published decisions issued after the U.C.C. amendments where courts have declined to enforce a cross-collateralization clause, the facts of those cases are distinguishable from the ones found here. In other cases decided after the amendments, courts have enforced cross-collateralization provisions in a consumer context, with the result that credit lines or deficiency balances were secured by the debtor's vehicle, and one court did so in spite of finding that the loans were adhesion contracts. Another court stated that a debtor's failure to read the loan documentation was an inadequate defense to the enforcement of these provisions. Here, the loan documents were clear about the cross-collateralization and the debtor (P) knowingly agreed to those terms. She has not submitted any evidence that the intent of the parties was anything other than as set forth in the documents, nor has she submitted any evidence of bad faith, overreaching or unconscionability. Therefore, the dragnet clauses found in the debtor's (P) loan documents

Continued on next page.

with Alaska USA (D) are valid and enforceable, and the Impala is collateral for both the debtor's (P) car loan and her credit line loan.

ANALYSIS

Under amended § 9-204, cross-collateralization clauses may not be enforced where they occur in a loan taken out by joint debtors and the creditor attempts to use the collateral to secure debt of just one of the debtors that is unrelated to the collateral. See, e.g., *In re Keeton*, 2008 Bankr. LEXIS 702, 2008 WL 686938 (Bankr. M.D. Ala. 2008), where the court held that a car loan taken out by joint debtors secured by the vehicle did not operate to secure the credit card liability of just one of the debtors. The court's rationale was that, where the loan defined "debtor" to mean both of the debtors, there was no indication that the parties intended the vehicle to secure the separate and individual obligations of just one of the debtor. Similarly, in *First National Bank of Izard County v. Garner*, 86 Ark. App. 213, 167 S.W.3d 664 (Ark. App. 2004), the court declined to apply a dragnet clause in a loan taken out by three debtors, secured by real property and a tractor, so that it would encompass a subsequent loan taken out by just one of the debtors individually. The court found that the subsequent loan was entirely unrelated to the first loan and could not have been within the contemplation of the parties at the time the first loan was taken out.

Quicknotes

BAD FAITH Conduct that is intentionally misleading or deceptive.

CHAPTER 7 BANKRUPTCY A legal proceeding whereby a debtor, who is unable to pay his debts as they become due, is relieved of his obligation to pay his creditors by liquidation and distribution of his remaining assets.

COLLATERAL Property that secures the payment of a debt.

CROSS-COLLATERAL CLAUSE Provision contained in a contract pursuant to which both parties provide security that performance will be rendered or that payment will be made.

DRAGNET CLAUSE A clause in a mortgage agreement making the property that is the subject of the agreement the security for past or future indebtedness.

SECURITY AGREEMENT An agreement creating a security interest on behalf of a creditor in certain personal property.

SECURITY INTEREST An interest in property that may be sold upon a default in payment of the debt.

STRICT SCRUTINY Method by which courts determine the constitutionality of a law, when a law affects a fundamental right. Under the test, the legislature must have had a compelling interest to enact the law and measures prescribed by the law must be the least restrictive means possible to accomplish its goal.

UNCONSCIONABILITY A situation in which a contract, or a particular contract term, is unenforceable if the court determines that such terms are unduly oppressive or unfair to one party to the contract.

In re Wild West World, L.L.C., Debtor

[Parties not identified.]

2008 WL 4642263, 66 U.C.C. Rep. Serv. 2d 1033 (Bankr. D. Kan. 2008).

NATURE OF CASE: Motion for summary judgment in adversary proceeding in bankruptcy to determine priority between creditors.

FACT SUMMARY: Larson (D), which delivered an amusement ride (the "Ride") to Wild West World (debtor (P)), contended that its sales contract, which provided that title remained with Larson (D) until the Ride was paid for in full, was not negated by the state's version of Uniform Commercial Code (U.C.C.) § 2-401(1), so that First National, which loaned money to debtor (P), could not have secured its loan with the Ride, and, therefore, Larson's (D) interest in the Ride was superior to that of First National.

RULE OF LAW

(1) Under U.C.C. § 2-401(1), once a creditor delivers goods to the debtor, the creditor's reservation of title is negated, leaving the creditor with only a purchase money security interest in the goods.

(2) Where a holder of a purchase money security interest fails to perfect its security interest within 20 days of delivery, it becomes subject to the general rules of priority between secured creditors.

FACTS: In November 2005, Wild West World (debtor (P)) entered into an agreement with Larson (D) for the purchase of an amusement ride (the "Ride"). In accord with the practice in the amusement ride industry, the purchase agreement provided that title to the Ride would not pass to debtor (P) until the Ride has been paid in full. The Ride was delivered to debtor (P) in March 2007, and Larson (D) filed a financing statement in June 2007. In the meantime, First National loaned over $6 million to debtor (P) for the construction of the amusement park in which the Ride would be used. In conjunction with the construction loan, debtor (P) and First National entered into a commercial security agreement in which debtor (P) granted a blanket security interest in debtor's (P) property. First National filed its financing statement in March 2006 perfecting a security interest in all of debtor's (P) business assets. Debtor (P) eventually declared bankruptcy. First National's lien secured a claim of $6,507,871; Larson (D) filed a proof of claim for $164,824. During the pendency of the bankruptcy, the Ride was liquidated and debtor (P) held net proceeds of $85,800, plus interest. Debtor (P) filed an adversary proceeding, and Larson (D) claimed that as an unpaid seller who reserved title to the Ride until being paid in full, it had an interest that primed that of the First National's lien perfected blanket security interest. First National argued that the state's version of U.C.C. § 2-401(1), Larson's (D) reservation of title in the delivered Ride was negated, so that all Larson (D) had was a security interest, and that, since Larson (D) filed its financing statement after First National filed its financing statement, First National had priority.

ISSUE:

(1) Under Uniform Commercial Code § 2-401(1), once a creditor delivers goods to the debtor, is the creditor's reservation of title negated, leaving the creditor with only a purchase money security interest in the goods?

(2) Where a holder of a purchase money security interest fails to perfect its security interest within 20 days of delivery, does it become subject to the general rules of priority between secured creditors?

HOLDING AND DECISION: (Nugent, C.J.)

(1) Yes. Under Uniform Commercial Code § 2-401(1), once a creditor delivers goods to the debtor, the creditor's reservation of title is negated, leaving the creditor with only a purchase money security interest in the goods. Section 2-401(1) provides in pertinent part: "Any retention or reservation by the seller of the title (property) in goods shipped or delivered to the buyer is limited in effect to a reservation of a security interest. Subject to these provisions and to Article 9, title to goods passes from the seller to the buyer in any manner and on any conditions explicitly agreed on by the parties." State case law precedent, as well as numerous decisions from other jurisdictions, holds that under § 2-401(1) the interest of an unpaid seller in goods already delivered to a buyer is subordinate to the interest of the holder of a perfected security interest in those same goods. Section 2-401(1) negates the ability to delay passage of title beyond delivery. Any express agreement of the parties or reservation of title in the seller is limited by the statute, which cannot be varied by custom and usage in the trade, course of dealing, or agreement. Therefore, Larson (D) cannot prevail on its argument that because it expressly reserved title until full payment under the purchase agreement, it avoids the operation of § 2-401(1). Larson (D) seizes upon the "unless otherwise explicitly agreed" language in the first sentence and the "title . . . passes . . . in any manner and on any conditions explicitly agreed on by the parties" language in the third sentence of § 2-401(1). However, it ignores the prefatory language in the statute: "Subject to these provisions and to Article 9. . . ." It is clear from this language that the ability to expressly agree on when title passes to the

Continued on next page.

buyer is subject to the second sentence of § 2-401(1), which limits reservation of title upon delivery. It is only when the seller has delivered the goods to the buyer that a seller's express reservation of title is limited to retention of a security interest. If there has been no delivery, the express reservation of title may be enforced. In accordance with these provisions, because Larson (D) voluntarily delivered the Ride to debtor prior to payment in full, Larson (D) retained only a security interest in the Ride. The question then becomes which secured creditor has priority.

(2) Yes. Where a holder of a purchase money security interest fails to perfect its security interest within 20 days of delivery, it becomes subject to the general rules of priority between secured creditors. The general rule is that the party that first files a financing statement in the same property has priority. An exception to this rule is that the holder of a purchase money security interest—such as Larson (D) here—has priority over a perfected non-purchase money security interest in the same collateral, provided the purchase money creditor perfects its security interest within 20 days of delivery of the collateral to the debtor. This special priority rule for purchase money security interests applies even if the non-purchase money security interest was perfected by filing prior to the purchase money security interest. Here, Larson (D) filed its financing statement a few months after delivery, and therefore does not come within the 20-day exception. Because First National was first to file its financing statement in the Ride, under the general rule, First National has priority. First National is entitled to the proceeds from the sale of the Ride held by debtor (P). Summary judgment for First National.

ANALYSIS

As this case demonstrates, a purchase money security interest (PMSI) in commercial goods must be perfected within a 20-day period following the buyer's possession of the goods for the PMSI to be given priority over earlier perfected interests. However, under U.C.C. § 9-309(1), where consumer goods are involved, the PMSI is perfected upon attachment, so the seller does not have to take any other steps to prevail over earlier or later interests.

Quicknotes

PURCHASE MONEY SECURITY INTEREST Security interest taken by a seller of the collateral to secure its purchase price.

SECURED CREDITOR A creditor, the repayment of whose loan is secured by collateral sufficient to repay the debt owed.

Kunkel v. Sprague National Bank

Bankruptcy trustee (P) v. Secured creditor (D)

128 F.3d 636 (8th Cir. 1997).

NATURE OF CASE: Adversarial proceeding in a bankruptcy case.

FACT SUMMARY: The trustee in bankruptcy (P) filed an adversarial proceeding to determine the superiority between competing interests of Hoxie Feeders, Inc., a purchase money secured creditor, and Sprague National Bank (D), in the net proceeds from the sale of the Morkens' livestock inventory.

RULE OF LAW

A purchase money security interest (PMSI) has superiority over an earlier perfected interest where: (a) the PMSI is perfected at the time the debtor receives possession of the inventory; (b) the PMSI creditor gives written notification to all holders of competing interests that had Universal Commercial Code (U.C.C.)-1 financing statements on file when the PMSI creditor filed its U.C.C.-1; (c) the competing secured creditor receives notification within five years before the debtor receives possession of the inventory; and (d) the notification state that the person expects to acquire a PMSI in the inventory of the debtor and describing such inventory.

FACTS: Sprague National Bank (Sprague) (D) made several loans to the Morkens pursuant to certain loan agreements and promissory notes. The Morkens executed a security agreement in favor of Sprague (D) in their inventory, farm products, equipment and accounts receivable. Hoxie Feeders, Inc. (Hoxie) finances and sells cattle. The Morkens purchased interests in approximately 1900 head of cattle from Hoxie. For each transaction, Morken executed a loan agreement and promissory note granting Hoxie a purchase money security interest (PMSI) in the cattle. Hoxie did not file a U.C.C.-1 financing statement but instead perfected its security interest by taking possession of the cattle pursuant to feedlot agreements. The Morkens filed a Chapter 11 bankruptcy case. Hoxie then sold the cattle and, after deducting the amounts owed Hoxie for care and feeding, $550,000 remained. The bankruptcy trustee (P) commenced a proceeding to determine whether Sprague (D) or Hoxie was entitled to the sale proceeds. Hoxie and the trustee reached a settlement. Hoxie and Sprague (D) filed cross-motions for summary judgment and the district court affirmed the bankruptcy court's summary judgment for Hoxie holding that Hoxie had priority over Sprague's (D) earlier security interest in the collateral. The district court also held that Sprague (D) did not have a security interest in the cattle under the U.C.C. because the debtor "lacked rights in the collateral." Sprague (D) appealed.

ISSUE: Does a purchase money security interest have superiority over an earlier perfected interest?

HOLDING AND DECISION: (Gibson, J.) Yes. A purchase money security interest has superiority over an earlier perfected interest where: (a) the PMSI is perfected at the time the debtor receives possession of the inventory; (b) the PMSI creditor gives written notification to all holders of competing interests that had U.C.C.-1 financing statements on file when the PMSI creditor filed its U.C.C.-1; (c) the competing secured creditor receives notification within five years before the debtor receives possession of the inventory; and (d) the notification state that the person expects to acquire a PMSI in the inventory of the debtor and describing such inventory. Under the U.C.C., a security interest attaches where: (a) either the secured party has possession of the collateral by agreement with the debtor or the debtor has signed a security agreement; (b) value has been given; and (c) the debtor has rights in the collateral. The U.C.C. fails to define the term "rights in the collateral." Courts consider such factors as the extent of the debtor's control over the property and whether the debtor bears the risk of ownership. Article 2 principles may also be considered. The district court erred in its interpretation of Article 2, since the sale and delivery of the cattle by Hoxie to Morken granted Morken "rights in the collateral." This was based on the fact that a sale has transpired, Hoxie had constructively delivered the cattle to Morken and had possession of the cattle on Morken's behalf, Morken had title to and owned the cattle, Hoxie merely retained a security interest in the cattle as bailee, Hoxie's U.C.C. Article remedy of refusing to deliver the cattle had been cut off, and Morken had rights in the collateral sufficient for Sprague's (D) security interest to attach. Thus, Sprague (D) had a perfected security interest in the cattle and the district court is reversed as to that issue. However, Hoxie's PMSI has superiority over Sprague's (D) interest under the Kansas U.C.C. § 84-9-312(3). The general rule is that the first creditor to perfect its security interest beats later perfected security interests. However, the PMSI provides an exception to the general rule and has superiority over an earlier perfected interest where: (a) the PMSI is perfected at the time the debtor receives possession of the inventory; (b) the PMSI creditor gives written notification to all holders of competing interests that had U.C.C.-1 financing statements on file when the PMSI creditor filed its U.C.C.-1; (c) the competing secured creditor receives notification within five years before the debtor receives possession of the inventory; and (d) the notification state that the person expects to acquire a PMSI in the inventory of the debtor

Continued on next page.

and describing such inventory. Sprague (D) argued that superiority status could not be obtained by a PMSI creditor who perfected its security interest by possession rather than filing. There is no support for this in the U.C.C. Next it must be determined whether Hoxie fulfilled the statutory requirements to obtain superiority. The only issue here is the timing of Hoxie's PMSI notice, which was received after the cattle were sold and this suit commenced. The notification requirement here is triggered by actual and not constructive possession of the inventory; thus, notification was timely. Sprague (D) also argued that the purpose of the statute is frustrated by granting superiority to as PMSI without requiring pre-perfection notification to prior filed secured creditors. The notification is required to state that the person expects or has a PMSI in the particular inventory; thus, the PMSI can wait to notify competing secured creditors until after it has acquired and perfected its security interest. Reversed as to the district court's holding that Sprague (D) did not have a security interest in the cattle and affirmed as to its judgment that Hoxie's security interest has priority.

ANALYSIS

Note that the 1999 revision of the U.C.C. elaborates the procedure for obtaining a PMSI in a debtor's livestock.

Quicknotes

PURCHASE MONEY SECURITY INTEREST Security interest taken by a seller of the collateral to secure its purchase price.

International Harvester Co. v. Glendenning

Corporation (P) v. Farmer (D)

Tex. Sup. Ct., 505 S.W.2d 320, 14 U.C.C. Rep. Serv. 837 (1974).

NATURE OF CASE: Appeal from denial of award of damages for conversion.

FACT SUMMARY: Glendenning (D) contended that he had purchased certain equipment in the ordinary course of business, even though he had been aware that the vendor had misrepresented certain aspects of the transaction.

RULE OF LAW

A vendee does not purchase in the ordinary course of business if he is aware of improprieties in the transaction.

FACTS: Barnes, an International Harvester Co. (P) dealer, sold to Glendenning (D), a farmer and occasional farm-equipment dealer, three tractors for $16,000. Glendenning (D) knew the tractors were worth about $22,500. When filling out the paper work, Barnes stated that the tractors had been sold for $24,700, $16,000 in cash and $9,700 worth of trade-in equipment. Glendenning (D), who had once been an International Harvester (P) dealer himself, knew that Barnes had done this to placate International Harvester (P), which had a purchase money security interest in the tractors he bought. Glendenning (D) later sold the tractors. International Harvester (P) brought a conversion action. The jury held Glendenning (D) to have been a purchaser in the ordinary course of business who took free of International Harvester's (P) lien. International Harvester (P) appealed.

ISSUE: Does a vendee purchase in the ordinary course of business if he is aware of improprieties in the transaction?

HOLDING AND DECISION: (Williams, C.J.) No. A vendee does not purchase in the ordinary course of business if he is aware of improprieties in the transaction. To be a buyer in the ordinary course of business within the meaning of Universal Commercial Code (U.C.C.) § 9-307 requires that the buyer act in good faith without knowledge that the sale to him is in violation of the rights of a third party. Here, Glendenning (D), an experienced seller of International Harvester (P) products, had ample reason to suspect that the reason for Barnes's falsification of the record of sale was to deceive International Harvester (P) into thinking that its security interest had not been impaired. This hardly constituted good faith. For that reason the jury was demonstrably wrong in its finding that Glendenning (D) had been a buyer in the ordinary course of business. Reversed.

ANALYSIS

U.C.C. & 9-307 does not define a buyer in the ordinary course of business. However, the section does refer to § 1-201(9). There, it is provided that such a buyer must purchase without knowledge that he is impairing the rights of a third party.

Quicknotes

ORDINARY COURSE OF BUSINESS The conducting of business in accordance with standard customs and practices.

PURCHASE MONEY SECURITY INTEREST Security interest taken by a seller of the collateral to secure its purchase price.

VENDEE Purchaser.

In re Western Iowa Limestone, Inc.

[Parties not identified.]

538 F.3d 858, 66 U.C.C. Rep. Serv. 2d 542 (8th Cir. 2008).

NATURE OF CASE: Appeal from bankruptcy appellate panel reversal of bankruptcy court judgment granting priority to purchasers of goods over a secured creditor in a bankruptcy proceeding to determine the distribution of proceeds from the sale of a debtor's inventory.

FACT SUMMARY: Dealers (P), who purchased agricultural lime ("ag lime") from Western Iowa Limestone, Inc. (WIL) and left their purchased ag lime on WIL's premises, contended that, under the state's version of Uniform Commercial Code (U.C.C.) § 1-201(9), they were buyers in the ordinary course of business (BIOC) because they had constructive possession of the ag lime, thus giving them priority over United Bank of Iowa (United Bank) (D), which held a secured interest in all of WIL's inventory.

RULE OF LAW

(1) For purposes of the definition of a buyer in the ordinary course of business in U.C.C. § 1-201(9), a buyer who purchases fungible goods from a seller but leaves the goods at the seller's premises satisfies, through constructive possession, the requirement that the buyer "take [] possession of the goods."

(2) A purchaser of goods retained by the seller as a bailee of the goods does not have to provide notice to a creditor who has a secured interest in the seller's inventory in order for the purchaser to constructively possess the goods.

FACTS: Various Dealers (P) purchased agricultural lime ("ag lime") from Western Iowa Limestone, Inc. (WIL). As was the custom in the industry, the Dealers (P) left their purchased ag lime on WIL's premises in one fungible pile until the Dealers (P) resold it to their customers and removed it from the premises. WIL filed for chapter 11 bankruptcy-protection. At that time, the Dealers (P) had not removed all the ag lime they had already paid for from WIL's premises. United Bank of Iowa (United Bank) (D) was WIL's largest secured creditor, and it had a security interest in all of WIL's assets, including its inventory, to secure a $6 million loan. The ag lime remaining on WIL's premises was sold in the bankruptcy proceedings as part of its inventory, and the Dealers (P) filed a joint objection to the proposed distributions from the sale of the inventory, claiming priority over United Bank (D) as buyers in the ordinary course of business (BIOC), as that term is defined in the state's version of U.C.C. § 1-201(9), to the extent of the value of the ag lime they had purchased but had not yet removed from WIL's premises. The bankruptcy court concluded that the Dealers (P) had taken constructive possession of the ag lime and had satisfied the requirements for BIOC status. The bankruptcy appellate panel (BAP) reversed, and the court of appeals granted review.

ISSUE:

(1) For purposes of the definition of a buyer in the ordinary course of business in U.C.C. § 1-201(9), does a buyer who purchases fungible goods from a seller but leaves the goods at the seller's premises satisfy, through constructive possession, the requirement that the buyer "take [] possession of the goods"?

(2) Does a purchaser of goods retained by the seller as a bailee of the goods have to provide notice to a creditor who has a secured interest in the seller's inventory in order for the purchaser to constructively possess the goods?

HOLDING AND DECISION: (Hansen, J.)

(1) Yes. For purposes of the definition of a buyer in the ordinary course of business in U.C.C. § 1-201(9), a buyer who purchases fungible goods from a seller but leaves the goods at the seller's premises satisfies, through constructive possession, the requirement that the buyer "take [] possession of the goods." Under the state's version of U.C.C. § 9-320(1), "a buyer in ordinary course of business . . . takes free of a security interest created by the buyer's seller, even if the security interest is perfected and the buyer knows of its existence." Thus if the Dealers (P) are entitled to BIOC status, they take free of United Bank's (D) prior security interest. As relevant here, under the definition of BIOC, only a buyer that takes possession of the goods may be a buyer in ordinary course of business. BIOC status also requires that the sale comport with the usual or customary practices for the kind of business involved. Thus, the key issue is whether a buyer who purchases fungible goods from a seller but leaves the goods at the seller's premises satisfies the requirement that the buyer "take [] possession of the goods. The term "possession" is not defined in § 1-201(9), nor does the statute elaborate on what it means to "take possession." Because the term "possession" could mean either constructive possession or physical possession, the statute is ambiguous, and, as is the practice in the state's courts, the common law is looked to for construing undefined terms. State case law holds that "possession" under some sections of the U.C.C. can encompass constructive possession, and there is no reason to believe that state courts would construe the undefined term "possession" to include constructive possession in some sec-

Continued on next page.

tions of the U.C.C. and not in others. Also, where the state's legislature intended to supplant the common law in the U.C.C., it specifically provided so. Thus, it can be inferred that the legislature intended courts to look to the common law to interpret undefined terms contained in the U.C.C. Under the state's common law, possession includes constructive possession. Therefore, possession in § 1-201(9) can include constructive possession. This conclusion is consistent with the purpose of the BIOC status and the fact that the transfer of possessory rights as between the buyer and the seller is a logical point at which to sever the security interest held by the seller's lender when the seller sells its goods in the ordinary course of its business. If only physical possession counted as possession, then a buyer who completed a sales transaction and placed goods with a bailee would not be considered a BIOC, but would continue to be subject to the lender's security interest. However, in this scenario, as between the buyer and the seller, the seller would have no authority for regaining possession of the goods from the bailee, and the buyer clearly would have the superior possessory interest as compared to the seller. Further, the lender would be secured by the proceeds of the sale and would no longer need the security provided by the goods themselves. The outcome should not differ based on whether the bailee is a third party or the seller, such as WIL was here. Reversed as to this issue.

(2) No. A purchaser of goods retained by the seller as a bailee of the goods does not have to provide notice to a creditor who has a secured interest in the seller's inventory in order for the purchaser to constructively possess the goods. The BAP believed that constructive possession could not be accomplished without such notice, and therefore held that the Dealers (P) did not have constructive possession. The BAP was wrong. The cases it relied on involved application of a statute that specifically required notice when a seller retained actual possession. That statute, however, is no longer on the books. Under state case law, constructive possession does not hinge on notice to the world; it is based on the knowledge and agreement of the parties rather than notice to the world. Moreover, the state's highest court has applied that interpretation to a different section of the U.C.C., and there is no reason to treat constructive possession differently for purposes of § 1-201(9). Applying this concept of constructive possession, the Dealers (P) here constructively possessed the ag lime. Title passed to them at the time of sale, the ag lime was identified to the contract, and delivery occurred at WIL's premises, where the parties agreed the ag lime would remain until removed. Because notice is not a requirement for constructive possession, the BAP erred in concluding that constructive possession required notice to the world. Finally, although there was conflicting evidence as to whether the sales of ag lime were conducted in a manner that was customary in WIL's business or in the industry, the bankruptcy court's finding that the sales were made in a manner consistent with the usual and customary practice in the industry was not clearly erroneous. For all these reasons, the Dealers (P) satisfied the requirements of being buyers in the ordinary course of business. Reversed as to this issue.

ANALYSIS

This decisions focused on the "takes possession" phrase portion of the definition of BIOC in § 1-201(9). However, to be a BIOC, the buyer must satisfy several other requirements, including that the buyer buys goods in good faith, without knowledge that the sale violates the rights of another person in the goods, and in the ordinary course from a person in the business of selling goods of that kind. The buyer must comport with the usual or customary practices in the kind of business in which the seller is engaged or with the seller's own usual or customary practices; and the buyer may not acquire the goods in a transfer in bulk or as security for or in total or partial satisfaction of a money debt. BIOC status also does not apply to a buyer buying farm products from a person engaged in farming operations.

Quicknotes

CHAPTER 11 BANKRUPTCY A legal proceeding whereby a debtor, who is unable to pay his debts as they become due, is relieved of his obligation to pay his creditors through reorganization and payment from future income.

ORDINARY COURSE OF BUSINESS The conducting of business in accordance with standard customs and practices.

POSSESSION The holding of property with the right of disposition.

SECURED CREDITOR A creditor, the repayment of whose loan is secured by collateral sufficient to repay the debt owed.

Clovis National Bank v. Thomas

Bank (P) v. Cattle broker (D)

N.M. Sup. Ct., 77 N.M. 554, 425 P.2d 726 (1967).

NATURE OF CASE: Appeal from denial of award of damages for conversion.

FACT SUMMARY: Clovis National Bank (P), having a security interest in certain cattle, allowed the debtor to retain possession thereof for sale.

RULE OF LAW

When a chattel mortgagee of livestock allows the debtor to possess the stock for sale, the sales broker will not be liable if the mortgagee loses his security.

FACTS: W.D. Bunch had a continuing relationship with Clovis National Bank (the Bank) (P) wherein the Bank (P) would advance monies to Bunch, to buy young cattle which he would raise and then sell, usually at auction. The Bank (P) would take a security interest in the cattle to secure the loans. The security agreement provided that Bunch would not dispose of the cattle without first obtaining the Bank's (P) approval. Nonetheless, Bunch regularly sold the cattle without notifying the Bank (P), a practice which the Bank (P) knew about without raising an objection. At one point, certain cattle purchased by Bunch received the brand of his son, and, when they were sold, the proceeds were paid to the son, who refused to turn any monies over to the Bank (P). The Bank (P) sued Thomas (D), the cattle broker/auctioneer, for conversion. The trial court found for Thomas (D), and the Bank (P) appealed.

ISSUE: When a chattel mortgagee of livestock allows the debtor to possess the stock for sale, will the sales broker be liable if the mortgagee loses his security?

HOLDING AND DECISION: (Oman, J.) No. When a chattel mortgagee of livestock allows the debtor to possess the stock for sale, the sales broker will not be liable if the mortgagee loses his security. The general rule is that when an auctioneer sells property on behalf of a principal who was not in fact legally authorized to convey title, the auctioneer is liable to any true owner or mortgagee, whether or not he had actual or constructive knowledge of that person's interest. However, it is also the rule that when a mortgagee under a chattel mortgage allows the mortgagor to retain possession of the property and sell the same at will, the mortgagee waives his lien as against third parties. This is precisely the case here. The Bank (P) was admittedly aware of Bunch's habit of selling the cattle without its consent. Consequently, it waived any rights it might have had against third parties, such as Thomas (D). Affirmed.

ANALYSIS

The significance of the farmer's role in American society is the basis for the Universal Commercial Code's deference shown farmers as debtors. Unlike with purchase of other kinds of goods, a buyer in the ordinary course who purchases farm products does not take free of the interest of another's secured interest in the goods purchased. The drafters of the code sought to encourage financial institutions to lend to farmers; in turn, their encouragement comes from the knowledge that this interest in the goods will not be lost if they are sold to a third party. In *Clovis*, only because the lender knew of the circumstances was the rule not applied, as that knowledge was deemed a valid waiver.

Quicknotes

CHATTEL An article of personal property, as distinguished from real property; a thing personal and moveable.

CONVERSION The act of depriving an owner of his property without permission or justification.

ESTOPPEL An equitable doctrine precluding a party from asserting a right to the detriment of another whom justifiably relied on the conduct.

SECURITY INTEREST An interest in property that may be sold upon a default in payment of the debt.

Farm Credit Bank of St. Paul v. F & A Dairy

Bank (P) v. Dairy farm (D)

Wis. Ct. App., 165 Wis. 2d 360, 477 N.W.2d 357 (1991).

NATURE OF CASE: Appeal from award of restitution for conversion.

FACT SUMMARY: In Farm Credit Bank of St. Paul's (the Bank) (P) action in conversion against F & A Dairy (D), the district court awarded the Bank (P) restitution for certain payments due it under a security-interest-satisfying payment obligation, even though F & A (D) was not privy to the agreement creating the interest.

RULE OF LAW

A buyer of farm products takes them subject to a security interest created by the seller where he receives written notice of this interest from the secured party within one year before the sale of the products.

FACTS: As collateral for a loan, Farm Credit Bank of St. Paul (the Bank) (P) obtained and perfected a security interest from the Bonneprises, covering all accounts arising from the sale or other disposition of their milk and milk products. The Bonneprises were selling milk to Land O' Lakes Dairy. In return for waiver of its lien, the Bank (P) executed an assignment with Land O' Lakes and the Bonneprises whereby Land O' Lakes would pay the Bank (P) $4,333 per month from the Bonneprises' milk proceeds. After the Bonneprises switched dairies and began selling their milk to F & A Dairy (D) in August 1988, the Bank (P) notified F & A Dairy (D) on and four days after August 22, 1988, of its assignment and security interest and demanded payments in accordance with the assignment. When F & A (D) refused to pay the Bank (P) for the months of August through November, the Bank (P) brought an action in conversion against F & A (D) to recover the amount due. The district court awarded restitution in that amount plus 5 percent interest. F & A (D) appealed.

ISSUE: Does a buyer of farm products take them subject to a security interest created by the seller where he receives written notice of this interest from the secured party within one year before the sale of the products?

HOLDING AND DECISION: (Cane, J.) Yes. A buyer of farm products takes them subject to a security interest created by the seller where he receives written notice of this interest from the secured party within one year before the sale of the products. This rule merely restates the principle articulated in 7 U.S.C. § 1631 of the Food Security Act. Where the buyer receives proper notice, including notice of any payment obligation, but fails to perform this obligation, he purchases the products subject to the security interest. Here, F & A (D) received notice of the Bank's (P) security interest in the milk it purchased from the Bonneprises, including notice of the $4,333 per month payment obligation but failed to comply with the obligation. Thus, the trial court did not err in requiring it to perform the obligation for the months it had adequate notice with interest. Affirmed in part; reversed in part; and remanded.

ANALYSIS

The financing statement a buyer files with the central filing office under the Food Security Act must be more detailed than the usual one filed under the Universal Commercial Code (U.C.C.) See § 1631(c)(4) for the definition of an "effective financing statement," which must include, among other things, the Social Security number of the debtor, the amount of farm products covered, and their location. See also "The Reborn Farm Products Exception Under the Food Security Act of 1985, 20 U.C.C.," *Sanford L. J.* 3 (1987). Assuming the proper guidelines are followed, if the buyer obtains either a release or waiver from the secured party (or follows his instructions as to payments), the buyer takes free of the security interest in the farm products.

Quicknotes

ASSIGNMENT A transaction in which a party conveys his or her entire interest in property to another.

CONVERSION The act of depriving an owner of his property without permission or justification.

RESTITUTION The return or restoration of what the defendant has gained in a transaction to prevent the unjust enrichment of the defendant.

SECURITY INTEREST An interest in property that may be sold upon a default in payment of the debt.

In re Arlco, Inc.

Creditor (P) v. Debtor (D)

239 B.R. 261, (Bankr. S.D.N.Y. 1999).

NATURE OF CASE: Motion in bankruptcy proceeding for summary judgment for reclamation.

FACT SUMMARY: Galey & Lord, Inc. (Galey) (P) sought to reclaim goods it had sold on credit to Arley Corp. (Arley) (D) (debtor), but CIT Group/Business Credit Inc. (CIT) held a perfected security interest in substantially all of Arley's (D) assets.

RULE OF LAW

A seller's reclamation claim to goods it has sold to a debtor in bankruptcy is subject to the claim of a holder of a perfected security interest in the debtor's assets and is rendered valueless upon sale of the goods where the secured claim exceeds the value of the reclamation claim.

FACTS: Galey & Lord, Inc. (Galey) (P) sold goods on credit to Arley Corp. (Arley) (D) (debtor). Before Arley (D) filed for bankruptcy under Chapter 11, Galey (P) sought to reclaim goods it had shipped to Arley (D). CIT Group/Business Credit Inc. (CIT) held a perfected security interest in substantially all of Arley's (D) assets, including inventory. After Arley (D) filed for bankruptcy, all of Arley's (D) assets as a going concern were sold under an asset purchase agreement. Galey (P) moved for summary judgment on its reclamation claim, which the bankruptcy Trustee opposed on several grounds, including that Galey's (P) right to reclamation was subject to CIT's perfected security interest.

ISSUE: Is a seller's reclamation claim to goods it has sold to a debtor in bankruptcy subject to the claim of a holder of a perfected security interest in the debtor's assets and rendered valueless upon sale of the goods where the secured claim exceeds the value of the reclamation claim?

HOLDING AND DECISION: (Gonzalez, J.) Yes. A seller's reclamation claim to goods it has sold to a debtor in bankruptcy is subject to the claim of a holder of a perfected security interest in the debtor's assets and is rendered valueless upon sale of the goods where the secured claim exceeds the value of the reclamation claim. The bankruptcy statute in § 546(c) recognizes any right of a seller to reclaim under applicable nonbankruptcy law. Universal Commercial Code (U.C.C.) § 2-702 forms the nonbankruptcy statutory right upon which sellers base their reclamation demand. In addition to providing that the seller must establish that statute's requirements, § 2-702 provides in subsection 3 that the seller's right to reclamation is subject to the rights of a good faith purchaser from the buyer. Most courts hold that a holder of a prior perfected, floating lien on inventory, like CIT here, is a good faith purchaser with rights superior to those of a reclaiming seller. Galey (P) argues that the language in § 2-702 ("under this Article") is applicable only to purchasers who acquire their interest under Article 2 of the U.C.C. An analysis of the Code, however, shows that the definition of purchaser is broad enough to include an Article 9 secured party. Thus, if CIT qualifies as a good faith purchaser for value, even if Arley (D) had voidable title to the goods, it could transfer good title to CIT, and Galey's (P) reclamation claim would be subject to CIT's interest. Notwithstanding debate by legal scholars as to whether reclaiming sellers should get priority against a prior secured lender with an after-acquired property interest, the court's task is to enforce the plain meaning of the statute. Under that plain meaning, a creditor with a security interest in after-acquired property who acted in good faith and for value, which includes acquiring rights as security for or in total or partial satisfaction of a pre-existing claim, is a good faith purchaser, and a reclaiming seller's claim is subject to the purchaser's claim. Here, CIT acted in good faith. Galey (P) argues that CIT's actions were not in good faith because it knew of Arley's (D) troubles and stopped funding Arley (D) without informing Arley's (D) other creditors. However, the U.C.C.'s good faith element does not require a secured creditor to continue to fund a business with enormous debt and losses. Such a decision is "clearly reasonable" and, therefore, there is no genuine issue as to CIT's good faith. There also is no issue that CIT gave value. Therefore, CIT qualifies as a good faith purchaser for value. Although Galey's (P) reclamation right is subject to CIT's rights, it is not automatically extinguished. Accordingly, Galey (P) argues that Galey (P) is entitled to an administrative claim or lien in lieu of its right to reclamation if there is any surplus collateral. The Trustee, however, argues that when the goods subject to the reclamation demand are liquidated and the proceeds are used to pay the secured creditor's claim, the reclaiming seller's subordinated right is rendered valueless, as opposed to being automatically extinguished. The majority approach is to give the reclaiming seller the right to reclaim, or an administrative claim or lien in lieu thereof, only when the goods or proceeds from those goods exceed the value of the secured party's claim. Here, all the goods Galey (P) sought to reclaim were sold and the proceeds were used to pay CIT—and even then a balance was due to CIT. Therefore, Galey's (P) claim was rendered valueless, as was any administrative claim or lien based on the reclamation claim.

Continued on next page.

ANALYSIS

Some legal scholars argue that § 2-702 gives a seller the rights of a purchase-money security holder for 10 days (the time period during which a seller may reclaim), and that a purchase-money lender "undoubtedly beats" a creditor with a security interest in after-acquired property. That view holds that a party with a security interest should only be considered a good faith purchaser for value if it has suffered detrimental reliance by extending new value (which CIT did not do here).

Quicknotes

AFTER-ACQUIRED PROPERTY Property acquired by a debtor after the security agreement, of which the property that is already owned by the debtor is the subject, has been perfected.

GOOD FAITH PURCHASER A party who purchases property in good faith and for valuable consideration without notice of a defect in title.

PERFECTED SECURITY INTEREST A security interest that is safeguarded against other claims to the collateral; perfection is generally accomplished by legal steps necessary to give other creditors notice of the interest.

SECURITY INTEREST An interest in property that may be sold upon a default in payment of the debt.

George v. Commercial Credit Corp.

Mobile home owner (D) v. Bank (P)

440 F.2d 551 (7th Cir. 1971).

NATURE OF CASE: Appeal from judgment upholding secured creditor's interest in a fixture.

FACT SUMMARY: In Commercial Credit Corp.'s (Commercial) (P) action against George (D), the district court ruled that despite George's (D) arguments that a mobile home, in which he as trustee in bankruptcy had an interest, was personalty and Commercial's (P) interest as mortgage was superior because the mobile home had become a fixture.

RULE OF LAW

Where personalty takes on the nature of real property, it becomes a fixture.

FACTS: After Foskett contracted to purchase a large mobile home, he executed a real estate mortgage to Highway Mobile Home Sales, Inc., which assigned the mortgage to Commercial Credit Corp. (Commercial) (P). Once the mobile home was delivered to Foskett's property, he applied for a homeowner's insurance policy, asked the seller to remove the home's wheels, and adapted it as his permanent residence. Moreover, the home was never again operated on or over the highways, and it was occupied by now-bankrupt Foskett continuously, until he was forced to vacate by order of George (D), trustee in bankruptcy. Commercial (P), however, challenged George's (D) interest in the mobile home, arguing that it had become a fixture under Wisconsin law. This, Commercial (P) asserted, made it a secured creditor with an interest superior to that of George's (D) in the home. The district court rejected George's (D) arguments that the mobile home was personalty and ruled in Commercial's (P) favor. George (D) appealed.

ISSUE: Where personalty takes on the nature of real property, does it become a fixture?

HOLDING AND DECISION: (Duffy, J.) Yes. Where personalty takes on the nature of real property, it becomes a fixture. This rule follows from examining applicable common law cases determining when personalty becomes affixed to real property. In *Auto Acceptance and Loan Corp. v. Keln*, 18 Wis. 2d 178 (1962), the court reaffirmed an earlier decision which stated the three tests for determining in a given case whether facilities remain personalty or have become fixtures. These tests are: (1) actual physical annexation to the realty; (2) application or adoption to the use or purpose to which the realty is devoted, and (3) the intention of the person making annexation to make a permanent accession to the freehold. In the instant case, since Foskett purchased a homeowner's insurance policy for his mobile home intent, requested the seller to have its wheels removed (permanence), and adapted it as his permanent residence (application), the district court did not err in determining that it had become a fixture under Wisconsin law. Affirmed.

ANALYSIS

The Universal Commercial Code has only the most limited definition of fixtures. Read § 9-313(1)(a) and 9-313(2) and official Comment 2. Obviously pre-Code state law defining fixtures is very important. State law tests ranged from a pure annexation test (measured by the difficulty of removal) to an "intention of the parties" test [for which the leading case is *Teaff v. Hewitt*, 1 Ohio St. 511 (1853)].

Quicknotes

FIXTURE An item of personal property that has become so attached to the real property that it is considered a part of the real property.

PERSONALTY Personal, movable property not attached to real estate.

Lewiston Bottled Gas Co. v. Key Bank of Maine

Seller of air conditioning (P) v. Bank (D)

Me. Sup. Jud. Ct., 601 A.2d 91, 17 U.C.C. Rep. Serv. 2d 282 (1992).

NATURE OF CASE: Appeal from declaratory judgment setting creditor priority to certain equipment.

FACT SUMMARY: Key Bank of Maine (D) contended that its security interest in after-acquired fixtures of a debtor had priority over one having a purchase-money security interest.

RULE OF LAW

A party with a security interest in after-acquired fixtures has priority over one supplying purchase-money credit on such fixtures, who had not complied with Article 9's financing statement rules.

FACTS: Key Bank of Maine (Key Bank) (D) loaned certain moneys to Grand Beach Inn, Inc. The loan was secured by liens attaching to the property, including after-acquired fixtures. Subsequent to this, Grand Beach contracted to purchase some 90 air-conditioning units from Lewiston Bottled Gas Co. (Lewiston) (P). These units were purchased on credit. Grand Beach gave a purchase-money security interest to Lewiston (P). The air conditioners were installed in the various units of the inn. The record owner of the property was DiBiase. Grand Beach's owner. Lewiston's (P) financing statement made no mention of DiBiase, only Grand Beach. Grand Beach defaulted, and Lewiston (P) brought a declaratory relief action to assert its lien. The trial court held Key Bank's (D) interest to have priority, and Lewiston (P) appealed.

ISSUE: Does a party with a security interest in after-acquired fixtures have priority over one supplying purchase-money credit on such fixtures, who had not complied with Article 9's financing statement rules?

HOLDING AND DECISION: (Clifford, J.) Yes. A party with a security interest in after-acquired fixtures has priority over one supplying purchase-money credit on such fixtures, who had not complied with Article 9's financing statement rules. One having a purchase-money security interest in fixtures will have priority over one having a pre-existing security interest in after-acquired fixtures. However, § 9-402(5) requires that the financing statement perfecting the interest list the name of the record owner of the property. Here, the units were undoubtedly fixtures. Fixtures, per Universal Commercial Code (U.C.C.) § 9-313(a), are goods physically annexed to real property, adapted to the use to which the real property is put, and intended to become part of the realty. The units in question fall within this definition. However, Lewiston's (P) financing statement did not mention DiBiase, the true owner of record. This being so, Lewiston (P) failed to comply with Article 9 and, thus, had no priority here. Affirmed.

ANALYSIS

The factors making personal property into fixtures enunciated in U.C.C. § 9-313(1) were taken from the common law. Of the three factors, intent is probably the most determinative. The code looks to "objective" intent (intent that can reasonably be inferred from the parties' conduct), not any subjective intent the parties may have had.

Quicknotes

DECLARATORY JUDGMENT An adjudication by the courts which grants not relief but is binding over the legal status of the parties involved in the dispute.

FIXTURE An item of personal property that has become so attached to the real property that it is considered a part of the real property.

LIEN A claim against the property of another in order to secure the payment of a debt.

SECURITY INTEREST An interest in property that may be sold upon a default in payment of the debt.

Maplewood Bank & Trust v. Sears, Roebuck & Co.

Bank (P) v. Department store (D)

N.J. Super. Ct., App. Div., 625 A.2d 537, 21 U.C.C. Rep. Serv. 2d 171 (1993).

NATURE OF CASE: Appeal from the dismissal of a counterclaim in an action to determine priority interests in a foreclosure sale.

FACT SUMMARY: Sears, Roebuck & Co. (D) took a security interest in certain kitchen fixtures it installed on the Capers's (D) property on which Maplewood Bank & Trust (P) had previously taken a purchase-money mortgage.

RULE OF LAW

A first mortgagee is entitled to priority over a fixture financier in the funds realized from a foreclosure sale of the mortgaged premises.

FACTS: Maplewood Bank & Trust (Maplewood) (P) was the holder of a first purchase-money mortgage dated September 20, 1988, and recorded on October 5, 1988, on the Capers' (D) property. On May 31, 1989, Sears, Roebuck & Co. (Sears) (D) filed a financing statement covering kitchen fixtures it installed on the mortgaged premises. When the Capers (D) defaulted on their loans, Maplewood (P) filed a complaint for foreclosure. Sears (D) filed an answer and counterclaim stating that it was entitled to priority over Maplewood (P) for the sums received in the foreclosure sale because of its fixture filing pursuant to Universal Commercial Code (U.C.C.) § 9-313, and that it was entitled to the difference between the price of the home with and without the new kitchen. Sears's (D) answer and counterclaim were stricken and an unopposed foreclosure sale ensued. Sears (D) appealed the dismissal of the counterclaim.

ISSUE: Is a first mortgagee entitled to priority over a fixture financier in the funds realized from a foreclosure sale of the mortgaged premises?

HOLDING AND DECISION: (Coleman, J.) Yes. A first mortgagee is entitled to priority over a fixture financier in the funds realized from a foreclosure sale of the mortgaged premises. Here, U.C.C. § 9-313 does not give Sears (D) priority over Maplewood (P) on the proceeds from the foreclosure sale. Sears's (D) perfected security interest was in the goods and chattels that became fixtures, and such interest attached to those goods before they became fixtures. Therefore, Sears's (D) superiority pursuant to U.C.C. § 9-313 applies only to those goods that became fixtures, and not the premises at large. Pursuant to U.C.C. § 9-313(8) as adopted in New Jersey, Sears's (D) remedy is to remove the goods from the premises and reimburse Maplewood (P) for any damage caused by the removal. In entering into this security agreement, Sears (D) knew of the risk it was taking and the remedy offered by state law. If the law is to be changed to allow creditors such as Sears (D) to have priority in similar foreclosure sale funds, that is to be determined by the state legislature. Summary judgment in favor of Maplewood (P) is affirmed.

ANALYSIS

Draft § 9-604(b), formerly § 9-501(g), states that "If a security agreement covers goods that are or become fixtures, a secured party, subject to subsection (c), may proceed under this part or in accordance with the rights and remedies with respect to real [estate] [property], in which case the other provisions of this part do not apply." This subsection is intended to clarify the notion that a security interest in fixtures may be enforced under any of the applicable provisions of Part 5. The subsection also serves to overrule cases holding that a secured party's only remedy after default is the removal of the fixtures from the real estate.

Quicknotes

COUNTERCLAIM An independent cause of action brought by a defendant to a lawsuit in order to oppose or deduct from the plaintiff's claim.

FIXTURE An item of personal property that has become so attached to the real property that it is considered a part of the real property.

Plymouth Savings Bank v. U.S. I.R.S.

Lienor (P) v. Lienor (D)

187 F.3d 203 (1st Cir. 1999).

NATURE OF CASE: Appeal from summary judgment on the priority of liens.

FACT SUMMARY: Plymouth Savings Bank (the Bank) (P) and the Internal Revenue Service (D) both held valid liens on money owed by Jordan Hospital (Hospital) to Shirley Dionne (Dionne) pursuant to a personal service contract, and each lienholder claimed priority.

RULE OF LAW

For purposes of the Federal Tax Lien Act's § 6323(c) safe harbor provisions for after-acquired property, a security interest in qualified contract rights covers the proceeds of those rights, even where such proceeds are an account receivable, and the proceeds fall within the scope of the safe harbor's protection.

FACTS: Shirley Dionne (Dionne) owed Plymouth Savings Bank (the Bank) (P) $64,465 on a loan. The Bank (P) had a security interest in all of Dionne's personal property, including contract rights and all cash and non-cash proceeds resulting from the rendering of services by Dionne. Dionne had executed an $85,000 promissory note in favor of the Bank (P) on April 13, 1994. Dionne also owed money to the Internal Revenue Service (IRS) (D), which filed tax liens against Dionne's property on December 19, 1994, and February 14, 1995. On March 31, 1995, Dionne entered into a personal services contract with Jordan Hospital (Hospital). The Hospital owed Dionne a $75,000 balance on the contract, and the Bank (P) sued the Hospital in state court to recover this unpaid balance. The state court held that the Bank (P) had a secured interest in the money because it was a "proceed" of services, but instead of awarding the Bank (P) the money, it directed the Bank (P) to bring a declaratory judgment to determine whether its interest had priority over other lienholders. The Bank (P) brought such an action. The IRS (D) claimed that its liens had priority, and the federal district court granted summary judgment in its favor. The Bank (P) appealed.

ISSUE: For purposes of the Federal Tax Lien Act's safe harbor provisions for after-acquired property, does a security interest in qualified contract rights cover the proceeds of those rights, even when such proceeds are an account receivable, and the proceeds fall within the scope of the safe harbor's protections?

HOLDING AND DECISION: (Cudahy, J.) Yes. For purposes of the Federal Tax Lien Act's § 6323(c) safe harbor provisions for after-acquired property, a security interest in qualified contract rights covers the proceeds of those rights, even where such proceeds are an account receivable, and the proceeds fall within the scope of the safe harbor's protection. The Federal Tax Lien Act (FTLA) grants the United States a lien on all the property of a person who fails to pay taxes, whether acquired before or after the lien is filed. Section 6323, however, gives certain commercial liens priority over federal tax liens, including security interests in a taxpayer's property that are "in existence" before filing of the notice of the tax lien. Section 6323(c) extends the priority of these prior security interests to certain "qualified property" (the 6323(c) safe harbor) that is acquired after the notice of the tax lien. To fall within the safe harbor, a security interest must be in property covered by a "commercial transactions financing agreement." A commercial transactions financing agreement is secured by "commercial financing security," which can include paper of a kind arising in commercial transactions—which includes "contract rights"—and accounts receivable. A commercial financing security must be acquired before the 46th day after the date of the tax lien filing. Here, Dionne entered the contract with the Hospital exactly 45 days after the tax lien was filed. Thus, the issue is whether she "acquired" the right to the money owed her by the Hospital; if she did, then Bank's (P) lien trumps the IRS's (D) lien because the Dionne-Bank agreement is a commercial transactions financing agreement, the Dionne-Hospital contract is a commercial financing security, the Bank's (P) security is in qualified property, and the money is after-acquired property that falls within the safe harbor. If, conversely, Dionne did not acquire rights to the money when she signed the contract, the IRS's (D) lien takes priority. Under IRS regulations, what Dionne acquired when she signed the contract with the Hospital was a "contract right" to be paid in the future because she had not as yet performed, and, therefore, the contract, and the rights under it, is qualified property covered by the Bank's (P) security interest and protected by the safe harbor. The next issue is whether the money itself is such qualified property. Under the tax regulations, "proceeds" are whatever is received when collateral is "exchanged." Proceeds are considered acquired at the time the qualified property is acquired. Here, therefore, the proceeds of the contract rights are considered to have been acquired by Dionne at the time she made the contract. However, the proceeds are an account receivable—the right to payment of the money upon performance. The IRS (D) correctly argues that Dionne did not earn the right to payment before the 45 days from the tax lien filing. Nonetheless, it is the contract and the contract rights under it, not the

Continued on next page.

account receivable, that constitute the qualified property, and the proceeds under that qualified property are deemed acquired at the time the qualified property was acquired. This results because the regulations do not distinguish between forms of proceeds. Moreover, the account receivable is proceeds because Dionne's performance "exchanged" her contract right into an account receivable. Here, the regulations make it clear that so long as the contract was entered into within 45 days of the tax lien filing, the rights under that contract and all the proceeds of those rights come within the protection of § 6323's safe harbor. This result is supported by the Universal Commercial Code, the principles of which Congress intended to incorporate into the tax lien provisions. Accordingly, the Bank's (P) lien trumps the IRS's (D). Reversed and remanded.

ANALYSIS

The IRS (D) argued that Dionne did not enter the contract in the "ordinary" course of her trade or business, as required by § 6323. The subject of the contract was the transfer of Dionne's business license, which, the IRS (D) argued, was not in the ordinary course of her business. However, the contract was a personal services contract, and such contracts were normally entered into in Dionne's business. The court left this issue of "ordinariness" for remand because it is a very fact-sensitive issue on which few facts had been developed, but it did note that if the IRS (D) characterized the transaction as a sale or transfer of a license, the proceeds from that transaction would clearly have entitled the Bank (P) to the money without having to "navigate § 6323(c)'s maze of definitions."

Quicknotes

LIEN A claim against the property of another in order to secure the payment of a debt.

ORDINARY COURSE OF BUSINESS The conducting of business in accordance with standard customs and practices.

SAFE HARBOR A tax code provision safeguarding the taxpayer from liability in respect to the payment of taxes, so long as he has made an effort to comply with the provisions of the code.

CHAPTER 23

Bankruptcy and Article 9

Quick Reference Rules of Law

PAGE

1. *In re Smith's Home Furnishings, Inc.* Payments made to a creditor by a debtor during 90 days before the debtor files for bankruptcy will not be avoided as preferential transfers where the creditor has a floating lien and it cannot be shown that the creditor received a greater amount by virtue of the payments than it would have received in a hypothetical bankruptcy liquidation. *222*

2. *James H. Rice Co. v. McJohn.* A conveyance of property will be set aside as null and void where the conveyance is a sham transaction that has been made for the sole purpose of preventing creditors from levying on the property. *224*

3. *Aptix Corp. v. Quickturn Design Systems, Inc.* There is sufficient evidence that a loan to a judgment debtor has been secured with the intent to hinder, delay, or defraud any creditor of the debtor where: the secured lender was an insider; before the transfer was made or obligation was incurred, the debtor had been sued or threatened with suit; and the debtor was insolvent or became insolvent shortly after the transfer was made or the obligation was incurred. *225*

In re Smith's Home Furnishings, Inc.

Bankruptcy trustee (P) v. Creditor (D)

265 F.3d 959 (9th Cir. 2001).

NATURE OF CASE: Appeal from affirmance of judgment in bankruptcy proceeding holding that transfer is not preferential.

FACT SUMMARY: Transamerica Commercial Finance Corp. (TCFC) (D) had a floating lien in the inventory of Smith's Home Furnishings, Inc. (Smith's). During the 90 days before Smith's filed for bankruptcy, Smith's paid TCFC (D) over $12 million in 36 payments. The bankruptcy trustee (P) sought to avoid these payments as preferences.

RULE OF LAW

Payments made to a creditor by a debtor during 90 days before the debtor files for bankruptcy will not be avoided as preferential transfers where the creditor has a floating lien and it cannot be shown that the creditor received a greater amount by virtue of the payments than it would have received in a hypothetical bankruptcy liquidation.

FACTS: Transamerica Commercial Finance Corp. (TCFC) (D) was one of the primary lenders for Smith's Home Furnishings, Inc. (Smith's). TCFC's (D) loans were secured by a first-priority floating lien on Smith's prime inventory and proceeds from it, with the inventory serving as collateral. When Smith's started to experience substantial losses, TCFC (D) reduced its line of credit, and Smith's made substantial paydowns of Smith's debt in 36 payments totaling over $12 million between May and August 22, 1995. On August 18, 1995, TCFC (D) declared a final default. For the first time, TCFC (D) also sought to require Smith's to segregate the proceeds from its collateral. On August 22, 1995, Smith's voluntarily filed for bankruptcy under Chapter 11, and TCFC (D) took possession of its collateral and liquidated it for $10,823,010.58, or $94,200.62 more than the amount Smith's still owed it. The case was converted to a Chapter 7 liquidation and the Chapter 7 trustee (P) discovered the over $12 million in payments that Smith's had made to TCFC (D) during the 90 days before the petition date ("preference period"). When TCFC (D) refused to return the payments, the trustee (P) sought to avoid the payments as preferential transfers. The bankruptcy court ruled that the trustee (P) had failed to meet his burden of proof. On appeal, the district court affirmed. The trustee (P) appealed to the court of appeals.

ISSUE: Will payments made to a creditor by a debtor during 90 days before the debtor files for bankruptcy be avoided as preferential transfers where the creditor has a floating lien and it cannot be shown that the creditor received a greater amount by virtue of the payments than it would have received in a hypothetical bankruptcy liquidation?

HOLDING AND DECISION: (Hall, J.) No. Payments made to a creditor by a debtor during 90 days before the debtor files for bankruptcy will not be avoided as preferential transfers where the creditor has a floating lien and it cannot be shown that the creditor received a greater amount by virtue of the payments than it would have received in a hypothetical bankruptcy liquidation. The Bankruptcy Code permits a trustee to avoid a transfer from a debtor to a creditor where such transfer enables the creditor to receive a "greater amount" than it would have received under a Chapter 7 proceeding if the transfer had not occurred. The parties dispute whether the over $12 million in payments made during the preference period enabled TCFC (D) to receive a "greater amount" than it would have if the transfer had not occurred and TCFC (D) received payments only pursuant to a Chapter 7 liquidation. The trustee (P), who had the burden of proof on this issue, made two arguments: first, that the over $12 million payments plus the amount that TCFC (D) received from the sale of its collateral was greater than the amount it received from the sale of the collateral alone (the "add-back" method); second, that TCFC (D) had not traced the source of the allegedly preferential payments to sales of its collateral. (A) With regard to the add-back method, the trustee (P) did not meet his burden. Pre-petition transfers to a creditor who is fully secured on the petition date are generally not preferential. Here, TCFC (D) was never undersecured at any time during the preference period because the value of the collateral exceeded Smith's indebtedness to TCFC (D). If TCFC (D) was never undercollateralized, then TCFC (D) could not have received more by virtue of the over $12 million payments than it would have received in a hypothetical liquidation without the payments. Because TCFC (D) had a floating lien, the collateral and indebtedness changed throughout the preference period, and, therefore, the trustee (P) could not prove that the amount of indebtedness was greater than the amount of collateral at some point during the preference period. Moreover, a floating lien does not shift the burden of proof on this issue to the creditor. The trustee (P) urges that the burden be shifted, but he is using § 547(c)(5), which is an affirmative defense provision. Here, TCFC (D) does not have to use an affirmative defense until the trustee (P) has initially proved that the creditor was

Continued on next page.

undersecured as of the petition date. Because the trustee (P) failed to carry its burden, there is no shift of burden. (B) As to the trustee's (P) argument that TCFC (D) had not traced the source of the allegedly preferential payments to sales of its collateral, the payments in the instant case came from commingled funds that were not all from the sales of goods subject to TCFC's (D) lien. Thus, the challenged payments were not made directly from the proceeds of the sales of TCFC's (D) collateral. Conversely, there was no evidence that Smith's did not sell off enough of TCFC's (D) collateral to account for all the challenged payments—but it is the trustee's (P) burden to prove whether or not the alleged preferential payments came from the proceeds of the sale of its own collateral. Here, the trustee (P) did not meet that burden. Affirmed.

ANALYSIS

The paramount policy behind § 547 of the Bankruptcy Code is to ensure equality of distribution among creditors of the debtor. If a floating lien creditor truly does not profit from a transfer made during the preference period, then the creditor should not be forced to repay the transferred payments. This section also attempts to discourage creditors from rushing to extract payments from the debtor shortly before the petition of bankruptcy is filed.

Quicknotes

CHAPTER 7 BANKRUPTCY A legal proceeding whereby a debtor, who is unable to pay his debts as they become due, is relieved of his obligation to pay his creditors by liquidation and distribution of his remaining assets.

CHAPTER 11 BANKRUPTCY A legal proceeding whereby a debtor, who is unable to pay his debts as they become due, is relieved of his obligation to pay his creditors through reorganization and payment from future income.

COLLATERAL Property that secures the payment of a debt.

PREFERENTIAL TRANSFER A transfer made by the insolvent debtor to a creditor prior to filing the bankruptcy petition, giving a priority to one creditor over others with respect to the debtor's assets.

James H. Rice Co. v. McJohn

Judgment creditor (P) v. Judgment debtor (D)

Ill. Sup. Ct., 244 Ill. 264 (1910).

NATURE OF CASE: Appeal in action to execute on a judgment. [The complete procedural posture of the case is not indicated in the casebook extract.]

FACT SUMMARY: James H. Rice Co. (company) (P) claimed that Joseph McJohn's (Joseph's) (D)'s conveyance of his real estate to Edward McJohn (Edward) (D) constituted a fraudulent transfer intended to prevent the company (P) and other creditors from levying on the property. [The complete factual and procedural posture of the case is not presented in the casebook extract.]

RULE OF LAW

A conveyance of property will be set aside as null and void where the conveyance is a sham transaction that has been made for the sole purpose of preventing creditors from levying on the property.

FACTS: James H. Rice Co. (the company) (P) obtained a judgment against Joseph McJohn (Joseph) (D), who owned certain real estate, but no other assets that could be levied upon. Before the company (P) obtained the judgment, but after the indebtedness on which the judgment was based had accrued, Joseph (D) purported to transfer the property to Edward McJohn (Edward) (D) for nominal consideration. The company (P), in attempting to execute on its judgment, brought suit against Joseph (D) and Edward (D), contending that the conveyance between Joseph (D) and Edward (D) of the property had been a sham transaction, entered into for the purpose of preventing the company (D) and other creditors from levying on the real estate, and that Edward (D), who had paid nothing for the property, held it in trust for Joseph (D). The company (D) sought to have the conveyance declared null and void and set aside. The state's highest court granted review. [The complete factual and procedural posture of the case is not presented in the casebook extract.]

ISSUE: Will a conveyance of property be set aside as null and void where the conveyance is a sham transaction that has been made for the sole purpose of preventing creditors from levying on the property?

HOLDING AND DECISION: [Judge not indicated in casebook extract] Yes. A conveyance of property will be set aside as null and void where the conveyance is a sham transaction that has been made for the sole purpose of preventing creditors from levying on the property. The conveyance here was a fraudulent conveyance that must be set aside as null and void. [The disposition of the case was not presented in the casebook extract.]

ANALYSIS

Under the widely adopted Uniform Fraudulent Transfer Act (UFTA), there are two types of fraudulent transfers that a creditor can avoid. The first is one where the transferee takes from an insolvent debtor without giving "reasonably equivalent value in exchange." The second is where the transferor and the transferee intend to defraud creditors. It seems that the transfer at issue in this case could have come within either type of fraudulent transfer dependent on the defendants' intent and whether Joseph (D) was insolvent.

Quicknotes

CONVEYANCE The transfer of property, or title to property, from one party to another party.

DEFRAUD A false representation of facts with the intent that another will rely on the misrepresentation to his detriment.

Aptix Corp. v. Quickturn Design Systems, Inc.

Judgment debtor (P) v. Judgment creditor (D)

148 Fed. Appx. 924 (Fed. Cir. 2005).

NATURE OF CASE: Appeal, in patent litigation, from the voiding of a security interest as fraudulent.

FACT SUMMARY: Mohsen, who loaned $9.7 million to his company, Aptix Corp. (Aptix) (P), contended that his obtaining a security interest in all of Aptix's (P) assets to secure the loan was not intended to defraud Quickturn Design Systems, Inc. (D), which had obtained a $4.2 million judgment against Aptix (P), but was, to the contrary, intended to help Aptix (P) pay its creditors, among other things.

RULE OF LAW

There is sufficient evidence that a loan to a judgment debtor has been secured with the intent to hinder, delay, or defraud any creditor of the debtor where: the secured lender was an insider; before the transfer was made or obligation was incurred, the debtor had been sued or threatened with suit; and the debtor was insolvent or became insolvent shortly after the transfer was made or the obligation was incurred.

FACTS: Mohsen founded Aptix Corp. (Aptix) (P) and was its majority shareholder, chief executive officer and chairman. Quickturn Design Systems, Inc. (Quickturn) (D) obtained a $4.2 million attorneys' fee judgment against Aptix (P) in patent litigation filed by Aptix (P). Soon thereafter, with Aptix (P) unable to borrow funds from outside sources, it borrowed $9.7 million from Mohsen pursuant to an agreement that gave Mohsen a security interest in all of the company's assets. According to Mohsen, the money was used to maintain Aptix's (P) operations by paying employees, vendors and other creditors. Prior to this loan, Mohsen had loaned the company $2 million on an unsecured basis. Applying the state's fraudulent transfer statute and determining that Aptix (P) granted the security interest to Mohsen with the intent to hinder or delay Quickturn's (D) satisfaction of the judgment, the district court voided Mohsen's security interest. The district court based its decision on three "badges of fraud," namely that Mohsen was an insider; the transfer occurred just before a substantial judgment was to be entered against Aptix (P); and Aptix (P) was insolvent at the time the transfer was made. The court of appeals granted review.

ISSUE: Is there sufficient evidence that a loan to a judgment debtor has been secured with the intent to hinder, delay, or defraud any creditor of the debtor where: the secured lender was an insider; before the transfer was made or obligation was incurred, the debtor had been sued or threatened with suit; and the debtor was insolvent or became insolvent shortly after the transfer was made or the obligation was incurred?

HOLDING AND DECISION: (Gajarsa, J.) Yes. There is sufficient evidence that a loan to a judgment debtor has been secured with the intent to hinder, delay, or defraud any creditor of the debtor where: the secured lender was an insider; before the transfer was made or obligation was incurred, the debtor had been sued or threatened with suit; and the debtor was insolvent or became insolvent shortly after the transfer was made or the obligation was incurred. The state's fraudulent transfer statute provides that a transfer made or obligation incurred by a debtor is fraudulent as to a creditor, whether the creditor's claim arose before or after the transfer was made or the obligation was incurred, if the debtor made the transfer or incurred the obligation with actual intent to hinder, delay, or defraud any creditor of the debtor. The three key factors relied on by the district court in determining that there was intent to defraud Quickturn (D) are known as "badges of fraud," and these three factors were among many others that were codified by the state after the court issued its order voiding the security interest. Mohsen argues that the granting of the security interest to Mohsen was intended to benefit not defraud creditors by keeping Aptix (P) operational. Borrowing a concept from bankruptcy cases, Mohsen argues that the ongoing operation of Aptix (P) was a "legitimate supervening purpose" such that the confluence of three badges of fraud was insufficient to establish actual intent to defraud. However, his reliance on the concept of a "legitimate supervening purpose" is misplaced. In bankruptcy proceedings, this concept is used to shift the burden of proof. Once multiple indicia or badges of fraud are established, the burden shifts to the transferee to prove that there was a "legitimate supervening purpose" for the transfer at issue. Here, Mohsen fails to rebut the presumption of fraudulent intent created by the three badges of fraud. The lending of the money explains why Aptix (P) entered into the loan arrangement with Mohsen, but it does not explain why it was necessary for Aptix (P) to grant Mohsen a security interest in substantially all of its assets when Mohsen had never required such an interest for his past loans. It also does not rebut the district court's finding that the arrangement was one by which Aptix (P) used the money to pay employee salaries and essential creditors in an effort to keep functioning, Mohsen received money back from Aptix on demand, and Aptix (P) paid unsecured creditors as it saw fit, while effectively avoiding its obligations toward a judgment

Continued on next page.

creditor. Also, while, as Mohsen contends, it is true that state law protects debtors who give security interests to creditors in preference over other creditors, state law does not do so where a debtor has granted the security interest with the intent to defraud creditors not party to the transaction. Also unconvincing is Mohsen's argument that there could be no fraud because the transaction was entered into for the benefit of some of Aptix's (P) creditors. However, this misreads the statute as if it requires that the debtor intend to defraud all of its creditors, whereas the language actually used in the statute mandates only that the debtor act with the actual intent to defraud any creditor. Finally, Mohsen argues that the security interest should not be voided because Aptix (P) "took in good faith and for a reasonably equivalent value" since it engaged in the security agreement in a good faith effort to stay in business and the amount of money loaned to Aptix (P) exceeded the value of the security granted in return. This argument fails, inter alia, because Mohsen only identifies evidence tending to show Aptix's (P) good faith in entering into the transaction and points to no evidence showing that Mohsen himself acted in good faith as required by the statute. Moreover, case law on which Mohsen relies does not stand for the proposition that a transfer made to enable an enterprise to stay in business cannot constitute a fraudulent transaction. Affirmed.

DISSENT: (Newman, J.) The preference granted by Aptix (P) to Mohsen over Quickturn (D) was not fraudulent. Here, the loan was not a sham, and the money loaned was used for legitimate purposes. In prior precedent, it was held that there was no fraud in a transfer made "with recognition that the transfer will effectively prevent another creditor from collecting on his debt." The majority bases its opinion largely on the fact that Mohsen required a security interest for the loan at issue, whereas previously, he had not required his smaller loans to be secured. However, it is surely not fraudulent to obtain security for a loan of over nine million dollars, whatever the relationship between the lender and the recipient, and knowledge of a potential adverse judgment does not establish fraudulent intent when making a loan to meanwhile keep the company alive and operating.

ANALYSIS

It is well-settled law that a transfer that establishes a preference is not thereby fraudulent, even its effect is to hinder or delay payment to other creditors, and even if the preferred creditor had knowledge that such consequence would follow the preference—since it is widely understood that a secured creditor has priority over unsecured creditors. Even if, as the district found here the transaction was not "innocent," as the dissent argues, there is a large space between absence of innocence, and deliberate fraud, especially where the transaction is on its face a legitimate business transaction, and clearly not a sham.

Quicknotes

FRAUD A false representation of facts with the intent that another will rely on the misrepresentation to his detriment.

INSIDER Any person within a corporation who has access to information not available to the public.

SECURITY INTEREST An interest in property that may be sold upon a default in payment of the debt.

CHAPTER 24

Proceeds

Quick Reference Rules of Law

Farmers Cooperative Elevator Co. v. Union State Bank

Feed supplier (P) v. Bank (D)

Iowa Sup. Ct., 409 N.W.2d 178, 4 U.C.C. Rep. Serv. 2d 1 (1987).

NATURE OF CASE: Appeal from ruling on motion denying priority to plaintiff's security interest.

FACT SUMMARY: In Farmers Cooperative Elevator Co. (Co-op) (P) action against Union State Bank (Union State) (D), the district court ruled that Union State's (D) security interest in certain livestock and their supplies was superior to Co-op's (P) competing interest since it was perfected prior to Co-op's (P).

RULE OF LAW

A purchase money security interest in collateral has priority over a conflicting security interest in the same collateral or its proceeds if it is perfected before the latter interest.

FACTS: After Cockrum formed a security agreement with Union State Bank (Union State) (D) covering his livestock and their supplies and Union State (D) perfected its interest, he entered into several purchase money agreements with Farmers Cooperative Elevator Co. (Co-op) (P) for livestock feed. When he subsequently defaulted on both obligations, Co-op (P) sued Cockrum, seeking possession of the hogs on the grounds that they were the proceeds of the feed. As a result, Union State (D) filed a statement of indebtedness and requested that its security interests be established as a first security lien on Cockrum's hog inventory. On Co-op's (P) motion to adjudicate law points, the district court ruled that Union State's (D) security interest in the hogs was prior and superior to Co-op's (P). Co-op (P) appealed.

ISSUE: Does a purchase money security interest in collateral have priority over a conflicting security interest in the same collateral or its proceeds if it is perfected before the latter interest?

HOLDING AND DECISION: (Larson, J.) Yes. A purchase money security interest in collateral has priority over a conflicting security interest in the same collateral or its proceeds if it is perfected before the latter interest. This rule merely restates the principle outlined in § 554.9312(4) of the Iowa Commercial Code. Section 554.9306 defines "proceeds" to include "whatever is received upon the sale, exchange, collection, or other disposition of collateral or proceeds." The "other disposition of collateral" language found in this section has been found not to include the consumption of feed since "there are no traceable proceeds to which the security interest may be said to have attached" once the feed is consumed. (See *First Nat'l Bank of Brush v. Bostron*, 564 P.2d 965, 966 (Colo. App. 1977).) Moreover, *Bostron* points out that feed eaten by cattle does not become commingled with them as contemplated by Universal Commercial Code (U.C.C.) § 9-315, the companion statute to Iowa's § 554.9315(1). In the instant case, the district court did not err in finding that the hogs were not the proceeds of their feed, and therefore, Union State's (D) security interest in them was superior to Co-op's (P). Affirmed.

ANALYSIS

In a related area concerning proceeds, Article 9 does not usually apply to security interests taken in either insurance policies or bank accounts as collateral. This is because the common law or other statutes regulate these transactions. However insurance payments or bank account moneys qualifying as "proceeds" are regulated by the U.C.C.

Quicknotes

SECURITY INTEREST An interest in property that may be sold upon a default in payment of the debt.

Helms v. Certified Packaging Corp.

Bankruptcy trustee (P) v. Transferee (D)

551 F.3d 675 (7th Cir. 2008).

NATURE OF CASE: In bankruptcy adversary proceeding, cross-appeals from reversal of judgment that proceeds of a tort settlement for failure to insure were not subject to a security interest, and from affirmance of judgment that proceeds of a tort settlement for business losses arising from negligence were subject to a security interest.

FACT SUMMARY: A $2 million transfer to Certified Packaging Corp. (Certified) (D) was avoided in bankruptcy, but LaSalle Bank (LaSalle), which held a security interest in Certified's (D) assets, contended that proceeds from two tort lawsuits initiated by Certified (D) were subject to its security interest. The suits arose from a fire at Certified's (D) plant, where the business losses far exceeded the damages to the plant and equipment. The first suit was against an insurance broker for having failed to list the plant on business-loss insurance; the second, still-pending suit, was against the electric utility company for negligence that allegedly started the fire. In its appeal from prior rulings, the trustee (P) contended that the proceeds from the first suit belonged to the estate because they were not proceeds from collateral. In a cross-appeal from prior rulings in the second suit, LaSalle argued the proceeds, if any, for business losses would be proceeds from the collateral.

RULE OF LAW

(1) In a tort action for damage to assets that serve as collateral as well as for business losses resulting from that damage, proceeds from the recovery of damages for the business losses are proceeds from the collateral, so that the proceeds are subject to the security interest in the collateral.

(2) Proceeds from settlement of a lawsuit for business losses brought against an insurance broker for having failed to list an insured's assets on a business-loss insurance policy do not constitute proceeds from collateral securing a loan, so that the proceeds are not subject to the security interest in the collateral.

FACTS: Sarah Michaels, Inc. (Michaels), was a customer of a packaging manufacturer Certified Packaging Corp. (Certified) (D). Michaels declared bankruptcy, and the bankruptcy trustee (P) brought an adversary proceeding against Certified (D) seeking to avoid transfers that Michaels had made to Certified (D) to pay for packaging. The trustee (P) obtained a default judgment for around $2 million. However, LaSalle Bank (LaSalle) claimed a security interest in Certified's (D) assets. An issue that arose was whether LaSalle's security interest covered proceeds from two lawsuits initiated by Certified (D), which arose from a fire at one of Certified's (D) plants and damaged equipment in it. The equipment was subject to LaSalle's security interest. The plant was shut down for several weeks, and the business losses resulting from the shutdown greatly exceeded the damage to Certified's (D) property. The first suit was against Certified's (D) insurance broker for negligence in having failed to list the plant on a business-losses insurance policy that the broker had procured for Certified (D). That suit was settled for $88,000 after deduction of attorneys' fees. The trustee (P) contended that the settlement money should belong to the bankrupt estate; LaSalle contended that the money should belong to it as proceeds of the collateral damaged in the fire. The bankruptcy court rendered judgment for the trustee (P), and the district court reversed. The second suit was against the electric utility. Certified (D) claimed that the fire had been due to the utility's negligence in maintaining one of its power lines. In that suit, which was pending, Certified (D) sought damages of $2,000,000 for property damage and business losses, the latter accounting for about 90 percent of the claimed damages. The bankruptcy court again ruled for the trustee (P), holding that the business-losses part of Certified's (D) claim belonged to the trustee (P), but this time the district court affirmed. The trustee (P) appealed the district court's ruling in the first suit, and LaSalle cross-appealed in the second. The court of appeals granted review.

ISSUE:

(1) In a tort action for damage to assets that serve as collateral as well as for business losses resulting from that damage, are proceeds from the recovery of damages for the business losses proceeds from the collateral, so that the proceeds are subject to the security interest in the collateral?

(2) Do proceeds from settlement of a lawsuit for business losses brought against an insurance broker for having failed to list an insured's assets on a business-loss insurance policy constitute proceeds from collateral securing a loan, so that the proceeds are subject to the security interest in the collateral?

HOLDING AND DECISION: (Posner, J.)

(1) Yes. In a tort action for damage to assets that serve as collateral as well as for business losses resulting from that damage, proceeds from the recovery of damages for the business losses are proceeds from the collateral, so that the proceeds are subject to the security interest

Continued on next page.

in the collateral. If a suit against someone who steals or damages collateral results in an award measured by the diminution in the value of the collateral caused by the defendant's wrongdoing, so that the award restores the original value of the collateral, the award, like an insurance payment for damaged collateral, constitutes "proceeds" of the collateral and is therefore covered by the lender's security interest. If Certified (D) prevails against the utility, it will be as if the utility converted around $200,000 of the collateral (10 percent of the total damages) for LaSalle's loan and was therefore obliged to repay it. The judgment so obtained would constitute proceeds of the collateral up to the collateral's value. However, replacing a business loss is not restoring the value of damaged collateral, and there is no necessary relation between the value of collateral and a business loss that results from its being destroyed or damaged—as demonstrated by this case, where the business losses were nine times the value of the equipment loss. Because the claim of a secured creditor to the proceeds of collateral cannot exceed the value of the collateral, the lower courts did not err in holding that the business-losses portion of the claim against the utility would not be proceeds from the collateral. Affirmed as to this issue.

(2) No. Proceeds from settlement of a lawsuit for business losses brought against an insurance broker for having failed to list an insured's assets on a business-loss insurance policy do not constitute proceeds from collateral securing a loan, so that the proceeds are not subject to the security interest in the collateral. The claim against the broker was for failure to obtain business-loss insurance. Replacing a business loss is not the same as restoring the value of damaged collateral. There is no necessary relation between the value of collateral and a business loss that results from its being destroyed or damaged. However, the claim of a secured creditor to the proceeds of collateral cannot exceed the value of the collateral. Therefore, the district court was wrong to treat the $88,000 settlement of Certified's (D) claim against the broker for failing to procure business-loss coverage as proceeds of damaged collateral. Reversed as to this issue.

ANALYSIS

Under the rules enunciated by the court, if the broker in this case had failed to obtain insurance coverage for damage to the physical assets that secured LaSalle's loan, the claim against the broker rather than for loss of business would be a claim to proceeds of the collateral.

Quicknotes

COLLATERAL Property that secures the payment of a debt.

SECURITY INTEREST An interest in property that may be sold upon a default in payment of the debt.

HCC Credit Corp. v. Springs Valley Bank & Trust Co.

Secured creditor (P) v. Bank (D)

Ind. Sup. Ct., 712 N.E.2d 952, 38 U.C.C. Rep. Serv. 2d 1066 (1999).

NATURE OF CASE: Suit to recover proceeds of sale.

FACT SUMMARY: HCC Credit Corp. (P) brought suit against Springs Valley Bank & Trust Co. (the Bank) (D) to recover payment due pursuant to its perfected security interest in Hesston tractors that were sold by Lindsey and the proceeds of which were paid to the Bank (D).

RULE OF LAW

A recipient of a payment made "in the ordinary course" by a debtor takes that payment free and clear of any claim that a secured party may have in the payment as proceeds, absent collusion intended to defraud the secured party.

FACTS: Lindsey purchased wholesale tractor equipment from Hesston for resale in its farm machinery sales and service business. HCC Credit Corp. (HCC) (P) provided financing for the purchases. Written contracts governed the relationship between the parties, including a security agreement. In the security agreement Lindsey granted HCC (P) a security interest in all equipment purchased from Hesston and in the proceeds from the sale of the equipment. Lindsey also agreed to pay HCC (P) immediately for equipment sold from the proceeds of the sale. The Indiana State Department of Transportation agreed to purchase 14 Hesston tractors from Lindsey. Lindsey received payment from the state and wrote a check payable to Springs Valley Bank & Trust Co. (the Bank) (D) for $212,104.75 to pay for debts owed by Lindsey to the Bank (D). Lindsey filed a bankruptcy liquidation proceeding and dissolved. HCC (P) sought to recover the $199,122 in proceeds from the sale of the Hesston tractors that the Bank (D) received from Lindsey. Both parties moved for summary judgment, which was granted in favor of the Bank (D). The court of appeals affirmed and HCC (P) appealed.

ISSUE: Does a recipient of a payment made "in the ordinary course" by a debtor take that payment free and clear of any claim that a secured party may have in the payment as proceeds, absent collusion intended to defraud the secured party?

HOLDING AND DECISION: (Sullivan, J.) Yes. A recipient of a payment made "in the ordinary course" by a debtor takes that payment free and clear of any claim that a secured party may have in the payment as proceeds, absent collusion intended to defraud the secured party. Under both the security agreement and Article 9 of the Universal Commercial Code (U.C.C.), HCC (P) had a valid and perfected security interest in the $199,122 proceeds from the sale of the tractors. The general rule is that the secured party, upon a debtor's default, has priority over all others except as otherwise provided by the U.C.C. priority rules. However, Comment 2(c) to Article 9 provides an exception to the general rule for "payments and transfers in the ordinary course" without any collusion on the part of the debtor. Thus, when "cash proceeds are covered into the debtor's checking account and paid out in the operation of the debtor's business, recipients of the funds of course take free of any claim which the secured party may have in them as proceeds." This was the rule followed by the trial court and the court of appeals. HCC (P) now argues that its perfected security interest entitles it to the proceeds. Commercial policy considerations support both the rights of the secured party and the rights of the transferee in the present situation. In *Citizens National Bank of Whitley County v. Mid-States Dev. Co.*, 177 Ind. App. 548, 557, 380 N.E.2d 1243, 1248 (1978), the court set forth commercial policy considerations supporting the rights of a secured party against a bank's right of set-off. There the court stated that a secured creditor should be able to rely on its compliance with U.C.C.'s perfection requirements as against the unrecorded interest of the setting-off bank, otherwise the secured creditor could not rely on recording. Conversely, there are also sound policy reasons for allowing third-party transferees to retain the proceeds of another's collateral. In *Harley Davidson Motor Co. v. Bank of New England-Old Colony, N.A.*, 897 F.2d 611, 620 (1st Cir. 1990), the court recognized that if "ordinary course" of business is defined too narrowly, the ordinary suppliers will find themselves called upon to return ordinary payments. Furthermore, these suppliers will have the burden of contacting secured creditors to obtain permission to take payment from the debtor's commingled bank account. Comment 2(c) was intended to resolve this conflict in competing interests. Whether a payment was made in the ordinary course will be a function of the extent to which the payment was made in the routine operation of the debtor's business and the extent to which the recipient was aware that it was acting to the prejudice of the secured party. Since imposing liability too readily on payees could impede the free flow of goods and services, the transfer will be free of any claim that a secured party may have in the proceeds, unless the payment would constitute windfall to the recipient. A windfall occurs when the recipient has no reasonable expectation of being paid ahead of a secured

Continued on next page.

creditor because of the extent to which the payment was made outside the ordinary routine of the debtor's business or because the recipient was aware it was acting to the prejudice of the secured party or both. Lindsey's payment to the Bank (D) here was not a payment in the ordinary course of the operation of Lindsey's business. The Bank (D) was aware that HCC (P) had a valid and perfected security interest in Lindsey's inventory. This was an extremely large payment, which Lindsey had never made before and was not in the ordinary course of its business. For the Bank (D) to prevail would result in a windfall since the Bank (D) had no reasonable expectation that Lindsey would liquidate its debt to the Bank (D) in advance of payment to HCC (P). Reversed and remanded.

ANALYSIS

The court lists several factors to be taken into consideration in determining whether a payment is routine, including its size, frequency, whether the debtor received any consideration in return, and whether the obligation was due. With respect to the awareness of prejudice prong, the nature of the relationship between the transferee and debtor may give rise to a presumption of awareness of prejudice, particularly if the transferee is a secondary lender whose debt is subordinated to the secured creditor. In such cases the secondary lender will be presumed to have actual knowledge of the prejudice to the secured creditor, since typically the secondary lender will have made the loan with the knowledge that the secured creditor has priority.

Quicknotes

ORDINARY COURSE OF BUSINESS The conducting of business in accordance with standard customs and practices.

PERFECTED SECURITY INTEREST A security interest that is safeguarded against other claims to the collateral; perfection is generally accomplished by legal steps necessary to give other creditors notice of the interest.

SECURED CREDITOR A creditor, the repayment of whose loan is secured by collateral sufficient to repay the debt owed.

CHAPTER 25

Default

Quick Reference Rules of Law

State Bank of Piper City v. A-Way, Inc.

Bank (P) v. Grain storage facility (D)

Ill. Sup. Ct., 115 Ill. 2d 401, 504 N.E.2d 737 (1987).

NATURE OF CASE: Review of order reversing dismissal of debt collection action.

FACT SUMMARY: State Bank of Piper City (P), after receiving partial satisfaction of a judgment on a note, brought an action to foreclose collateral securing the note.

RULE OF LAW

An action to recover on a note does not preclude a subsequent action to foreclose upon collateral securing the note.

FACTS: State Bank of Piper City (State Bank) (P) obtained a judgment against Brenner in the amount of $131,083.91. Learning that Brenner had stored certain grain with A-Way, Inc. (D), upon which State Bank (P) had a security interest, State Bank (P) demanded that A-Way (D) make an accounting. A-Way (D) listed 5,141.20 bushels, which were valued at $11,310.64. Mistakenly equating the volume with the value, State Bank (P) obtained an order mandating that A-Way (D) pay it $5,141.20, which it did. Realizing its mistake eight months later, State Bank (P) brought an action to enforce its security interest. The trial court dismissed, holding the foreclosure action barred by the prior judgment. The court of appeal reversed, and the Illinois Supreme Court granted review.

ISSUE: Does an action to recover on a note preclude a subsequent action to foreclose upon collateral securing the note?

HOLDING AND DECISION: (Ward, J.) No. An action to recover on a note does not preclude a subsequent action to foreclose upon collateral securing the note. Universal Commercial Code § 9-501 (1) permits a secured creditor either to reduce a claim to judgment or to foreclose upon or otherwise proceed against the collateral. The section specifically states that the remedies are cumulative. The effect of this language is to permit a creditor to proceed against an obligation or any security thereon, at the creditor's option, without any fear of the subsequent suit being barred by the doctrine of merger. Here, State Bank (P) went first against the obligation and then against the balance owing through an action against collateral. This it was entitled to do. Affirmed.

ANALYSIS

Merger (a subset of the doctrine of res judicata) is an old common law concept. Essentially, it provides that a judgment will bar any claim which could have been brought along with the suit underlying the judgment. The rule still has much vitality; unless a statutory exception to it exists, it will be applied in an appropriate situation.

Quicknotes

DOCTRINE OF RES JUDICATA The rule of law, that a final judgment by a court precludes subsequent litigation between the parties regarding the same cause of action.

MERGER The acquisition of one company by another, after which the acquired company ceases to exist as an independent entity.

Klingbiel v. Commercial Credit Corp.

Car buyer (P) v. Car repossessor (D)

439 F.2d 1303 (10th Cir. 1971).

NATURE OF CASE: Appeal from award of damages for conversion.

FACT SUMMARY: Commercial Credit Corp. (D) repossessed Klingbiel's (P) car without notice or demand for performance even though he was not behind in his payments.

RULE OF LAW

A creditor may accelerate the maturity of a debt when he deems himself insecure, but he must make demand or give notice to purchaser before he repossesses the collateral.

FACTS: Klingbiel (P) entered into an installment contract with a dealer for the purchase of a new car. The contract provided that, if the purchaser defaulted or the dealer felt itself or the vehicle insecure, the unpaid balance would, without notice, become due. Furthermore, the contract permitted the mortgage to be foreclosed in any lawful manner and allowed the dealer, without notice or demand for performance, to lawfully take possession of the vehicle. The dealer assigned the contract to Commercial Credit Corp. (Commercial) (D). Before Klingbiel's (P) first monthly installment was due, Commercial (D) felt itself insecure and repossessed the car without notice to Klingbiel (P). Klingbiel (P) sued Commercial (D) for unlawful conversion. The jury found for Klingbiel (P) and awarded actual and punitive damages. Commercial (D) appealed, contending that no notice or demand was necessary prior to repossession.

ISSUE: Must a creditor who accelerates the maturity of a debt make demand or give notice to the purchaser before he repossesses the collateral?

HOLDING AND DECISION: (Brown, J.) Yes. A creditor may accelerate the maturity of a debt when he deems himself insecure but must make demand or give notice to the purchaser before he repossesses the collateral. In the contract in this case, the clause that allowed the seller to take possession of the car without notice or demand followed the clause that required notice/demand before seller could act on a declared acceleration. According to the sequential language of the contract, Commercial (D) could have entered Klingbiel's (P) premises and taken possession of his car without notice, i.e., stealthily, in the dead of night, but only upon default, that is, only after Klingbiel (P) had either failed or refused to perform after receiving notice and demand for performance. Here, Klingbiel (P) was not given a chance to do either; his car simply disappeared without any contact from Commercial (D) before or after the repossession. Failure of notice/demand made Commercial's (D) repossession an unlawful conversion. Affirmed.

ANALYSIS

"Insecurity clauses" like the one in this case are expressly authorized by Universal Commercial Code (U.C.C.) § 1-208. Some jurisdictions interpret the clauses to permit acceleration at the whim of the creditor, while others allow acceleration only if a reasonable, prudent creditor would consider himself insecure. U.C.C. § 1-208 simply requires that the secured party act in "good faith."

Quicknotes

COLLATERAL Property that secures the payment of a debt.

CONVERSION The act of depriving an owner of his property without permission or justification.

Hilliman v. Cobado

Cattle raiser (P) v. Cattle seller (D)

N.Y. Sup. Ct., 499 N.Y.S.2d 610, 1 U.C.C. Rep. Serv. 2d 327 (1986).

NATURE OF CASE: Action seeking replevin of repossessed chattel.

FACT SUMMARY: Cobado (D) repossessed certain cattle belonging to Szata (P) in a highly confrontational manner.

RULE OF LAW

One having a security interest in chattel may not foreclose thereon in a confrontational manner.

FACTS: Cobado (D) sold Szata (P) certain cattle. He took a purchase-money security interest. Later, believing Szata (P) to be impairing his security by selling some of the cattle, Cobado (D) elected to repossess, as his security instrument permitted him to do. He showed up at Szata's (P) ranch unannounced and began rounding up the cattle. Szata (P) protested that he was not in default. A police officer appeared and ordered Cobado (D) to desist, but he continued anyway. Szata (P) later brought a replevin action, seeking return of the repossessed cattle.

ISSUE: May one having a security interest in chattel foreclose thereon in an confrontational manner?

HOLDING AND DECISION: (Horey, J.) No. One having a security interest in chattel may not foreclosure thereon in a confrontational manner. Under § 9-504 of the Universal Commercial Code (U.C.C.), one having a security interest in chattel may use self-help and repossess the security when the debtor defaults or impairs the security. However, the U.C.C. clearly states that such repossession must be effected without a breach of the peace. Such breach of the peace means not only actual violence but any act likely to produce violent reaction. In this case, Cobado (D) without doubt did effect his repossession in a manner likely to produce violence, particularly by ignoring Szata's (P) demands that he leave the property and his failure to obey a policeman's orders. Since the repossession was effected in an illegal manner, it was invalid, and the cattle must be returned. So ordered.

ANALYSIS

For the most part, self-help is looked upon with disfavor in all areas of the law. Repossession is the most notable exception to general rules against self-help. Generally, the requirement that repossession be effected peaceably is strictly enforced.

Quicknotes

CHATTEL An article of personal property, as distinguished from real property; a thing personal and moveable.

REPLEVIN An action to recover personal property wrongfully taken.

REPOSSESSION The taking back of an item paid for under an installment contract when payment of an installment is not made.

SECURITY INTEREST An interest in property that may be sold upon a default in payment of the debt.

R & J of Tennessee, Inc. v. Blankenship-Melton Real Estate, Inc.

Secured party (P) v. Debtor (D)

Tenn. Ct. App., 166 S.W.3d 195, 55 U.C.C. Rep. Serv. 2d 278 (2005).

NATURE OF CASE: Appeal from deficiency judgment after foreclosure obtained by a secured party against a guarantor.

FACT SUMMARY: Blankenship-Melton Real Estate, Inc. (D), a guarantor on a loan in default held by R & J of Tennessee, Inc. (R & J) (P), contended that he did not receive proper notice of the foreclosure sale and that the sale was not conducted in a commercially reasonable manner, so that a deficiency judgment following the foreclosure sale should not have been granted to R & J (P).

RULES OF LAW

(1) A debtor or guarantor of a loan may not waive the right to notification of disposition of collateral in the guaranty agreement itself.

(2) A debtor or guarantor of a loan is not given statutorily sufficient notice regarding the public sale of the loan collateral where, despite the security holder's knowledge of the debtor's or guarantor's current address, the notice is sent to the debtor's or guarantor's former address listed in the guaranty so that the debtor or guarantor does not receive actual notice of the sale and the holder of the security proceeds with the sale notwithstanding a failure to receive confirmation that the debtor or guarantor has received the notice.

(3) A foreclosure sale of collateral is not conducted in a commercially reasonable manner where the secured party has not acted in good faith by: delaying the sale and thereby permitting the collateral to depreciate; not advertising the sale; permitting the collateral to be used and the deficiency to increase; and not having an independent appraisal of the collateral.

FACTS: Blankenship-Melton Real Estate, Inc. (Blankenship-Melton) (D) borrowed around $40,000 from the Bank of Henderson County (the Bank). The loan was secured by a truck, a tractor, a boat, and a mobile home, which were owned by Blankenship-Melton (D) and together had a value of at least $40,000. Blankenship (D), Larry Melton and Steve Melton each executed a guaranty promising to be personally liable on the promissory note. Eventually, the loan, after having been extended a few times, went into default, and Larry and Steve Melton asked Johnny Melton, the majority owner of R & J of Tennessee, Inc. (R & J) (P) for help with the loan. R & J (P) purchased the promissory note from the Bank for around $26,500. By this time, the boat had been sold and the proceeds used to repay some of the loan, so only the other vehicles were left as collateral. When R & J (P) purchased the note, Steve Melton had been living in the mobile home, and he never paid rent to Blankenship-Melton (D) during his periods of occupancy. Larry Melton had possession of the truck and drove it on a daily basis. The tractor remained in Larry Melton's possession, was stored at his personal residence, and was inoperable. Over seven months after R & J (P) had obtained the promissory note, during which time Steve Melton and Larry Melton were permitted to use the collateral, Johnny Melton, acting as R & J's (P) agent, commenced foreclosure proceedings. He posted a copy of the notice of sale at R & J's (P) office, the courthouse, and on the collateral. He also sent a notice to Blankenship (D) by certified mail at the address listed in the promissory note indicating that the collateral would be sold at a public sale within ten days. Blankenship (D), however, had moved in the meantime and had not informed the Bank of the change of address, so he never actually received the notice. Despite having not received a return receipt indicating successful delivery of the notice, R & J (P) went ahead with the sale of the collateral as planned, and only a week later did it receive the notice back from the postal service with an indication that it was undeliverable. In addition, it appeared that Johnny Melton knew Blankenship's (D) current address, since it was correctly entered on the complaint filed on the sale date. At the sale, at which only Johnny Melton and Larry Melton were present, R & J (P) purchased the mobile home for $8,000, the truck for $11,000, and the tractor for $1,000—based on Johnny Melton's appraisal of the collateral. Steve Melton and Larry Melton continued to use the collateral during this period of time. R & J (P) then brought suit against Blankenship (D) for a deficiency judgment on the personal guaranty of around $13,000. The trial court's first decision was for Blankenship (D), but on a rehearing, a deficiency judgment of close to $11,000 was rendered in R & J's (P) favor. The state's intermediate appellate court granted review.

ISSUE:

(1) May a debtor or guarantor of a loan waive the right to notification of disposition of collateral in the guaranty agreement itself?

(2) Is a debtor or guarantor of a loan given statutorily sufficient notice regarding the public sale of the loan collateral where, despite the security holder's knowledge of the debtor's or guarantor's current address, the notice is sent to the debtor's or guarantor's former

Continued on next page.

address listed in the guaranty so that the debtor or guarantor does not receive actual notice of the sale and the holder of the security proceeds with the sale notwithstanding a failure to receive confirmation that the debtor or guarantor has received the notice?

(3) Is a foreclosure sale of collateral conducted in a commercially reasonable manner where the secured party has not acted in good faith by: delaying the sale and thereby permitting the collateral to depreciate; not advertising the sale; permitting the collateral to be used and the deficiency to increase; and not having an independent appraisal of the collateral?

HOLDING AND DECISION: (Highers, J.)

(1) No. A debtor or guarantor of a loan may not waive the right to notification of disposition of collateral in the guaranty agreement itself. The Universal Commercial Code (U.C.C.) expressly provides that such waiver may occur only in an agreement entered into after default—which did not happen here, so Blankenship (D) did not waive his right to notification.

(2) No. A debtor or guarantor of a loan is not given statutorily sufficient notice regarding the public sale of the loan collateral where, despite the security holder's knowledge of the debtor's or guarantor's current address, the notice is sent to the debtor's or guarantor's former address listed in the guaranty so that the debtor or guarantor does not receive actual notice of the sale and the holder of the security proceeds with the sale notwithstanding a failure to receive confirmation that the debtor or guarantor has received the notice. U.C.C. § 9-611(b) provides that a secured interest holder disposing of collateral by public sale "shall" send to debtors and guarantors reasonable notification of such disposition. Based on this language, Blankenship (D) argues that receipt of notice is mandatory. R & J (P) responds to this argument by saying that it sent the notice to the address it had, so that it is Blankenship's (D) responsibility that he did not receive the notice because he failed to alert the Bank of his new address. The official comment to § 9-611(b) indicates that notification must be reasonable as to timing, manner and content. The timing of the notice is not at issue here. Thus, the issue of reasonableness attaches to the manner of sending, including where the notice was sent. Whether a secured party must resend a notice after learning that the first try failed is a question left to judicial determination. Based on the U.C.C.'s definition of "send" and the general meaning of "notice" as it is used in the U.C.C., it is clear that this state's case law requires something more than a mere "sending" for a secured party to be in compliance with the statute. The sending of the notice by certified, return receipt requested mail is reasonable, and getting back the signed return receipt permits the secured party to assume the debtor or guarantor received the notice. However, the state's case law provides that while absolute proof of receipt of notice may not be required in every instance, a creditor, who only makes one attempt to contact the debtor or guarantor, and is left uncertain of receipt of the notice, has not fulfilled its obligation to the debtor or guarantor when it proceeds with a disposition less than two weeks from mailing its first notice. Moreover, a secured party is not required to prove that the debtor or guarantor actually received the notice. Applying these principles here, the attempt to notify Blankenship (D) by Johnny Merton was not commercially reasonable. Reversed as to this issue.

(3) No. A foreclosure sale of collateral is not conducted in a commercially reasonable manner where the secured party has not acted in good faith by: delaying the sale and thereby permitting the collateral to depreciate; not advertising the sale; permitting the collateral to be used and the deficiency to increase; and not having an independent appraisal of the collateral. Lack of reasonable notice of a sale of collateral is only one factor bearing on the commercial reasonableness of the sale, and the determination of whether the sale has been conducted in a commercially reasonable manner is made on a case-by-case basis based on all the facts and circumstances. Throughout the sale process, the secured party is bound by the duty of good faith and must effect the sale in a commercially reasonable way. The secured party has the burden of proving commercial reasonableness. The state's case law has specified six factors by which the statute requirements may be measured: (1) the type of collateral involved; (2) the condition of the collateral; (3) the number of bids solicited; (4) the time and place of sale; (5) the purchase price received or the terms of the sale; and (6) any special circumstances involved. Applying these factors here, R & J's (P) delay in conducting the sale was commercially unreasonable because the loan was already in default and R & J (P) could provide no justification for waiting over seven months before commencing the sale and letting Larry Melton and Steve Melton use the collateral during that period. Here, use of the items of collateral would cause them to depreciate more rapidly, and would increase the deficiency. Permitting such use was also indicative of bad faith. Here, too, although R & J (P) placed notices on the collateral and in the courthouse, it failed to advertise the sale in the local press, and failed to use an experienced auctioneer. Such failure is indicative of commercial unreasonableness. And while an independent appraiser is not required in every case, here, coupled with the other conduct, the lack of an independent appraiser is indicative of commercial unreasonableness. Thus, the aggregate of circumstances in this case demonstrates that the sale of the collateral conducted by R & J (P) was not conducted in good faith or in a

Continued on next page.

commercially reasonable manner. Accordingly, Blankenship (D) may be entitled to statutory damages, and R & J (P) must overcome a rebuttable presumption (under the state's "rebuttable presumption rule") that the extent of those damages is the full deficiency by showing that the fair market value of the collateral exceeds those damages. The trial court, on remand, must make these determinations. R & J (P) must bear the costs of this appeal. Reversed and remanded.

ANALYSIS

The rebuttable presumption rule provides that in the event the creditors foreclose upon security interest in collateral and conduct a commercially unreasonable sale, there is a presumption that the debtor is damaged to the extent of the deficiency claimed. The fact of an unreasonable sale does not result in the extinguishment of any deficiency whatsoever. This presumption shifts the burden of proving to the creditor the amount that should reasonably have been obtained through sale conducted according to the law. However, not every state uses a rebuttable presumption rule where a secured party has failed to send reasonable notification or conduct the disposition sale in a commercially reasonable manner. Some states use the "absolute bar rule" where the secured party is completely barred from recovering a deficiency, while others permit the debtor to offset (without the use of a rebuttable presumption) his damages from the secured party's noncompliance against the deficiency.

Quicknotes

COLLATERAL Property that secures the payment of a debt.

DEFICIENCY JUDGMENT A judgment against a mortgagor for the difference between the amount obtained at a foreclosure sale and the amount of the mortgage debt that is due.

FORECLOSURE An action to recover the amount due on a mortgage of real property where the owner has failed to meet the mortgage obligations, terminating the owner's interest in the property which must then be sold to satisfy the debt.

GRANTOR Conveyor of property or settlor of a trust.

Coxall v. Clover Commercial Corp.

Debtor (P) v. Secured interest holder (D)

N.Y. Civ. Ct., 4 Misc. 3d 654, 781 N.Y.S.2d 567 (2004).

NATURE OF CASE: Action for unlawful repossession of an automobile consolidated with action for judgment of deficiency after foreclosure sale.

FACT SUMMARY: Jason Coxall (P), who had given Clover Commercial Corp. (Clover) (D) a security interest in his vehicle, contended that Clover (D) had unlawfully repossessed his car, while Clover (D) contended that Jason Coxall (P) and Utho Coxall, who had both signed the security agreement, owed it a deficiency after it had sold the repossessed car.

RULE OF LAW

(1) A secured party does not provide reasonable notification of a foreclosure sale to a debtor in a consumer transaction where the notification does not contain all information required by the Universal Commercial Code (U.C.C.) and where the notification is sent 11 days before the sale and there is no indication that such a prompt sale is necessary for obtaining the best price.

(2) A foreclosure sale is not commercially reasonable where a repossessed vehicle is sold back to the dealer from which it was bought at 18.5 percent of the original purchase price and where there is no evidence of the fair market value of the vehicle or of other potential buyers.

(3) In a consumer transaction case, a secured party's failure to provide reasonable notification of a disposition sale or to provide a commercially reasonable sale bars the secured party from obtaining a deficiency from a debtor.

(4) In a consumer transaction case, where the secured party has not complied with U.C.C. Article 9 enforcement provisions, the debtor is entitled to the minimum statutory damages.

FACTS: Jason Coxall (P) and Utho Coxall purchased a used car from a car dealer. The "cash price" on the contract was $8,100, against which the Coxalls made a "cash down payment" of $3,798.25 and financed the balance of $4,970. The contract was assigned to Clover Commercial Corp. (Clover) (D). The Coxalls were required by the contract to make monthly payments of $333.68 each, but because Jason Coxall (P) experienced mechanical difficulties with the car, no payments were made. On the third month that a payment was due, Clover (D) repossessed the car. The car had not sustained any damage during the four months it was in Jason Coxall's (P) possession. The day following repossession, it mailed two letters to Jason Coxall (P), one informing him that he could redeem the vehicle with a payment of $5,969.28, exclusive of storage charges and a redemption fee, the other giving him notice that the vehicle would be offered for private sale after 12:00 noon on the 11th day from the date of the letter. No such letters were sent to Utho Coxall. The contract between the Coxalls and Clover (D) provided that after repossession, Clover (D) could sell the vehicle after 10-days' notice, and that "notice will be reasonable if . . . sent . . . to your current address . . . at least 10 days . . . before seller acts on the notice." On the stated sale date, the car was sold back for $1,500 (i.e., only 18.5 percent of the purchase price) to the car dealer from which the car had been purchased by the Coxalls. Over a month later, Clover (D) wrote to Jason Coxall (P) demanding that he pay the remaining balance of $4,998.09. A week later, Jason Coxall (P) filed suit against Clover (D) for unlawful automobile repossession, seeking $8,000 with interest from the date of repossession. Less than two months later, Clover (D) filed suit against Jason Coxall (P) and Utho Coxall for $4,630.62 with interest from the date of purchase plus reasonable attorney fees. The contract provided that the debtor had to pay the "cost of repossession, storage and preparation for sale" and "an attorney's fee of up to 15 percent of the amount due . . . unless the court sets a smaller fee." The actions were consolidated for joint trial.

ISSUE:

(1) Does a secured party provide reasonable notification of a foreclosure sale to a debtor in a consumer transaction where the notification does not contain all information required by the U.C.C. and where the notification is sent 11 days before the sale and there is no indication that such a prompt sale is necessary for obtaining the best price?

(2) Is a foreclosure sale commercially reasonable where a repossessed vehicle is sold back to the dealer from which it was bought at 18.5 percent of the original purchase price and where there is no evidence of the fair market value of the vehicle or of other potential buyers?

(3) In a consumer transaction case, does a secured party's failure to provide reasonable notification of a disposition sale or to provide a commercially reasonable sale bar the secured party from obtaining a deficiency from a debtor?

(4) In a consumer transaction case, where the secured party has not complied with U.C.C. Article 9 enforcement

Continued on next page.

provisions, is the debtor entitled to the minimum statutory damages?

HOLDING AND DECISION: (Battaglia, J.)

(1) No. A secured party does not provide reasonable notification of a foreclosure sale to a debtor in a consumer transaction where the notification does not contain all information required by the U.C.C. and where the notification is sent 11 days before the sale and there is no indication that such a prompt sale is necessary for obtaining the best price. The notification must be reasonable as to timeliness, manner, and content, and whether the notification is reasonable is a question of fact under the circumstances. For non-consumer transactions, 10-days' notice is reasonable. Also, in all transactions, the form of notification is prescribed and must contain certain information. In a consumer case, if any of that information is missing, the notification is unreasonable as a matter of law. Here, even if the two letters sent to Jason Coxall (P) are read in combination, they did not provide all the information required by U.C.C. since they did not state that he was "entitled to an accounting of the unpaid indebtedness" nor stated "the charge, if any, for an accounting." Also, 11-days' notice in a consumer transaction does not seem reasonable where there is no evidence that a prompt sale is necessary for obtaining the best price, since even if the debtor receives the notification five days before the sale, that does not provide him with enough time to arrange for alternate financing. For these reasons, the notification was unreasonable. Moreover, it is not necessary to decide in this case whether the contract term between the parties providing for 10-days' notice is reasonable.

(2) No. A foreclosure sale is not commercially reasonable where a repossessed vehicle is sold back to the dealer from which it was bought at 18.5 percent of the original purchase price and where there is no evidence of the fair market value of the vehicle or of other potential buyers. Every aspect of a disposition of collateral must be reasonable. Private sales are not unreasonable, and, in fact, are encouraged by the U.C.C., as it is generally believed they provide the best price. The burden of proving reasonableness is on the secured party, and the test for reasonableness is whether the secured party acted in good faith in the mutual best interests of the parties. While private sales of repossessed automobiles to car dealers have been held to be commercially reasonable, here the sale was to the original seller. Here, Clover (D) presented no evidence of its procedure for the sale, its identification of prospective buyers, or any other details of the sale, except for the price. Thus, the only evidence of reasonableness is the price, i.e., $1,500 for a vehicle that four months earlier had been purchased for $8,100 and that had not sustained any damage in the interim. Where a price is significantly lower than the purchase price, it must be carefully scrutinized. While a low price might by merely an indication that the collateral has depreciated greatly, it can also be an indication of self-dealing. Given that there was no justification for the wide disparity between the disposition price and the purchase price, and that there was ample room here for self-dealing, Clover (D) has not met its burden of proof in showing that the sale price was commercially reasonable.

(3) Yes. In a consumer transaction case, a secured party's failure to provide reasonable notification of a disposition sale or to provide a commercially reasonable sale bars the secured party from obtaining a deficiency from a debtor. In this judicial department, the appellate courts adopted an absolute bar rule, which bars the secured party that has failed to send reasonable notification or has not disposed of the collateral in a commercially reasonable manner—or both, as here—from obtaining a deficiency judgment against the debtor. Other appellate departments adopted other rules, so there was a conflict between the departments. Revised U.C.C. Article 9, however, resolved this conflict in non-consumer cases, so that a rebuttable presumption rule is in effect for such non-consumer transactions. However, the U.C.C. left to the courts the discretion of which rule to apply in consumer cases. Since the department had adopted the absolute bar rule, which was not legislatively changed, that rule still applies. Applying this rule here, Clover (D) is barred from obtaining a deficiency. Even if the rebuttable presumption rule was used, however, Clover (D) would still not be entitled to a deficiency since it did not present any evidence that would rebut the presumption that it is not entitled to a deficiency. However, although it cannot recover a deficiency, Clover (D) is still entitled to the amounts owed to it prior to repossession, as well as the costs of repossession—the Coxalls are not relieved from all their liability because of Clover's (D) failure to comply with Article 9. The amount owed prior to repossession, including contractual late fees, is $1,101.15. Thus, Jason Coxall (P) and Utho Coxall are jointly and severally liable for this amount. Clover (D) did not present evidence on its entitlement to repossession and storage costs or attorneys' fees, so it is not entitled to these.

(4) Yes. In a consumer transaction case, where the secured party has not complied with U.C.C. Article 9 enforcement provisions, the debtor is entitled to the minimum statutory damages. Under the common law, a repossessing seller did not have to make any repayment to the defaulting debtor. If, however, the seller did not comply with statutory obligations, the seller had to make complete or partial repayment. Under revised Article 9, a person is liable for damages in the amount of any loss caused by a failure to comply with the statute, and the

Continued on next page.

debtor is entitled to damages sustained as a result of the noncompliance. In non-consumer cases, however, a debtor whose deficiency has been eliminated or reduced may not recover such damages. The law in this jurisdiction, prior to revised Article 9, was that a debtor could recover noncompliance damages even if relieved of paying all or some of a deficiency. Since revised Article 9 does not displace existing law in consumer cases, that rule is still in effect for consumer cases. Therefore, a debtor is entitled to statutorily-prescribed minimum damages. Those damages are calculated as "an amount not less than the credit service charge plus 10 percent of the principal amount of the obligation or the time-price differential plus 10 percent of the cash price." Here, these amounts, the definition of which is to be decided by the courts, totals $1,846.24. Therefore, in the first action, Jason Coxall (P) is entitled to the difference between this amount and what he owes on the contract ($1,101.15) for a total of $745.09. The complaint in the second action is dismissed against Jason Coxall (P), but judgment of $1,101.15 is entered against Utho Coxall, with interest.

ANALYSIS

Revised U.C.C. § 9-625(d) provides that "[A] debtor . . . whose deficiency is eliminated or reduced under Section 9-626 may not otherwise recover . . . for noncompliance with the provisions . . . relating to . . . enforcement." This provision "eliminates the possibility of double recovery or other over-compensation," but because Section 9-626 does not apply to consumer transactions, the statute is silent as to whether a double recovery or other over-compensation is possible in a consumer transaction. Respected commentators have argued that double recoveries or other windfalls should be denied in consumer cases as well. See White and Summers, *Uniform Commercial Code*, § 25-13, at 919 (5th ed. 2000). Obviously, the court in this case disagreed, and held that at least statutorily prescribed minimum damages should be available in such situations to discourage noncompliance.

Quicknotes

DEFICIENCY JUDGMENT A judgment against a mortgagor for the difference between the amount obtained at a foreclosure sale and the amount of the mortgage debt that is due.

FORECLOSURE An action to recover the amount due on a mortgage of real property where the owner has failed to meet the mortgage obligations, terminating the owner's interest in the property which must then be sold to satisfy the debt.

SECURITY AGREEMENT An agreement creating a security interest on behalf of a creditor in certain personal property.

Reeves v. Foutz & Tanner, Inc.

Erstwhile owners of jewelry (P) v. Pawnshop (D)

N.M. Sup. Ct., 94 N.M. 760, 617 P.2d 149 (1980).

NATURE OF CASE: Appeal from reversal of award of surplus proceeds from a foreclosure sale.

FACT SUMMARY: After sending Reeves (P) and Begay (P) a notice of intent to retain the jewelry they had pawned, Foutz & Tanner, Inc. (D) sold it in the regular course of its business.

RULE OF LAW

A secured party who intends to sell the collateral in the normal course of his business must account to the debtor for any surplus, even if strict foreclosure has occurred.

FACTS: Reeves (P) and Begay (P) left their Navaho jewelry as collateral with Foutz & Tanner, Inc. (Foutz) (D), a pawnshop, in return for a loan, which they promised to repay in 30 days. The jewelry was worth several times the amount they borrowed. When Reeves (P) and Begay (P) defaulted on the loan, Foutz (D) sent each of them a notice of intent to retain the collateral. When neither Reeves (P) nor Begay (P) objected to the retention, Foutz (D), in accordance with its normal business practice, sold the jewelry. Foutz (D) did not account to Reeves (P) or Begay (P) for any surplus; Reeves (P) and Begay (P) brought suit against Foutz (D). The trial court applied Universal Commercial Code (U.C.C.) § 9-504, requiring that Foutz (D) return any surplus from the sale of the jewelry to Reeves (P) and Begay (P). The appellate court reversed, and Reeves (P) and Begay (P) appealed.

ISSUE: Must a secured party who intends to sell the collateral in the normal course of his business account to the debtor for any surplus, even if strict foreclosure has occurred?

HOLDING AND DECISION: (Sosa, C.J.) Yes. A secured party who intends to sell the collateral in the normal course of his business must account to the debtor for any surplus, even if strict foreclosure has occurred. A secured party in possession of collateral may choose one of two courses of action upon default by the debtor: (1) pursuant to U.C.C. § 9-504, he may sell the collateral, but he must account to the debtor for any surplus, or (2) pursuant to U.C.C. § 9-505(2), he may strictly foreclose by retaining the collateral for his own use in satisfaction of the obligation. However, waiver of surplus rights under § 9-505(2) is appropriate only when prompt resale of repossessed collateral in the ordinary course of business is not contemplated by the creditor. Since, in this case, Foutz (D) did intend to sell the jewelry in its normal course of business, he must comply with § 9-504 and account for any surplus. Court of Appeals reversed and trial court affirmed.

ANALYSIS

One of the advantages of strict foreclosure over resale of the collateral is that the secured party need not worry about later challenges regarding the fairness of a resale price, as sometimes occurs under § 9-504. *Reeves* appears to eliminate this advantage, at least in those cases where the intention of the secured party to resell the collateral can be shown.

Quicknotes

COLLATERAL Property that secures the payment of a debt.

Glossary

Common Latin Words and Phrases Encountered in the Law

A FORTIORI: Because one fact exists or has been proven, therefore a second fact that is related to the first fact must also exist.

A PRIORI: From the cause to the effect. A term of logic used to denote that when one generally accepted truth is shown to be a cause, another particular effect must necessarily follow.

AB INITIO: From the beginning; a condition which has existed throughout, as in a marriage which was void ab initio.

ACTUS REUS: The wrongful act; in criminal law, such action sufficient to trigger criminal liability.

AD VALOREM: According to value; an ad valorem tax is imposed upon an item located within the taxing jurisdiction calculated by the value of such item.

AMICUS CURIAE: Friend of the court. Its most common usage takes the form of an amicus curiae brief, filed by a person who is not a party to an action but is nonetheless allowed to offer an argument supporting his legal interests.

ARGUENDO: In arguing. A statement, possibly hypothetical, made for the purpose of argument, is one made arguendo.

BILL QUIA TIMET: A bill to quiet title (establish ownership) to real property.

BONA FIDE: True, honest, or genuine. May refer to a person's legal position based on good faith or lacking notice of fraud (such as a bona fide purchaser for value) or to the authenticity of a particular document (such as a bona fide last will and testament).

CAUSA MORTIS: With approaching death in mind. A gift causa mortis is a gift given by a party who feels certain that death is imminent.

CAVEAT EMPTOR: Let the buyer beware. This maxim is reflected in the rule of law that a buyer purchases at his own risk because it is his responsibility to examine, judge, test, and otherwise inspect what he is buying.

CERTIORARI: A writ of review. Petitions for review of a case by the United States Supreme Court are most often done by means of a writ of certiorari.

CONTRA: On the other hand. Opposite. Contrary to.

CORAM NOBIS: Before us; writs of error directed to the court that originally rendered the judgment.

CORAM VOBIS: Before you; writs of error directed by an appellate court to a lower court to correct a factual error.

CORPUS DELICTI: The body of the crime; the requisite elements of a crime amounting to objective proof that a crime has been committed.

CUM TESTAMENTO ANNEXO, ADMINISTRATOR (ADMINISTRATOR C.T.A.): With will annexed; an administrator c.t.a. settles an estate pursuant to a will in which he is not appointed.

DE BONIS NON, ADMINISTRATOR (ADMINISTRATOR D.B.N.): Of goods not administered; an administrator d.b.n. settles a partially settled estate.

DE FACTO: In fact; in reality; actually. Existing in fact but not officially approved or engendered.

DE JURE: By right; lawful. Describes a condition that is legitimate "as a matter of law," in contrast to the term "de facto," which connotes something existing in fact but not legally sanctioned or authorized. For example, de facto segregation refers to segregation brought about by housing patterns, etc., whereas de jure segregation refers to segregation created by law.

DE MINIMIS: Of minimal importance; insignificant; a trifle; not worth bothering about.

DE NOVO: Anew; a second time; afresh. A trial de novo is a new trial held at the appellate level as if the case originated there and the trial at a lower level had not taken place.

DICTA: Generally used as an abbreviated form of obiter dicta, a term describing those portions of a judicial opinion incidental or not necessary to resolution of the specific question before the court. Such nonessential statements and remarks are not considered to be binding precedent.

DUCES TECUM: Refers to a particular type of writ or subpoena requesting a party or organization to produce certain documents in their possession.

EN BANC: Full bench. Where a court sits with all justices present rather than the usual quorum.

EX PARTE: For one side or one party only. An ex parte proceeding is one undertaken for the benefit of only one party, without notice to, or an appearance by, an adverse party.

EX POST FACTO: After the fact. An ex post facto law is a law that retroactively changes the consequences of a prior act.

EX REL.: Abbreviated form of the term "ex relatione," meaning upon relation or information. When the state brings an action in which it has no interest against an individual at the instigation of one who has a private interest in the matter.

FORUM NON CONVENIENS: Inconvenient forum. Although a court may have jurisdiction over the case, the action should be tried in a more conveniently located court, one to which parties and witnesses may more easily travel, for example.

GUARDIAN AD LITEM: A guardian of an infant as to litigation, appointed to represent the infant and pursue his/her rights.

HABEAS CORPUS: You have the body. The modern writ of habeas corpus is a writ directing that a person (body) being detained (such as a prisoner) be brought before the court so that the legality of his detention can be judicially ascertained.

IN CAMERA: In private, in chambers. When a hearing is held before a judge in his chambers or when all spectators are excluded from the courtroom.

IN FORMA PAUPERIS: In the manner of a pauper. A party who proceeds in forma pauperis because of his poverty is one who is allowed to bring suit without liability for costs.

INFRA: Below, under. A word referring the reader to a later part of a book. (The opposite of supra.)

IN LOCO PARENTIS: In the place of a parent.

IN PARI DELICTO: Equally wrong; a court of equity will not grant requested relief to an applicant who is in pari delicto, or as much at fault in the transactions giving rise to the controversy as is the opponent of the applicant.

IN PARI MATERIA: On like subject matter or upon the same matter. Statutes relating to the same person or things are said to be in pari materia. It is a general rule of statutory construction that such statutes should be construed together, i.e., looked at as if they together constituted one law.

IN PERSONAM: Against the person. Jurisdiction over the person of an individual.

IN RE: In the matter of. Used to designate a proceeding involving an estate or other property.

IN REM: A term that signifies an action against the res, or thing. An action in rem is basically one that is taken directly against property, as distinguished from an action in personam, i.e., against the person.

INTER ALIA: Among other things. Used to show that the whole of a statement, pleading, list, statute, etc., has not been set forth in its entirety.

INTER PARTES: Between the parties. May refer to contracts, conveyances or other transactions having legal significance.

INTER VIVOS: Between the living. An inter vivos gift is a gift made by a living grantor, as distinguished from bequests contained in a will, which pass upon the death of the testator.

IPSO FACTO: By the mere fact itself.

JUS: Law or the entire body of law.

LEX LOCI: The law of the place; the notion that the rights of parties to a legal proceeding are governed by the law of the place where those rights arose.

MALUM IN SE: Evil or wrong in and of itself; inherently wrong. This term describes an act that is wrong by its very nature, as opposed to one which would not be wrong but for the fact that there is a specific legal prohibition against it (malum prohibitum).

MALUM PROHIBITUM: Wrong because prohibited, but not inherently evil. Used to describe something that is wrong because it is expressly forbidden by law but that is not in and of itself evil, e.g., speeding.

MANDAMUS: We command. A writ directing an official to take a certain action.

MENS REA: A guilty mind; a criminal intent. A term used to signify the mental state that accompanies a crime or other prohibited act. Some crimes require only a general mens rea (general intent to do the prohibited act), but others, like assault with intent to murder, require the existence of a specific mens rea.

MODUS OPERANDI: Method of operating; generally refers to the manner or style of a criminal in committing crimes, admissible in appropriate cases as evidence of the identity of a defendant.

NEXUS: A connection to.

NISI PRIUS: A court of first impression. A nisi prius court is one where issues of fact are tried before a judge or jury.

N.O.V. (NON OBSTANTE VEREDICTO): Notwithstanding the verdict. A judgment n.o.v. is a judgment given in favor of one party despite the fact that a verdict was returned in favor of the other party, the justification being that the verdict either had no reasonable support in fact or was contrary to law.

NUNC PRO TUNC: Now for then. This phrase refers to actions that may be taken and will then have full retroactive effect.

PENDENTE LITE: Pending the suit; pending litigation under way.

PER CAPITA: By head; beneficiaries of an estate, if they take in equal shares, take per capita.

PER CURIAM: By the court; signifies an opinion ostensibly written "by the whole court" and with no identified author.

PER SE: By itself, in itself; inherently.

PER STIRPES: By representation. Used primarily in the law of wills to describe the method of distribution where a person, generally because of death, is unable to take that which is left to him by the will of another, and therefore his heirs divide such property between them rather than take under the will individually.

PRIMA FACIE: On its face, at first sight. A prima facie case is one that is sufficient on its face, meaning that the evidence supporting it is adequate to establish the case until contradicted or overcome by other evidence.

PRO TANTO: For so much; as far as it goes. Often used in eminent domain cases when a property owner receives partial payment for his land without prejudice to his right to bring suit for the full amount he claims his land to be worth.

QUANTUM MERUIT: As much as he deserves. Refers to recovery based on the doctrine of unjust enrichment in those cases in which a party has rendered valuable services or furnished materials that were accepted and enjoyed by another under circumstances that would reasonably notify the recipient that the rendering party expected to be paid. In essence, the law implies a contract to pay the reasonable value of the services or materials furnished.

QUASI: Almost like; as if; nearly. This term is essentially used to signify that one subject or thing is almost analogous to another but that material differences between them do exist. For example, a quasi-criminal proceeding is one that is not strictly criminal but shares enough of the same characteristics to require some of the same safeguards (e.g., procedural due process must be followed in a parole hearing).

QUID PRO QUO: Something for something. In contract law, the consideration, something of value, passed between the parties to render the contract binding.

RES GESTAE: Things done; in evidence law, this principle justifies the admission of a statement that would otherwise be hearsay when it is made so closely to the event in question as to be said to be a part of it, or with such spontaneity as not to have the possibility of falsehood.

RES IPSA LOQUITUR: The thing speaks for itself. This doctrine gives rise to a rebuttable presumption of negligence when the instrumentality causing the injury was within the exclusive control of the defendant, and the injury was one that does not normally occur unless a person has been negligent.

RES JUDICATA: A matter adjudged. Doctrine which provides that once a court of competent jurisdiction has rendered a final judgment or decree on the merits, that judgment or decree is conclusive upon the parties to the case and prevents them from engaging in any other litigation on the points and issues determined therein.

RESPONDEAT SUPERIOR: Let the master reply. This doctrine holds the master liable for the wrongful acts of his servant (or the principal for his agent) in those cases in which the servant (or agent) was acting within the scope of his authority at the time of the injury.

STARE DECISIS: To stand by or adhere to that which has been decided. The common law doctrine of stare decisis attempts to give security and certainty to the law by following the policy that once a principle of law as applicable to a certain set of facts has been set forth in a decision, it forms a precedent which will subsequently be followed, even though a different decision might be made were it the first time the question had arisen. Of course, stare decisis is not an inviolable principle and is departed from in instances where there is good cause (e.g., considerations of public policy led the Supreme Court to disregard prior decisions sanctioning segregation).

SUPRA: Above. A word referring a reader to an earlier part of a book.

ULTRA VIRES: Beyond the power. This phrase is most commonly used to refer to actions taken by a corporation that are beyond the power or legal authority of the corporation.

Addendum of French Derivatives

IN PAIS: Not pursuant to legal proceedings.

CHATTEL: Tangible personal property.

CY PRES: Doctrine permitting courts to apply trust funds to purposes not expressed in the trust but necessary to carry out the settlor's intent.

PER AUTRE VIE: For another's life; during another's life. In property law, an estate may be granted that will terminate upon the death of someone other than the grantee.

PROFIT A PRENDRE: A license to remove minerals or other produce from land.

VOIR DIRE: Process of questioning jurors as to their predispositions about the case or parties to a proceeding in order to identify those jurors displaying bias or prejudice.

Casenote® Legal Briefs